The Enlightened Law of Moses

The Enlightened Law of Moses

A Christian Review of the Remarkable System of Old Testament Law

Mark P T Robertson

STONEHOLME BOOKS

Copyright © 2024 Mark P T Robertson

Published by Stoneholme Books, PO Box 7123, Redland Bay, Queensland Australia 4165. info@stoneholmebooks.com.

All rights reserved. No part of this publication may be reproduced or transmitted in any form or by any means, including electronic or mechanical, including photocopy, recording, or any information storage, without the prior written permission of the publisher.

Unless otherwise indicated, Scripture quotations are taken from the New King James Version® (NKJV). Copyright © 1982 by Thomas Nelson. Used by permission. All rights reserved.

Scripture quotations marked ESV are from The Holy Bible, English Standard Version, copyright © 2001 by Crossway, a publishing minister of Good News Publishers. Used by permission. All rights reserved.

Scripture quotations marked NLT are from the *Holy Bible, New Living Translation*, copyright © 2015 by Tyndale House Foundation. Used by permission of Tyndale House Publishers, Inc, Carol Stream, Illinois 60188. All rights reserved.

Copyediting by East Gate Editing

Cover art by Geoff Robertson

ISBN 978-1-7636717-1-3

2503

To my loving wife Lani and family

*The entirety of Your word is truth,
and every one of Your righteous judgments
endures forever.* —Ps. 119:160

Contents

Preface .... *v*

Introduction 1

PART 1: Background — 7

What Is the Law of Moses? 8
What the Law of Moses Is Not 14
How Credible Is Moses? 19
Comparing Jesus and Moses 24

PART 2: Key Perspectives from Historical Sources — 31

Jesus' Perspective of the Law 32
Jesus and the Sermon on the Mount 40
Moses' Perspective of the Law 47
Ancient Israel and the Law in Practice 53
David's Perspective of the Law 60
Paul's Perspective of the Law 65

PART 3: Getting to Know the Lawgiver — 73

God's Character Is Knowable 74
Unchanging Values 78
Motivated by Love 82
Rational and Coherent 88
A Lover of Freedom 94
Just and Righteous 99
In Touch with the Reality of Life 107
A Great Master Plan 114
Focused on the Individual 118
Unlike Our Imagination 123
The Lawgiver Summarized 132

PART 4: Foundational Principles — 133

God's Intent and Purpose for the Law 134

The Overall Structure and Format	141
The Ten Commandments	146
The Application of the Judgments	155
Key Principles of Justice	164
Eye for Eye, Tooth for Tooth	171
Mercy and the Written Law	179
The Importance of Faith	187
The Centrality of the Family	192
Women and the Law of Moses	200
Firstborn and Firstfruits	208

PART 5: The Law and the Nation — 213

The Unique Structure of Government	214
Civil Rights and Freedom	223
What It Meant to Be a Citizen of Israel	234
The Structure of the Judicial System	240
Sentencing and Penalties	248
The Redeeming Kinsman	255
Tort Laws	262
Sexual Morality	269
Sabbatical Cycles and the Jubilee	278
The Economic System	287
The Social Welfare System	300
The Importance of Education	308
The Issue of Slavery	315
The Public Health System	331
Caring for the Environment	341

PART 6: The Worship System — 347

The Key: God's Holiness	348
The Tabernacle	354
The Priesthood	361
The Sacrificial System	372
The Holy Days	380
Ceremonial Uncleanness	395

PART 7: More Difficult to Understand   403

     Why the Attraction of Paganism? 404
     What about the Canaanites? 412
     Sins of the Fathers 422
     The Trial by Ordeal for Jealousy 426
     Love Your Enemies. Really? 429
     God Hardens Hearts? 435
     Hard-to-Understand Mosaic Laws 440
     New Testament Terminology 446

PART 8: Final Perspectives   451

     Why Was It Written This way? 452
     Why the Old Covenant Failed 458
     The Law and the Kingdom of God 462
     The Law of Moses Today 466

Appendices   473

     Appendix: Law of Moses or Law of God? 474
     Appendix: Laws Before Moses 477
     Appendix: Biblical Terms for the Law 479
     Appendix: The Hebrew Calendar 482
     Appendix: Further Insights from the Psalmist 484

Bibliography 487
Index of Subjects 496
Index of Scriptures 503

Preface

In my search for works on the law of Moses, I came across a book written over 100 years ago. When I read the author's opening preface, I laughed out loud:

> It would not be possible in the present temper of the public mind, to offer a more uninteresting book than a treatise on the law of Moses. The feeling of the general reader is that the subject belongs not only to the ancient, but the antiquated, not only to the old, but the obsolete, not only to the lifeless, but to the discredited and untrue.
> —*The Law of Moses*. R. Roberts. 1899[1]

If that was the sentiment in the nineteenth century, how many *more* reasons do people have today to reject another book on such an uninteresting topic? "You've got to be kidding!" would be a common response. "What possible relevance does that archaic and oppressive law of Moses have to life in the twenty-first century?"

It was this negativity directed toward the Old Testament law that captured my attention some years ago. Something seemed amiss. If the God of the Bible is God, and Jesus was a perfect reflection of God's unchanging character, how is it that his Old Testament law system seemed so out of step with both the reality of life and the standards Jesus espoused? After all, this was a law system that God delivered *personally* to Moses and the people at Mount Sinai. Yet it's thought of in all sorts of negative terms—harsh, burdensome, impractical, petty—and is presented as a stumbling block to agnostics and atheists accepting the Bible as God's word. The general sentiment, even within Christianity, is the world is fortunate to be free of it. Some even blame the law (at least in part) for ancient Israel's demise.

But if that's the case, how did God get it so wrong?

In talking to Christians over the years, most are either ignorant of the topic or embarrassed by aspects of the Mosaic law. They either apologize for those parts of the Bible or sweep them under the carpet. (Even though it seems few have read the books of Moses in any depth.)

Some years ago, I set out to understand the law of Moses (as it is called) in light of this contradiction. This book is a result of that personal journey. It's a study

---
[1] Bibliog: (Roberts 1899, preface)

that has led me to view the law of Moses in a dramatically different light. Far from being opposed to Jesus' teachings, I now realize the law of Moses provided the foundation of everything he had to say.

In the pages ahead I hope to introduce you to what was a truly enlightened system far ahead of its time. It was not just a brilliant system of moral, civil, and ceremonial law but a teaching framework that opens our eyes to understanding God and his purpose for humankind. Even more surprising is its relevance to life in the twenty-first century.

Hopefully, you will find this book encouraging and an aid to deepening your faith in God and strengthening your walk in Christ.

Mark P T Robertson

Introduction

Moses is a giant in biblical terms, his name forever associated with freedom and the struggle to escape oppression and bondage. The narrative of ancient Israel leaving Egypt and their journey to the promised land has inspired many people, none more so than the founding fathers of the United States of America. They regularly referenced Moses as the gold standard for leadership against tyranny.

But mention the system of law that Moses delivered to the Israelites, and you'll generally get a different response. The extensive pages of "laws" outlined in the early books of the Bible have become some of the most denigrated parts of the Bible.

Putting aside the Ten Commandments, many commentaries describe aspects of the law of Moses in negative terms. The nineteenth-century American theologian Albert Barnes calls them "rites" that were "numerous, expensive, requiring much time, much property, and laborious."[1] He continues, saying they were "burdensome, expensive, and painful, and oppressive" and that "they were attended with great inconvenience and many transgressions, as the consequence." He states we should "rejoice at any evidence that the people of God might be delivered from them."[2] Matthew Henry's eighteenth-century historic commentary sums it up similarly to Barnes, noting that Moses' law was "a heavy yoke; they and their fathers found it difficult to be borne, so numerous, so various, so pompous, were the institutions of it."[3]

Powerful words that seem at odds with the ideals of the liberator Moses! Moses frees his people from affliction, inspires them with the hope of the promised land, and then introduces a burdensome legal system that ends up oppressing his people for centuries? Something doesn't seem quite right with such a scenario.

Certainly, there are aspects of the Mosaic law that are recognized as progressive and sound, but other parts are seen as confusing, regressive, and impractical—even irrational. Start reading the books of Leviticus or Numbers, and you'll get right into it: ceremonial sacrifices, rituals, cleansings, dietary laws, vows, laws of priesthood—things we would have a hard time relating to today. In

---

[1] Bibliog: (Barnes 1983, ref Matt. 24:3)
[2] Bibliog: (Barnes 1983, ref Acts 15:10)
[3] Bibliog: (M. Henry 1994, ref Acts 15:10)

2 The Enlightened Law of Moses

these same books of Moses, critics will point to laws regulating slavery, polygamy, capital punishment, and other things our society today would reject outright. And then there's the "eye for an eye, tooth for a tooth" directive—a recipe for a blind and toothless world we are told. These concepts invoke thoughts of a harsh and legalistic system, out of sync with our modern world.

> *This law code came from ... a God of truth, wisdom and unchanging character and values.*

But there's an even bigger problem. The Bible tells us this law code came from the mouth of God himself, an eternal God who describes himself as merciful, gracious, and kind, a God defined by John as the epitome of love—a God of truth, wisdom, and unchanging character and values.

The Legacy of Jesus

In contrast to the reputation of Moses' law, there is little negativity associated with the life and teachings of Jesus. The way Jesus lived, his character, and his demeanor carry a positive reputation far beyond the scope of Christianity. Millions of believers and nonbelievers have admired his teachings and profound insights on the key issues of life.

Far from being oppressive or harsh, Jesus is seen as a true liberator when it comes to the interpretation of law. Jesus was refreshingly pragmatic. Leaving aside the outward shows of religious pretense, he sat down to meals, ignoring the confusing handwashing rituals of the religious hierarchy, and ate despite their criticism. If someone needed help or healing on the Sabbath day, he didn't hesitate to act. He spoke to gentiles, women, children—whoever—ignoring Jewish segregation rules. His compelling manner attracted flawed people from all walks of life. Unlike the authoritarian religious leaders of the day, he didn't condemn these imperfect people but instead inspired them to change and become greater than they were.

Jesus was someone who deeply understood the reality of life.

Reconciling the Differences

How do we reconcile these seemingly different perspectives of the Old and the New? The assumption implied by some, that Jesus and the God of the Old were somehow at odds, doesn't hold any credence. Jesus confirmed multiple times that the Godhead was, and always will be, in perfect harmony (John 10:30; 14:7; 17:21).

We could assume that God got some aspects of the old law wrong or that he changed his values by the time of Jesus. But neither of those ideas works theologically. God doesn't change his standards, nor does the eternal God make errors of judgment. If he did either, we could never have any confidence in him again.

Others have suggested that God's motivation for giving such laws was to demonstrate that people could *not* live under such a legalistic system. Therefore, they would need to look forward to being liberated by the arrival of Jesus Christ some thousand years into the future. The problem with this idea of Israel "being set up to fail" is that it ignores the people involved. Millions of ordinary people made in God's image who supposedly lived out their lives under a burdensome system to prove a point to a future yet-to-be-born generation? It paints a worrying picture of a seemingly loving and just God. There is rightful pushback at such an idea. God cares for the individual and always has. Each person who lived before Christ, both great and small, was just as important to him as any person alive today. That is evident within the law of Moses itself, with God expressing his concern for the lowest and most vulnerable in society.

What is also clear when reading the books of Moses is that the law code God gave Israel was not some half-hearted project where he was careless with the details and made it up as he went along. God was closely and emotionally invested in the nation of Israel. He deeply cared and was passionately involved at the big-picture level and the small, showing enormous attention to detail and taking a personal interest in minute aspects of the ceremonial system and tabernacle design.

> *God was closely and emotionally invested in the nation of Israel*

Even more surprising, God strongly hoped the Israelites would *love* the way of life described in the law system he gave them: the commandments, statutes, judgments, rituals, ceremonies, sacrifices—the whole package! He saw his law in a very positive light, quite the opposite of most people's perspective today.

Finding the Correct Approach

What approach should we take to harmonize the law of Moses with the standards of Jesus? Rather than put God in the dock, as Christian apologist C. S. Lewis postulated,[4] and taking the position that the old law system was

---

[4] Bibliog: (Lewis. 1996)

flawed, a far more reasonable approach is to assume that it's our *understanding* and *interpretation* of the system that's at fault—not God nor the law he gave.

Later we will see that Jesus had no criticism of Moses or his law, but he did strongly criticize the religious leaders of his day. Jesus and the Pharisees had the same written words of Moses, but Jesus' *interpretation* of that same law was *dramatically different* than theirs. He rebuked them for distorting and adding to the law's original intent to the point it was unrecognizable. He even went so far as to say that they were *not even keeping* the law of Moses (John 7:19)!

Their hard hearts had blinded them from knowing the true God. They didn't understand his values or standards. And because they didn't know God, they didn't recognize Jesus as the Messiah. Jesus was nothing at all like they understood God to be, even though he was, in fact, the perfect reflection of the God they claimed to worship and the one predicted by Moses.

The Journey Starts with Jesus

Understanding God's original intent for the law is not as easy as one might think. The practices of ancient Israel don't help us a great deal. Even a cursory reading of their history shows the Israelites didn't obey God for any substantial period of time. Israel was far more captivated by the pagan religions around them than they were in doing what God asked them to do. Later, after the return from captivity, the Jewish leaders took the law off on another tangent, taking it to places God never intended. So historically we have little to rely on.

So how are we to understand what the system was *supposed* to look like in practice, the way God intended? The answer is to start with the character and values of God, the Lawgiver. Only by knowing the heart of God is it possible to properly understand his purpose for the law and how he wanted it to be interpreted, administered, and applied in people's lives.

And while a person can come to know the true God through the Old Testament Scriptures, the best way for us to come to know him is through Jesus. We have the record of Jesus' life and teachings and the way he perfectly reflected his Father in heaven. He is the door, the starting point of understanding. The prophet Isaiah predicted that the Messiah would come and "exalt the law and make it honorable" (ESV "magnify his law and make it glorious") (Isa. 42:21). The clear implication is that the law had lost its glory and honor and needed to be restored and uplifted. We will see that Jesus did not come to disparage or contradict Moses and certainly not to diminish the God of Israel. All his teachings were based on the Hebrew Scriptures. He taught from them, quoted from them, and upheld them. He came to correct, expound, and realign a system of law that had veered from God's original intent.

As we later work through the law of Moses, it will become clear that it was indeed an enlightened system, revolutionary in its day. The law of Moses was a recipe for greatness, not mediocrity. Had it been implemented and sustained, it would have created a free and open society with truth, justice, and compassion at its heart. It included many key principles and values we hold dear today in our Western countries: the rule of law, equality under law for all, impartiality, proportionality of justice, respect for women, social welfare for the vulnerable, laws for debt relief, laws for public health, laws for the environment, reformation of criminals—the list goes on.

> *The law of Moses was a recipe for greatness, not mediocrity.*

Why Another Book?

There have been many deep and valuable theological dissertations on the Old Testament law, but too often they are written with an underlying premise that the law of Moses was flawed in some way, that it was always doomed to fail.

The goal of this book is to put aside the baggage of history and take a fresh and practical look at the law of Moses from the *gracious perspective* that Jesus spoke about, believed in, and epitomized so strongly. A perspective of grace and love, justice, mercy, and faith. To look at the law in this way, we'll have to look beyond the poor example of Israel, beyond the religious power-mongers of Jesus day, beyond legalistic rabbinic interpretations, and beyond the negativity of so many commentators to see if we can get to the heart of the spirit and intent that God had in mind all along for his system of law.

This book is not meant to be a treatise on the entire law of Moses, nor does it profess to have all the answers. But it does aim to explore all the key elements of the law, particularly those areas invoking criticism. I hope you will find the pages ahead encouraging and a reinforcement of the consistent, gracious, loving God of the Bible.

6 The Enlightened Law of Moses

1

PART 1: **Background**

The term "law of Moses" can mean different things to different people, so for the context of this book, it is important to first define what is meant by the term.

This section will also briefly explore the law's origins and context and Moses' role in delivering the law to the nation. It will be helpful to consider Moses' historical credibility and compare him to Jesus, who was prophesied to be that second great prophet like Moses.

What Is the Law of Moses?

Come up to Me on the mountain and be there; and I will give you tablets of stone, and the law and commandments which I have written, that you may teach them.
—Exodus 24:12

The book of Exodus describes the dramatic circumstances surrounding the receiving of the law of Moses. The Israelites had arrived at the base of Mount Sinai after a demanding journey across the desert from Egypt (Exod. 19). Moses directed the people to set up camp to prepare to meet the God who had miraculously rescued them from centuries of bondage. This great being was going to come down to these descendants of Abraham and outline the standards he required of them and what he promised in return. On offer was a covenant, an agreement, where God promised to do great things for this insignificant nation if they trusted him and did as he asked.

The first words God proclaimed from the mountain announced that it was *he* who had rescued them from Egypt. There could be no doubt that this God was real and personal. He then proceeded to outline his core Ten Commandments (Exod. 20).

And the people were terrified. The lighting, the shaking of the mountain, the heavenly trumpets, and the booming voice were nothing like they had experienced before. They asked Moses to intercede for them and for him to receive the words from God on their behalf (Exod. 20:18–20). And so Moses went up the mountain to receive the Lord's instructions.

What Moses received in this and later interactions with God has become known as the law of Moses. Moses wrote down what he received and taught it to the children of Israel.

The Books of Moses

We find the writings of Moses in the first books of our modern Bible. Genesis, Exodus, Leviticus, Numbers, and Deuteronomy are known as the Books of Moses. These books are collectively known as the Torah (Hebrew: "teaching" or "instruction") and as the "Pentateuch" (Greek: "five books").

New Testament Scripture often refers to these five books as the "Law" when referencing how the Jews structured the Hebrew canon.[1] Jesus used similar expressions when he referenced the Hebrew Scriptures as "the Law, Prophets

---
[1] The Jewish *Tanakh*.

and the Psalms" or sometimes just "the Law and the Prophets" (Luke 24:44; Matt. 5:17).

Although the five books of Moses are collectively called the "Law," actual laws make up only about one-third of their content. In addition to laws, these books contain narrative history, literature, and genealogies. Actual *codified laws* are only found in portions of the books of Exodus, Leviticus, Numbers and Deuteronomy. It is these laws we will be reviewing in this book.

God's High Aspirations

What is eminently clear from God's words to Moses is that he had high expectations for the way of life outlined in his system of law. He had selected Israel to be his holy people and a special treasure above all the people of the earth (Deut. 7:6). His aspiration was for them to be a vibrant and morally sound people who would be a light and a blessing to the nations around them (Deut. 4:5–6; Gen. 12:3). He wanted them to be a people who would develop a heart like his, who reflected his own values and standards in a reciprocal loving relationship (Deut. 6:5). And all this was not to be without earthly benefits: his promised blessings for obedience were to include great wealth and power in the region (Deut. 28:1–14).

Such high ambition and lofty goals would require the Israelites to learn a way of life that was dramatically different from the surrounding nations. This was the intent of the law of Moses. At times the law of Moses is demeaned as being small-minded and legalistic—but a system like that could never achieve the greatness God had in mind for his people.

Good laws create strong, vibrant, and prosperous societies and confident individuals. Bad laws corrupt societies and stifle the human spirit.

A Remarkable Law System

The effect a system of law has on a nation cannot be overstated. Laws are foundational to a nation's stability and development, and without a sound fabric of law, a society cannot properly function. Good laws create strong, vibrant, and prosperous societies and confident individuals. Bad laws corrupt societies and stifle the human spirit.

Ancient Israel was unique not only in how they received their new law but also in its scope. Laws in most countries develop and evolve over centuries or are inherited from an imperial nation or conquering power. After centuries of Egyptian domination, the natural outcome for Israel would have been to retain a mix of Egyptian practices and Abrahamic traditions and for a hybrid system of law to slowly morph into place over time. But this did not happen, and for a good reason: God wanted the ways of Egypt taken entirely out of Israel. He wanted the nation to have a clean and decisive break from the shackles of the past and be a truly enlightened people who exhibited a morally sound and godly culture. *This could only occur by the decisive introduction of a complete and far-reaching system of law.*

Remarkably, Israel's law was delivered over a short period of time in the wilderness and included not only 1) a comprehensive structure of civil law and 2) a detailed worship system but also 3) a standard of moral law for the individual. *Nothing like this has ever happened in history*. Law systems do not normally have such a far-reaching scope where even the values to be held in people's hearts and minds are defined. This in itself is a powerful confirmation that the law was not the work of human beings.

To suggest, as some critics do, that the law of Moses developed over centuries as a variant of ancient Near East legal codes not only defies the internal biblical record but also ignores major differences that made the law of Israel so unique and advanced for its day.

The Constitution of Israel

It is surprising how the word "law" today has such a negative connotation when it comes to religion but in other contexts is highly esteemed. The law of Moses has taken the brunt of this anti-law criticism. Much of this negativity arises from a misunderstanding as to what the law of Moses actually represented.

The law of Moses was not the legalistic control and punishment set of rules that many imagine it to be. It was, in the truest sense of the word, the *constitution* of the nation of Israel. A constitution is, by definition, a document that outlines the fundamental principles by which a nation is to be governed. A constitution is designed to be the supreme law of the land—a big-picture document, establishing the character of the nation. That is exactly what God gave to Israel. Yet despite being delivered by God himself, ancient Israel

> *A constitution is designed to be the supreme law of the land—establishing the character of the nation.*

pushed against God's law code and it has been largely denigrated since.

In contrast, the Constitution of the United States of America is also the supreme law of the land but is hallowed by its citizens. It is regarded as the main source of enlightenment that set America on course to become a great nation and is held up as an example of the benefits a well-thought-out law system can have on a nation's success. It is this same constitution that American citizens and immigrants swear oaths to protect and defend. It is seen as a document of inestimable value protecting and defending the nation.

Why such opposing perspectives? We can understand some of the reasons by considering the state of both nations at the time of their founding.

Perspective of American Law

There were major societal differences present at the time of the founding of America compared to the situation at Mount Sinai. One of these fundamental differences is demonstrated by the words of the Declaration of Independence:

> We hold these truths to be *self-evident*, that all men are created equal, that they are endowed by their Creator with certain unalienable Rights, that among these are Life, Liberty and the pursuit of Happiness.

The founding fathers could confidently state that such truths were "self-evident" because of their background in the Judeo-Christian standards of the mother country of England. Otherwise, history demonstrates that values such as equality of man are *not* self-evident at all. Ideas such as *life, liberty,* and *the pursuit of happiness* have *not* been deemed inherent rights for most people. History is full of empires, nations and fiefdoms that were founded on the exact opposite principle of *inequality* between the rich and poor. Ancient Israel as a newly freed slave nation would also have had little chance of understanding principles such as equality being "self-evident." (Even after ratifying these words in their founding declaration, America struggled with the issue of equality for well over 150 years.)

The American founding fathers had another major advantage. Again, because of their English heritage, the new nation of America was able to inherit and maintain the English common law system, which was in place at the time of the War of Independence.[2] In doing so, they dramatically simplified the scope of their new nation's legal structure. Because laws regulating social and moral

---
[2] Bibliog: (G. Hughes 1996, 9-26)

behavior were extant in the existing common law of the land, there was no need to include such directives in the new American Constitution. This can be verified by simply reading the document. The American Constitution primarily concerns itself with structures and actions of government, not the ethics of the individual citizen.

The legal precedents contained in English common law were based on biblical values incorporated in law at the time of King Alfred the Great (ca. 850 CE). Alfred established a legal code (Book of Dooms) that melded the Ten Commandments and many of the laws of Moses with a code of Saxon laws. He also included concepts from Jesus' Sermon on the Mount.[3] Churchill explains how this system of law further developed in his *History of the English-Speaking Peoples*:

> The Laws of Alfred, continually amplified by his successors, grew into that body of customary law administered by the shire and hundred courts which, under the name of the Laws of St. Edward (the Confessor), the Norman kings undertook to respect, and out of which, with much manipulation by feudal lawyers, the Common Law was founded.[4]

These common law precedents continued to flow through the American legal system even after the separation from England.

The *Great Awakening* spiritual revival of the eighteenth and nineteenth centuries had a further major influence, reinforcing and strengthening biblical values in the New World society before and after American independence. These key factors help explain why the Ten Commandments and biblical law were so strongly reflected in the government and judicial system of the new nation.

America has been looked up to by much of the world as an enlightened nation, but most do not acknowledge the source of that enlightenment. It was not due to the inherent genius of a special people. The fact that America was founded with migrants from many nations proves this beyond dispute. Although it is increasingly being disregarded, it was the *values* that originated from the nation's Judeo-Christian heritage that were held by the founders and allowed to flourish, that created the culture and environment that immigrants found so attractive. These values became a part of the American law code and in

---

[3] Bibliog: (Lee 2006, 12-13)
[4] Bibliog: (W. S. Churchill 1956, 94-95)

conjunction with the Constitution, were at the heart of the success of the United States as a nation.

Israel Needed a Complete Reset

Unlike America, the new nation of Israel had no precedent or parent country to fall back on. The moral standards and laws passed down through the fathers of Israel had become fuzzy during their years of captivity. They had absorbed many of the customs of Egypt where they had been for hundreds of years (Lev. 18:3; Josh. 24:14).

God, therefore, had to give Israel not only a set of national laws for the law and order of the nation—more importantly, he needed to teach the people *personal values* that were dramatically different from the values they had learned during their long captivity. He wanted Israel to adopt his values, not the values of Egypt or the surrounding nations—or those rising from their own innate desires.

God wanted Israel to adopt his values, not the values of Egypt or the surrounding nations—or those arising from their own innate desires.

Counteracting the negative influence of hundreds of years was never going to be easy and Israel was not receptive to change, but God was prepared to be patient. Far from wanting to control or put burdens on these people, God wanted to teach them an enlightened way of life that would lead to true success. This is why the law God gave to Israel was so important and so key to everything he had in mind.

What the Law of Moses Is Not

Whatever I command you, be careful to observe it; you shall not add to it nor take away from it. —Deuteronomy 12:32

Because the Gospels present Jesus frequently in conflict with the religious leaders of his day, people often assume that Jesus' criticisms were directed at those following the law of Moses. But when we look more closely at the practices of these Jewish religious leaders, we find that many of their added traditions had no basis in the law of Moses at all. Some were, in fact, in direct contradiction to the written law. Even more off base were their attempts to use the law in ways that were never intended. Somewhere in the intervening centuries since the return from exile in Babylon their interpretation of the law of Moses had taken a seriously wrong turn.

Because of this confusion between the relatively concise set of *written* laws of Moses and the *extrabiblical* practices of what became rabbinic Judaism (with its extensive rules and regulations), it is important to distinguish between the two.

Judaism and the Oral Law

The term "law of Moses" can mean different things to different people. The Pharisees of Jesus' day believed that God had given Moses many oral instructions in addition to the laws in the written Torah. They believed that Israel passed these oral laws down via word of mouth over the centuries and maintained them through the years of captivity and after their return from exile.[1]

By the time of Jesus and the apostles, the Pharisees in particular, had blurred the line between the written laws of Moses and their oral traditions. To them, the law of Moses included these traditions. Jewish scholar Alfred Edersheim (1825-1889) studied and documented the tedious and legalistic religious practices of the Judaism of Jesus' day. He notes that in the first century, "Traditionalism went further and placed the oral (law) actually above the written Law."[2]

This oral law, or "Oral Torah," was not fully documented until hundreds of

---

[1] The Pharisees were the major sect of Judaism at the time of Jesus. The Pharisees arose on the scene in the second century BC and had begun formalizing what they understood as the oral law. Other Jewish factions (Sadducees, Essenes, Zealots, etc.) had different perspectives on the law.
[2] Bibliog: (Edersheim 1993, p69)

years after the destruction of the temple in Jerusalem in 70 CE. The Talmud today consists of the Mishnah (ca. 200-300 CE) and the Gemara (ca. 500 CE) and provides the basis for modern rabbinic Judaism.

One of the world's leading Talmudical scholars, Rabbi Adin Steinsaltz, confirmed the importance of these extrabiblical writings to Judaism. He wrote:

> If the Bible is the cornerstone of Judaism, then the Talmud is the central pillar, soaring up from the foundations and supporting the entire spiritual and intellectual edifice. *In many ways the Talmud is the most important book in Jewish culture,* the backbone of creativity and of national life. No other work has had a comparable influence on the theory and practice of Jewish life, shaping spiritual content and serving as a guide to conduct.[3]

Considering that these "oral traditions" have been developing for well over 2,000 years, it is not surprising that the religion of the Jews has diverged significantly from the teachings of the original Hebrew Scriptures that Jesus referenced.

Arguments against an Oral Law

Contradicting the idea of an "oral law," the Bible tells us that Moses *wrote* down *everything* that God had told him. There is no hint in Scripture that there was an additional set of undocumented oral laws:

> So Moses came and told the people all the words of the LORD and all the judgments. ... *And Moses wrote all the words of the LORD.* (Exod. 24:3–4)

> So *Moses wrote this law and delivered it to the priests*, the sons of Levi, who bore the ark of the covenant of the LORD, and to all the elders of Israel. (Deut. 31:9)

Shortly after entering the promised land, Moses' successor, Joshua, confirmed that every single word of the law was in written form, which he was able to read out loud:

There is no hint in Scripture that there was an additional set of undocumented oral laws.

---

[3] Bibliog: (Steinsaltz 1976, 3)

> He *read all the words of the law*, the blessings and the cursings, according to all that is written in the Book of the Law. *There was not a word of all that Moses had commanded which Joshua did not read* before all the assembly of Israel. (Josh. 8:34–35)

Despite being transcribed for posterity, even this written law was sometimes in danger of being lost. Hundreds of years after Moses, in the time of king Josiah, the southern nation of Judah had strayed so far from God that the Book of the Law was forgotten. When a copy was found hidden in the temple and brought to King Josiah, he was shocked to learn what it contained (2 Chron. 34:14–18). If the actual written law of Moses had been so neglected and forgotten that it was nearly lost, how could an oral law (if such a thing had existed) have survived during these same years?

Jesus' Support of Written Law

Further pushing back at the idea of an additional oral law is Jesus' clear response to the practices of the Jews of his day. In many of his dialogues with the religious leaders, Jesus criticizes them for their traditions being in *direct conflict* with the written law. Jesus makes the clear distinction between written Scripture and the (oral) traditions of the elders:

> Thus you have made the commandment of God of no effect by your tradition. ... And in vain they worship Me, *teaching as doctrines the commandments of men*. (Matt. 15:6–9)

> He said to them, "All too well you reject the commandment of God, that you may keep your tradition." (Mark 7:9)

At one time Jesus' apostles were taken back by his strong response against the Jewish religious leaders, and they let him know that the Pharisees were offended at what he had said (Matt. 15:12). Jesus' response was blunt: "Let them alone. They are blind leaders of the blind. And if the blind leads the blind, both will fall into a ditch" (v. 14).

In contrast to his attitude toward their traditions, Jesus was highly respectful and supportive of the written Scripture. When tempted by Satan in the wilderness, Jesus countered Satan's proposals with the words "It is written." In the same vein, his regular response when challenged by religious leaders was to refer to the Hebrew Scriptures with the introduction "It is written." When questioned, Jesus would respond with: "What is written in the law? What is your reading of it?" (Luke 10:26).

This is the great benefit of a written law. It allows an individual of any time period to go directly to the source document and verify what is being taught. Even if it did exist, an oral law would always carry doubt as to the veracity of the handed-down message.

Judaism Was Not the Religion of the Old Testament

Jesus' words and actions make it eminently clear that there was something seriously off track with the religion practiced by the religious sects of his day. The Jews had created a religion of men—maybe with the best intentions of "protecting the law"—but one that had gone off the rails to the point where the original intent and purpose of the law had been lost.

Paul later highlighted how his zeal for the misguided religion of Judaism had led to his persecution of the followers of Jesus (Gal. 1:13–14). He later warned Titus about these Jewish teachings, calling them *fables*:

> *Judaism had become a different religion to the one God delivered to Moses at Sinai.*

> Therefore, rebuke them sharply ... not giving heed to *Jewish fables and commandments of men* who turn from the truth. (Titus 1:13–14)

Judaism had become a different religion to the one God delivered to Moses at Sinai.[4]

The 613 Commandments

As a further example of adding tedium to the law, many centuries *after* Christ, the idea started circulating that there were 613 specific commandments in the Torah. Certain Jewish rabbis had extracted every minor directive and nuance in the law and compiled them into a list. Other rabbis came up with different totals, but by the twelfth century CE, the 613 number had gained traction.[5]

But breaking down the law code in such a way is an artificial, manmade construct that does not enlighten, and in fact can mislead. Laws are taken out of context and the overarching importance of major principles of the law are lost in the detail.

The 613 idea was certainly not how Jesus understood or taught the law. It misses the big picture of God's intent for the law and is not a way to gain

---

[4] This is not referring to the cultural traditions of the Jewish people, but the religion and system of worship that developed in the post-Babylonian era.
[5] Bibliog: (Herman 2017)

understanding.

Simplicity of the Law Lost

The rabbis have detracted from the simplicity of the law of Moses by overanalyzing the words of the law and granulating them down to the point where the original intent and context were often lost. A simple test the reader can do is to compare the size of the first five books of the Bible with the thousands of pages and millions of words of the Jewish Talmud. This alone should set off alarm bells. *Was this God's intention?* Israel was specifically commanded *not* to add to what God had given them:

> Whatever I command you, be careful to observe it; *you shall not add to it* nor take away from it. (Deut. 12:32)

The Pharisees were clearly in breach of this instruction of Moses, and rabbinical Judaism has continued this same course to the present.

The additional baggage and legalistic approach of rabbinical Judaism has confused the scope of the system of law God gave Israel. The only laws we will be referring to in this book are the laws that were *written* down by Moses and preserved and transmitted to us in the first five books of our Bibles.

How Credible Is Moses?

For if you believed Moses, you would believe Me; for he wrote about Me.
—John 5:46

The early books of the Bible are traditionally attributed to a man called Moses. But was Moses really a historical figure? How much confidence can we have in the narrative of these ancient events?

Secular scholars reject any sort of divine revelation in these early books of the Bible and go so far as to question whether a man called Moses ever existed. Moses is often presented as a mythical and legendary figure created much later than the timeline Scripture provides. The general secular position is that the laws included in these first five books of the Bible are an invention of men developed over many centuries and finally codified somewhere around the eighth century BCE.[1] As a matter of principle, secular scholars negate the supernatural and generally seek to find alternate explanations as to the source of these documents.

Considering the widely accepted stance against a historic Moses, it will be helpful at the outset to present a brief defense of Moses' life and authorship—and why we can have confidence that his testimony is accurate and true.

Internal Biblical Confirmation

Several major problems arise when dismissing both the historical person called Moses and the God he identifies with originating the law.

Firstly, both the Old and New Testaments state that a man called Moses actually lived, was a liberator of his people, and authored these early books of the Bible. The Bible outlines his lineage precisely for us, and his parents, Amram and Jochebed, are identified (Exod. 6:16–20). The dramatic circumstances of Moses' birth, his concealing and rescue by Pharaoh's daughter, and the origin of his name are provided (Exod. 2:1–10). Moses' first wife, Zipporah (Exod. 2:21), his father-in-law, Jethro (Exod. 18:5), and his children are named (Exod. 2:22; 18:4). His sons are identified as serving in the priesthood, and some of his grandchildren are also named (1 Chron. 23:14–17). If Moses was purely mythical, such carefully recorded personal details would not likely have been given.

David and later prophets also reference Moses as a real person:

---
[1] Bibliog: (Bakers 2013, Documentary Hypothesis p 450)

> He sent *Moses His servant*, and Aaron whom He had chosen. (Ps. 105:26)
>
> We have acted very corruptly against You, and have not kept the commandments, the statutes, nor the ordinances which You commanded *Your servant Moses*. (Neh. 1:7)
>
> Who led them by the *right hand of Moses*, with His glorious arm, dividing the water before them to make for Himself an everlasting name. (Isa. 63:12)
>
> Then the LORD said to me, "*Even if Moses and Samuel stood before Me*, My mind would not be favorable toward this people. Cast them out of My sight, and let them go forth. (Jer. 15:1)
>
> Remember the Law of *Moses, My servant*, which I commanded him in Horeb for all Israel, with the statutes and judgments. (Mal. 4:4)

The New Testament also references Moses as a historical person:

> By faith Moses, when he was born, was hidden three months by his parents, because they saw he was a beautiful child; and they were not afraid of the king's command. By faith Moses, when he became of age, refused to be called the son of Pharaoh's daughter. (Heb. 11:23–24)
>
> Yet Michael the archangel, in contending with the devil, when he disputed about the body of Moses, dared not bring against him a reviling accusation. (Jude 9)

Jesus Confirms Moses

Secondly, we have the testimony of Jesus himself. Jesus confirmed both the existence of Moses, and that it was he who wrote the words of the law. Jesus spoke of Moses as a real human being on multiple occasions:

> For if you believed Moses, you would believe Me; for *he wrote about Me*. (John 5:46)
>
> But even Moses showed in the burning bush passage that the dead are raised. (Luke 20:37)
>
> And as Moses lifted up the serpent in the wilderness. (John 3:14)

Jesus confirmed that Moses was the one that delivered the laws to Israel:

> Did not *Moses give you the law*? (John 7:19)

Moses also significantly appeared with Jesus in vision (Matt. 17:3).

To reject the man Moses as a historical individual is to discredit the testimony of Jesus Christ. The credibility of Jesus and the man Moses stand or fall together.

Historical Evidence

Thirdly, despite theoretical textual analysis to the contrary, no external evidence exists that the first books of the Bible were written over centuries by multiple authors nor that the laws of Moses developed over hundreds of years. Documentary Hypothesis theories (such as JEDP) remain just that—theories that contradict the internal biblical record and turn godly people of old into fictional characters.

Within the books of Moses are records of nations, historical events, cities and locations, and even conversations. These records include the complete history of the rise of Israel as a nation. Archaeology and secular sources have confirmed many locations and events recorded in the biblical books, including the existence of ancient nations, early towns and cities, customs and religious practices of the peoples, and idioms of the day. These details would be nearly impossible to correctly insert centuries later out of context.

Jesus confirmed both the existence of Moses, and that it was he who wrote the words of the law.

Scripture confirms that Moses was academically qualified to write, having received formal training. Stephen refers to him as being *mighty in word* and deed and *learned in all the wisdom of the Egyptians* (Acts 7:21–22). Scholars have noted various writing styles in the books of Moses, but these can be explained in several ways—including that Moses wrote these words over forty years. Over that time he wrote with a range of perspectives, emotions, and contextually different poetic and prose styles.

Those using a critical textual approach to dismiss the written text often ignore the big picture. When Jesus and other writers confirm Moses' authorship, they're not doing so from a technical, deconstructive, textual criticism approach used in our scientific world today. They were simply confirming that Moses was indeed the principal overseer and author of the work.

An Honest Record

Fourthly, in the record of Moses and Israel, no one (Moses and his family included) comes out looking good except God. This gives us confidence that these books represent an honest record of what occurred. From the outset, there is no attempt to cover up these peoples' failures, and we are given multiple frank and blunt assessments of Israel's faithlessness (Exod. 16:28; Num. 14:11; Deut. 9:13; etc.).

Moses is presented as a man with fears and failings, not in the heroic terms we might expect if the story was fabricated. Our first introduction to Moses is someone who kills an Egyptian and then flees in fear (Exod. 2:11–15). Moses is then described as a reluctant messenger for God (Exod. 4:10–14) and a man criticized by his wife (Exod. 4:25–26). Moses' close brother, Aaron, loses his reputation for reliability when he builds a golden calf for the Israelites (Exod. 32:4), and Moses' sister, Miriam ends up with leprosy because of her complaining (Num. 12:10). Toward the end of his life, Moses loses his temper and ends up being excluded from the promised land, even after pleading his case with God to enter (Num. 20:10–12; Deut. 3:23–26).

Authors fabricating these events centuries later would have no reason to include such disparaging passages of the man who was to be Israel's hero. The fact that they are included is a mark of an honest and humble man, someone accountable to a higher power and not on an ego trip. These understandable failings of a human being give us confidence that the words we read are a true testimony of what occurred.

The same is true of the entire Old Testament. It is a record of Israel, both good and bad. The uncomfortable truths of history are not glossed over as they were in the histories of other nations. Israel's failures in war are presented as equally as their victories. Israelites are presented as hardhearted, fearful, and ungrateful people. What nation would fabricate and maintain such a negative and disparaging account of their history? The remnants of the kingdom of Judah (the Jewish people) became the custodians of these writings after their return from captivity. If it was a contrived narrative written much later, as some scholars suggest, why would it have not been presented more favorably? The only plausible answer is that the writings represent an honest record of what happened to both Moses and the nation of Israel.

Profound Nature

Finally, and most convincingly, as we work through the laws of Moses, we will see that many aspects of the law are too profound in their application to have come from the minds of men—especially those supposedly fabricating events over multiple centuries. Laws about caring for strangers and the poor and the widows, laws ensuring that everyone is equal under the law, whether rich or poor, laws on the cancellation of debts, laws protecting servants and strangers—these things go beyond anything seen in any society of the day.

Many of the laws of Moses also work against those in the position of power, and this is a highly unusual and rare thing to find historically. For most of history, men and women in positions of power have aimed to reinforce their own status and position. Yet the laws of Moses insist on the rule of law for great and small without partiality (Deut. 17:19–20).

Many aspects of the law are too profound in their application to have come from the minds of men

Some suggest that the law of Moses was developed from other law codes—such as the Code of Hammurabi or the Code of Ur-Nammu of Mesopotamia. But all law codes overlap in key antisocial behavior areas by necessity. In reality, the comparatives with other ancient law codes are few. The law of Moses had superior human rights, and its scope covers a much broader range of moral, societal, and religious issues, not just civil and criminal matters. It is in that sense absolutely unique.

In summary, the Bible authoritatively confirms that the man Moses was real and was the person responsible for recording the narrative of Israel's history and transcribing the law that God delivered through him to the nation.

Comparing Jesus and Moses

I will raise up for them a Prophet like you [Moses] from among their brethren, and will put My words in His mouth. —Deuteronomy 18:18

Jesus and Moses are often presented as contrasting individuals with opposing ideas of law and grace. Many people's image of Moses comes from the 1960s Cecil B. DeMille movie *The Ten Commandments*. Charlton Heston portrays a grey-bearded Moses who changes from a vibrant and caring leader of men into a stern, detached, religious type after meeting God at the burning bush. In the movie, his wife complains about Moses being distant from his family. "I lost him when he found his God," Zipporah laments. Moses is presented as severe, even angry at times—and somewhat critical of the wrathful God he met on the mountain. This sort of portrayal of both God and Moses does *not* align with Scripture.

Similarly, the persona of Jesus is often portrayed as the opposite of Moses—a "meek and mild" soft individual who focuses only on love, who turns the other cheek and teaches against the harsh laws of the Old Testament. Again, such caricatures of Jesus do not align with the gospel accounts of his life.

Moses and Jesus were probably far more similar than we would otherwise imagine.

Moses and Jesus were probably far more similar than we would otherwise imagine.

One Like Moses

Long before Jesus, God gave Moses a prophecy of a future great prophet who would be like Moses. This prophet was to be someone of such importance that anyone who ignored what he had to say would be held to account by God himself:

> I will raise up for them a Prophet like you *(Moses)* from among their brethren, and will put My words in His mouth, and He shall speak to them all that I command Him. And it shall be that whoever will not hear My words, which He speaks in My name, I will require it of him. (Deut. 18:18–19)

Both Jesus and the apostles confirmed that Jesus was indeed this prophet like Moses (Luke 24:27; John 1:45; Acts 3:22–26), and there are striking parallels between the two, including:

- Both were born at times when the Israelites were under oppression.
- Jesus, like Moses, had to be protected and hidden from the harsh edict of a king's order to kill all the male children.
- Both had a connection with Egypt.
- Both performed public miracles.
- Moses was the physical leader who rescued his people from bondage, paralleling what Jesus would do at a spiritual level.
- Moses was the mediator of the old covenant between God and the people. Jesus was the mediator of the new covenant.
- Moses interceded for his people as Jesus did for all people.
- Both were strong and bold teachers of law and values.

Jesus was like Moses, yet there are differences. For one, Moses was not technically a Jew. He was not of the tribe of Judah as Jesus was; he was a Levite from the tribe of Levi.[1]

But where the two diverge in most people's opinion is in the areas of law and grace. Moses has the reputation of being more legalistic, with a strong focus on *judgment*, whereas Jesus is more often associated with *mercy* and *grace*. Jesus was known to be a friend of sinners, something never associated with Moses.

The Man Moses

We don't know a lot about the personality of Moses, but we do have some clues. He was a prince of Egypt and a leader of men (Acts 7:22). Despite his impressive background, he did not have an overly inflated opinion of himself. When God appears to him in the burning bush and offers him a job, Moses replies, "Who am I that I should go to Pharaoh?" (Exod. 3:11). He argues against taking the job. He is later described as the humblest of men (Num. 12:3). His humility did not mean a lack of courage. Moses was bold and strong with Pharaoh in the face of adversity. He even stood firm with God himself when he held a different opinion (Exod. 32:11–13).

Those who accuse Moses of harshness forget the tough job he was called to do—managing Israel out of Egypt and into the promised land. It was not an easy job, despite God being on his side. The people were ungrateful, fearful, and constantly complained. They frustrated Moses immensely. A lesser man would have given up. God himself reached the end of his tether with the

---

[1] The definition of the word "Jew" changed over the timeline of the Bible. It can mean either an individual of the tribe of Judah, a citizen of the nation of Judah, a descendant of Jacob, or a practitioner of the religion of Judaism.

Israelites several times.

We also see a softer side to Moses in his despair at seeing Miriam with leprosy (Num. 12:11–14) and his prayers for his milder brother, Aaron (Deut. 9:20). Moses often sat for days at a time, personally guiding and teaching the people (Exod. 18:13). Amazingly, he even put his own eternal life on the line for the ungrateful Israelites (Exod. 32:32). He was a bold and caring role model for the people to follow. He was not the harsh and inflexible overlord he is sometimes depicted as. It was Moses who stood in the gap between God's anger and the people. Moses often fell on his face, pleading to God for the rebellious Israelites' lives. When he could have had a personal lineage, he graciously asked God to spare these undeserving people (Exod. 32:9–11).

Jesus Like Moses

Like Moses, Jesus was also a man of action. He was a strong man—a builder[2] used to dealing with timber and stone. Twice he boldly strode into the outer court of the temple driving out the moneychangers with a whip in full view of the religious leaders. He was decisive, even feisty at times, and spoke bluntly when needed. He had no time for hypocrites. He offended the Pharisees on multiple occasions, and as his arrest drew near, he spoke even more fearlessly. At the same time, Jesus was caring and kind to society's most vulnerable. He was meek in the true definition of the word. He loved children, and they loved him (Mark 10:14; Matt. 21:15–16). He was a bold individual with perfect clarity of his purpose and mission. He was not the mild, soft-spoken person many people imagine.

Moses appeared beside Jesus in the Transfiguration with another bold character, Elijah (Matt. 17:1–3). Moses represented the law, and Elijah the prophets. The vision demonstrates Jesus' strong support for both men and what they stood for.

Key Difference Between Moses and Jesus

There is one key reason Jesus has more of a reputation for mercy and grace than Moses, but it has nothing to do with different standards of values and principles—it has to do with jurisdiction.

Jesus and Moses both taught extensively on law. But Jesus, teaching in the Roman-occupied province of Judea, primarily focused on moral law and the importance of the individual's response to God. Moses, on the other hand, was

---

[2] Greek *Tekton*.

responsible for the entire scope of law for a nation—including the civil, ceremonial, and moral law.

The failure to recognize these differences of jurisdiction has led to many unreasonable and invalid comparisons between Moses and Jesus.

Moses was the executive leader of the physical nation of Israel. He was called by God and given the mission of leading the people out of Egypt and into the promised land (Exod. 3:15–17). Under God, Moses was the supreme leader of the nation. In that capacity, he filled many executive and administrative roles. He was essentially the president of the nation, chief justice, commander-in-chief, and a priest all rolled into one. He had the authority to judge the people and appoint other judges. He oversaw the setup of the administrations of the tabernacle and the tribes. It was his role to anoint his brother Aaron and establish the Levitical priesthood (Exod. 30:30; Ps. 99:6).

> *The failure to recognize these differences of jurisdiction has led to many unreasonable and invalid comparisons between Moses and Jesus.*

Moses was unique because no other physical leader in Israel's history was ever given this level of jurisdiction and authority. God specifically said that Moses' successor, Joshua, would not have the same relationship with him that Moses had. Only some of Moses' authority would be given to him (Num. 27:18–21; Deut. 34:10).

Jesus, in contrast, did not claim any executive or administrative authority in this physical world. Unlike Moses, whose nation *was* of this world, Jesus made it clear that his kingdom *was not* of this world:

> Jesus answered, "My kingdom is not of this world. If My kingdom were of this world, My servants would fight, so that I should not be delivered to the Jews; but now My kingdom is not from here." (John 18:36)

At one stage the people tried to make Jesus king, but he escaped (John 6:15). Worldly power was not part of his mission. It was the same with legal authority. As a judge of his people, Moses spent long hours judging the cases that the Israelites brought before him (Exod. 18:13–14). In contrast, Jesus claimed no such legal authority to judge people during his earthly ministry (Luke 12:14).

Most of the perceived differences between Moses and Jesus come down to this simple but significant point of jurisdiction: Jesus was not a judge, nor a Levitical priest, and neither did he assume any worldly power. He let the forces of evil overtake him for a great purpose.

This was something that puzzled the apostles for a long time. They assumed all along that Jesus had come to establish his kingdom. At one time they asked Jesus to call down fire in judgment (Luke 9:54). They wanted him to demonstrate his power and execute authority. For this reason, his arrest, trial, and death were a massive shock to them. They thought all hope was lost. Even after his resurrection, the establishment of his physical kingdom was still foremost in their minds (Acts 1:6–7). It took them some time to put Jesus' sojourn into its correct perspective.

> *Unlike Moses, whose nation was of this world, Jesus made it clear that his kingdom was not of this world.*

Jesus can be rightly compared to Moses as a ruler of Israel, but in his first coming, his focus was the establishment of his spiritual assembly: the church (Heb. 12:22–24). When he comes again, he will come as King of kings with *executive power*, not just over Israel, but over all the nations of this earth (Matt. 24:30–31; 26:64; Dan. 7:13–14; Rev. 1:7). That future coming will be dramatically different from his first visit to this earth—"Of the increase of that government there will be no end" (Isa. 9:7).

Grace and Truth before Jesus

In the Gospel of John, one particular verse is often interpreted as Moses and Jesus being at different ends of a spectrum:

> For the law was given through Moses, grace and truth came through Jesus Christ. (John 1:17)

One might get the impression that John was implying here that there was no grace or truth prior to Jesus. Some translations include a "but" (i.e., "the law came from Moses, *but* grace and truth came through Jesus") as if to emphasize a major contrast between Moses and Jesus. But this insertion of "but" creates a false dichotomy not in the original text. There *was* grace and truth in Old Testament times, long before Moses. Grace was at the heart of God's relationship with Noah, Abraham, and the fathers of Israel. He graciously rescued undeserving Israel from Egypt. He announced himself as merciful and gracious to Moses on Mount Sinai (Exod. 34:6). Likewise, "truth" was not new with the coming of Jesus. God has always been the source of truth—he has never been otherwise.

John was simply emphasizing Jesus as the *ultimate expression* of God's grace and truth. Only through the life and death of Jesus can a person come to the *full* understanding of God's grace and his plan of salvation for humanity. Jesus didn't just teach the truth—he *is* the way and the truth (John 14:6).

There was grace and truth in Old Testament times, long before Moses.

Knowing that Jesus was *that great prophet like Moses* affirms we should look to Jesus for understanding the original purpose and intent of the law of Moses. Fortunately for us, Jesus had much to say about the topic.

2

PART 2: Key Perspectives from Historical Sources

This section will consider the viewpoints of primary and secondary historical sources who were impacted by the Mosaic law in their lives and culture. The perspectives of such close sources can add greatly to a person's understanding—especially considering how distant modern readers are from those times.

These sources, starting with Jesus himself, provide a valuable reference point to ensure our perspective of the law and its impact on people's lives is historically sound.

Jesus' Perspective of the Law

You ... have neglected the weightier matters of the law: justice and mercy and faith. These you ought to have done, without leaving the others undone.
—Matthew 23:23

Jesus provides the ideal reference point for putting the law of Moses into its correct perspective. He had both the foreknowledge of being with God in the beginning and a perfect understanding of the law's original intent.

From a practical point of view, the law of Moses was also a major influence in Jesus' life and ministry. While the cultural environment he lived in was not a full implementation of Mosaic civil law, the Romans did allow "Jewish law" (as they called it) to operate when it didn't conflict with Roman law (John 18:31; Acts 18:15). The law of Moses was a regular topic of discussion, and Jesus had plenty to say about it, both to his disciples and to the religious leaders of his day. And Jesus was truthful and bold, not afraid to "tell it like it is."

Jesus Criticizes the Religious Leaders

At the time of Jesus, the Pharisees and scribes sat in what was called "Moses' Seat" (Matt. 23:2). Those sitting in the symbolic "seat of Moses" were in positions of authority—as teachers, judges, and interpreters of the law of Moses. People came to these men for advice and judgments, and this gave them enormous influence over the lives of ordinary people.

The problem was that Jesus identified many of these religious leaders as hypocrites. They taught one thing and did another. They had an external pious appearance, but according to Jesus, they were "whitewashed tombs" riddled with hypocrisy. As his ministry progressed, he became increasingly vocal in his criticism of their understanding and application of the law. These religious leaders regarded themselves as disciples of Moses, but Jesus had a diametrically opposite view of their relationship with Moses.

Jesus had a diametrically opposite view of their relationship with Moses.

It came to a head at the temple one day late in his ministry. In Matthew 23, Jesus confronted the Pharisees with such a hard-hitting diatribe that it must have sent shock waves through them and everyone listening. He started his discourse by affirming that though the scribes and the Pharisees were indeed in a position of authority, they were abusing that position because of their hypocritical actions:

> Then Jesus spoke to the multitudes and to His disciples, saying: "The scribes and the Pharisees *sit in Moses' seat.* Therefore whatever they tell you to observe, that observe and do, *but do not do according to their works;* for they say, and do not do." (Matt. 23:1–3)[1]

He talked about the burdens *they* were putting on the people with their observances, and sharply rebuked them for what they were doing:

> For *they* bind heavy burdens, hard to bear, and lay them on men's shoulders; but they themselves will not move them with one of their fingers. But all their works they do to be seen by men. (Matt. 23:4–5)

According to Jesus, this was not how things were supposed to be done. He criticized their hypocrisy and the enormous damage they were doing in people's lives—many who looked up to them as their spiritual guides:

> But woe to you, scribes and Pharisees, hypocrites! For you shut up the kingdom of heaven against men; for you neither go in yourselves, nor do you allow those who are entering to go in. (Matt. 23:13)

There is no suggestion that Jesus was criticizing the written laws of Moses or that the law of Moses was troubling the people. Rather, he had his sights squarely on the hypocritical men who were overloading the people with burdensome, hypocritical rules, and judgmental attitudes.

Jesus Highlights Foundational Principles

In this same polemic against the Pharisees, Jesus highlighted key principles that must be applied by administrators and judges of the law if they were going to meet the standards of governance that God expected:

> Woe to you, scribes and Pharisees, hypocrites! For you pay tithe of mint and anise and cummin, and have *neglected the weightier matters of the law: justice and mercy and faith.* These you ought to have done, without leaving the others undone. (Matt. 23:23)

The law he was talking about here was the law of Moses. His whole discourse from the start of Matthew 23 was directed at the teachers of the law who sat in Moses' seat. Jesus strongly stated that there was no excuse for their lack of

---

[1] "Sitting in Moses' seat" was to carry the authority of Moses. This is a reference to the Pharisees reading and teaching from the *written* law of Moses. It cannot be a reference to their *unwritten* oral traditions because Jesus rejected those on multiple occasions.

understanding of these important foundational matters of *justice*, *mercy*, and *faith*.

Note that Jesus did not present these three principles as new ideas, nor did he imply that the concepts were beyond them; he otherwise would not have come down so hard on them as he did. Jesus says, as teachers of the law, they *should have understood* these weightier principles. The prophet Micah, for example, had previously highlighted these same foundational principles:

> And what does the LORD require of you but to do *justly*, to love *mercy*, and to *walk humbly with your God*? (Mic. 6:8)

By calling the religious leaders "hypocrites" Jesus confirms they knew better. He went on to *berate* them for their myopic and hypocritical interpretation of the law and for missing these major principles. He was so fired up that he pronounced woes on them if they didn't change their ways (Matt. 23:25–33). In Luke's account of an earlier interaction, Jesus phrases his criticism a little differently, stating that they were also missing the "love of God" in their administration:

There is no suggestion that Jesus was criticizing the written laws of Moses or that the law of Moses was troubling the people.

> But woe to you Pharisees! For you tithe mint and rue and all manner of herbs, and *pass by justice and the love of God.* These you ought to have done, without leaving the others undone. (Luke 11:42)

From Jesus' perspective, the problem was not with the law itself—it was with the doctrine of the Pharisees. The Pharisees were not administering the Mosaic law to the standard that God had originally established. They claimed to trust in Moses, but they ended up being condemned by the very Scripture they professed to believe in:

> Do not think that I shall accuse you to the Father; *there is one who accuses you—Moses, in whom you trust*. For if you believed Moses, you would believe Me; for he wrote about Me. *But if you do not believe his writings, how will you believe My words?* (John 5:45–47)

Understanding Jesus' perspective is important because it is the *right* perspective. People have often looked at the law of Moses and criticized it for its lack of love and mercy—yet Jesus berated the religious leaders of his day for not applying the principles of love and mercy that he says were *foundational to understanding the original law*!

Jesus Rejects Traditions of Men

Jesus didn't just talk about the law in a theoretical sense. He wanted his listeners to understand how the principles of love, justice, mercy, and faith were supposed to be implemented in life. In doing so Jesus demonstrated his disdain for misguided rules and regulations which were directly opposed to the original intent of the law of Moses.

Jesus went out of his way at times to deliberately ignore other Pharisaical "religious" practices that served no purpose other than to prop up the self-righteousness of the individual. One time, the religious leaders challenged Jesus as to why he didn't follow their rules:

The problem was not with the law itself—it was with the doctrine of the Pharisees.

> For the Pharisees and all the Jews do not eat unless they wash their hands in a special way, holding the tradition of the elders. When they come from the marketplace, they do not eat unless they wash. And there are many other things which they have received and hold, like the washing of cups, pitchers, copper vessels, and couches. Then the Pharisees and scribes asked Him, *"Why do Your disciples not walk according to the tradition of the elders, but eat bread with unwashed hands?"* (Mark 7:3–5)

Again, such tedious procedures do not come from the law of Moses. They were created as extensions of the law by misguided teachers. Jesus could have gone along with these things to avoid offense, but he pushed back at them in no uncertain terms:

> He answered and said to them, *"Well did Isaiah prophesy of you hypocrites,* as it is written: 'This people honors Me with their lips, but their heart is far from Me. And *in vain they worship Me, teaching as doctrines the commandments of men.'* For laying aside the commandment of God, you hold the tradition of men—the washing of pitchers and cups, and many other such things you do." (Mark 7:6–8)

Jesus called these legalistic practices "commandments of men" and confirmed that such invented religious rituals worked *against* the commandments of God. This is a strong affirmation that the law of Moses did not support such tedium in the daily life of an Israelite.

Jesus consistently taught that God had *always* been primarily interested in the heart (Mark 7:6). It wasn't a new idea with him. The religion of the Pharisees was about outward appearance based on pretense and hypocrisy:

> Then He said to them in His teaching, "Beware of the scribes, who desire to go around in long robes, love greetings in the marketplaces, the best seats in the synagogues, and the best places at feasts, who devour widows' houses, and for a pretense make long prayers. These will receive greater condemnation." (Mark 12:38–40)

The distorted interpretations of Moses continued after Jesus' death. A faction of the Pharisees who eventually accepted Jesus as the Messiah still clung to wrong interpretations of Moses. Many of the issues that Paul had to address in the New Testament church related to their legalistic practices.

Jesus Rejects Segregation

The Pharisees had many misguided rules and regulations, but the ones related to the treatment of non-Jews stand out for particular criticism. The Pharisees had developed a regime of segregation from gentiles and they strongly criticized Jesus for ignoring these rules. It's a law that Peter later referred to:

> You know how *unlawful* it is for a Jewish man to keep company with or go to one of another nation. (Acts 10:28)

People often assume that the law being referred to came from the law of Moses. But this Jewish law, like many others, was directly *opposed* to Moses. The Mosaic law required *all* people, including strangers and foreigners, to be treated *equally* and *impartially* under the law (Num. 15:16). Strangers were to be loved as one loves oneself:

> The stranger who dwells among you shall be to you as one born among you, and *you shall love him as yourself.* (Lev. 19:34)

Jesus ignored Jewish laws of segregation and interacted with foreigners, women, children, etc., as he saw fit. The way he treated people perfectly aligned with the law of Moses and reflected the impartiality of God (Deut. 10:17). His speaking to the Samaritan woman at the well is another example of Jesus rejecting such negative manmade traditions (John 4:9). His apostles, who had grown up with the Jewish laws of separation, marveled that he took the time to dialogue with her (v. 27).

In the same vein, when challenged by the Pharisees on why he spent time with "sinners and tax collectors," Jesus' response was to tell them to "go and learn," confirming they *should have understood these things* from Scripture:

> When Jesus heard that, He said to them, "Those who are well have no need of a physician, but those who are sick. *But go and learn what this means:* 'I desire mercy and not sacrifice.'" (Matt. 9:12–13)

It is sometimes difficult to separate the added baggage of the Pharisees from the simple written structure of law given by Moses. But one thing is clear: the religion of the Pharisees was not the religion of the Old Testament that God gave through Moses. A simple comment by Jesus says it all:

Did not Moses give you the law, yet none of you keeps the law?

> Did not Moses give you the law, yet none of you keeps the law? (John 7:19)

Jesus and the Sabbath

Jesus' interactions on the Sabbath day are particularly insightful and highlight the disparity between Jesus' understanding of the law with that of the religious leaders. The administration of the Sabbath day at the time of Jesus was one of rigid rules, which would have turned the Sabbath into a day of dread for many. Yet the description of the day in the written law of Moses describes it as one of celebration and liberty, a day to remind the people that God had freed them from oppression (Deut. 5:15).

God did not intend for the Sabbath to be burdensome, but a day of rest and release. This is how Jesus understood the intent of the day. He pushed back strongly against manmade Sabbath rules to the point the religious leaders accused him of breaking the Sabbath (John 9:16). But their accusation was off base. Jesus confirmed the correct perspective of the Sabbath:

> [Jesus] said to them, "The *Sabbath was made for man*, and not man for the Sabbath." (Mark 2:27)

It was not the Sabbath Jesus had a problem with—it was the religious leaders. Jesus explained that the Sabbath day was a gift from God, yet the Pharisees had turned the law of the Sabbath upside down, thinking it was a measure of their own righteousness.

Jesus' teachings about the Sabbath provide the perfect example of the pragmatic way God originally expected the Sabbath to be applied. Jesus taught that it was lawful to do good on the Sabbath:

> What man is there among you who has one sheep, and if it falls into a pit on the Sabbath, will not lay hold of it and lift it out? Of how much more value then is a man than a sheep? *Therefore it is lawful* to do good on the Sabbath. (Matt. 12:11–12)

Even though there is no specific allowance in the law of Moses to rescue or water animals on the Sabbath, Jesus confirmed that doing so was a sensible and perfectly acceptable judgment to make. He used the Pharisees' own practices to drive home his point:

> Hypocrite! Does not each one of you on the Sabbath loose his ox or donkey from the stall, and lead it away to water it? (Luke 13:15)

On another Sabbath occasion, Jesus' hungry disciples were picking and eating heads of grain. The Pharisees accused them of doing something unlawful (Matt. 12:1–2). Jesus' response to this alleged "law-breaking" is also insightful. He could have rightfully countered the Pharisees by stating that their criticism was baseless, and that there was nothing in the written law to support their position. Instead, he references an obscure Old Testament story involving David to drive home a more fundamental point. When David was on the run from Saul, he and his men ate holy shewbread which was technically unlawful for lay persons to eat (Matt. 12:3–4; 1 Sam. 21:1–6). Yet Jesus said David was "guiltless."

Some read this as a new interpretation of the administration of the law of Moses, but Jesus went on to again say that the Pharisees *should have understood* these things because of something the law itself demonstrated: that at times the issues of life *must take precedence over rules*:

> Or *have you not read in the law* that on the Sabbath the priests in the temple profane the Sabbath, and are blameless? Yet I say to you that in this place there is One greater than the temple. *But if you had known what this means*, "I desire mercy and not sacrifice," you would not have condemned the guiltless. (Matt. 12:5–7)

Jesus confirmed that Sabbath keeping was to be approached pragmatically and with mercy on those who had extenuating circumstances. Even under the old covenant, God would not condemn a person for making sensible judgments on the application of the law.

Respect for Moses' Words

There are many other examples of Jesus and the law of Moses that could be commented on. One additional example is worth noting. In the well-known parable of Lazarus and the rich man, Jesus describes the rich man calling out to Abraham from his place of torment, asking him to send Lazarus back to his family to warn them to change their ways. Abraham's response in the parable is revealing:

> Abraham said to him, *"They have Moses and the prophets; let them hear them."* And he said, "No, father Abraham; but if one goes to them from the dead, they will repent." But he said to him, *"If they do not hear Moses and the prophets, neither will they be persuaded though one rise from the dead."* (Luke 16:29–31)

Jesus' implication was clear: the books of Moses and the prophets contain the words of life.

There were many other occasions in his ministry where Jesus could have criticized the law of Moses if he had a mind to do so, but he never did. In every case, his criticism was for the misguided teachers who had both distorted and added to the written law.

There is no hint in Jesus' teachings that he was trying to start an entirely new religion.

From the start of his ministry, Jesus set out to present the true and right perspective of the laws of the Old Testament. This was something that the Messiah was prophesied to do. He would be one to "magnify the law and make it glorious" (Isa. 42:21 ESV). There is no hint in Jesus' teachings that he was trying to start an entirely new religion. Everything he taught was based on the foundation written in the Hebrew Scriptures.

Jesus and the Sermon on the Mount

Therefore whatever you want men to do to you, do also to them, for this is the Law and the Prophets. —Matthew 7:12

Jesus' famous discourse, commonly called the Sermon on the Mount, is a lengthy sermon given early in Jesus' ministry. The sermon is found in chapters 5, 6, and 7 of the book of Matthew. (A shorter version of a similar discourse is found in Luke 6.) In this sermon, Jesus covers the central principles of his ministry and sets the stage for many of his other teachings. A common perception of this sermon is that of Jesus teaching a new standard of personal and moral behavior that wasn't previously understood or taught under the old covenant.

But a closer look at what Jesus said shows that the key points of his sermon were built on principles *already included* in Scripture. Certainly, the way in which Jesus delivered this sermon was new and insightful, but the underlying concepts he presented were based on the Law, the Prophets, and the Writings of what we call the Old Testament. When put in its correct perspective, Jesus' sermon is a powerful demonstration of the respect that he had for the written law of Moses.

> *Jesus' sermon is a powerful demonstration of the respect that he had for the written law of Moses.*

The Beatitudes

The Sermon on the Mount starts with eight blessings—commonly called the "Beatitudes" (Matt. 5:1–11). The eight principles underlying these blessings align with the written Scriptures of the Old Testament. Many study Bibles in fact provide references to Old Testament verses against each of these blessings. For example, "Blessed are the meek, for they shall inherit the earth" is a direct reference to Psalm 37:11. Being poor in spirit is a theme mentioned multiple times in Scripture (e.g., Isa. 66:2; Ps. 34:18), and the importance of being merciful is extensively noted (e.g., 2 Sam. 22:26; Ps. 18:25).

All of the concepts Jesus referred to—of being poor in spirit, meek, humble, pure, merciful, seeking God with the whole heart, being a peacemaker, etc.—are principles that were taught and implied throughout the Hebrew Scriptures. They reflect God's standards, which are consistent and unchanging. They are principles that all the godly people of old understood.

Jesus had the unique ability to express these timeless principles in a memorable and concise way that his listeners could appreciate and retain.

For the people listening to Jesus' discourse, many of these principles would have been in stark contrast to the practices of their religious teachers who were so often at odds with the Scripture they professed to follow.

You Have Heard It Was Said

Before launching into the core message of the sermon, Jesus made a definitive statement aimed at setting the context for what he was about to teach:

> Do not think that I came to destroy the Law or the Prophets. I did not come to destroy but to fulfill. For assuredly, I say to you, till heaven and earth pass away, one jot or one tittle will by no means pass from the law till all is fulfilled. (Matt. 5:17–18)

Jesus knew that when his audience heard the words he was about to speak, some would wrongly think that he *was* contradicting the law and the prophets. He therefore made it clear that was not his intent. He was going to be controversial, but his debate was not with the written word.

In this part of his sermon, Jesus referenced six well-known sayings of the day, which he introduced with the words: "You have heard that it was said ..." (Matt. 5:21, 27, 31, 33, 38, 43). His response to each saying was corrective: "But I say to you ..." With each use of the word "but," Jesus was taking a different position to what was being said. But who or what was he taking issue with?

A first-time reader might assume that Jesus was taking issue with the law of Moses, but this is not the case. Jesus' issue was with what was being *said*, not what was *written*. Nowhere in his ministry did Jesus ever have an issue with what was *written* in the law, but he often took issue with what was being *taught*. His goal was to correct certain faulty teachings of the day. His opening statement to this section clarifies who he had a problem with:

> *Nowhere in his ministry did Jesus ever have an issue with what was written in the law, but he often took issue with what was being taught.*

> For I say to you, that unless your righteousness exceeds the righteousness of *the scribes and Pharisees*, you will by no means enter the kingdom of heaven. (Matt. 5:20)

The Pharisees and the scribes had developed religious practices and sayings that did not align with the original teaching of Scripture but they were enormously influential. As first-century Jewish historian Josephus noted, "Through their doctrines they were greatly able to persuade the body of the people."[1]

Sayings Supported in the Law of Moses

A brief examination of Jesus' six teachings that follow reveal a contrast between the oral teachings and practices of the Pharisees and the way God intended for the written law of Moses to be understood.

1. **Murder/Hatred**—Jesus taught:

> You have heard that it was said to those of old, "You shall not murder, and whoever murders will be in danger of the judgment." *But* I say to you that whoever is angry with his brother without a cause shall be in danger of the judgment. (Matt. 5:21–22)

Jesus was clearly not taking issue with the law against murder. The "but" in Jesus' comment was addressing the wrong idea that murder could be narrowly defined—that it was ok to hate someone in your heart as long as you didn't actually commit murder. In this he had the support of the written law. The law specifically taught against hatred and harboring grudges against others:

> You shall *not hate your brother in your heart. ...nor bear any grudge* against the children of your people, but you shall love your neighbor as yourself. (Lev. 19:17–18)

Jesus was affirming God's original standards. Hatred against another has *always* been the spirit of murder. The religious leaders of his day interpreted the law of murder strictly to the letter, ignoring the broader intent. We see that demonstrated in the way they were often filled with anger and hatred (Acts 5:33; 7:54)—the most obvious example being their unreasonable hatred of Jesus (Luke 6:11; John 5:18; Matt. 12:14).[2]

2. **Adultery**—Jesus taught:

> You have heard that it was said to those of old, "You shall not commit adultery." *But* I say to you that whoever looks at a woman to lust for

---

[1] Bibliog: (Whiston 1989, 477 Bk 18(3))
[2] Jesus elsewhere criticized the narrow, legalistic way the Pharisees interpreted the law, missing the overall intent. "Many such things they do," he said (Mark 7:9–13).

her has already committed adultery with her in his heart. (Matt. 5:27–28)

People often assume that the sin of adultery being defined this way was a new idea with Jesus. But the law supported Jesus' teaching, clearly noting that lust had always been a sin:

> You shall not covet your neighbor's wife ... nor anything that is your neighbor's. (Exod. 20:17)

Jesus was emphasizing the importance of what went on *inside* a person. He rejected the legalistic idea that it was ok to think lustfully as long as it did not result in physical contact. Jesus again reaffirmed the written law and God's intent from the beginning.

3. **Divorce**—Jesus taught:

> Furthermore it has been said, "Whoever divorces his wife, let him give her a certificate of divorce." *But* I say to you that whoever divorces his wife for any reason except sexual immorality causes her to commit adultery; and whoever marries a woman who is divorced commits adultery. (Matt. 5:31–32)

Jesus wasn't changing God's law on divorce. God has always hated divorce:

> For the LORD God of Israel says that He *hates divorce.* (Mal. 2:16)

In a later statement, Jesus made it clear that Moses only allowed divorce because of the hard-heartedness of the people but that it was never God's ideal:

> He said to them, "Moses, because of the hardness of your hearts, permitted you to divorce your wives, but *from the beginning it was not so.*" (Matt. 19:8)

The Pharisees, on the other hand, had distorted and misapplied the divorce provisions of Moses. Their historical divorce practices have been well documented.[3] They interpreted the law as allowing divorce on almost any grounds. They had turned Moses' instructions on divorce into a license to legalistically dispose of a wife when it suited them. Jesus reaffirmed the importance of the marriage institution.

---

[3] Bibliog: (Edersheim 1993, 704-706)

4. **Oaths**—Jesus taught:

> Again you have heard that it was said to those of old, "You shall not swear falsely, but shall perform your oaths to the Lord." *But* I say to you, do not swear at all: neither by heaven, for it is God's throne; nor by the earth, for it is His footstool; nor by Jerusalem, for it is the city of the great King. Nor shall you swear by your head, because you cannot make one hair white or black. But let your "Yes" be "Yes," and your "No," "No." For whatever is more than these is from the evil one. (Matt. 5:33–37)

Again, Jesus was not taking issue with the law of Moses. Believers were still taking vows decades after Christ (Acts 18:18; 21:23). Marriage and baptism vows are still taken to this day. But such things are a serious matter. Jesus was teaching that oaths and vows should have no place in the daily life of a believer. A person's word should be their bond without having to swear an oath.

What the Pharisees were doing at that time makes a whole study of itself. They had a confusing and contradictory regime of oaths for which Jesus later derided them (Matt. 23:16–22). It seems that they created their bizarre hierarchy of oaths so that they could break their word when it suited them.

5. **Retaliation**—Jesus taught:

> You have heard that it was said, "An eye for an eye and a tooth for a tooth." But I tell you not to resist an evil person. But whoever slaps you on your right cheek, turn the other to him also. If anyone wants to sue you and take away your tunic, let him have your cloak also. And whoever compels you to go one mile, go with him two. Give to him who asks you, and from him who wants to borrow from you do not turn away. (Matt. 5:38–42)

Jesus here was not taking issue with the legal and justice system of the law of Moses. He was addressing the issue of *personal retaliation*. God did not give individuals the "eye for an eye" principle so they could take personal vengeance on someone who was treating them badly. Personal vengeance, even holding grudges against others, was forbidden in the law of Moses:

> *You shall not take vengeance*, nor bear any grudge against the children of your people. (Lev. 19:18)

The Pharisees and other religious leaders were distorting the original intent of the law and using it to justify their personal vindictive attitudes.[4]

6. **Hatred of Enemies**—Jesus taught:

> You have heard that it was said, "You shall love your neighbor and hate your enemy." *But* I say to you, love your enemies, bless those who curse you, do good to those who hate you, and pray for those who spitefully use you and persecute you, that you may be sons of your Father in heaven; for He makes His sun rise on the evil and on the good, and sends rain on the just and on the unjust. (Matt. 5:43–45)

The law of Moses did not teach that it was acceptable to hate your enemies. Jesus was referencing what was being "said" by the teachers of that time. In contrast, the law of Moses taught the following:

> If you meet your *enemy's* ox or his donkey going astray, you shall surely bring it back to him again. If you see the donkey of one *who hates you* lying under its burden, and you would refrain from helping it, you shall surely help him with it. (Exod. 23:4–5).

Later Old Testament Scriptures built on this principle:

> If your enemy is hungry, give him bread to eat; and if he is thirsty, give him water to drink; for so you will heap coals of fire on his head, and the LORD will reward you. (Prov. 25:21–22)

The Golden Rule

Jesus continued with his historic sermon, correcting misguided ideas of pretentious giving, ostentatious prayers, judging others, grasping for wealth, worrying, etc. and contrasted these ideas with how a believer should act.

Near the end of his sermon, Jesus summed up with a highly significant statement that confirmed all his teachings were supported by the underlying foundation of the law of Moses. It is a statement often referred to as the "Golden Rule":

> *Therefore,* whatever you want men to do to you, do also to them, *for this is the Law and the Prophets.* (Matt. 7:12)

This is an important statement. Loving others *was the law and the prophets*, according to Jesus. He later called this the second great commandment (Matt. 22:39–40). It is a strong confirmation that the way of life outlined in the

---
[4] Refer to the chapter "Eye for Eye, Tooth for Tooth."

Mosaic law and reflected in the prophets was founded on the principle of love toward other people. All the laws, therefore, must be interpreted and applied with that intent. This explains why Jesus made such a strong statement at the outset of his sermon—that he was not there to destroy the law but to fill it up and restore its original intent (Matt. 5:17).

Loving others was the law and the prophets, according to Jesus.

Unfortunately, people not familiar with the contents of the law of Moses will assume that Jesus' sermon was a criticism of the Old Testament system. But this was not the case. Jesus' issue was only with the misguided religious teachers of his day. Jesus taught in a unique way and magnified the law by giving us a deeper understanding of the intent, but his foundation was solidly in line with the written words delivered to Moses.

Moses' Perspective of the Law

Be careful to observe [these statutes] for this is your wisdom and your understanding in the sight of the peoples who will hear all these statutes, and say, "Surely this great nation is a wise and understanding people."
—Deuteronomy 4:6

Moses' personal perspective concerning the law is important to consider. After all, it was Moses who received the law and was tasked to oversee its implementation in the nation. When the people had questions about administration, it was Moses who sought answers from God. When the people complained, it was again Moses who stood between the people and God. And he did this for 40 years, through numerous trials and tribulations, right up to the time of his death.

Moses His Own Man

It's natural to assume that Moses would be an automatic cheerleader for the laws he had been given, that he would maintain a positive spin even if he thought the law code was the burdensome or unkeepable system that some critics have claimed.

But Moses was clearly no puppet. We see numerous examples of Moses having no hesitation in expressing his thoughts to God and querying points of law when they arose. If Moses had a question or doubts on any matter, he was never shy in making his position clear. Even in the presence of God's anger, Moses didn't hesitate to speak his mind (Exod. 32:11; Num. 14:11–13).

> *Even in the presence of God's anger, Moses didn't hesitate to speak his mind.*

On one occasion Moses unloaded on God his deep frustration with these people who continually complained and pushed back at everything he asked them to do. His bluntness in speaking to God is startling:

> So Moses said to the LORD, "Why have You afflicted Your servant? And why have I not found favor in Your sight, that You have laid the burden of all these people on me? Did I conceive all these people? Did I beget them? ... Where am I to get meat to give to all these people? ... I am not able to bear all these people alone, because the burden is too heavy for me. If You treat me like this, please kill me here and now." (Num. 11:11–15)

Moses' brutal honesty on this and many other occasions gives us confidence in his perspective. Here was a person who did not hesitate to tell God exactly what he really thought.

Moses Supported the Law

So what do we find? Do we find Moses complaining about God's teachings or in any way implying that they were burdensome or exacerbating his difficulties in managing the Israelites? We find no such complaint.

At no point does Moses criticize the law or imply that it was too difficult or impossible for the people to keep—quite the opposite. Moses was an enthusiastic supporter of the way of life God had outlined. Even though there was ongoing pushback from these faithless people, Moses had confidence that this system of law would be positive for the nation if they would only keep it.

It is especially significant to read Moses' sentiments in the book of Deuteronomy. Deuteronomy is an outline of a sermon Moses gave to the people nearly forty years after God gave the initial law at Mount Sinai. After all these years Moses was still extremely positive and supportive of the system:

> Surely I have taught you statutes and judgments, just as the LORD my God commanded me, that you should act according to them in the land which you go to possess. Therefore be careful to observe them; for this is your wisdom and your understanding in the sight of the peoples who will hear all these statutes, and say, "Surely this great nation is a wise and understanding people." For what great nation is there that has God so near to it, as the LORD our God is to us, for whatever reason we may call upon Him? And what great nation is there that has such statutes and righteous judgments as are in all this law which I set before you this day? (Deut. 4:5–8)

At the time Moses wrote these words, the nation had already lived under these statutes and judgments for a couple of generations since Mount Sinai. If it was becoming oppressive, Moses might not have been so enthusiastic and generous with his words. Yet he was so confident in the outcomes of the law system, *he thought that other nations would admire Israel and see them as a wise people!*

Moses never thought what God was asking Israel to do was beyond their capabilities or too complex:

> For this commandment which I command you today is *not too mysterious for you, nor is it far off*. It is not in heaven, that you should

say, 'Who will ascend into heaven for us and bring it to us, that we may hear it and do it?" Nor is it beyond the sea, that you should say, "Who will go over the sea for us and bring it to us, that we may hear it and do it?" *But the word is very near you, in your mouth and in your heart, that you may do it.* (Deut. 30:11–14)

The old covenant and its laws were evidently within Israel's ability to keep. Otherwise, Moses would never have made such a statement. God's desire for Israel was for the nation to be a light to the world, and clearly, both God and Moses were confident that these laws outlined a positive and enlightened way of life.

> *God and Moses were confident that these laws outlined an inspired and enlightened way of life.*

Moses Expected Positive Outcomes

Moses also understood that the law system wasn't designed as a way of "religious rigor" with no earthly rewards. From the outset in Egypt, God had made it clear to Moses that he had a positive future in mind for this nation of Israel in their new land. He wanted to bless them and see them prosperous and happy in a plentiful land of their own (Exod. 3:8).

Moses confirmed that God had nothing but the best interests of these people at heart, and if they did what God asked, Moses promised *positive outcomes* for them and their children:

> Then it shall come to pass, because you listen to these judgments, and keep and do them, that the LORD your God will keep with you the covenant and the mercy which He swore to your fathers. And *He will love you and bless you and multiply you;* He will also bless the fruit of your womb and the fruit of your land, your grain and your new wine and your oil, the increase of your cattle and the offspring of your flock, in the land of which He swore to your fathers to give you. *You shall be blessed above all peoples;* there shall not be a male or female barren among you or among your livestock. (Deut. 7:12–14).
>
> Therefore keep the words of this covenant, and do them, that you may *prosper in all that you do.* (Deut. 29:9)

Moses also included a series of extraordinary national blessings from God if they would keep the law (Deut. 28:1–14). There were no implied negatives for keeping the law, but there were major negative consequences for the nation if they ignored it:

> But it shall come to pass, if you *do not obey* the voice of the LORD your God, to observe carefully all His commandments and His statutes which I command you today, that *all these curses will come* upon you and overtake you. (Deut. 28:15)

Moses also included a series of extraordinary national blessings from God if they would keep the law.

This was the simple reality of the life they would face without God's blessing. Many of the curses were the natural consequences they would bring upon themselves if they followed the ways of the nations around them.

Personal Contentment

The positive sentiments Moses expressed about the law at a national level were also anticipated to extend into the lives of the individual Israelite. Moses stated that it was God's desire for Israel to be a happy and uplifting place for both native-born and strangers to live:

> *Happy are you, O Israel!* Who is like you, a people saved by the LORD, the shield of your help and the sword of your majesty! (Deut. 33:29)

The law included statutory festivals with specific commands for the people to rejoice:

> And you shall take for yourselves on the first day the fruit of beautiful trees, branches of palm trees, the boughs of leafy trees, and willows of the brook; and *you shall rejoice before the LORD your God for seven days.* (Lev. 23:40)

> So you shall *rejoice in every good thing which the LORD your God has given to you* and your house, you and the Levite and the stranger who is among you. (Deut. 26:11)

Commanding people to rejoice has a hollow ring of pretense if not reflected in reality. We have all seen images of controlled dictatorial environments where people smile and rejoice in public displays of enthusiasm for their despotic leader. God, on the other hand, has never been interested in pretense. He was genuine in his desire for the children of Israel to be a deeply contented people.

No Change of Sentiment

Some commentators have expressed the idea that the early law given at Sinai was positive, but after the rebellion of the golden calf and the incident of the ten spies, God added burdensome rituals to the law as some sort of punishment.

We will look at the ceremonial aspects of the law in a later chapter, but the point to make here is that regardless of the scope of the law at any point in time, we find no evidence that God or Moses ever thought the law would be anything but positive for the people. Toward the end of his life,

> *Moses stated that it was God's desire for Israel to be a happy and uplifting place to live.*

decades after the golden calf incident, Moses still felt confident that the law God had given was a positive system they could love from the heart.

> The LORD your God will make you *abound in all the work of your hand*, in the fruit of your body, in the increase of your livestock, and in the produce of your land for good. For the LORD *will again rejoice over you for good* as He rejoiced over your fathers, if you obey the voice of the LORD your God, to keep His commandments and His statutes which are written in this Book of the Law, and if you turn to the LORD your God with all your heart and with all your soul. (Deut. 30:9–10)

After Moses' death, God personally reminded their new leader Joshua of the potential positive outcomes, if they just stayed the course and follow the structure that he had outlined for them:

> Only be strong and very courageous, that you may observe to do according to all the law which Moses My servant commanded you; do not turn from it to the right hand or to the left, *that you may prosper wherever you go.* This Book of the Law shall not depart from your mouth, but you shall meditate in it day and night, that you may observe to do according to all that is written in it. *For then you will make your way prosperous, and then you will have good success.* (Josh. 1:7–8).

Law Was a Blessing

The words of Moses consistently present the idea that the law was a great blessing to both the nation and the individual. There is no hint of any sort of "bondage" connected to the law. God had freed the people from bondage in Egypt. and he desired to lift their heavy yoke from them, not add another one:

> I am the LORD your God, who brought you out of the land of Egypt, that you should not be their slaves; I have *broken* the bands of your yoke and made you walk upright. (Lev. 26:13)

Looking back some years later, God spoke through the prophet Hosea and affirmed the perspective of Moses, that his approach to Israel was that of a caring, gentle, loving father who wanted his family to be truly free and content:

> When Israel was a child, I *loved* him, and out of Egypt I called My son. ... I drew them with *gentle cords*, with *bands of love*, and I was to them as those *who take the yoke* from their neck. I stooped and fed them. (Hosea 11:1, 4)

Ancient Israel and the Law in Practice

The women and the children also rejoiced, so that the joy of Jerusalem was heard afar off. —Nehemiah 12:43

Often those who make negative assumptions about the law of Moses don't stop to consider the actual record of the ancient Israelites who lived under the law. In different forms, the nation of Israel lived under the system for an enormous period of time: from Sinai to the Babylonian captivity of Judah many centuries later. How they responded to the system provides an important reference point for our understanding.

Because of their poor track record in keeping the law, most of the Old Testament record relates to Israel's failures, not successes, so it's not often we see the law working as it was designed. Nevertheless, we do see glimpses of the system in action in the narrative of Judges, Samuel, Kings, Chronicles, Ezra, and Nehemiah. We also have the extensive writings of the prophets commenting on societal conditions. These records provide some insight into how the people received the law.

We also have confidence that the Old Testament is a true and honest account because it presents an honest "warts and all" record of the nation. There is no attempt to cover up social issues or problems. If Israel had concerns or complaints about the law being onerous, we would certainly read about them.

When we examine the Old Testament narrative, we find no evidence to support the idea that the original law of Moses was oppressive or a burden to the people. In fact, we see the opposite. Curses and problems came when the nation *broke* the law, not when they kept it. We will look at the reasons for the people's rejection of God in later chapters, but for now, consider the historical record of life under the old covenant.

God Challenges Israel to List their Grievances

One point is clear in Scripture: the Israelites were never shy at bringing their complaints to God, their leaders, or anyone else for that matter. If nothing else, they were a transparent people who complained whenever an issue bothered them. And they obviously had no fear to do so. Many times, post the exodus, the people cried out because of lack of food, lack of water, or fear of being attacked by other nations. Their complaints drove God himself to weariness (Num. 14:27). Over the centuries the people's demeanor never changed. Jesus, Paul, and others noted how the same attitude was still present in the people of their day (Matt. 13:14–15; Acts 28:25–28).

There was also no reticence by the people in making representation to Moses when the law wasn't working as well as it should. For example, the people voiced issues related to the Passover and complained about inheritance laws when some felt they were missing out (Num. 9:7; 27:2–4). In these situations, God took on board their complaints and adjusted the law accordingly. Later they complained to Samuel they wanted a king like all the other nations—and God relented (1 Sam. 8:4–5).

> *If there were complaints about the law, we would have a record of them. Yet we find no complaints of any substance.*

All this affirms that if there were complaints about the law, we would have a record of them. Yet we find no complaints of any substance. After approximately seventy years of living under the old covenant, Joshua made the following observation:

> Behold, this day I am going the way of all the earth. And you know in all your hearts and in all your souls that *not one thing has failed of all the good things* which the LORD your God spoke concerning you. *All have come to pass for you;* not one word of them has failed. (Josh. 23:14)

All the positive blessings God outlined in the covenant had been delivered.

Centuries later, as if to challenge the perception that he had somehow let them down or burdened them, God encourages them to bring their complaints forward:

> O My people, what have I done to you? And how have I wearied you? Testify against Me. (Mic. 6:3)

> Thus says the LORD: "*What injustice have your fathers found in Me*, that they have gone far from Me, have followed idols, and have become idolaters?" (Jer. 2:5)

God's challenge for Israel to list their grievances remained unanswered. The consistent internal evidence of the Old Testament is that problems came to the people when they *forgot* the law, not when they kept it.

The Reality of Ceremonial Occasions

The ceremonial days and the system of worship are often presented as a major part of the "burdensome" system. However, the historical narrative does not support that viewpoint. We have the record of several occasions when Mosaic religious sacrifices and ceremonial rituals were in full operation.

One such event is recorded at the time of King Hezekiah. Hezekiah was a king of Judah who turned to God and was determined to keep the ceremonies God had instructed (2 Chron. 31:20). He revived the law that had been neglected under former kings and reimplemented the statutory holy days. He invited the entire country to keep the weeklong festival of Unleavened Bread, even extending the invitation to the remnant tribes of the northern nation of Israel (2 Chron. 30:1).

The people's attitude during all this ritual and ceremony was recorded for us:

> So the children of Israel who were present at Jerusalem kept the Feast of Unleavened Bread seven days with *great gladness*; and the Levites and the priests praised the LORD day by day, singing to the LORD, accompanied by loud instruments. And Hezekiah gave encouragement to all the Levites who taught the good knowledge of the LORD. (1 Chron. 30: 21–22)

Here was the nation sacrificing to God, fulfilling all the temple rituals, enjoying the fellowship and food that was a part of the law, and having a joyous time! These were not somber celebrations—they were uplifting. The people so enjoyed the festivity that *everyone* agreed to keep it another seven days:

> Then the whole assembly agreed to keep the feast another seven days, and they kept it another seven days *with gladness*. (v. 23)

An event of this scale had not been held in Jerusalem since the days of Solomon:

> *So there was great joy in Jerusalem*, for since the time of Solomon the son of David, king of Israel, there had been nothing like this in Jerusalem. (v. 26)

The "great joy" they had experienced during Solomon's time occurred some 200 years prior at the dedication of the First Temple. At that time thousands of sheep and bulls were sacrificed during the dedication ceremony and for the

Feast of Tabernacles, which occurred at that time. The people's attitude was recorded:

> Then the king and all Israel with him offered sacrifices before the Lord. ... On the eighth day he sent the people away; and they blessed the king, and went to their tents *joyful and glad of heart* for all the good that the LORD had done for His servant David, and for Israel His people. (1 Kings 8:62, 66)

There was no negativity associated with such ceremonies. The three annual holy day periods were designed to be highlights of the annual calendar, and it's not hard to understand why the people enjoyed these celebrations.

The ceremonies were a delight to young and old.

The people reacted similarly in the days of Nehemiah after the temple had been rebuilt. They rededicated the temple and kept the festival, and the people were so enthused that the noise of the uplifted crowd (including children) was heard a long way off:

> Also that day they offered great sacrifices, and rejoiced, for God had made them rejoice with great joy; *the women and the children also rejoiced, so that the joy of Jerusalem was heard afar off.* (Neh. 12:43)

> Then the children of Israel, the priests and the Levites and the rest of the descendants of the captivity, celebrated the dedication of this house of God *with joy*. And they offered sacrifices at the dedication of this house of God, one hundred bulls, two hundred rams, four hundred lambs, and as a sin offering for all Israel twelve male goats, according to the number of the tribes of Israel. ... And they kept the Feast of Unleavened Bread seven days *with joy*; for the LORD made them joyful. (Ezra 6:16–17, 22)

These glimpses of occasions where Israel did what God commanded, show the celebrations as a delight to young and old. The ceremonies carried deep meaning and were combined with food and fellowship.

One problem we have in understanding the environment of the worship system of ancient Israel is our cultural bias. Some practices outlined in the laws of Moses are so foreign to us that we assume they were a burden. But considering we are thousands of years removed, many ancient practices will naturally appear bizarre and off-putting to us. Even in the modern world, we can have a similar negative reaction to the practices and celebrations of other nations. Only by taking the time to thoroughly investigate another culture can we begin to appreciate the differences. Many a traveler has delighted in getting to know and understand the historical celebrations and ceremonial practices of foreign nations that are held with great enthusiasm by the people concerned.

No Evidence Sacrificial System Was a Burden

Neither is there any evidence of the sacrificial system being a burden to the people. Far from being put off by the concept of sacrifices, Israelites were continually making *additional* sacrifices at the old pagan high places in Canaan, even when God told them *not* to do so (Deut. 12:2–4; 2 Kings 14:4; 15:35; 16:4; 17:10; etc.). Clearly, the concept of sacrificing was culturally and religiously acceptable to the people.

The historical record also shows that Israel was consistently attracted to the pagan religions of the nations around them. Some commentators assume that this was an escape from the Mosaic ceremonial rituals. But visit any museum of ancient history and read and observe the practices of the pagan religions of the Levant. In every case, you will find similar, and usually *far more onerous*, ceremonial sacrificial regimes—the most extreme impost being the human/child sacrifice practiced by some of the nations of the day.

The concept of sacrificing was culturally and religiously acceptable to the people.

Israel Loved the Ceremonial System

We have strong confirmation of just how much the Israelites loved the ceremonial system in the days following the rule of King Solomon. Because of Solomon's sins, God said he would divide the nation of Israel into two, with the northern ten tribes retaining the name *Israel* under a new King Jeroboam, and the southern kingdom called *Judah* remaining under David's grandson, King Rehoboam. The central place of worship at that time was the temple in Jerusalem within the kingdom of Judah.

Jeroboam in the north knew that God was behind the split, but he also knew the people would be *attracted back* to the temple in the south because of all the celebrations and sacrifices that went on there:

> If these people go up to offer sacrifices in the house of the LORD at Jerusalem, then the heart of this people will turn back to their lord,

Rehoboam king of Judah, and they will kill me and go back to Rehoboam king of Judah. (1 Kings 12:27)

Jeroboam was so concerned about the situation that he decided to set up a *competing* system of worship and ceremony! He added sacrifices and a new holy day one month after God's statutory time because he knew that the people enjoyed these days of ceremony.

> Jeroboam ordained a feast on the fifteenth day of the eighth month, *like the feast that was in Judah,* and offered sacrifices on the altar. ... And he ordained a feast for the children of Israel, and offered sacrifices on the altar and burned incense. (1 Kings 12:32–33)

This is unambiguous confirmation that the system of worship was not a stumbling block to the people at all. It was attractive to them!

> *The system of worship was not a stumbling block to the people at all. It was attractive to them.*

Years later, King Asa of Judah decided to put his trust in the God of Israel. He held a great feast in Jerusalem to rededicate the nation to God. Many from the breakaway northern kingdom came over when they heard what was happening:

> Then he gathered all Judah and Benjamin, and those who dwelt with them from Ephraim, Manasseh, and Simeon, *for they came over to him in great numbers from Israel when they saw that the* LORD *his God was with him.* ... And all Judah *rejoiced* at the oath, for they had sworn with all their heart and sought Him with all their soul; and He was found by them, and the LORD gave them rest all around. (2 Chron. 15:9, 15)

This passage again reinforces that Israel's ceremonial system was something the people loved and enjoyed.

Ceremony Is Important

Every nation in history has had its special days of ceremony and ritual. Such celebrations are greatly prized as part of a nation's heritage. Even today, our national holidays continue to be accompanied by pomp and pageantry with uniforms, parades, and meaningful speeches. It's a natural desire in people to love these types of events.

God understood how receptive people are to this type of event, and he gave Israel special days and celebrations of great significance and meaning. There was no hint of negativity in the way they were implemented. Some days were solemn (e.g., the Day of Atonement), similar to the more somber tone of Memorial Day celebrations, while other days were celebrated with great excitement and ample food and drink for everyone.

In the New Testament, the parables of Jesus and the book of Revelation offer glimpses of ceremonies in God's future kingdom—wedding suppers, tabernacles, chorales, and fabulous attire. Such celebratory events have always been a part of God's plan for people to learn from and enjoy.

David's Perspective of the Law

I delight to do Your will, O my God, and Your law is within my heart.
—Psalm 40:8

As one of the few leaders of Israel who put his trust in God, David's perspective of the law of Moses is highly relevant to our understanding. David was the sovereign king of the nation, and in his day the Mosaic law was the moral, ceremonial, and civil law of the nation, unlike the corrupted and limited version of Mosaic law operating at the time of Jesus.

Furthermore, David took the time to study and take an interest in the law, something the kings of Israel were supposed to do, but few did (Deut. 17:18–20). And David didn't do this half-heartedly. He was a passionate individual who, by all accounts, put into practice the greatest commandment of the law of Moses—loving God with all his heart and soul (Deut. 6:5).

> *David took the time to study and take an interest in the law.*

Who Was David?

David was the second king of Israel who reigned for forty years in what is sometimes called the "Golden Age" of Israel. King David was an unusual man with a great love of God. God says he chose David as a youth because he was a person "after God's own heart" (1 Sam. 13:14).

David was also unique among the few other righteous kings of Israel in that he provides insight into his deepest thoughts in the form of psalms. Of the one hundred and fifty psalms in the book of Psalms, seventy-five are biblically noted as being the work of David.[1]

In his psalms, David passionately expounds his love of God and how he came to deeply understand his Creator. David's psalms are studied and highly regarded by Christians because they reflect a deep understanding of the theology of God. They touch on subjects such as faith and righteousness, justification, mercy, salvation, and forgiveness. Many of the psalms of David are quoted in the New Testament.

---

[1] In addition, a number of the anonymous psalms have been traditionally attributed to David. For some of these, modern scholarship suggests later authorship.

David's View of the Law of Moses

Like Moses, David was an honest and transparent man without pretense—a man who spoke what was in his heart. David loved God from his youth. He also loved the values of God as expressed in the law.

There is no hint in his psalms that the Mosaic system of law was burdening him or his people. Quite the opposite—David saw the law as liberating and empowering, and a blessing to him and the nation.

> I delight to do Your will, O my God, and *Your law is within my heart.* (Ps. 40:8)

And there's no doubt what law he was talking about. He refers to every aspect of the law of Moses in his psalms:

> The law of the LORD is perfect, converting the soul; the testimony of the Lord is sure, making wise the simple; the *statutes* of the LORD are right, *rejoicing the heart;* the *commandment* of the LORD is pure, enlightening the eyes; the fear of the LORD is clean, enduring forever; the *judgments* of the LORD are true and righteous altogether. *More to be desired are they than gold,* yea, than much fine gold; sweeter also than honey and the honeycomb. Moreover by them Your servant is warned, and in keeping them there is great reward. (Ps. 19:7–11)

He expressed his desire for God to teach him more of his ways:

> Show me Your ways O LORD; Teach me Your Paths. Lead me in Your truth and teach me, For You are the God of my salvation; On You I wait all the day. …The humble He teaches His way. All the paths of the LORD are mercy and truth. To such as keep His covenant and His testimonies. (Ps. 25:4–5, 9–10).

David was someone in Old Testament times who achieved the goal that God outlined for Israel—that of putting the laws of God into both his heart and mind, showing it was possible under the old covenant.

> The mouth of the righteous speaks wisdom, and his tongue talks of justice. The law of his God is in his heart. (Ps. 37:30–31)

Psalm 119

Psalm 119, the longest chapter in the Bible, is an intense focus on the law of Moses. While the authorship of the psalm is not noted, it has traditionally been attributed to David by older Christian commentators and earlier rabbis. The psalm is written with Davidic tones and expressions—and is of an acrostic style which David used in other psalms. Modern scholars have suggested the psalm may have been written much later by an individual such as Ezra, Nehemiah or even Daniel.

If we assume Davidic authorship, the words of Psalm 119 complement and expand on David's love of God's teachings as expressed in his other psalms:

> *I have rejoiced in the way of Your testimonies,* as much as in all riches. I will meditate on Your precepts, and contemplate Your ways. *I will delight myself in Your statutes;* I will not forget Your word. (Ps. 119:14–16)

> Teach me, O LORD, the way of Your statutes, and I shall keep it to the end. Give me understanding, and I shall keep Your law; indeed, I shall observe it with my whole heart. Make me walk in the path of Your commandments, *for I delight in it.* Incline my heart to Your testimonies. (Ps. 119:33–36)

> I will speak of Your testimonies also before kings and will not be ashamed. And I will *delight myself* in Your commandments, *which I love.* My hands also I will lift up to Your commandments, *which I love,* and I will meditate on Your statutes. (Ps. 119:46–48)

> *How sweet are Your words to my taste,* sweeter than honey to my mouth! (Ps. 119:103)

The psalmist credited the law for bestowing him with understanding, wisdom, and insight:

> You, through Your commandments, *make me wiser than my enemies;* for they are ever with me. I have *more understanding than all my teachers,* for Your testimonies are my meditation. *I understand more than the ancients, because* I keep Your precepts. (Ps. 119:98–100)

> I am Your servant; *give me understanding,* that I may know Your testimonies. ... *Therefore I love your commandments* more than gold, yes, than fine gold! (Ps. 119:125, 127)

> Through Your precepts I get understanding. (Ps. 119:104)

The law was a guide for the psalmist's life:

> Your word is a lamp to my feet and a light to my path. (Ps. 119:105)

Even if we assume non-Davidic authorship, the message of Psalm 119 is a powerful testimony of the positive and empowering nature of the law of Moses.[2]

Psalm of Repentance

One of David's most notable psalms is Psalm 51, written after he had an affair with Bathsheba and then had her husband Uriah murdered. It is a prayer of deep repentance, where David demonstrates profound sorrow for his actions. The psalm touches on many deep principles that Christians understand today, including:

- The importance of trusting in God and not in our own righteousness
- That without God's mercy and grace, we have no hope for salvation
- Only God can make us clean—it is not something we can do on our own
- The understanding that the sacrificial system was merely an outward manifestation and that what goes on in a person's heart is the true measure of a person

It is a passionate psalm that gets to the heart of an individual's relationship with God:

> Have mercy upon me, O God, according to Your lovingkindness; according to the multitude of Your tender mercies, blot out my transgressions. … For You do not desire sacrifice, or else I would give it; You do not delight in burnt offering. The sacrifices of God are a broken spirit, a broken and a contrite heart—these, O God, You will not despise. (Ps. 51:1, 16–17)

David understood that God's forgiveness was not dependent on penance or works of the law but on God's undeserved mercy to someone with a repentant heart:

> Blessed is he whose transgression is forgiven, whose sin is covered. Blessed is the man to whom the LORD does not impute iniquity. (Ps. 32:1–2)

These and many other words of David show a deep understanding of the true theology of God. They perfectly align with Jesus' teachings and demonstrate a consistent message across the old and new covenants.

---

[2] Refer to Appendix *Further Insights from the Psalmist*.

Meditating on the Law

A strategy David repeatedly emphasizes in his writings is the need to meditate. His clear implication is that by meditating and thinking about God and his works and his words, a person can come to a deeper understanding of their Creator:

> When I remember You on my bed, I meditate on You in the night watches. (Ps. 63:6).

> I remember the days of old; I meditate on all Your works; I muse on the work of Your hands. (Ps. 143:5).

In Psalm 19, David describes the power of the law of God to enlighten and make a person wise (vv. 7–11), and concludes with these words:

> Let the words of my mouth and the *meditation of my heart* be acceptable in Your sight, O LORD, my strength and my redeemer. (Ps. 19:14)

David understood that there was a deeper wisdom and meaning to the law beyond its face value.

Meditating on the law was a joy to David. He understood the teachings of God were far more than just a list of dos and don'ts—*otherwise, there could be nothing to meditate on.* He understood that there was a deeper wisdom and meaning to the law beyond its face value. As the opening of the book of Psalms states:

> Blessed is the man who walks not in the counsel of the ungodly. …His delight is in the law of the Lord, And in His law he meditates day and night. (Ps. 1:1–2)

As one of the few leaders of Israel who did seek to understand and apply God's intent for the law, David's life and writings provide compelling evidence that the law of Moses was a truly enlightened system.

Paul's Perspective of the Law

Therefore the law is holy, and the commandment holy and just and good.
—Romans 7:12

The apostle Paul is a giant in New Testament terms and is regarded as the most influential Christian teacher after Jesus. Paul's epistles comprise a large portion of New Testament Scripture and have enormously influenced the understanding of Christian doctrine. In his letters, Paul makes many references to the law of Moses in one form or another, and he does so from the unique position of both a trained expert in the law and a deeply converted man.

The purpose of this chapter is not to be drawn into theological Pauline arguments about the law (of which there are many) but simply to consider Paul's perspective of the law of Moses. With his background as a Pharisee of the highest order and then as a Christian with a calling direct from God, Paul provides valuable insight into where the Jews went wrong with their understanding of Moses.

> *Paul provides valuable insight into where the Jews went wrong with their understanding of Moses.*

People often assume that there was tension between the teachings of Paul and the law of Moses. But Paul's criticism was never of Moses or the law itself but of the religion of Judaism and later Jewish converts who were presenting a distorted version of the law and its role in the life of a believer.

Paul's Background

Paul (originally Saul) was a highly trained scholar and expert in the Hebrew Scriptures. He was born and raised a Jew in Tarsus, and from his youth was trained in the sect of the Pharisees (Acts 26:4–5). He studied at the feet of Gamaliel, a respected and esteemed Jewish rabbi. Paul describes Gamaliel as a teacher of the "strictest interpretation" of the law of their fathers (Acts 22:2–3). As part of his training, Bible scholars have suggested Paul may have memorized large portions of the Torah.

After God called him, the apostle Paul became a deeply converted Christian who understood the true intent of the law of Moses in the light of God's grace. As a Pharisee, Paul had formerly believed that the righteousness of law-keeping would be his justification. Because the Pharisees thought this way, their leaders put in a colossal amount of detailed study and discussion to ensure they were precise in their practices. Their centuries of study meant they could often expound minute nuances of the law in countless scenarios, but their false premise meant they often missed the overall intent.

His new understanding of God's grace changed everything for Paul—he now viewed the Scriptures he knew so well in a dramatically new light. With his mind now opened by the Holy Spirit, his knowledge of Scripture was of enormous value when it came to understanding the true intent and meaning behind the laws God had given. He now knew that God had no intention to burden people with complex rules and regulations in some sort of spiritual IQ test. That had never been God's intention.

Faith and the Law

Jesus had strongly criticized the religious teachers of his day for ignoring the important foundational pillars of the law of Moses (Matt. 23:23; Luke 11:42). Before his conversion Paul was of the same ilk. He had neglected justice, mercy, faith, and the love of God. Despite his lifelong study of Scripture, his understanding of the law was on the wrong track. Instead of humbly putting his faith in God's righteousness, his confidence was firmly based on his own righteousness. Looking back years later he could see it so clearly:

> If anyone else thinks he may have *confidence in the flesh, I more so*: circumcised the eighth day, of the stock of Israel, of the tribe of Benjamin, a Hebrew of the Hebrews; concerning the law, a Pharisee; concerning zeal, persecuting the church; *concerning the righteousness which is in the law, blameless.* (Phil. 3:4–6)

When he heard those fateful words of Jesus, "*Saul, Saul, why are you persecuting Me?*" his whole world view collapsed (Acts 9:4–5). Jesus' words cut deep. Paul was a highly intelligent individual who had felt that something wasn't adding up. He had been fighting against his conscience and trying to suppress his doubts. By God's grace, he now saw the futility of his former ways:

> But what things were gain to me, these I have counted loss for Christ. Yet indeed I also count all things loss for the excellence of the knowledge of Christ Jesus my Lord, for whom I have suffered the loss of all things, and count them as rubbish, that I may gain Christ and be found in Him, *not having my own righteousness, which is from the law, but that which is through faith in Christ, the righteousness which is from God by faith.* (Phil. 3:7–9)

The contrast with Paul's old belief system was stark. He now understood how foolish the idea of trusting in his own righteousness had been. Because of this, Paul spent more time writing about the correct perspective of the law than any other New Testament writer—from an intellectual as well as a deeply personal perspective.

Paul Explains the Example of Abraham

Paul came to understand that keeping the law had *never been a means of salvation at any time in history*. He proved this by going right back to the father of the faithful, Abraham. One of the most profound insights into how righteousness is to be understood is a verse Paul references from the book of Genesis:

> *Paul came to understand that keeping the law had never been a means of salvation at any time in history.*

> And (Abram) believed in the LORD, and He accounted it to him for righteousness. (Gen. 15:6)

This statement is a reference to a vision God gave to Abraham while he was still childless. In that vision, God told Abraham that his descendants would be like the stars of heaven. Abraham *believed* what God said, even though at that time he had no children and was over eighty years of age. Paul referenced this verse in his epistle to the Romans and explained that it was not Abraham's works that made him righteous before God but his *faith* in God.

> For if Abraham was justified by works, he has something to boast about, but not before God. For what does the Scripture say? *"Abraham believed God, and it was accounted to him for righteousness."* (Rom. 4:2–3)

This is the key to understanding righteousness. The Pharisees, who taught and lived a works-based religion, did not understand this deeper principle despite it being right in front of them in Scripture. Paul goes on to show that David also understood this principle:

> Just as David also describes the blessedness of the man to whom God imputes righteousness apart from works: "Blessed are those whose lawless deeds are forgiven, and whose sins are covered; blessed is the man to whom the Lord shall not impute sin." (Rom. 4:6–8)

He further drives home the point that Abraham was declared righteous *before* he was circumcised, showing again that circumcision was not the key measure of righteousness:

> For we say that faith was accounted to Abraham for righteousness. How then was it accounted? While he was circumcised, or uncircumcised? Not while circumcised, *but while uncircumcised*. (Rom. 4:9–10)

The Law Had Never Justified Anyone

Over the centuries, after Israel's return from captivity, the religious leaders of Israel had developed an added system of law that lost sight of the true basis of a relationship with God. Their new religion might have started with the best intentions, but it veered so far off track that it became *opposed* to the very principles the law of Moses stood for. By the time of Jesus, the religion of the Jews had redefined the definition of righteousness away from God to the law. They had come to trust in themselves and their own law-keeping as a way of earning their salvation. Their added rules, which they installed to "protect" the law, became their stumbling block.

The heart of the law of Moses had *always* been based on the righteousness of God. Paul said ancient Israel was *misguided* to not seek it by faith:

> But Israel, pursuing the law of righteousness, has not attained to the law of righteousness. Why? Because they did not seek it by faith, but as it were, by the works of the law. (Rom. 9:31–32)

Paul was talking in the *past tense* here. He wasn't introducing a new teaching about the law. He was clarifying where the Jews had gone astray. Their trust was in their own works and not in God himself. Paul said a similar thing to the Jews when he was in Galatia:

> Therefore let it be known to you, brethren, that through this Man is preached to you the forgiveness of sins; and by Him everyone who believes is justified from all things *from which you could not be justified by the law of Moses*. (Acts 13:38–39)

Faith in God, not works, has *always* been at the heart of true righteousness.

> Where is boasting then? It is excluded. By what law? Of works? No, but by the law of faith. Therefore we conclude that a man is *justified by faith apart from the deeds of the law*. (Rom. 3:27–28)

Israel's *unbelief* was the issue that caused God grief, not the nation's failure to keep the law perfectly (Heb. 3:19).

Paul now understood that the law of Moses had never been a works-based religion. No one could earn salvation or be justified in the eyes of God by works under the old covenant any more than they can under the new covenant.

No one could earn salvation or be justified by works under the old covenant any more than they can under the new covenant.

Interestingly, in nearly all civilizations across history, man has created works-based religions as the default. Humans innately want to trust in their own rites, ceremonies, and offerings to prove they are worthy to their gods. The Jews also turned the law of Moses into a religion of works. But the God of Israel was different and had never put ritual over the substance of a believing heart (Isa. 1:11; Hosea 6:6).

Paul's Respect for the Law

The law had a purpose, and Paul was not denigrating it because it could not justify. In his epistles, he reinforced what Jesus had taught about the core tenets of the law—that they were an expression of how to love one's neighbor:

> For the commandments, "You shall not commit adultery," "You shall not murder," "You shall not steal," "You shall not bear false witness," "You shall not covet," and if there is any other commandment, are all summed up in this saying, namely, "You shall love your neighbor as yourself." *Love does no harm to a neighbor; therefore love is the fulfillment of the law.* (Rom. 13:9–10)

> For all the law is fulfilled in one word, even in this: "You shall love your neighbor as yourself." (Gal. 5:14)

He credits the law for teaching him what sin is:

> What shall we say then? *Is* the law sin? Certainly not! On the contrary, I would not have known sin except through the law. For I would not have known covetousness unless the law had said, *"You shall not covet."* (Rom. 7:7)

And he gives the law the respect it deserves:

> Therefore the law *is* holy, and the commandment holy and just and good. (Rom. 7:12)

Paul saw clearly that the problem was not with the law but how it was being misused. As he wrote to Timothy:

> We know that the law is good if one uses it lawfully. (1 Tim. 1:8)

Paul Rejects his Former Belief System

When writing to the Galatians, Paul distanced himself from his former belief system, which he specifically identified as the religion of *Judaism*:

> For you have heard of my former conduct in *Judaism*, how I persecuted the church of God beyond measure and tried to destroy it. And I advanced in *Judaism* beyond many of my contemporaries in my own nation, being more exceedingly zealous for the traditions of my fathers. (Gal. 1:13–14)

Unfortunately, the New Testament church included Pharisees who had converted to Christianity but wanted to maintain certain viewpoints and practices that were not aligned with written Scripture and church teaching. Paul knew exactly where this wrong mindset was coming from. The Pharisees had a distorted view of the role of the law; they were a disruptive force in the early church and were referred to as those "of the circumcision" (not because they were circumcised, but among other things, they taught that circumcision was necessary for salvation). These Pharisees brought conflict into the church with their judgmental and unscriptural rules and practices. Paul strongly warned Titus about them:

The problem was not with the law but how it was being used.

> For there are many insubordinate, both idle talkers and deceivers, *especially those of the circumcision*, whose mouths must be stopped. (Titus 1:10–11)

Paul Grieved over His People

The general failure of the Jews to accept Jesus was an emotional subject for Paul. They were his people, and it bothered him greatly that the chosen ones, the descendants of Abraham, had rejected Jesus (Rom. 9:1–5). Paul also understood that his own hard-heartedness was only broken by the grace of

God—otherwise, he, too, would have been in the same situation (1 Cor. 15:9–10).

Paul understood what Jesus said in his parables: that God would use Israel's hard-heartedness as an opportunity for gentiles to receive the gospel. Israel, whom God had chosen to be first, would be last. And the gentiles, who were last, would be first (Matt. 21:28–46; 22:1–14). By taking the gospel to the gentiles, he hoped to provoke the Jews to "jealously" return to the God of Israel (Rom. 11:11).

Israel's hard-heartedness goes a long way in explaining why the understanding of the law of Moses veered so far off base and why it remains so to this day. Paul used the metaphor of the veil Moses wore after his face radiated from being in God's presence as a type of the hard-heartedness of his people:

> But their (Israel's) minds were blinded. For until this day the same veil remains unlifted in the reading of the Old Testament, because the veil is taken away in Christ. But even to this day, when Moses is read, a veil lies on their heart. Nevertheless when one turns to the Lord, the veil is taken away. Now the Lord is the Spirit; and where the Spirit of the Lord is, there is liberty. (2 Cor. 3:14–17).

While this is a criticism of the Israelites, it is not exclusive to them. A hard heart will always make it difficult to understand the true purpose and intent of the law of Moses. When a person trusts in Jesus for their salvation, God removes the veil, and the true meaning behind the law can be seen in the positive light God intended.

God designed both the old and new covenants to fulfill their intended objectives. The new covenant is the better covenant with better promises based on the surety of Jesus (Heb. 7:22; 8:6). But the old was still glorious in what it could have achieved for the people of Israel, if they had only put their trust in God (2 Cor. 3:7–11).

3

PART 3: Getting to Know the Lawgiver

It would be a mistake to dive into the detail of the law of Moses without first seeking to know the heart and mind of God the Lawgiver. Only when one considers the character and values of God is it possible to correctly discern his purpose and intent for the law—and how he intended it be interpreted, administered, and applied in people's lives.

This section will examine key attributes of God's character that have a direct bearing on how the law of Moses was to be understood. These are attributes that Jesus perfectly reflected in his life and ministry.

God's Character Is Knowable

For My people are foolish, they have not known Me. —Jeremiah 4:22

At their foundation, all laws are conceived and derived from the values of the lawgiver. Values are the standards and principles the lawgiver deems most important and directly affect how laws are developed and administered.

In a democracy, the people are the ultimate lawgiver, and the laws reflect the collective values of society. As Australian Chief Justice James Allsop notes: "These values find their expression not only in the formal law but also in societal expectations, behavior, and actions."[1] As societal values shift, new legislation is proposed, and laws are changed to suit. Over the last century, the Western world has seen major changes in societal values, affecting marriage, family, sexual morals, capital punishment, abortion, social welfare etc., resulting in many laws today that previous generations would have rejected outright.

The law of Moses also reflected the values of the Lawgiver. But unlike a democracy, where core values will change over time, God's values are timeless and unchanging. The law is described in such grand terms as *truth, righteousness, justice,* and *wisdom*—values that can only originate from the higher character of God. We see this in the testimony of Scripture. Despite being written by dozens of authors over an enormous period of time, the core values of God never changed. These values, including the "weightier matters," as Jesus called them, were constant—and remain so today because they were based on the values of an eternal God.

> *Without knowing the character of the God of Israel and his standards and values, it is not possible for a person to properly understand how the law was supposed to be interpreted, administered, and applied.*

Therefore, if we want to correctly understand the law of Moses and its intent, we must first seek to understand the values of God. Failing to look behind the law to the values of the Lawgiver has led to no end of misguided interpretations of Mosaic law. Without knowing the character of the God of Israel and his standards and values, it is not possible to properly understand

---

[1] Bibliog: (Allsop 2016)

Law Is an Extension of God's Values

People can lose sight of the original intent of the lawgiver in any law system. They can look at the written words of a law without reference to the underlying intent of the original authors and end up with dramatically different interpretations of the law. For this purpose, nations have established supreme courts, high courts, appeal courts, etc., to consider the original intent and scope of the law. With fallible men, such interpretations can vary according to judges' ideologies and changing societal standards. But the reference point for the law of Moses must always return to the character and values of an unchanging God. Cultures, people, and context will change, but God's core values will not.

The consequences of not properly knowing the God of Israel were amply demonstrated during Jesus' ministry. The religious leaders of the time had lost sight of the true God and his values. And because they didn't know God or the values he considered most important, they misunderstood, misinterpreted, and misapplied his law. The same can happen today when a person reads the law of Moses. For this reason, we must first seek to know the character of God as revealed through Scripture and the life of Jesus.

> *God himself declares that his character and the values he holds dear to his heart are knowable and understandable.*

God Desires to be Understood

Seeking to know God is not a futile exercise, as some think. God confirmed his desire to be known at the outset of creation by creating humankind in his own image. He made humans with minds capable of understanding, and a world capable of being understood. Being made in the image of God has been a standing invitation since creation for people to seek to know and understand their Creator.

That's not to imply that everything about God is understandable. His divine nature and eternal magnificence are clearly beyond our understanding despite people contending over such topics for millennia. But esoteric discussions on the nature of God should not pull us away from the most important characteristics of God that we *can* confidently know and understand. God himself declares that his *character* and the *values* he holds dear to his heart *are* knowable and understandable:

> Thus says the LORD: "Let not the wise man glory in his wisdom, let not the mighty man glory in his might, nor let the rich man glory in his riches; but let him who glories glory in this, *that he understands and knows Me, that I am the* LORD, *exercising lovingkindness, judgment, and righteousness in the earth.* For in these I delight," says the LORD. (Jer. 9:23–24)

God castigated Israel and the priests for *not* knowing him:

> The priests did not say, "Where is the LORD?" *And those who handle the law did not know Me.* (Jer. 2:8)

> For My people are foolish, *they have not known Me.* They are silly children, and they have no understanding. They are wise to do evil, but to do good they have no knowledge. (Jer. 4:22)

The problem was still extant at the time of Jesus. The religious leaders knew of the God of Israel by name but did not know who he truly was at heart:

> Jesus answered, *"You know neither Me nor My Father.* If you had known Me, you would have known My Father also." (John 8:19)

Because of their misguided and false perceptions of both God and the law, the religious leaders failed to recognize Jesus as the Son of God. This was despite the miracles and the clear prophetic signs he fulfilled. He didn't look or act anything like the God they had come to worship. Jesus reflected a standard of behavior so different from their ideas of God that they accused him of breaking the law—*when he was keeping it perfectly*! Yet all along they had the Scriptures that revealed God's consistent character.

We Must Know Him

If we are going to know the God of Israel and learn to appreciate the law he gave through Moses, we must first get to know who he is and what he stands for. The entire structure of law must then be interpreted in the light of his eternal values and character.

It has been rightly said that we become what we worship.[2] God wanted Israel to trust him and love him *personally*. To take his words into their hearts so that they became a part of who they were at their core (Deut. 6:6). By wanting his

---

[2] Bibliog: (Beale 2008)

law system to be a part of people's innermost being, God was expressing his desire to shape the hearts of individuals with a set of moral values different from the other cultures around them—values that would align with God's own holy standards:

> Speak to all the congregation of the children of Israel, and say to them: *"You shall be holy, for I the* LORD *your God am holy."* (Lev. 19:2)

Not surprisingly, the New Testament presents the same perspective:

> As He who called you is holy, you also be holy in all your conduct, because it is written, "Be holy, for I am holy." (1 Pet. 1:15–16)

Today in our Western societies, we see an increasing move away from Judeo-Christian values and a resulting decline in the standards that God expresses. We are moving to the point where the teachings the Bible espouses are not just being ignored; they are seen as negative. History amply demonstrates that when people lose sight of God, anything is possible.

The entire structure of law must then be interpreted in the light of God' eternal values and character.

Even within the broader church, as the study and appreciation of the Word of God declines, aspects of God's character and values are less understood than in previous generations. This is particularly evident in relation to the Old Testament. One goal of this book is to encourage a deeper understanding of the unchanging character of God and Jesus to help provide a rock-solid foundation and reference point for a Christian life.

Unchanging Values

You know neither Me nor My Father. If you had known Me, you would have known My Father also. —John 8:19

In his final published work *Farewell to God*, Christian-turned-atheist Charles Templeton summarized his perception of the God of the Old Testament:

> The God of the Old Testament is utterly unlike the God believed in by most practicing Christians. He is an all-too-human deity with the human failings, weaknesses, and passions of men—but on a grand scale. His justice is, by modern standards, outrageous, and his prejudices are deep-seated and inflexible. He is biased, querulous, vindictive, and jealous of his prerogatives.[1]

While holding this negative view of the God of the Old Testament, Templeton surprisingly held a high opinion of Jesus. He believed what many agnostics and atheists also believe—that Jesus was a truly outstanding individual, quite unlike the capricious God of Israel. In his later years, Templeton is quoted as saying:

> (Jesus) was the greatest human being who has ever lived. He was a moral genius. His ethical sense was unique. He was the intrinsically wisest person that I've ever encountered in my life or in my readings. His commitment was total and led to his own death, much to the detriment of the world. What could one say about him except that this was a form of greatness. ... Everything good I know, everything decent I know, everything pure I know, I learned from Jesus.[2]

Quite a contrast! In a major difference of opinion, one of Templeton's contemporaries, Billy Graham, presented the following perspective:

> God is the same from one end of the Bible to the other. His character is unchanging, His love is unchanging, His purity is unchanging—and His plan for the human race is unchanging. The Bible says, "I the Lord do not change."[3]

It's as if Templeton and Graham are talking about two different books and two different beings! How can people reading the same words come to such

---

[1] Bibliog: (Templeton 1996, 71)
[2] Bibliog: (Strobel 2000, 21)
[3] Bibliog: (Graham 2013)

different conclusions? What Templeton may not have considered is this: If the God of old was truly the negative and vindictive being he described, then Jesus would be a hypocrite to praise and honor him as he did. And more to the point, if the God of the Old Testament and Jesus are indeed so different, then Christianity has a colossal problem—one of a God of internal conflict and changing standards. As Jesus said, a kingdom divided against itself cannot stand (Mark 3:24), and neither can Christianity stand if its foundations are so unstable.

The Harmony of the Godhead

Directly contradicting the idea of any clash of standards between the God of old and Jesus is the testimony of Jesus himself. He described the perfect harmony of the godhead:

> I and My Father are one. (John 10:30)

> If you had known Me, you would have known My Father also; and from now on you know Him and have seen Him. (John 14:7)

His mission was totally focused on doing the will of his heavenly Father:

> For I have come down from heaven, not to do My own will, but the will of Him who sent Me. (John 6:38)

> Jesus said to them, "My food is to do the will of Him who sent Me, and to finish His work." (John 4:34)

Everything Jesus taught and the standards he expressed in his ministry perfectly aligned with the one who had sent him:

> Jesus answered them and said, "My doctrine is not Mine, but His who sent Me." (John 7:16)

Focusing on the Negative

Where do the negative views of God in the Old Testament come from? They come from focusing on specific sections of Scripture where God seems to be uncaring or harsh in his words or actions. These verses are then presented as "proof" of the "moral failings" of the old covenant God, while the many positive examples of God's kindness, mercy, and grace are ignored.

But it's easy to cherry-pick Scripture. We could do the same with Jesus, focusing on his verbal "abuse" of religious leaders, his claims of self-importance, his use of whips to chase people out of the temple, his refusal to help the Samaritan woman in distress, etc. We could also point to Jesus' prophesied future return, graphically outlined in the last book of the Bible—showing him in a robe dipped in blood, striking the nations with a sword, and treading "the winepress of the fierceness and wrath of Almighty God" (Rev. 19:11–16). If that is all we knew about Jesus, he, too, would be a fearful person to know.

But highlighting attributes that bother us or isolating specific incidents without taking the time to understand the context, is not the way to gain a true perspective of a person. Using the same fault-finding approach, we could make any great person in history look bad, no matter how highly revered.

Unchanging Character

Jesus did not come with radical new ideas on morality that were different or at odds with the previous standards of the Mosaic lawgiver as some present. It is a fundamental tenet of Christianity, and one supported throughout Scripture, that God's values are eternally consistent and unchanging because they emanate from his innermost core being:

> For I am the LORD, *I do not change*. (Mal. 3:6)

> Every good gift and every perfect gift is from above, and comes down from the Father of lights, with whom there is *no variation or shadow of turning*. (James 1:17)

> Jesus Christ is the *same* yesterday, today, and forever. (Heb. 13:8)

God's values are eternally consistent and unchanging because they emanate from his innermost core being.

The way Jesus was during his life and ministry perfectly reflected the nature of God. Any thought that the God of Israel operated to different standards flies in the face of his nature. God must be consistent—otherwise, neither we nor the host of heaven could ever have any confidence in him again.

If a person wants further proof of God's consistency, they must also consider who Jesus said he was. Jesus declared himself as the great "I Am" (John 8:58), the same being that spoke to Moses out of the burning bush (Exod. 3:13–14). To know Jesus is to know the one who spoke to Abraham, Isaac, Jacob, and Moses. He was the *logos* (the Word) who was there from the outset:

> In the beginning was the Word, and the Word was with God, and the Word was God. He was in the beginning with God. (John 1:1–2)

> God, who ... has in these last days spoken to us by His Son, whom He has appointed heir of all things, through whom also He made the worlds; who being the brightness of His glory and *the express image of His person* ... sat down at the right hand of the Majesty on high. (Heb. 1:1–3)

When a Scripture at first reading calls God's character into question, the answers are found by seeking to better understand the circumstances or issues involved, not assuming that God is at fault.

> This is the message which we have heard from Him and declare to you, that God is light and in Him *is no darkness at all.* (1 John 1:5)

The confidence for ancient Israel and Christians today lies in the immutability of God.

No tension exists between Jesus and the God of Israel. Jesus was the embodiment of the positive character and values God has always stood for. Those same values and standards are reflected in the law that was delivered to Israel through Moses.

For those who think there is a difference, the problem is with their understanding—not with God.

Motivated by Love

Yes, I have loved you with an everlasting love; therefore with lovingkindness I have drawn you. —Jeremiah 31:3

From a new covenant perspective, it is well known that God is a god of love. The apostle John describes him as the very essence of love:

> He who does not love does not know God, *for God is love.* (1 John 4:8)

The word John used for love is the Greek *agape/agapao*, which is different from the love found between friends and family (Greek: *phileo*). *Agape* love is an outgoing, selfless concern for others. It implies a decision to love with no expectation of love in return. God's selfless love is epitomized by the giving of his own Son while we were yet sinners (John 3:16).

But God's love in the Old Testament is not as appreciated, especially by critics of the law of Moses. Yet God's character has never changed.

Hebrew also has more than one word to describe love. Although Hebrew does not have a direct equivalent word to the Greek *agape*, the Hebrew word *chesed* (*hesed*) is used extensively throughout the Hebrew Scriptures to define the same enduring nature of God's love. As the *Expository Dictionary of Biblical Words* explains:

> *Hesed* constitutes one of the most significant theological terms in the Hebrew Scriptures. … When applied to Yahweh, *hesed* is fundamentally the expression of his loyalty and devotion to the solemn promises attached to the covenant. … With reference to Yahweh, *hesed* commonly refers to his "steadfast love," signifying an irrevocable commitment to his promise to fashion a people to serve him, whom he in turn promised to love and protect.[1]

Like *agape*, *chesed* is a difficult word to fully express in English. It is variously translated as lovingkindness, mercy, goodness, or love. For example:

> And the LORD passed before him and proclaimed, "The LORD, the LORD God, merciful and gracious, longsuffering, and *abounding in goodness* (*chesed*) and truth." (Exod. 34:6)

---

[1] Bibliog: (Renn 2005, 633-634)

> The LORD is longsuffering and *abundant in mercy (chesed)*, forgiving iniquity and transgression. (Num. 14:18)
>
> Have mercy upon me, O God, according to Your *lovingkindness (chesed)*; according to the multitude of Your tender mercies, blot out my transgressions. (Ps. 51:1)

God's *chesed* nature—a motivation of *pure, selfless, steadfast love*—was at the heart of everything he did for ancient Israel. The entire law must be evaluated in this light. As *Vines Expository* notes:

> The entire history of Yahweh's covenantal relationship with Israel can be summarized in terms of *hesed*. It is the one permanent element in the flux of covenantal history.[2]

A motivation of pure, selfless, steadfast love—was at the heart of everything God did for ancient Israel.

In his love, God had rescued an undeserving nation from bondage and offered them an incredible relationship. It was not because of anything they had done:

> The LORD did not set His love on you nor choose you because you were more in number than any other people, for you were the least of all peoples;[8] *but because the LORD loves you,* and because He would keep the oath which He swore to your fathers, the LORD has brought you out with a mighty hand, and redeemed you from the house of bondage, from the hand of Pharaoh king of Egypt. (Deut. 7:7–8)

Not only were they insignificant—they were decidedly unworthy:

> Therefore understand that the LORD your God is *not giving you this good land to possess because of your righteousness*, for you are a stiff-necked people. (Deut. 9:6)

The basis of the old covenant was God's love, grace, mercy, and kindness to an undeserving people. By grace they were saved from Egypt. The narrative of Israel is the essential parallel for a Christian—the rescuing of an undeserving people from captivity and the offer of an incredible future—*despite* who we are and what we have done.

---

[2] Bibliog: (Vine 1996, 143 Loving-Kindness)

A Two-Way Relationship

God didn't want his love for Israel to be a one-way affair. He greatly desired that the people would respond with a deep heartfelt love in return. And the love God desired was not some sort of "ritualistic" or "technical" love—he was genuinely hoping that they would love him deeply and emotionally and take his instruction into their hearts:

> You shall love the LORD your God with all your heart, with all your soul, and with all your strength. And these words which I command you today *shall be in your heart*. (Deut. 6:5–6)

Here at the heart of the old covenant is the clear statement of God's greatest desire: to receive a deep and abiding love from these people in response to the undeserved love he had given to them.

This alone should put the law of Moses into perspective. Love and respect can't be demanded. Bullies and hard taskmasters never win over hearts and minds—they breed resentment and contempt. God was clearly hopeful that the care he had demonstrated to the nation and the way of life he outlined to them through his law would develop into a loving response in return. And he wanted this selfless love to extend throughout society and be reflected in how Israelites treated one another.

> *God greatly desired that the people would respond with a deep heartfelt love in return.*

Jesus affirmed the importance of these two great principles of love—love of God and love of man—and that they are the foundational principles of the entire law: "On these two commandments hang all the Law and the Prophets" (Matt. 22:36–40).

Critics have misunderstood why loving God comes first. This was not the God of Israel seeking attention—he *is* a God of love, and only by loving him can a person learn to properly love their neighbor.

Commanded to Love?

The way in which the law of Moses refers to love seems strange from our modern perspective. God *commanded* Israel to love him. It wasn't a suggestion or hope but a "you *shall!*" Jesus used the same imperative when he referred to these directives to love as "*commandments*" and emphatically stated, "You *shall* love the Lord your God" and "You *shall* love your neighbor as yourself" (Matt. 22:37–39).

How is it possible for God to *command* someone to love him or anyone else for that matter? And why would he find it necessary to decree such a command? Shouldn't loving another, whether it be God or another person, be left up to our natural feelings and desires? Not according to Scripture!

We can deduce two things from God's command to love: Firstly, how God defines the word "love" must differ from how it is generally defined in our modern society. It must be something beyond feelings alone. Secondly, loving God and man must *not* be the natural way of humankind; otherwise, no such commands would be necessary.

How God defines the word "love" differs from how it is generally defined in our modern society.

The Bible consistently confirms these two points.

It should be self-evident that is not up to humans to determine how to love the One who created us. It is God's absolute prerogative to define how he wants to be loved and how we are to love others. After all, he loved us first. He knows what works in the long run and what doesn't. Both Scripture and life teach us that: "There is a way that seems right to a man, but its end is the way of death" (Prov. 14:12). Relying on our human feelings alone is a recipe for losing our way.

Scripture teaches that the *agape* love God personifies—a love of outgoing concern for others—is not innate to man. Jesus stated that godly love even involves showing love to one's enemies (Exod. 23:4; Matt. 5:44). Clearly, this type of love is neither natural nor intuitive.

Therefore, to be of any value, the word "love" must be defined. Otherwise "love" is simply a moral platitude. The societal definition of "loving" our fellow man has changed enormously over time. Even within the wider Christian world there are a variety of different ways in which people profess their love of God.

It is God's absolute prerogative to define how he wants to be loved and how we are to love others.

True Love Must Be Taught

Considering the context of the time of Moses, God's command to love and the need for him to define what love meant in practice made perfect sense. Israel had come out of a foreign society with a corrupt set of values and a confused view of God. How the Egyptians and the Canaanites "loved" their gods dramatically differed from how the true God desired to be loved. And how their cultures selectively loved and hated other human beings was also nothing like what God had in mind for the society of Israel.

Those who assume that the natural man will eventually arrive at an enlightened understanding of selfless love without revelation from God are defying the lessons of history. They are also denying the Bible's teaching, which says the natural ways of humankind cannot be trusted:

> The heart is deceitful above all things, and desperately wicked; who can know it? (Jer. 17:9)

> He who trusts in his own heart is a fool, but whoever walks wisely will be delivered. (Prov. 28:26)

Selfishness, judging and condemning others, are natural; loving others is not. God had to teach Israel his ways, including how to love him and their fellow man in line with his standards.

The entire Mosaic law was an expression of God's love.

This was the core intent of law of Moses. Far more than a prescriptive set of "rules," the law of Moses taught what the true love of God and love of man looked like in practice. The entire Mosaic law was an expression of God's love. This included the core Ten Commandments, the judgments, the statutes, and the ceremonial system of worship—all of which fell under the umbrella of the great principles of love of God and love of fellow man as Jesus confirmed (Matt. 22:40). God wanted the people to understand that these laws were a blessing from him and *for their own good*:

> What does the LORD your God require of you ... to keep the commandments of the LORD and His statutes which I command you today *for your good.* (Deut. 10: 12–13)

> The LORD commanded us to observe all these statutes, to fear the LORD our God, *for our good always.* (Deut. 6:24)

> You shall therefore keep His statutes and His commandments which I command you today, that it *may go well with you* and with your children after you, and that you may prolong your days in the land which the LORD your God is giving you for all time. (Deut. 4:40)

Love Is a Decision

By commanding Israel to love him, God was teaching Israel that true *agape* love starts with a decision, not a feeling. By deciding to commit to the One True God of Israel—to trust him and obey him, as an expression of that love—the nation, over time, would develop a deep, heartfelt love for the God who loved them deeply and had done so much for them.

In the same way, in a family, a small child first learns to obey their parents, who desire nothing but the best for them. Then, as the child grows in understanding, the relationship develops into deep, emotional love toward the

> *True agape love starts with a decision, not a feeling.*

parents who loved them first. In many ways, ancient Israel paralleled the story of an immature child rebelling against a caring parent:

> Do you thus deal with the LORD, O foolish and unwise people? *Is He not your Father,* who bought you? Has He not made you and established you? (Deut. 32:6)

> For My people are foolish, they have not known Me. *They are silly children*, and they have no understanding. They are wise to do evil, but to do good they have no knowledge. (Jer. 4:22)

Like unruly children, Israel pushed back at God when he always had their best interests in mind. As a parent to the nation, God knew that keeping his law would result in positive fruit in their lives if they obeyed.

Love Was Central

Knowing God's steadfast love was at the heart of the old covenant and the law of Moses should dramatically change a person's perspective of the law. God wasn't looking for Israel to approach him with the legalistic, fear-driven formulas of pagan religions. He desired a reciprocal love originating from the innermost being of the individual Israelite. The entire law system must be interpreted in the light of that desired outcome.

Rational and Coherent

I do not feel obliged to believe that the same God who has endowed us with sense, reason, and intellect has intended us to forgo their use. —Galileo Galilei

When asked to identify the greatest command in the law of Moses, Jesus responded by quoting a verse from the book of Deuteronomy:

> You shall love the Lord your God with all your heart, with all your soul, and with *all your mind.* (Matt. 22:37)

By confirming God wanted a connection with the *mind*, Jesus reinforced what we already know about God from observing his creation: he is *rational*. The universe's structure is founded on predictable laws of science and mathematics that reflect a supremely intelligent and coherent Creator.

Secondly, Jesus' statement teaches us something important about the nature of the relationship God desired with ancient Israel. God was looking for a bond with the holistic person—mind, heart, and body[1]—demonstrating the high value God placed on the complete feeling and thinking person.

Thirdly, making such a statement in the context of the law of Moses was a declaration that God wanted his people to *understand* the law and the rationale behind it. It confirms a foundational principle of the law of Moses: that both the Lawgiver and the law are understandable. This was in contrast to pagan religions and their often random and illogical universe of their gods.[2]

> *Jesus strongly reinforced the rationality of the law of Moses.*

An Intelligent and Coherent Law

Jesus strongly reinforced the rationality of the law of Moses. In his ministry, he was challenged and questioned on the law multiple times. His responses in those encounters showed that he saw the law as something far more than a set of imposed rules or a religious checklist. At every opportunity he encouraged his listeners to *think* and *discern* and *meditate* on what he was saying. His explanations made good sense, unlike many of the practices of the Pharisees. There is no hint that Jesus supported a concept of mindless obedience.

"Let us reason together" God at one time entreated through his prophet.

---

[1] Described as *all your heart, all your soul, and all your strength* in Deut. 6:5.
[2] One has only to consider the pantheons of the Ugaritic gods and the Greek and Roman gods.

"Present your case, bring forth your strong reasons" (Isa. 1:18; 41:21). "The fear of the LORD is the beginning of knowledge, but fools despise wisdom and instruction" (Prov. 1:7). These and many other statements of Scripture confirm God as a rational being with rational principles that people of all ages have a right to question and seek to understand. As American philosopher and educator, Mortimer Adler observed:

> I suspect that most of the individuals who have religious faith are content with blind faith. They feel no obligation to understand what they believe. They may even wish not to have their beliefs disturbed by thought. But if the God in whom they believe created them with intellectual and rational powers, that imposes upon them the duty to try to understand the creed of their religion. Not to do so is to verge on superstition.[3]

God's desire to be engaged with the mind has profound consequences and, again, by necessity, must change our perspective of the law of Moses. It confirms that the law must fundamentally satisfy a *rational enquiring mind*. It must also reflect what we might call "common sense" and implies there had to be an intelligent and coherent basis in all aspects of the law.

> *Loving God with the mind remains a standing invitation for a person to explore the deeper principles held within the law of Moses.*

Loving God with the mind remains a standing invitation for a person to explore the deeper principles held within the law of Moses—principles that may not always be obvious at first reading.

Problem with Arbitrary Laws

Some have subscribed to the idea that at least some aspects of the law of Moses were arbitrary rules designed to control or test the people. But how could keeping a set of arbitrary laws develop greatness in a nation? How could meaningless obedience lead to anything of true value in the character of a people? Lawmakers have confirmed for centuries that arbitrary laws without rational purpose, given at the whim and fancy of the lawgiver, are destructive for a society.

Arbitrary laws have sometimes been used in history by despots to control

---

[3] Bibliog: (James-Clark 1993, 207)

people and test whether they were "loyal" or not. Ultimately such laws lead to no good in a society. American founding father James Madison correctly observed that incoherent, unpredictable, and arbitrary law "poisons the blessings of liberty itself."[4] Interestingly, nonsensical laws are banned in some national constitutions, and a legal test of rationality is in place in most countries, including the United States.[5]

Not all religions are rational in their doctrines. In Jesus' day, the Pharisees embraced the idea that the sheer act of legalistic obedience was of some value in God's eyes, even when what they were doing was inherently illogical. For example, they had created a bizarre regime of contradictory oaths, which Jesus derided them for:

> Woe to you, blind guides, who say, "Whoever swears by the temple, it is nothing; but whoever swears by the gold of the temple, he is obliged to perform it." Fools and blind! For which is greater, the gold or the temple that sanctifies the gold? And, "Whoever swears by the altar, it is nothing; but whoever swears by the gift that is on it, he is obliged to perform it." Fools and blind! For which is greater, the gift or the altar that sanctifies the gift? (Matt. 23:16–19)

In the centuries prior, the Pharisees and their religious colleagues had drifted away from the fundamental principle of rationality that underpinned the entire law system. Many of their religious rules and rituals made no sense and were contradictory. In contrast to the religion of the Jews, Jesus always encouraged his listeners to consider what was *written* and to *think*, search out *meaning*, and make *sensible* judgments. His responses to questions about the law invited deep thought, unlike the Pharisees who in many areas operated by rote and legalistic interpretation.

For Your Wisdom and Understanding

The law of Moses went beyond simple rationality—it was designed to be a source of *wisdom* and *understanding*. For this reason David could say:

> The fear of the LORD is the *beginning of wisdom*; a *good understanding* have all those who do His commandments. (Ps. 111:10)

Wisdom is the ability to discern a present situation and make choices that are beneficial and productive in the long run. There can be no wisdom or

---

[4] Bibliog: (Madison, Federalist No 62 1788)
[5] Bibliog: (Cornell 2023)

understanding in some random set of "rules." For laws to contain wisdom and understanding, they must be inherently sound and based on the realities of life. Only then can they be a source of understanding and long-term reward.

Moses stated that the wisdom and understanding contained in the law would be evident—even attractive to other nations—when they saw these laws in action:

> For this is *your wisdom and your understanding* in the sight of the peoples who will hear all these statutes, and say, "Surely this great nation is a *wise and understanding people.*" (Deut. 4:6)

After Moses' death, God spoke to the new leader, Joshua, and reaffirmed the depth of meaning in the law by advising Joshua to meditate on it as a part of his daily life (Josh. 1:8). If the words are worth meditating on, they must contain wisdom and understanding. If the law of Moses was little more than a religious IQ test or a rule-bound obedience test, there would be nothing at all to meditate on. This was the issue Jesus was so often confronted with in his day—religious leaders who didn't discern the situation but blindly applied a rule. Yet all along the law of Moses was there encouraging a person to *think*! Observing the law was supposed to have a positive, real-life value:

The law of Moses went beyond simple rationality—it was designed to be a source of wisdom and understanding.

> Set your hearts on all the words which I testify among you today, which you shall command your children to be careful to observe—all the words of this law. *For it is not a futile thing for you, because it is your life*, and by this word you shall prolong your days in the land which you cross over the Jordan to possess. (Deut. 32:46–47)

The starting point for true success was for Israel to listen carefully to the wisdom of their Creator who could see the end from the beginning (Isa. 46:10). When a society rejects the revelation from God, as Israel eventually did, there can be no wisdom. This is what made the law itself so important in the nation and why law was central to the old covenant.

Aligned to Reality

Another aspect of God's rationality has a direct bearing on how we should interpret his system of law. God describes himself as "abounding in goodness and *truth*" (Exod. 34:6), someone who speaks what is always *right* and *true*

(Isa. 45:19). Because truth and reality are inherently tied together, we should, therefore, expect the law of Moses to align with the reality of life.

In other words, the law had to not only be rational, but it also had to be in harmony with the observable laws of cause and effect that operate in nature. As the influential English philosopher John Locke correctly wrote:

> Laws human must be made according to the general laws of nature, and without contradiction to any positive law of Scripture, otherwise they are ill made.[6]

Locke, called the Father of Liberalism (i.e., as in *freedom*), understood that good laws must work with the reality that God has built into his creation. Just as observable laws of physics and chemistry make up our universe, so, too, universal moral laws exist that all people have understood to at least a minimal degree. C. S. Lewis used the existence of this naturally understood moral reality as a powerful proof of the existence of God because it has no worldly explanation.[7] Paul commented on this "natural law" as it is sometimes called when writing to the Romans:

> For when gentiles, who do not have the law, *by nature do the things in the law*, these, although not having the law, are a law to themselves, who show the work of the law written in their hearts, their conscience also bearing witness, and between themselves their thoughts accusing or else excusing them. (Rom. 2:14–15)

In other words, people generally know from the reality of life that morally destructive behaviors such as murder, stealing, lying, greed, adultery, etc. destroy relationships and result in negative outcomes for individuals and societies. When a person applies outgoing love for others, positive things flow in their life. Selfishness, on the other hand, does not produce long-term joy as it should according to a materialistic view of the world. These causes and effects can be observed outside religion.[8]

Christian author and medical doctor Dr. Timothy Jennings uses the term "design law" in contrast to man's idea of "imposed law" and expresses it this way:

> The Bible writers understood that God, as Creator, built the universe

---

[6] Bibliog: (Locke 1690, Ch XI)
[7] Bibliog: (Lewis 2002, 3-8)
[8] There are religions that claim that murder and violence in this life can lead to nirvana, but they are defying observable reality.

to operate in harmony with himself. He did not construct reality to be at variance to himself. Therefore God's design law is an expression of his character of love. ... The law of love is not a rule; it is a design protobuilt into the fabric of reality.[9]

God did not simply impose a system of law on Israel. It was an extension of God's worldview of truth and reality. The major tenets of the law of Moses perfectly align with God's creation. The Ten Commandments represent how God optimally designed society to operate and following them creates strong and caring communities. The rest of the law also reflected logical and coherent principles that direct an individual toward these same positive outcomes. As Jesus stated, the law can be summed up as the love of God and the love of man. The entire law must be analyzed and understood in this light.

> *God did not simply impose a system of law on Israel. It was an extension of God's worldview of truth and reality.*

Entire Law Had Meaning

The rationality and coherence of God must be kept in mind when working through the law of Moses. The command to love God with the *mind* was a directive for the people to think and meditate and seek to understand his laws intelligently.

If any aspect of the Old Testament law seems illogical or contradictory to sound reasoning to us today, then just like the ancient Israelites, we have the right to question, explore, and seek understanding. The answer may lie in cultural differences, the historical context, or the specific circumstances at hand. Knowing that the law was given by a wise and sovereign God for Israel's wisdom and understanding is the starting point. We will later see that the *entire* law (including the ritual and ceremonial law) had deep meaning and was designed to teach Israel about God, his values, and his great plan for humanity.

---

[9] Bibliog: (Jennings 2017, 39,41)

A Lover of Freedom

The rights of man come not from the generosity of the state but from the hand of God.—John F. Kennedy, Inaugural Address, 1961

The founding document of the nation of America, the *Declaration of Independence*, based its legal authority to establish the new nation on the "self-evident" truth that the God who created humankind endowed them with "unalienable rights," of which "life, liberty, and the pursuit of happiness" were paramount. They wrote that these were rights that "the Laws of Nature and of Nature's God entitle them."[1] The source of the rights they were referring to is historically clear: the Judeo-Christian heritage of divine law as outlined in the Bible—rights that originate from man being made in the image of God.

Made in the Image of God

God, the author of the law of Moses, is also our Creator. Humans are the pinnacle of his creation, epitomized by that profound statement in Genesis "Let us make man in our own image" (Gen. 1:26). Being made in the image of God is to be given hearts and minds that have the potential to understand and relate to God personally. It also includes the gift of freewill that allows humans to accept God or reject him, love him, or hate him. Our modern world believes that mankind is causally bound by our physical atoms, but our Creator says otherwise. We are his children.

God didn't have to make humans this way. He could have made us like animals, operating on instinct, but he instead chose to make us free—free to ask and explore the great questions of life. Even God's servants, the angels, were given freewill. *Freedom has been one of God's fundamental guiding principles from creation.*

> *Those who imagine God giving Israel a law system based on control, coercion, and micromanagement are greatly mistaken.*

Those who imagine this freedom-loving God giving Israel a law system based on control, coercion, and micromanagement are greatly mistaken. Firstly, it would be incompatible with his nature. Secondly, such a system could never have achieved the outcomes God sought in his people. Unless God gave the Israelites the free will to choose or

---

[1] Bibliog: (National Archives 1776)

reject him, any concept of a deep connection of the heart would be impossible. God had no interest in *forcing* Israel to do what was right. He wanted to shape their hearts so that they *desired* to do right. This is what he was looking for in ancient Israel and what he is looking for in Christians today: a connection to our deepest desires and emotions. And such a connection can only come from the *voluntary* and *free choice* of the individual.

However, the problem with granting free choice is that it comes with great risks and can result in harsh consequences and pain when wrong decisions are made. Any parent knows this well when they choose to bring a child into the world. The child has the potential to be a source of great joy but may also make choices that bring great heartache. As the parent of Israel, God experienced such pain firsthand when his children repeatedly rejected him (Deut. 32:6; Mal. 1:6).

Freedom Requires Law

Freedom is not as simple to define as some think. Freedom is sometimes interpreted as the unrestrained right of an individual to do whatever they want, but this definition quickly fails. No one wants a society where people are free to disrupt and cause havoc. Neither will a person who wants to harm others be allowed to remain loose. They will be quickly restrained. Even criminals would reject such a society because it would soon deteriorate into chaos.

Without boundaries of law and order, there can be no freedom, only anarchy. We have our freedoms in our societies today only because we have laws. Freedom always starts with a structure of law. It's never "Liberty *without* law; it's always "Liberty *under* law." In recent years, some "nation-building" experiments in foreign countries have amply demonstrated this. Dictators have been removed in the name of freedom, and after the initial dancing in the streets and the promise of a better life, violence emerges, and day-to-day life deteriorates to worse than before the dictator was removed. Only when a *rule of law* is established can any quality of life be restored.

Bad laws can certainly suppress freedom, but good laws do not erode freedom; they defend freedom.

Bad laws can certainly suppress freedom, but *good laws do not erode freedom; they defend* freedom. Good laws create strong, vibrant, and prosperous societies.

But establishing the correct balance between civil order and individual freedom is difficult, and boundaries must be defined. Such boundaries extend even to the mind of the individual. Even outside religion, medical professionals recognize that an unrestrained mind consumed in negative emotions such as hate, lust, anger, or jealousy is destructive for the individual and those around them. What happens within the confines of an individual mind *can* and *will* hurt others—and hurt badly.

Even personal freedom must be based on a system of law with boundaries that guide a person morally in the way they live their life. Freedom will never come from a totally unrestrained mind.

Freedom Must be Defined

True freedom, therefore, must be defined; it is not something that naturally flows by simply removing restraints. It must be defined firstly as a standard of moral behavior for the individual, and secondly as a set of external standards for society if both are to achieve their best potential. The laws defining freedom must also be based on values that work and align with the realities of life; otherwise they will work against the natural order of things and frustrate those under their jurisdiction.

Who better to define freedom than the one who created humankind and gave us our freedom in the first place? As Thomas Jefferson expressed:

> The God who gave us life gave us liberty. Can the liberties of a nation be secure when we have removed a conviction that these liberties are the gift of God?[2]

Today our Western world has been deceived into thinking that freedom is permissiveness and licentiousness. But such freedoms have always led to rising social problems and the eventual collapse of society. As Jesus said, only *truth* will set a person truly free (John 8:32). Lies may be attractive, but in the long run, they will never set anyone free.

True Freedom Based on Moral Virtue

The author of the law of Moses is often underestimated and misrepresented as someone who did not understand freedom. Yet freedom was central to the law. But God knew from the outset that to have a truly free nation, the people of Israel would need to be people of virtue.

---

[2] Bibliog: (Jefferson 1786)

This link between freedom and morality is a topic that the founding fathers of America commented extensively on. They understood the simple truth that without virtue and morality, a people will never be truly free nor empowered. Their comments are insightful:

> Only a virtuous people are capable of freedom. —Benjamin Franklin[3]

> Liberty can no more exist without virtue and independence than the body can live and move without a soul. —John Adams[4]

> Public liberty will not long survive the total extinction of morals. —Samuel Adams[5]

> But a republic once equally poised must either preserve its virtue or lose its liberty. —John Witherspoon[6]

> No free government, or the blessings of liberty, can be preserved to any people but by a firm adherence to justice, moderation, temperance, frugality, and virtue; and by a frequent recurrence to fundamental principles. —Patrick Henry[7]

To have a truly free nation, the people of Israel would need to be people of virtue.

> Human rights can only be assured among a virtuous people. —George Washington[8]

> Our Constitution was made only for a moral and religious people. It is wholly inadequate to the government of any other. —John Adams[9]

> Their minds are to be informed by education what is right and what wrong; to be encouraged in habits of virtue and to be deterred from those of vice ... These are the inculcations necessary to render the people a sure basis for the structure and order of government. —Thomas Jefferson[10]

It was the moral standards and laws that came from the Bible that laid the

---

[3] Bibliog: (Franklin 1840)
[4] Bibliog: (J. Adams 1775)
[5] Bibliog: (S. Adams 1778)
[6] Bibliog: (Witherspoon 1906)
[7] Bibliog: (P. Henry 1776)
[8] Bibliog: (Washington 1939)
[9] Bibliog: (J. Adams 1798)
[10] Bibliog: (Jefferson 1819)

groundwork for America's rise. They gave the impetus to the founding fathers to define a free society where the people could have confidence in the legal structures, the justice system, property rights, and their safety and security.

God has always known that true freedom is not the freedom to do whatever evil a person wills to do, but the freedom to *worship the true God and do what is right*—a privilege many people in history have been unable to do. It is the legacy of history that those who have tried to follow the true God have so often been persecuted. Even in Old Testament times, in the actual land of Israel, the prophets of God and God-fearers were often mistreated.

Freedom Creates a Bold People

One strong proof of the value God put on individual freedom is the response of righteous people of the Old Testament who put their trust in him. They were not a timid, fearful people cowering under a controlling God. Rather, we see a boldness that is startling. The closer they got to God, the more secure and confident they were to be themselves and speak boldly to God and others. The righteous were indeed "bold as a lion" (Prov. 28:1). A dictatorial framework of law based on control would never have created such confidence in a people. It would have instead resulted in an underlying fear and timidity as controlling environments and fear religions always do.

He designed the laws he gave to Moses to bolster the freedoms of the individual Israelite, not suppress them.

God has always wanted his people to be free. He designed the laws he gave to Moses to bolster the freedoms of the individual Israelite, not suppress them. Later we will see just how different these laws were to those of the surrounding nations and most nations in history. Collectively they were designed to create what could have been the freest nation that had ever existed.

Just and Righteous

I am the LORD, exercising lovingkindness, judgment, and righteousness in the earth. For in these I delight. —Jeremiah 9:24

God is a God of justice, a standard that flows from his character: "For I, the LORD, love justice" he proclaims (Isa. 61:8). Justice is at the foundation of his throne, the way he judges all people. God's judgment is not capricious—it is based on truth and his own standard of unchanging righteousness:

> He is the Rock, His work is perfect; for all His ways are justice, a God of truth and without injustice; righteous and upright is He. (Deut. 32:4)

Godly justice is not simply a matter of *judgment,* as the Mosaic law is so often interpreted, it is inherently tied to God's character of *righteousness*.

Godly Justice Defined

Two Hebrew words are commonly used in conjunction with each other to describe godly justice. They are words not easily expressed in English. They are variously translated as "judgment and justice," "justice and righteousness," or "justice and equity" as translators tried to reflect the original intent.

Consider the use of these words in summarizing David's reign:

> So David reigned over all Israel; and David administered *judgment* and *justice* to all his people. (2 Sam. 8:15)

The words *judgment* and *justice* may seem redundant, but in Hebrew, they represent two concepts of law:

Mishpat (Heb.)	Act of sitting as a judge, hearing a case, and rendering a proper verdict.[1] The rule of law.
Tzedakah (Heb.)	To be righteous, be in the right, be justified, be just.[2]

These two words come together to describe godly justice. David not only judged the people in reference to the written law (*mishpat*), he also delivered those judgments with *righteousness* (*tzedakah*), according to God's *intent*. This

---

[1] Bibliog: (Vine 1996, To Judge. mispat p 126)
[2] Bibliog: (Vine 1996, To Be Righteous. p 205)

is what God desires—*righteous judgment*:

These two concepts are tightly paired together in many places in the Hebrew Scriptures including in the law itself:

> You shall do no injustice in *judgment* ... In *righteousness* you shall judge your neighbor. (Lev. 19:15)

> He loves *righteousness* and *justice*; the earth is full of the goodness of the LORD. (Ps. 33:5)

> "Hear the cases between your brethren, and *judge righteously* between a man and his brother or the stranger who is with him." (Deut. 1:16)

These two concepts were understood at the time of Abraham:

> For I have known him, in order that he may command his children and his household after him, that they keep the way of the LORD, to do *righteousness* and *justice*." (Gen. 18:19).

They will still be valid for Jesus' rule in his kingdom:

> Of the increase of His government and peace there will be no end, upon the throne of David and over His kingdom, to order it and establish it with *judgment* and *justice* from that time forward, even forever. (Isa. 9:7)

Righteous judgment requires two components: a standard of law, and a judge with wisdom who understands the character and values of God. Godly justice has never been served by blindly applying a penalty—not in today's world nor back in the time of Moses. A police officer today will be rightly criticized for issuing a ticket to a driver speeding to the hospital with a gravely ill child. That is legalism. This is how the Pharisees interpreted the law, and Jesus pushed back at them strongly for not applying righteous judgment (John 7:24). God has never been a legalist because legalism is not righteousness.

God has never been a legalist because legalism is not righteousness.

Godly justice will at times require punishment to the full extent of the law, and at other times will call for mercy.

This is a common mistake made by critics of the law of Moses. They read the law and interpret it *strictly to the letter* and then present that as the way the law was always to be interpreted. Or they point to a specific case where someone receives a harsh punishment and then present that as the standard judgment for all. This is a false representation of the intent of the Lawgiver. Godly justice was to be achieved by considering both the context and the individuals concerned, and then applying the correct balance of judgment and mercy to achieve a righteous decision. This is how God judges all people:

> *Righteousness* and *justice* are the foundation of Your throne; mercy and truth go before Your face. (Ps. 89:14)

These concepts arise from the heart and character of God:

> But let him who glories glory in this, that he understands and knows Me, that I am the LORD, exercising *lovingkindness, judgment, and righteousness* in the earth. For in these I delight," says the LORD. (Jer. 9:24)

Justice and Mercy

In the same vein, justice and mercy are often presented as opposites. But they are not. The opposite of justice is *injustice*, not mercy. Godly justice can *include* mercy. Because God is just, he is also gracious and merciful. The prophets understood that the two virtues are inherently linked:

> Therefore the LORD will wait, that He may be gracious to you; and therefore He will be exalted, *that He may have mercy on you. For the LORD is a God of justice.* (Isa. 30:18)

> He has shown you, O man, what is good; and what does the LORD require of you *but to do justly, to love mercy*, and to walk humbly with your God? (Mic. 6:8)

C. S. Lewis beautifully expresses this tie between mercy and judgment:

> Mercy, detached from Justice, grows unmerciful. That is the important paradox. As there are plants which will flourish only in mountain soil, so it appears that Mercy will flower only when it grows in the crannies of the rock of Justice.[3]

If there was no potential for judgment, mercy would be meaningless. If there was no mercy, there would be no hope for anyone. It should be of enormous comfort that God's mercy will always take precedence over judgment as the previous Scriptures confirm. As James also wrote when talking about the law:

---

[3] Bibliog: (Lewis. 1996, Essay: The Humanitarian Theory of Punishment. p 500)

For judgment is without mercy to the one who has shown no mercy. *Mercy triumphs over judgment.* (James 2:13)

This preeminence of mercy over judgment is implied directly in the law of Moses, with mercy offered to a *thousand generations of those who love him* (Deut. 7:9). God has always been primarily interested in exacting repentance and a changed heart, not punishment. Even as the people of Israel became corrupt, he was always hopeful of a change and often deferred his judgment on them.

> *God has always been primarily interested in exacting repentance and a changed heart, not punishment.*

But while God is merciful, his mercy is not something a sinner can demand. Mercy is not a right; it is God's prerogative. At times he will be tough on high-handed sinners and those who know better. Not every sinner will be given mercy in this life. This is what Paul highlighted when writing about the hard-hearted Israelites:

> For He says to Moses, "I will have mercy on whomever I will have mercy, and I will have compassion on whomever I will have compassion." (Rom. 9:15; Exod. 33:19)

This should not be interpreted that God's mercy is arbitrary—he will always be merciful and forgiving to a humble and contrite sinner. But whether he is merciful to unrepentant sinners is his decision to make. Either way, as the one who gives life and takes it away, we can have confidence that God's righteous justice will prevail. As the judges of old would say in cases of capital punishment, "May God have mercy on your soul," correctly acknowledging that God will have the final say.

The Spirit versus the Letter of the Law

There is a false idea held by some that the old covenant was focused on the "letter of the law" while the new covenant focuses on the "spirit of the law." But this is not supported in Scripture. God's standard of justice has never changed. By necessity the law of Moses was written "in the letter" as all law codes must be, but from the outset, God desired his people to seek out the *intent* of the law and use wisdom and discernment in its application. The law had to be applied with mercy and judgment so that righteous judgment could be applied. Those in positions of judgment were supposed to deeply understand and meditate on these matters in the law so that they were *just* in their rulings.

Jesus castigated the religious leaders for not understanding this most fundamental of points. On one occasion he was particularly incensed with the Pharisees for legalistically defrauding their parents in the name of God (Matt. 15:3–9). While they may have been technically keeping the *letter* of the law, they had broken the *spirit* of the law and dishonored their parents. When correcting them, he referenced the Old Testament prophet Isaiah:

> Hypocrites! Well did Isaiah prophesy about you, saying: "These people draw near to Me with their mouth, and honor Me with their lips, but their heart is far from Me." (Matt. 15:7–8)

This is the message throughout the Old Testament. The prophets consistently stated that the God of Israel was not interested in ritual for ritual's sake. Many times the prophets addressed this false idea of outward religious show without cleaning up the heart:

> For I desire mercy and not sacrifice, and the knowledge of God more than burnt offerings. (Hosea 6:6)

> With what shall I come before the LORD, *and* bow myself before the High God? Shall I come before Him with burnt offerings, with calves a year old? Will the LORD be pleased with thousands of rams, ten thousand rivers of oil? Shall I give my firstborn *for* my transgression, the fruit of my body *for* the sin of my soul? He has shown you, O man, what *is* good; And what does the LORD require of you but to do justly, to love mercy, and to walk humbly with your God? (Mic. 6:6–8)

God wanted Israel to understand and apply the spirit and intent of the law.

> I hate, I despise your feast days, and I do not savor your sacred assemblies. Though you offer Me burnt offerings and your grain offerings, I will not accept *them,* nor will I regard your fattened peace offerings. Take away from Me the noise of your songs, for I will not hear the melody of your stringed instruments. *But let justice run down like water, and righteousness like a mighty stream.* (Amos 5:21–24)

God wanted Israel to understand and apply the spirit and intent of the law. Outward shows of ritual and religious pretense have never been of any value to him.

A God of Vengeance

There are times when God's judgment should be feared because God is just, and evil needs to be addressed. For unrepentant workers of evil, when the God of justice eventually decides to act, Scripture warns us not to take it lightly:

> He repays those who hate Him to their face, to destroy them. He will not be slack with him who hates Him; He will repay him to his face. (Deut. 7:10)

> God is jealous, and the LORD avenges; the LORD avenges and is furious. The LORD will take vengeance on His adversaries, and He reserves wrath for His enemies. (Nah. 1:2)

Critics of the Old Testament point to these and similar verses while ignoring those passages emphasizing God's mercy and patience. They accuse God of being harsh and swift in his punishment, acting with an eagerness, even a delight, in bringing down judgment on evildoers. This is patently false. Consider how quickly God agreed with Abraham to potentially avoid the destruction of Sodom (Gen. 18:22–32). How responsive he was to Nineveh's turnaround (Jon. 3–4). How long he pleaded with Israel to change. God will take every opportunity to defer punishment.

Critics also fail to note that the New Testament presents God in identical terms, with the apostle Paul warning us to consider both "the kindness *and the severity* of God" (Rom. 11:22)—kindness toward those who turn to him but serious consequences for those who continue to hate him, who consciously and willingly reject him. As the writer of Hebrews warns:

> For we know Him who said, "Vengeance is Mine, I will repay," says the Lord. And again, "The LORD will judge His people." It is a fearful thing to fall into the hands of the living God. (Heb. 10:30–31)

Vengeance is a word we recoil at today. We associate vengeance with retaliation and vindictiveness, but that is not the meaning of the word when used in conjunction with God. As *Baker's* commentary notes:

> A close study of the biblical term suggests that vengeance has to do with the administration of justice.[4]

God makes no apologies for being a God of vengeance. He described himself to ancient Israel as the ultimate avenger (Deut. 32:35). Vengeance is when God

---

[4] Bibliog: (Bakers 2013, Vengeance p 1687)

punishes his adversaries who refuse to acknowledge the error of their ways. While God's justice is sometimes hard, it has an end goal in mind, which is not just to punish but to restore and make things right wherever possible. As Baker's further comments:

> God's justice is counterbalanced by his love. For that reason his vengeance on his covenant people is often more corrective than punitive and anticipates their repentance, redemption, and restoration.

This is the message of the Old Testament and the New. This is the same God who:

> Is longsuffering toward us, not willing that *any* should perish but that all should come to repentance. (2 Pet. 3:9)

> Did not send his Son into the world to condemn the world, but that the world through him might be saved. (John 3:17)

Neither did God send his prophets to ancient Israel to condemn but instead to entreat his people to turn from their sins and be restored. When punishment came, it was not the end of the story. From the earliest times God always promised to deliver his people and restore them (Deut. 4:25–29).

God makes no apologies for being a God of vengeance.

God's justice is ultimately focused on restoration and reconciliation, not retribution. Again, this reflects God's character. He is not the vindictive, vengeful God who needs his wrath appeased as some critics suggest. He has always primarily desired a changed heart, not punishment, and has never taken any pleasure in the death of the wicked (Ezek. 33:11). He yearned for Israel to turn around and was willing to forgive the most heinous of their sins. Even as he warned the nation that they would be punished for their evil ways, he continually invited them to repent and spoke of their eventual restoration and healing (Jer. 33:6–9).

God's Unchanging Standards

Jesus expressed the same balance of judgment and mercy in his earthly ministry. He was merciful to sinners, but hard on those who hated him—calling them fools, hypocrites, blind guides, whitewashed tombs, sons of murderers, and a brood of vipers (Matt. 23). He warned them of the judgment to come if they did not change.

God's justice has always been tempered with compassion. But for God to be a God of justice, judgment must eventually fall on those who refuse to change. He is long-suffering, not forever-suffering. He will eventually bring down judgment on nations and individuals who knowingly continue in their immoral and idolatrous ways.

At the core of it, justice has to do with how people are ultimately treated. Justice must be based not on the whims of a fallible lawgiver or on changing societal standards, but on divine truth and a consistent standard of moral righteousness. To be just, a law system must demonstrate fairness, impartiality, and consistency. This is the character of God and how he desired the law of Moses to be administered.

In Touch with the Reality of Life

Keep the words of this covenant, and do them, that you may prosper in all that you do. —Deuteronomy 29:9

Jesus has the reputation of being down-to-earth and pragmatic—someone who understood the realities of life. He was not constrained by narrow interpretations of the Mosaic law when common sense would imply a better course of action. He often demonstrated that it was sensible (and lawful) to make practical decisions about how to apply the law to real life. This is particularly evident in Jesus' understanding of the Sabbath (Matt. 12:1–13). To the Pharisees, Jesus was a Sabbath-breaker, yet Jesus kept the entire law without sin. It was the Pharisees who had the wrong idea about how to approach the Sabbath—Jesus was simply reflecting the graciousness of God as he has always been.

Even today, many think that God in Old Testament times had more in common with the Pharisees than Jesus, that he was inflexible and impractical when it came to the application of the law. But this idea is not supported in the law itself nor in the recorded interactions of God with his people. It would also suggest a being who was unable to foresee a future time when his law would have to be administered in different social environments and under different governing structures.

The gracious and pragmatic God of Israel well understood that the law had to be adaptable across cultures and times to remain relevant.

Even from when God first gave the law at Mount Sinai, when Israel lived in a camp environment, to the time they entered the permanency of the promised land, there was a need to adapt the administration of the law. And from the time of Joshua to the time of the apostles, Israel underwent further structural change: the period of the judges, the period of the monarchy, a divided nation, living as captives in a foreign land, living as a vassal state, etc. Each period impacted the implementation of civil and ceremonial law, and judgments had to be made on how to apply the law. Jesus himself lived under a hybrid cultural mix of Roman and Jewish law, and discernment was needed to understand how the law of God was to be applied in such an environment. The gracious and pragmatic God of Israel well understood that the law had to be adaptable across cultures and times to remain relevant.

Adjusting to the Concerns of the People

Even before they entered the promised land, God showed his willingness to listen and adapt the law to the concerns and petitions of his people. This is evident in his response to a complaint about Passover.

The Passover was a highly significant ceremony that was to include all of Israel (Exod. 12). God had given Moses precise details about when this important Passover service was to be kept (Num. 9:2–4)—with no allowance for keeping the ceremony at any other time. But one particular year after Israel had kept the Passover, some men came forward who had missed out on the ceremony because they were ceremonially unclean due to a burial. Their attitude was right, but they felt it was unfair that they missed out on this important service, so they brought the problem to Moses (Num. 9:7). Note that Moses, who knew God's character well, didn't simply refer them to the prescribed law—he thought these men had a valid case. So he brought the matter before God and told the men to wait and see what God might say on the matter. God's response is revealing:

> Then the LORD spoke to Moses, saying, "Speak to the children of Israel, saying: 'If anyone of you or your posterity is unclean because of a corpse, or is far away on a journey, *he may still keep the LORD's Passover. On the fourteenth day of the second month, at twilight, they may keep it.*'" (Num. 9:9–11)

God listened to the problem the men put forward and provided a judgment. He advised Moses that the Passover could be postponed for a month for people unable to keep it at the appointed time.

We might wonder why God hadn't thought of this situation in advance and why it took a query by these men to bring it to his attention. Possibly he had considered the matter and simply wanted to demonstrate he valued his people's input. Regardless, this decision reveals an approachable God who will make a practical judgment in the spirit of the original law when needed.

Inheritance Laws Adjusted

Another example in the same vein is in the book of Numbers. God directed Moses to count the households of Israel in readiness to divide the land of Canaan along male family inheritance lines (Num. 26:55). The daughters of Zelophehad realized that because their father had died in the wilderness, they would miss out on an inheritance. So they boldly went to Moses and asked:

> Why should the name of our father be removed from among his family because he had no son? Give us a possession among our father's brothers. (Num. 27:4)

Again, it is noteworthy that the women were fearless in bringing their petition to Moses, even though the inheritance laws had already been announced. Moses again considered their case valid and brought the matter before God. God's response is both surprising and heart-warming:

> And the LORD spoke to Moses, saying: *"The daughters of Zelophehad speak what is right;* you shall surely give them a possession of inheritance among their father's brothers, and cause the inheritance of their father to pass to them." (Num. 27:6–7)

What is particularly revealing here is God's statement that these women "speak what is right." God was not reticent in crediting the women for their sensible idea. Again, we might wonder why God hadn't included this scenario in advance and why he waited until these women made their case. Regardless, he saw that what they were saying made sense, and he listened and responded to what they had to say. God subsequently laid out a revised set of inheritance laws for the nation (Num. 27:8–11). Sometime later a further adjustment was made to the laws to clarify what would happen if the women married outside their tribe (Num. 36).

> *God has always been reasonable and willing to adapt his law to the demands and realities of real life.*

These examples demonstrate the mind of God and his willingness to be reasonable in the application of his law to the demands and realities of real life. Judgments within the spirit and intent of the law will always be needed to allow for the issues of life. God himself set the example. This is the same mindset Jesus demonstrated in his approach to applying the law during his day. Jesus understood that the law had to work in real-life situations.

Laws Created because of Hardness of Heart

When considering that God himself authored the law, our natural reaction might be to assume that laws given to Israel by Moses would be a perfect set of laws for a perfect society. But there is a big problem with that line of reasoning: the Israelites. They were far from perfect. Therefore, God's willingness to adapt his law to the realities of life was not always based on positive scenarios. Many judgments of the law of Moses were given for the opposite reason—to manage negative social issues. Again, they demonstrate the pragmatic mind of God.

Jesus highlighted this in an interaction with the Pharisees who had come to him with a question relating to the laws for divorce:

> Is it lawful for a man to divorce his wife for just any reason? (Matt. 19:3)

Jesus' answer was unequivocal, and he confirmed that divorce was *never* God's intention for a married couple:

> And He answered and said to them, "Have you not read that He who made them at the beginning 'made them male and female,' and said, 'For this reason a man shall leave his father and mother and be joined to his wife, and *the two shall become one flesh*'? So then, they are no longer two but one flesh. Therefore what God has joined together, let not man separate." (Matt. 19:4–6)

The Pharisees thought that they had Jesus trapped in a contradiction. But Jesus immediately cut to the heart of the matter and pinpointed the real reason these laws for divorce existed:

> They said to Him, "Why then did Moses command to give a certificate of divorce, and to put her away?" He said to them, "Moses, *because of the hardness of your hearts, permitted you to divorce your wives*, but from the beginning it was not so." (Matt. 19:7–8)

Jesus' reply teaches us an important additional insight into how to understand the law of Moses. Divorce, as we know, is clearly outside God's own standards. It's something he never wanted. In the book of Malachi, God goes so far as to say that he *hates* divorce (Mal. 2:16). Yet, despite this, the people still divorced for various reasons. (God himself "divorced" Israel because of their infidelities as a nation, Jer. 3:8.) And so through Moses, God provided rules for divorce so that this less-than-ideal situation could be managed in an orderly way (albeit the Pharisees had missed the intent of this law and interpreted it for their own convenience).

It is equally clear from Jesus' same statement of the "two becoming one" (quoted from Genesis) that polygamy did not align with God's ideal. From the beginning God said marriage was to be between one man and one woman who joined together as "one flesh" (Gen. 2:24). This defined an exclusive, intimate, and lifelong relationship of two people, not multiple women to one man as practiced by many of old.[1] Yet the law of Moses again included laws to manage polygamous situations.

The key point to understand is this: just because regulations on certain negative behavior existed in the Mosaic law, did not imply that such behavior was to be looked on favorably. In fact, we have many examples of the negative—sometimes disastrous—effects of polygamy on the lives of Old Testament characters who were in such relationships.

This principle of creating laws to manage less-than-ideal situations is widely extant in our society today. We have laws to regulate all sorts of negative situations we never imagined would even exist years ago. The simple point is this: sin leads to more sin, which leads to more laws to manage the after-effects. If people were without sin, many laws could be deleted. It was the same for the law of Moses.

> *Just because regulations on certain negative behavior existed in the Mosaic law, did not imply that such behavior was to be looked on favorably.*

Adjusting to Imperfect People

Why didn't God simply make laws against divorce, polygamy, and some other negative situations we will later come across? The answer again lies in God's character. God describes himself as merciful and gracious, and so he is. He is also a believer in the freedom of the individual and knew his law had to operate in the real world of hard-hearted Israel.

We see a working example of this in how God addressed the matter of a physical king. God was clear that he did not want Israel to have a human king because he himself was their king. But God knew the people would one day want to be like the other nations around them and have a physical leader they could look up to. Many years later, when the people finally approached the prophet Samuel to ask for a king, God's response was revealing:

> Heed the voice of the people in all that they say to you; for they have not rejected you, but *they have rejected Me*, that I should not reign over them. According to all the works which they have done since the day that I brought them up out of Egypt, even to this day—with which they have forsaken Me and served other gods—so they are doing to

---

[1] Polygamy faded out in the New Testament era as the church considered Jesus' interpretation of the law in the light of Genesis 2:24. No change to the written law was necessary.

you also. *Now therefore, heed their voice. However, you shall solemnly forewarn them*, and show them the behavior of the king who will reign over them. (1 Sam. 8:7-9)

Despite knowing that such a request was a rejection of himself as king, and that it would lead to negative consequences in the nation, God told Samuel to go ahead and heed their request, albeit with warnings. He even chose their first king, Saul, and their second king, David.

Even more surprising, hundreds of years previously God had planned for the day when Israel would one day have a king. This was even before they had entered the promised land. In Deuteronomy, we find laws for a future king even though God knew all along that a physical king would be to the detriment of the people (Deut. 17:14-20). This is another example of God accommodating the hard-heartedness of man. If the people were going to insist on a king, then God at least wanted to outline how the king should behave to ensure that the situation was managed in the best possible way. At the time, God also made it clear that polygamy was not an acceptable practice for a future king:

Neither shall he multiply wives for himself, lest his heart turn away; nor shall he greatly multiply silver and gold for himself. (Deut. 17:17)

Yet we find even the righteous Kings David and Solomon copied the nations around them. David's actions of multiplying wives and concubines to himself caused major grief in his family, and Solomon's outrageous number of wives eventually led him away from the true God (1 Kings 11:3). Both paid a heavy price for ignoring God's directives.

God, on the other hand, in line with his merciful and gracious manner, was still willing to work closely with both kings despite their polygamous behavior. It was his idolatry that God later judged Solomon harshly on, not his polygamous behavior. God has always worked with imperfect people and continues to do so today.

> *God has always worked with imperfect people and continues to do so today.*

God Is Gracious

God has always shown a willingness to listen to his people and adapt the application of the law to deal with the issues of life. It is a part of his gracious nature. He understood from the outset that once sin had entered the world, life could become complex for those who are sincerely striving to do his will. God's grace was not a license for Israel to distort and push against his law, but to allow for sensible judgments to be made in line with the original intent, just as Jesus did in his ministry. This was how God designed the law to be administered from the outset.

A Great Master Plan

Indeed I have spoken it; I will also bring it to pass. I have purposed it; I will also do it. —Isaiah 46:11

In one of the most significant books of the twentieth century, *Man's Search for Meaning*, Dr. Viktor Frankl, an Auschwitz Holocaust survivor and psychiatrist, concluded that life is never made unbearable by circumstances but only by lack of meaning and purpose.[1] He observed that people could overcome terrible persecution and suffering when they had something worth living for. Frankl had also known people surrounded by physical wealth and success who had taken their own life after experiencing a deep void and lack of purpose.

The deepest longing of the human heart is the desire for purpose and meaning. As Solomon observed, God has put eternity in the hearts of all men (Eccles. 3:11)—a longing for meaning. And there can be no greater meaning in life than the one given by our Creator. It is a purpose inferred in the first chapter of Genesis with those incredible words: "Let us make man in our image; according to our likeness" (Gen. 1:26). These are not the words of a detached god a deist might describe, but a God with a purpose and plan in mind. It is a profound statement that hints at an enormous potential for humankind. It's a plan of salvation shadowed throughout the Old Testament Scriptures and, more specifically, in the ceremonial system God outlined to Moses.

> *The deepest longing of the human heart is the desire for purpose and meaning.*

Zealous and Motivated

From the outset of the Bible, God is presented as a passionate and motivated being. At the end of his creation, "God saw everything that He had made, and indeed it was *very good*" (Gen. 1:31). Calling the creation "very good" is a massive understatement. The creation is the work of a super-intellect. It is magnificent in the extreme, far beyond any "evolutionary" necessity. Today, with more understanding of our world and our universe than ever before, we continue to be astonished at the complexity, beauty, design, and engineering marvel of all we observe.

Atheists point disparagingly to the insignificance of our planet Earth, the

---

[1] Bibliog: (Frankl 2008)

frailty of man, and our ongoing social problems as proof that the God of the Bible can't be real. They question why a supposed great God (if he indeed did exist) would have even the remotest interest in our world when we are so small in comparison to this enormous universe.

They do have a point—man is indeed small, but it's a point that proves nothing. The true God is not like the gods created in the minds of men. King David also felt small looking into the enormity of the night sky, and he too queried, "What is man that you are mindful of him?" (Ps. 8:3–4). His answer was not to assume God didn't care, but to praise God when he realized how undeserved humans were for his attention. The entire story from Genesis to Jesus confirms that there is indeed something enormous going on here below, with humankind at its center.

Moses described God as a "consuming fire" (Deut. 4:24). He is a being filled with purpose. He is also described as *jealous*, not in the negative sense of envy but someone eager to protect what is precious to him. Jesus was also filled with zeal, reflecting the same energetic persona we read about in Old Testament times. Reading through the gospel records, we see Jesus on a mission, filled with energy and enthusiasm for a great divine purpose. No one who encountered Jesus could ever say otherwise. Even as a child, he was about his "father's business" (Luke 2:49)—a business that was about giving humanity meaning and hope. As Jesus said, "I have come that they may have life, and that they may have it more abundantly" (John 10:10). Jesus' death on the cross was the ultimate demonstration of just how important humankind is to God.

> *God has always been a big-picture person—a grand thinker.*

Plan from the Beginning

What has all this to do with the law of Moses? An enormous amount. Some look at the law of Moses and see random rules, unusual ceremonies, and rituals as some sort of anomaly from an out-of-touch God, as if he lost his way for a while but finally got back on track when his son arrived. But nothing could be further from the truth. God has never been small-minded or fixated on trivia. God has always been a big-picture person—a grand thinker.

A closer look at the early books of the Bible shows a deeply thought out and consistent, multifaceted plan for humankind that is threaded throughout the *entirety* of Scripture. It starts in Genesis with the creation of male and female in the image of God and ends in the book of Revelation with a kingdom overseen by his own redeemed family members (Rev. 22).

This plan is outlined in some detail within the law of Moses. The ceremonial system foreshadowed a great master plan for humanity—a plan God had in mind from the outset of creation. A plan that would start its fulfillment through the family of Abraham, with his descendants becoming a blessing to *all* nations (Gen. 12:3).

Christians now see the centrality of Jesus in the ceremonial system: the sacrificial system that foreshadowed the atoning role of the Messiah, the structure of the priesthood, the typology that looked to Jesus as the true High Priest of God (Heb. 6:20), and the tabernacle that pictured the spiritual realm of God's throne (Heb. 8:1). The design of the outer court, inner court, and veil all had spiritual significance related to the Messiah (Heb. 9).

None of these, or the many other details of the ceremonial system, were random or irrelevant. God designed them to be *revelatory* with their deeper meaning becoming clearer as history progressed.

The statutory holy days also outlined how God's plan would unfold. The perfect alignment of Passover with the death of Jesus, the significance of firstfruits on the day of Pentecost, the Feast of Trumpets, the Day of Atonement ceremonies, and the Feast of Tabernacles had meaning and purpose—and outlined a great plan for humanity far beyond simple earthly significance.

> *Such a well-thought-out and consistent plan could never have come from the minds of men.*

The people of old could not have fully understood the meaning behind this typology. But these celebratory days still taught the ancient people powerful lessons about God's forgiveness and the future hope he offered to the faithful. As Jesus said, many of these things were kept secret from the foundation of the world until his arrival (Matt. 13:35).

Such a well-thought-out and consistent plan could never have come from the minds of men. No group of humans could have sustained such a consistent and deep narrative over so many thousands of years of history. It is a powerful affirmation of the veracity of Scripture.

More importantly, what is outlined in the law of Moses demonstrates just how important this whole "project humankind" is to God. It gives us insight into his motives, his methodology, and his ultimate end goal. It is a plan he has been passionately committed to from the outset:

> I am God, and there is none like Me, declaring the end from the beginning, and from ancient times things that are not yet done, saying, "My counsel shall stand, and I will do all My pleasure" ... Indeed I have spoken it; I will also bring it to pass. I have purposed it; I will also do it. (Isa. 46:9–11)

The law of Moses included many concepts that were a *shadow of things to come*. They add to the depth and wisdom in the written law and are strong evidence that God is a God of purpose and meaning. While God's plan involves peoples and nations, at its heart it has always been focused on the individual—an invitation from the Creator of this universe to a deep and meaningful, permanent relationship with those made in his image.

Focused on the Individual

For what great nation is there that has God so near to it, as the LORD our God is to us. —Deuteronomy 4:7

A personal relationship with God is considered a distinctly New Testament Christian idea. Jesus was intensely personal and invited his followers into a close loving relationship of the heart and mind (John 14:23). This is in contrast to most religions in history where the gods are either scary, detached, or a nebulous "force" without a persona.

What about the God of Israel? Was there any concept of a personal relationship under the old covenant? The Hebrew Scriptures present God as having a distinct character and personality, but many consider him more concerned with national issues rather than the individual Israelite. How much of this is reality versus perception? Jesus comes across as more personal than God in the Old Testament because he came in the flesh, and we have the gospel narratives of his life, family, personality, and interactions with people.

God has always sought out and responded to individuals who turned to him with a loyal heart.

The Hebrew Scriptures were not written along the same biographical style as the Gospels, so we must dig deeper to see the personal interactions of the God of Israel—and there are many. While the old covenant was a national covenant, it also spoke to the individual Israelite. God has always sought out and responded to *individuals* who turned to him with a loyal heart:

> For the eyes of the LORD run to and fro throughout the whole earth, to show Himself strong on behalf of those whose heart is loyal to Him. (2 Chron. 16:9)

The Personal God

The founding fathers of the nation of Israel—Abraham, Isaac, and Jacob—had a surprisingly personal relationship with God. They knew him, spoke to him, and interacted with him. They even ate with him in his human form (Gen. 18:1–15). Although their interactions were somewhat irregular, they were common enough that they recognized him and spoke to him with confidence. Both Abraham and Sarah laughed in God's presence, showing a remarkably strong relationship (Gen. 17:15–17; 18:12; 21:6). Abraham was called a friend of God (Isa. 41:8). While God was possibly not as personal in his interactions with Isaac and Jacob, he undoubtedly had a close interest in their lives. They knew him and had direct revelations from him.

Moses had a very personal relationship with God, and spoke "face to face, as a man speaks to his friend" (Exod. 33:11). Although Joshua would never have such a close relationship with God, at one time the Lord did appear to him in person (Josh. 5:14–15). God gave focused attention to these and other individuals in the books of Moses.

God's Intention for Israel

It was also God's original intention to be close to the nation of Israel. He desired to dwell among the people and be their God and their king (Exod. 25:8; 29:45). He wanted Israel to be near him and be the example for other nations to learn from:

> For what great nation is there that has God so near to it, as the LORD our God is to us, for whatever reason we may call upon Him? (Deut. 4:7)

In a symbolic sense, God wanted to dwell right in their midst, and while in the wilderness, the *tabernacle* was in the center of the camp (Num. 2). By necessity God's glory meant that people had to be kept at a distance, and the tabernacle had off-limit areas. But one of the primary purposes of the ceremonial system and its structures was to foreshadow how the future Messiah would bridge that great gulf through to the "Holy of Holies" so that God could have the deep and personal relationships with his future spiritual sons and daughters that he had planned from the outset.

But things did not pan out as God had hoped. It wasn't God who distanced himself from the people. It was the people who rejected God's advances. God could no longer be so close to such an unbelieving people, so he told Moses to move the tent of meeting outside the camp (Exod. 33:3–7). He despaired many times and asked Moses how long the people would continue to reject him and not believe him (Num. 14:11). He wanted to be "near" to Israel, but they didn't want to be near their God and pushed him further and further away.

Later the nation rejected God as their king and demanded a man to govern over them (1 Sam. 8:7). In the centuries that followed, Israel completely forsook the God of Israel—and the temple, which represented his closeness to the nation, fell into disrepair and was eventually destroyed. But this failure of

The Old Covenant and the Individual

The old covenant was a national agreement, but God wanted a buy-in from the individual Israelites. Moses and the leaders of Israel did not sign the old covenant in secret on behalf of the people. The covenant was presented directly to *all the people*, and they verbally agreed to the terms of the covenant in a public ceremony (Exod. 24:3–8; see also Deut. 29:10–15). It was a national contract founded on the *individual* agreeing to the covenant and being *personally* faithful to God.

The foundational law, the Ten Commandments, were also personal. Each commandment was addressed to the individual ("*you* shall") and was spoken to the people directly. God wanted these laws to reside deep within each person and become a part of their personal value system.

> *The old covenant was a national agreement, but God wanted a buy-in from the individual Israelites.*

Jesus confirmed this personal nature of the law of Moses when he focused on the two key commands that underpin the entire system of law (Matt. 22:36–40). The command to love God with all the heart, soul, and strength, and the command to love a neighbor as oneself are directives that could only apply to an individual. They involve a person's heart and mind to respond to such a call.

We see the personal nature of the covenant in the sacrificial system. While there were times of national ceremony, most sacrifices were focused on the individual Israelite. It was the individual's responsibility to consider their own relationship with God and respond accordingly.

Before he died, Moses reinforced the importance for each Israelite to *personally* take the words of the law into their innermost being:

> You shall love the LORD your God with all your heart, with all your soul, and with all your strength. *And these words which I command you today shall be in your heart.* You shall teach them diligently to your children. (Deut. 6:5–7)

> Therefore you shall lay up these *words of mine in your heart and in your soul*, and bind them as a sign on your hand, and they shall be as

frontlets between your eyes. (Deut. 11:18)

The idea that these laws could be held in a person's heart puts the law of Moses into a different category than other law systems of the time. Laws held inside the heart are *values*. Values are the views people hold most dear and believe to be the most important in life. God's idea was for the strength of the nation to be built on moral individuals whose hearts were strong for him, unlike other nations of the time who built their civilizations on governmental power and control.

> *God's idea was for the strength of the nation to be built on moral individuals whose hearts were strong for him.*

David also understood God's focus was on the hearts of individuals:

> The LORD is near to all who call upon Him, to all who call upon Him in truth. (Ps. 145:18)

Supporting these and similar statements from the prophets, we have evidence of those many individuals, some important and others insignificant, whom God took notice of because their hearts were strong for him. People like Caleb, who stood strong for God under pressure and was rewarded (Josh. 14). Phinehas, whose zeal restrained God's wrath on the nation (Num. 25). Rahab, whose family was protected in Jericho because of her faith (Josh. 6). Jabez, who God blessed in his ventures (1 Chron. 4:10). Hannah, who cried out to God for a child and was heard (1 Sam. 1). Ruth and Naomi, poor widows God blessed and honored (Ruth 1–4). The seven thousand who held strong for him during the time of Ahab (1 Kings 19:18). Righteous people like Simeon and Anna who looked forward to the Messiah (Luke 2:25–38). Each of these and the many others God heard and responded to are testimony of his focus on the individual.

God Is Personal

When considering God's interactions with humans throughout history, it is clear he has never changed. He has always desired to be close and intimate to those he made in his image. Christian writer Philip Yancey summarizes God's Old Testament personage well:

> God is not a blurry power living somewhere in the sky, not an abstraction like the Greeks proposed, not a sensual super-human like the Romans worshiped, and definitely not the absentee watchmaker

of the Deists. God is *personal*. He enters into people's lives, messes with families, shows up in unexpected places, chooses unlikely leaders, calls people to account. Most of all, God loves.[1]

The law of Moses must be read and interpreted in this light. God meant it to be personal, not abstract. He wanted it to speak squarely to the hearts and minds of individual Israelites so that they could come to know him personally. And although only a minority took God's words to heart, we nonetheless have the record of that *great cloud of witnesses* who did, and set the example for Christians today to follow (Heb. 11–12:1).

---

[1] Bibliog: (Yancey, The Bible that Jesus Read, p33)

Unlike Our Imagination

"For as the heavens are higher than the earth, so are My ways higher than your ways, and My thoughts than your thoughts." —Isaiah 55:8–9

To fully appreciate the heart and mind of the being who gave his law to Moses, there is one additional characteristic that must be considered. It is a characteristic unlike anything we would naturally expect from such a supreme and majestic being—something so extraordinary and unexpected that most have never grasped its enormous significance. It is an attribute perfectly illustrated in the life and character of Jesus.

The Unexpected Messiah

Consider how unusual Jesus was. Almost nothing in his physical life aligned with the expectations of the predicted Messiah.

He was born of unassuming parents, in humble surroundings, without pomp and circumstance. No adoring crowds or important religious leaders were present at his birth, just a handful of shepherds who came to pay homage to this seemingly ordinary baby. It would be difficult to imagine a lowlier start in life. As he grew, Jesus' life was normal for a Jewish boy of that time. Other than the incident in the temple when Jesus was twelve, Scripture does not provide any extraordinary details about his young life. He was a humble carpenter's son who worked out of a small, nondescript village in Galilee.

When he commenced his ministry around age thirty, his reputation grew, but his way of life remained simple. He mingled with the sinners of the world, the despised, the forgotten—even lowly lepers, the outcasts of society. This was not how a future king or prince would normally build his kingdom! His motley group of followers seemed to be chosen simply because they were ordinary—it's hard to otherwise find any pattern of significance. Finally, just when his ministry seemed to be gaining traction and Jesus was receiving the attention he deserved, everything came to an unexpected and shocking end as Jesus was publicly humiliated, subjected to terrible beatings, and died a death fitting for the worst of criminals.

Nothing could be more opposite to the Jewish idea of the promised Messiah. Where was the power and might to defeat Rome? Where was the worldly glory expected from so important an individual? The Jews were so programmed to think of the Messiah a certain way they didn't recognize him when he was in their very midst.

The gentiles were equally skeptical but for different reasons. The Greco-Roman world despised humility. It was associated with failure and shame. The very suggestion that any human, let alone one who died in such ignominy could be divine, invited ridicule and rejection. The gods were supposed to be beautiful and powerful and far beyond human reach. Yet here was Jesus, who "made Himself of no reputation, taking the form of a bondservant, and coming in the likeness of men" and being found in appearance as a man, "humbled Himself and became obedient to the point of death, even the death of the cross" (Phil. 2:7–8).

> *Nothing could be more opposite to the Jewish idea of the promised Messiah.*

It was such a shocking idea (even blasphemous to some) that the people of his day struggled to come to terms with it. Paul knew how foolish this sounded to both the average Jew and gentile:

> For Jews request a sign, and Greeks seek after wisdom; but we preach Christ crucified, to the Jews a stumbling block and to the Greeks foolishness. (1 Cor. 1:22–23)

Even today the idea of a god presenting himself in such a way is mocked by educated people such as Richard Dawkins:

> It's a horrible idea that God, this paragon of wisdom and knowledge, power, couldn't think of a better way to forgive us our sins than to come down to Earth in his alter ego as his son and have himself hideously tortured and executed.[1]

Yet all this was part of a plan conceived by God from the foundation of the world (Rev. 13:8). Clearly, he is a being utterly unlike our natural assumptions. And God himself knows this to be true:

> "For My thoughts are not your thoughts, nor are your ways My ways," says the LORD. "For as the heavens are higher than the earth, so are My ways higher than your ways, and My thoughts than your thoughts." (Isa. 55:8–9)

Jesus Reveals the Heart of God

We rightly praise and honor Jesus for his incredible sacrifice, but how often do we consider the mind and heart of the God who planned all this in advance? Why would anyone, let alone a being of such immense power and glory, have

---

[1] Bibliog: (Dawkins 2012, Min. 3:28)

his precious son arrive on this earth in such lowly circumstances and be so ordinary in life and so demeaned in death? What core value would he have to hold to come up with such an idea?

One value God consistently prized throughout the Bible is humility. The prophets wrote about it, and the men and women of God modeled it. The great Moses was called the humblest man of his day (Num. 12:3).

"For My thoughts are not your thoughts, nor are your ways My ways," says the LORD.

The Bible also teaches that it is the humble who this great God wishes to associate with:

> For thus says the High and Lofty One Who inhabits eternity, whose name is Holy: "*I dwell in the high and holy place, with him who has a contrite and humble spirit*, to revive the spirit of the humble, and to revive the heart of the contrite ones." (Isa. 57:15)

> "For all those things My hand has made, and all those things exist," says the LORD. "*But on this one will I look: on him who is poor and of a contrite spirit*, and who trembles at My word." (Isa. 66:2)

Why would the great Creator God of the universe have such an interest in those who are poor and of a contrite spirit? What is it about humility and lowliness that so attracts his attention? Yet that is exactly the style of person he focuses on throughout Scripture—and it aligns closely with one of Jesus' key teachings:

> Assuredly, I say to you, unless you are converted and become as little children, you will by no means enter the kingdom of heaven. Therefore whoever humbles himself as this little child is the greatest in the kingdom of heaven. (Matt. 18:3–4)

When we read these words of Jesus our first thought might be: *Of course! We are nothing in comparison to God. To be humble is to accept the reality of our inferior position.* And that is certainly true. We are truly insignificant compared to our great God.

But there is something far deeper here. It has to do with not just the heart of man but the heart of God. Jesus spoke to this point when he made a deep and personal statement. When we meditate on what he is saying, it really is one of the *most astonishing statements in Scripture*:

> Come to Me, all you who labor and are heavy laden, and I will give you rest. Take My yoke upon you and learn from Me, *for I am gentle and lowly in heart,* and you will find rest for your souls. (Matt. 11:28–29)

The immediate assumption is that Jesus made this comment about his *gentle and lowly heart* because he was in the flesh. But he is referring to his *heart*, his innermost core, which doesn't change. Jesus is the same yesterday, today and forever. And as noted earlier, Jesus told his disciples that if they had seen him, they had seen the Father (John 14:7). Gentle and lowly of heart is how Jesus has always been.

> *When we meditate on what Jesus is saying, it really is one of the most astonishing statements in Scripture.*

What Jesus is saying here is truly extraordinary. He is confirming something evidenced throughout Scripture but often hard to accept: *that God himself is meek and lowly of heart*!

This is a profound and deep insight into the heart of the great God. It explains why such a great being would be so attentive to those this world might despise. This great God, who values humility so highly, does so—*not* because he wants us to "know our place," to see us grovel, or to reinforce his own superiority—but because *he too*, has a humble heart and wants his spiritual sons and daughters to be like him!

In simple terms, God is looking for those of a *kindred spirit*.

A God Unlike Our Expectations

The idea that the God of Israel is gentle and lowly in heart may be hard to accept at face value, but it perfectly matches his interactions with man throughout the Old Testament period. Just as Jesus did, the God of Israel often worked with the lowly, the sinners, and the outcasts of society, people such as Rahab, Jephthah, Samson, Barak, and Ruth. Rarely did he choose the high and mighty for his work. He included gentiles and outcasts in

> *In simple terms, God is looking for those of a kindred spirit.*

the lineage of Jesus. Gideon and David were the least in their father's household. King Saul was from the most insignificant family of the most insignificant tribe. Israel was the least among the nations. His prophets were, again, mostly simple, unpretentious people. This is the surprising heart and mind of God.

One particular incident with Moses demonstrates the meek and lowly nature of God's heart. It was the time when the people created a golden calf and began a decadent celebration while Moses was atop Mount Sinai with God (Exod. 32:1–6). When God saw the situation, he was very upset and made his intentions clear to Moses:

> And the LORD said to Moses, "I have seen this people, and indeed it is a stiff-necked people! Now therefore, *let Me alone*, that My wrath may burn hot against them and I may consume them. And I will make of you a great nation." (Exod. 32:9–10)

When the Creator of this universe, emanating enormous power, says in an angry voice, "let me alone," any normal human being would do well to leave him alone! But Moses did not leave God alone. He stood his ground and spoke strongly back to God:

> LORD, why does Your wrath burn hot against Your people whom You have brought out of the land of Egypt with great power and with a mighty hand? Why should the Egyptians speak, and say, "He brought them out to harm them, to kill them in the mountains, and to consume them from the face of the earth"? *Turn from Your fierce wrath, and relent from this harm to Your people.* (Exod. 32:11–12)

Moses's courage is amazing—but even more astonishing is God's response to Moses' corrective plea:

> So the LORD relented from the harm which He said He would do to His people. (v. 14)

For Moses to talk so bluntly to God and have the effect he did is astounding.[2] Such a great being taking counsel from his creation! And this is not the only time he did so. Scripture is full of God listening and taking heed of his creation in both the angelic and human realms. This is an attribute of God that the natural human mind would never imagine of an infinitely superior being. Our automatic assumption is that the supreme God of this universe would be aloof, unteachable, and determined to do his own will—certainly not someone to take any advice or correction from mere mortals or angels. Yet clearly he does and has done so many times throughout the history of his creation.

---

[2] Some have assumed that God was bluffing and had no real intention to do as he said. But bluffing is a form of lying, something God is incapable of. God doesn't play-act anger. He means what he says. On a later occasion, he again became angry at the people, and thousands died before Moses intervened (Num. 16:44–49).

Abraham was called a friend of God (Isa. 41:8), and he, too, understood this surprising nature of God. When God revealed to Abraham his intention to destroy Sodom and Gomorrah, Abraham spoke in a similarly blunt fashion to God:

> Far be it from You to do such a thing as this, to slay the righteous with the wicked, so that the righteous should be as the wicked; *far be it from You!* Shall not the Judge of all the earth do right? (Gen. 18:25)

Considering who Abraham was talking to, it is again astonishing that God would accept such a blunt, corrective tone, yet he did. He took no offense and allowed Abraham to continue to barter for people's lives.

So many of God's other interactions are amazing when we consider them in the same light. At one stage God told Abraham that he would have a child when he was old, and Abraham fell down laughing in God's presence (Gen. 17:17). Sarah also laughed (Gen. 18:11–15). Yet God took no offense.

> *So many of God's other interactions are amazing when we consider them in the same light.*

Many prophets had outbursts against God. Moses complained strongly to God on more than one occasion, as did Elijah. Some, like Job, even accused God of being unfair (Job 9:22–24). Yet he took it all in stride with grace.

When King David told the prophet Nathan that he wanted to build a beautiful temple for the God of Israel, God's response to David speaks enormously of who he is at heart:

> Would you build a house for Me to dwell in? For I have not dwelt in a house since the time that I brought the children of Israel up from Egypt, even to this day, but have moved about in a tent and in a tabernacle. Wherever I have moved about with all the children of Israel, have I ever spoken a word to anyone from the tribes of Israel, whom I commanded to shepherd My people Israel, saying, "Why have you not built Me a house of cedar?" (2 Sam. 7:5–7)

What an incredible thing! David said he wanted to make God a beautiful temple fitting for such a great God. And God's response was essentially, "Well, that's never been too important to me; I'm happy in my temporary dwelling." God then graciously turned the proposal around and told David he would make *him* a permanent house (v. 11).

Man has built great edifices to honor God—and that might be good and proper at times—but these things have never been of great importance to him. God has always been far more interested in people's hearts. When the most evil of the kings of Israel, Ahab, humbled himself for a brief period, God eagerly accepted his contrite attitude (1 Kings 21:27–28). There was no suspicion or resentful attitude one might expect, considering the harm this man had done. It was more of a childlike enthusiasm that here was something positive.

A God Who Is Softhearted

Jesus' parable of the prodigal son affirms this same attribute of God. In the parable, a father gives his son his inheritance, and the son wastes it. Yet when the son finally returns home, his deeply offended father does not exhibit even a hint of pride. Instead, the father was overjoyed to see his son coming home and *ran* toward him.

> And he (the wayward son) arose and came to his father. But when he was still a great way off, his father saw him and had compassion, *and ran* and fell on his neck and kissed him. (Luke 15:20)

It is an outrageous thought that a patriarch would run toward a wayward son. Patriarchs didn't run—they were more dignified than that. But as the parable tells us, this humble father didn't care what others thought. He ran toward his son when he saw him a long way off and embraced him.

This parallels what happened to Israel. God gave his children their inheritance and they despised it. Over and over they turned against God and prostituted themselves to other nations and gods. Yet despite their outrageous behavior and rejection of him, just like the father in the parable, God was always willing to have them back:

> The LORD said also to me ... "Have you seen what backsliding Israel has done? She has gone up on every high mountain and under every green tree, and there played the harlot." *And I said, after she had done all these things,* "*Return to Me.*" (Jer. 3:6–7)

Only a softhearted being who is lowly in heart would ever say such a thing. If the God of Israel was the way many people seem to view him, he would have destroyed not only Israel but all humankind, millennia ago.

A God That Man Does Not Recognize

Philip Yancey makes an interesting observation of God's humility in action. Quoting English playwright Dorothy Sayers, he writes:

> Dorothy Sayers has said that God underwent three great humiliations in his efforts to rescue the human race. The first was the incarnation when he took on the confines of a physical body. The second was the cross, when he suffered the ignominy of public execution. The third humiliation, Sayers suggested, is the church. In an awesome act of self-denial, God entrusted his reputation to ordinary people.[3]

How incredible it is that God chose to do things this way. Throughout Scripture we see a God whose heart is nothing like the manmade "gods" of people's imagination. Humility is at the heart of who he is. It's a heart that is selfless and forgiving, receptive to anyone of a humble and contrite spirit. Jesus was like this. He saw the world differently from those around him. In a crowd of people, he didn't see the rich with all their flowing robes and impressive gifts. Instead, he focused on the unseen—the poor widow woman who quietly gave two small copper coins (Luke 21:1–4).

> *Throughout Scripture we see a God whose heart is nothing like the manmade "gods" of people's imagination.*

Jesus reflected the eternal God who has values unlike the natural ways of man, and this is the type of people he chooses to associate with:

> But God has chosen the foolish things of the world to put to shame the wise, and God has chosen the weak things of the world to put to shame the things which are mighty; and the base things of the world and the things which are despised God has chosen, and the things which are not, to bring to nothing the things that are. (1 Cor. 1:27–28)

As one modern philosopher paraphrased, "People don't find God because they aren't looking low enough."[4] There's a lot of truth in that statement. People simply don't understand the true heart of God. God's magnificence and splendor are beyond comparison, but how he measures greatness is nothing at all like this world imagines.

---

[3] Bibliog: (Yancey, Disappointment with God 1988, p162)
[4] Bibliog: (Peterson 2018, Minute 24)

Everything about the God of the Bible and Jesus, his son, is counterintuitive. Yet, for this reason, they invite our close attention. As C. S. Lewis insightfully wrote in his most famous work *Mere Christianity*:

> Reality, in fact, is usually something you could not have guessed. That is one of the reasons I believe Christianity. It is a religion you could not have guessed. If it offered us just the kind of universe we had always expected, I should feel we were making it up. But, in fact, it is not the sort of thing anyone would have made up. It has just that queer (sic.) twist about it that real things have.[5]

A Reflection of God's Heart

The law of Moses reflected the approachable heart of God. It put great emphasis on caring for the smallest and most vulnerable in society—widows, orphans, strangers, and the poor. It responded to a humble and repentant heart with forgiveness and mercy. It was designed to create an environment without fear, where people could openly express themselves and feel confident and secure.

For those who came to truly know the God of Israel, it would have taken their love and respect to a deep and personal level. It would be a place where a person could find "rest for their soul" as Jesus so beautifully expressed (Matt. 11:29).

---

[5] Bibliog: (Lewis 2002, p41)

The Lawgiver Summarized

For I know the thoughts that I think toward you, says the LORD, thoughts of peace and not of evil, to give you a future and a hope. —Jeremiah 29:11

Knowing the heart and mind of the God of Israel must by necessity change our perspective of the system of law he gave his people.

Here is a consistent, unchanging being who can be trusted. A God of grace and truth. A God epitomized as love itself. A God who values individual freedom—who doesn't desire to control and coerce, but instead wants to inspire and motivate people to be greater than they are. A God who is rational and pragmatic—inherently sensible. A God who is just, who will surely bring to judgment those who are evil—but also a God who is full of grace, mercy, and compassion toward those who seek his forgiveness. A God willing to put aside the worst of sins and erase them from his mind.

> *Looking at the law of Moses through the character and values of this great being indeed changes everything.*

This is a big-picture God, not petty like the gods of people's imagination. He is a God of zeal and purpose who adds meaning to life. He is a God who, at the foundation of this world, laid out a great, positive plan for the salvation of humanity—an invitation to be a part of his family. And most endearingly, he is a personal God who is meek and lowly of heart, willing to listen and respond to the smallest in his creation.

A God like this could never be anything like the harsh, detached, and legalistic being so often presented by those who reject the God of the Old Testament. How could such a lawgiver have anything other than positive outcomes in mind?

Looking at the law of Moses through the character and values of this great being indeed *changes everything.*

4

PART 4: Foundational Principles

The law given to Israel was unlike any other law code in history. As Jesus confirmed, it was a product of God's love and founded on his character, with justice, mercy, and faithfulness at its heart.

It was not just a civil code. The character and values of God himself and the moral standards he established for the individual were central to the law. He desired to build a strong, caring society based on his values that would be a light to the world and lead other nations to him. The law also included constructs that foreshadowed God's great master plan for humanity.

God's Intent and Purpose for the Law

Oh, that they had such a heart in them that they would fear Me and always keep all My commandments, that it might be well with them and with their children forever! —Deuteronomy 5:29

God had ambitious plans for his law. He wanted to shape the people of Israel's values to align with his own character. God's values include love, mercy, kindness, graciousness, justice, truth, humility—and much more. Being made in the image of God has always been a mandate for humankind to imitate and image these same characteristics. Moses described this in terms of having the *words of God laid up in the heart*. This is where we see the inherent link between God's values and the laws he gave to Israel:

> And these words which I command you today *shall be in your heart*. (Deut. 6:6)

> *Set your hearts on all the words* which I testify among you today, which you shall command your children to be careful to observe—all the words of this law. (Deut. 32:46)

> But the word is very near you, in your mouth *and in your heart*, that you may do it. (Deut. 30:14)

In biblical terms, the heart is where the innermost character and values of a person reside.

It is sometimes expressed that the law of Moses was focused more on ritual and the outward form, whereas the way of life Jesus taught was focused on the heart. But God's standards have never changed, and neither do the Hebrew Scriptures support that viewpoint. God has *always* considered the heart as the true measure of the state of a person:

> For the LORD does not see as man sees; for man looks at the outward appearance, *but the LORD looks at the heart*. (1 Sam. 16:7)

> Behold, You desire truth *in the inward parts*. (Ps. 51:6)

> I, the LORD, *search the heart*, I test the mind, even to give every man according to his ways, according to the fruit of his doings. (Jer. 17:10)

It was the same at the time of Moses. One of God's key objectives was searching his people's hearts and knowing who they were deep down:

> And you shall remember that the LORD your God led you all the way these forty years in the wilderness, to humble you and test you, *to know what was in your heart,* whether you would keep His commandments or not. (Deut. 8:2)

God was confident that his way of life had the potential to do great things for the nation, but it couldn't simply be forced onto these people. He wanted to inspire them to believe in and love the principles he was outlining. Therefore, he had to give them the freedom to choose or reject what he was offering.

Meaning of "Torah"

One reason people have misunderstood God's intent for the Mosaic system is the use of the word "law." Law is often associated with legal judgment, enforcement, and punishment. Law has a particularly negative connotation when used in the context of religion, implying rules and regulations that seek to control people and inhibit their freedoms. It has created the impression that the God of Israel must have been highly legalistic to make law so central to the old covenant. It is the same impression some people have when they hear the word "*torah,*" a word often wrongly associated with the tedious Jewish rabbinic traditions and regulations.

> *One reason people have misunderstood God's intent for the Mosaic system is the use of the word "law."*

None of this describes the sort of "law" God had in mind. The word translated "law" in the Old Testament is the Hebrew word *torah*. While "The Torah" (capitalized) is an official title for the first five books of the Bible, the Hebrew word simply means "instruction" or "teaching." The word does *not* carry the implication of controlling or punishing people but of providing guidance, direction, and education. Commentators explain how the translation of the word *torah* as *law* is somewhat misleading:

Encyclopedia Judaica notes:

> Torah is derived from the (Hebrew) root which means "to teach." The meaning of the word is therefore "teaching," "doctrine," or "instruction"; the commonly accepted "law" gives a wrong

impression. The word is used in different ways, but the underlying idea of "teaching" is common to all.[1]

The *Jewish Encyclopedia* provides insight into how the word came to be translated "law":

> The Torah receives its title from its contents, the name itself connoting "doctrine." The Hellenistic Jews, however, translated it as "law" whence came the term "law-book"; this gave rise to the erroneous impression that the Jewish religion is purely nomistic, so that it is still frequently designated as the religion of law. In reality, however, the Torah contains teachings as well as laws, even the latter being given in ethical form and contained in historical narratives of an ethical character.[2]

The *Ancient Hebrew Research Center* further explains:

> One of the most misunderstood words in the Hebrew Bible is the Hebrew word *torah*. This word is usually translated as "law," which by definition is a set of rules and regulations established by a government and are enforced with the threat of fines or imprisonment. However, the word *torah* literally means "teachings," a set of instructions given by a teacher or parent in order to foster maturity and is enforced with discipline and encouragement.[3]

The books of Moses do contain laws and legal standards, which are needed for all civil societies, but their primary intent was not as a mechanism for control or punishment. They were designed to teach truth and godly principles to lead people to success. This is what good laws do—they guide the individual for the benefit of themselves and the nation.

> *The books of Moses do contain laws and legal standards, but their primary intent was not as a mechanism for control or punishment.*

This is what Jesus aimed to convey in the insightful way that he taught. His focus was never on the "rules" or the letter of the law but on the underlying *principles* that would help a person develop a heart and mind in sync with God. This is how the psalmist understood the law. He

---

[1] Bibliog: (Rabinowitz 2007, 39 Torah)
[2] Bibliog: (Jacobs and Blav 1906 (orig), Torah)
[3] Bibliog: (Benner 2022, What is Torah)

described it as a *lamp to his feet and a light to his path* (Ps. 119:105).

Law Was an Expression of God's Grace

Another misconception that has distorted the true purpose of the law of Moses is the later Pharisaical teaching that the law was the means of salvation. As we saw earlier, the apostle Paul understood the fallacy of this idea simply by considering the life of Abraham. Abraham was declared righteous in God's eyes when he chose to trust in God—not because of his law-keeping (Gen. 15:6; Rom. 4:3).

In the same way, God had graciously saved Israel from Egypt *before* he gave them his law. It was by the atoning blood of the lambs and God's grace that they were rescued. They were, in fact, the least of all people yet were offered the incredible opportunity to be a holy and special people above all the people of the earth (Exod. 19:5). This grace of God is evident in his grand opening statement to the Ten Commandments. He sets the scene by reminding the children of Israel what he had *already* done for them:

> And God spoke all these words, saying: "I am the LORD your God, *who brought you out of the land of Egypt, out of the house of bondage.*" (Exod. 20:1–2)

God also instructed Israel to ensure future generations understood the connection between His grace and why they had such a great system of law:

> When your son asks you in time to come, saying, "What is the meaning of the testimonies, the statutes, and the judgments which the LORD our God has commanded you?" *then* you shall say to your son: "*We were slaves of Pharaoh in Egypt, and the LORD brought us out of Egypt with a mighty hand;* and the LORD showed signs and wonders before our eyes, great and severe, against Egypt, Pharaoh, and all his household. Then He brought us out from there, that He might bring us in, to give us the land of which He swore to our fathers." (Deut. 6:20–23)

The law itself was a further demonstration of God's grace. It included the revelation of an enlightened way of life that would lead to true success:

> And now, Israel, what does the LORD your God require of you, but to fear the LORD your God, to walk in all His ways and to love Him, to serve the LORD your God with all your heart and with all your soul,

> and to keep the commandments of the LORD and His statutes which I command you today *for your good*? (Deut. 10:12–13)
>
> You shall therefore keep My statutes and My judgments, which if a man does, *he shall live by them:* I am the LORD. (Lev. 18:5)

The law also revealed much more. It revealed who the true God was, his values and standards, how to approach him, and, importantly, how to be forgiven and welcomed into his presence. All of this was given to a wholly undeserving people.

Response to God's Grace

Keeping the law was therefore, not about the children of Israel proving their own righteousness. Rather, it should have been the grateful response of a people who had *already* found unmerited grace in God's sight. God had shown them undeserved love and kindness and desired that they should love him in return by listening to his instructions and doing as he asked:

> He is your praise, and He is your God, who has done for you these great and awesome things which your eyes have seen. Your fathers went down to Egypt with seventy persons, and now the LORD your God has made you as the stars of heaven in multitude. ... *Therefore* you shall love the LORD your God, and keep His charge, His statutes, His judgments, and His commandments always. (Deut. 10:21–22; 11:1)

Changing their hearts would involve ongoing voluntary participation and effort on *their* part. God could not simply change their hearts by decree. He wanted them to diligently read and meditate on the words he was giving them and teach those laws and principles to their children—and make God's word a part of their daily lives until it became a part of their own value system:

> Therefore *you* shall lay up these words of mine in your heart and in your soul, and bind them as a sign on your hand, and they shall be as frontlets between your eyes. *You* shall teach them to your children, speaking of them when you sit in your house, when you walk by the way, when you lie down, and when you rise up. And *you* shall write them on the doorposts of your house and on your gates. (Deut. 11:18–20)

This learning principle of immersion is well understood in all fields of endeavor. Over time, making God's words central to their lives and living out his principles and laws would train and shape their hearts to reflect the character of God.

God realized that this would not be easy. They would need to be diligent. Paul writes about circumcision of the heart in the New Testament as an expression of God's desire for his elect (Rom. 2:29). This was also God's directive to ancient Israel. Again, notice that it was the responsibility of the *owner* of the heart to respond to God's advances by softening their heart and humbling themselves before God:

> Therefore *circumcise the foreskin of your heart,* and be stiff-necked no longer. (Deut. 10:16)

When the people did as God required of them, it demonstrated their *believing loyalty* and reflected God's righteousness in their lives:

> *Then it will be righteousness for us, if we are careful to observe all these commandments before the* LORD *our God, as He has commanded us.* (Deut. 6:25)

Through all this, God was under no illusions that Israel would somehow be able to keep his law perfectly at all times. That was never his expectation—clearly demonstrated by the system of forgiveness he built into the ceremonial and sacrificial system. He knew all people fail at times and would need to repent of sin—and he provided the means to do so.

> *God was under no illusions that Israel would somehow be able to keep his law perfectly at all times.*

Aligned to God's Standards

The old covenant was unique in the ancient world. It was a covenantal relationship between a God and his people. God wanted to teach his chosen people standards and values that would align with his and that would lead to great success for the individuals and for the nation. The laws he gave to Moses were the means to achieve this goal.

As stated earlier, the importance of law on a nation's destiny cannot be overstated. For a nation to be truly great, it must embody quality values in its system of law and *inspire* its citizens to believe in those values, cherish them, and desire to pass them down to following generations.

This is what good laws do: they don't simply impose restraints on their citizens—they teach and guide the individual for the benefit of themselves and the nation. The law of Moses includes laws and legal standards needed for all civil societies, but the foundation of those laws are the values and principles by which God himself operates and which were given to direct the Israelites toward an enlightened way of life.

The Overall Structure and Format

On these two commandments hang all the Law and the Prophets.
—Matthew 22:40

The normal starting point in analyzing something as important as a system of law would be to present a high-level view of its scope and structure. But when approaching the law of Moses in this way, we are presented with a problem. The actual sections of codified law spread throughout Exodus, Leviticus, Numbers, and Deuteronomy do not seem logically structured. To our modern minds they appear disorganized and untidy and do not conform to our expectations for a work of such significance. Today we demand a defined structure and consistency of writing styles in all official documents. This is especially the case in the context of law codes, which are generally laid out in order of precedence, carefully categorized, and subtitled.

The loose structure and irregular format of the law of Moses have been the source of much scholarly criticism and have added to the popular idea that it was written and edited by multiple authors over a long time. But our modern disciplined approach to such matters is a relatively recent phenomenon, and we cannot hold the ancient world to our standards of scholarship. Most importantly, regardless of whether the format of the law aligns with our requirements for technical discipline, the content itself must take precedence.

> *The loose structure and irregular format of the law of Moses have been the source of much scholarly criticism.*

In a later chapter, we will consider why the law was written in the way that it was.[1] In the meantime, when considering how to present a framework or an outline of the law of Moses, we must, by necessity, approach it differently than we might a modern work.

Internal Categorization of Law

An obvious starting point to approaching the structure of the law is to take God's lead. At Mount Sinai, God opened his presentation to the people with the Ten Commandments—the first and only words he spoke out loud to the nation (Exod. 20). The Ten Commandments were of such importance they became symbolic of the entire law and covenant. They were later carried inside

---
[1] Refer to the chapter *Why Was It Written This Way?*

the ark of the covenant as a testimony to the agreement between the people and God.

More than just a symbol, the Ten Commandments provide the first major category of law. They represented the foundational moral code for the nation, addressing both the people's relationship with God and with each other. The Ten Commandments were not designed to be interpreted narrowly but were principles on which the other categories of law rested.

The two other major categories within the law are commonly called the "statutes" and the "judgments."[2] (e.g., Lev. 18:5; Deut. 8:11; 11:1).

Statutes are decrees or ordinances. They generally relate to those parts of the law that outline specific rituals, procedures, festivals, and customs. They include specific ordinances for the Levitical priests for their service in the tabernacle and for individual Israelites in their worship. They also include the statutory holy days.

Judgments are a type of case law. They provided a type of precedent and guidance for legal and moral decisions. Judgments were not designed to be narrowly interpreted as legalistic rules or regulations. Instead, they existed to teach *principles* on making wise and discerning judgments within the spirit and intent of the law.[3] They built on the foundational tenets of the Ten Commandments.

Each of these three categories of law—the Ten Commandments, the statutes, and judgments—must be understood in their context and application. While the usage of the terms is not always precise, they provide one way of framing the structure of the Mosaic law.

Traditional Classification

A more traditional approach used by theologians since the Reformation is to frame the law into three broad classifications according to their scope and application:

Moral laws:	Laws related to personal moral behavior. The Ten Commandments are seen as primarily moral. A large portion of the judgments are moral in nature.

---

[2] The word *judgments* is translated "rules, regulations, or ordinances" in some Bible translations reflecting the difficulty in English translation. The Hebrew word is *mishpatim* from the lemma *mishpat* meaning "judgment" or "rights" and the word *shapat* meaning "to judge."
[3] Refer to the chapter *The Application of the Judgments*.

Judicial/civil laws:	Laws for managing society and the nation. These include laws related to criminal justice, punishment, debt management, social welfare, public health, indemnity and liability, land ownership, etc.
Ceremonial laws:	These are customs, rituals, and laws related to the worship of God. These include laws related to the tabernacle, priesthood, sacrifices, annual holy days, food laws, etc.

This traditional trifold classification might be a helpful approach when presenting a broad analysis of the law, but if the intent is to use this classification to isolate the moral code from the civil and ceremonial, it is highly problematic. Many laws do not fit neatly into a single classification, while other laws overlap into multiple categories. Many ceremonial and civil laws have strong underlying moral teachings. For example, the laws of gleaning are civil judgments applying to managing a harvest, yet they carry a direct moral teaching of caring for the poor. Judgments related to the treatment of employees and servants likewise have both a civil component and a moral teaching. Many ceremonial laws carry civil obligations. The Sabbath has civil, moral, and ceremonial relevance. Therefore, trying to silo segments of the law into one of the three categories can become somewhat arbitrary and subjective.

In an attempt to define clear boundaries, some designate the Ten Commandments as the preeminent and only permanent moral laws. Yet when asked to identify the greatest commandment of all, Jesus quoted a moral law from the heart of the book of Leviticus: "Love your neighbor as yourself" sits right in the middle of a section of ceremonial and judgment laws (Lev. 19:18). The entire chapter of Leviticus 19 is a perfect example of the intermixing of moral, civil, and ceremonial laws, all presented in one discourse from God. The entire system of law is closely intertwined and interdependent and impossible to deconstruct tidily.

We return to the initial observation that the law appears somewhat disorganized. Perhaps the lesson to be learned is to take the law holistically and resist the temptation to compartmentalize. The apostle Paul confirmed that the entirety of Scripture has value:

> *All Scripture* is given by inspiration of God, and is profitable for doctrine, for reproof, for correction, for instruction in righteousness,

> that the man of God may be complete, thoroughly equipped for every good work. (2 Tim. 3:16–17)

This was the holistic way Jesus referenced the law. He did not attempt to dissect it into sections. Instead, he presented a different way to frame the law.

Jesus' Approach to the Law

Rather than deconstructing the law into various components or categories, Jesus brings the *entire* system together under two great moral commands:

> "Teacher, which is the great commandment in the law?" Jesus said to him, "'You shall love the LORD your God with all your heart, with all your soul, and with all your mind.' This is the first and great commandment. And the second is like it: 'You shall love your neighbor as yourself.' *On these two commandments hang all the Law and the Prophets."* (Matt. 22:36–40)

Although the law is not summarized so succinctly as this in the Old Testament, Jesus' response does not suggest he was presenting some new concept. He was citing these two commandments from within the law of Moses itself (Deut. 6:5; Lev. 19:18). The importance of loving God with all the heart is stressed many times (Deut. 10:12; 11:13; 13:3; 30:6). Jesus was confirming how the law was designed from the outset.

Surprisingly, a scribe who questioned him, an "expert" in the law, agreed with Jesus' answer, showing that others under the old covenant also understood the significance of those commands:[4]

> So the scribe said to Him, "Well said, Teacher. You have spoken the truth, for there is one God, and there is no other but He. And to *love Him with all the heart, with all the understanding, with all the soul, and with all the strength, and to love one's neighbor as oneself, is more than all the whole burnt offerings and sacrifices."* (Mark 12:32–33)

Jesus confirmed that this scribe's understanding was right on target:

> Now when Jesus saw that he [the scribe] answered wisely, He said to him, *"You are not far from the kingdom of God."* (Mark 12:34)

---

[4] Hillel the Elder, a Jewish rabbi who lived just before the time of Jesus, is reported as saying: "That which is hateful to you, do not do to your fellow. That is the entire Torah and the rest is its commentary." Bibliog: (Chabad. Menachem Posner. 2022)

It was an expression of God's love to give Israel the law and an expression of the people's love to keep the law in response. The entire system was based on this premise. Jesus had earlier said a similar thing in his Sermon on the Mount:

> Therefore, whatever you want men to do to you, do also to them, *for this is the Law and the Prophets.* (Matt. 7:12)

By confirming that love was the overarching intent of the Mosaic law, Jesus teaches us that the law was designed not simply as a code of conduct but as a call to a *relationship* with God and with one another. It was never about self-righteousness but about *outgoing love* of God and neighbor. *All* the components of the law were designed to work to that effect. This is what God wanted the people of Israel to understand: A focus that was not on technical interpretation of rules, nor on control and punishment, but on understanding the character of God and the deeper intent which was reflected throughout the entirety of the law.

> *Jesus teaches us that the law was designed not simply as a code of conduct but as a call to a relationship with God and with one another.*

A Foundation of Love

Combining Jesus' big-picture insight with the foundational principles of justice, mercy, and faith—which Jesus taught must also be present when applying the law—provides a way of approaching the law in line with God's original intent. Instead of analyzing the law into compartments and trying to determine which parts are relevant and which are not, the far more valuable approach is to seek the relevancy of all of Scripture. The entire law can be "profitable for doctrine, for reproof, for correction, for instruction in righteousness" when one seeks the deeper meaning and purpose God had in mind.

The entire framework of ceremonial, civil, and moral laws must be considered in the light of the foundation of love from which "all the law and the prophets" hang. While the law was given in the context of an ancient civilization with a format that may not align with modern expectations, the system contains timeless values, principles, and teachings.

Even those laws with no direct relevance to us today can give insight into the heart and mind of God and his great plan of salvation. To discard those sections is to do God's words to Moses a great injustice.

The Ten Commandments

And when He had made an end of speaking with him on Mount Sinai, He gave Moses two tablets of the Testimony, tablets of stone, written with the finger of God.
—Exodus 31:18

The Ten Commandments were the first and most important component of the law God gave to Israel. Spoken out loud and written by God himself on two tablets of stone, they were of such significance that they were later stored in the ark of the covenant (Exod. 20:1; 32:15–16; 40:20–21). They are referred to as The Testimony, a symbolic witness of God's entire agreement with Israel (Exod. 31:18; 32:15).[1]

The Ten Commandments were more than symbolic. They laid the foundation for a moral life. They were not to be read narrowly but as key *principles* that would teach people the basics on how to practically apply the two great principles of the law: that of loving God and their fellow man.

The Uniqueness of the Commandments

The Ten Commandments make the law of Moses truly unique. Rather than focusing on the requirements of the state as per other national law codes, the Ten Commandments are directed at the moral behavior of the individual. It made the heart of the law *very personal*. The Ten Commandments also reinforced an often-overlooked truth: that an enduring, free society can only be built with a moral people. History has shown that societies with declining moral standards can only be held together by authoritarian rule and will eventually fail.

Even those who do not formally acknowledge the Ten Commandments can't deny the soundness of the moral provisions they contain. The directives against murder, stealing, and lying are nearly universally accepted. The value of respecting parents and the damage that adultery can have on families and relationships are again accepted in most cultures. People will push back at the idea of a law against coveting, yet there is no denying the damaging effects of jealousy, greed, lust, etc. on mental health, which will almost always result in a negative outward expression in that person's life.

The first three commandments, which acknowledge one supreme God, will

---

[1] Within the books of Moses, the Ten Commandments are more precisely referred to as *the Ten Words* (Exod. 34:28). Most times the English word "commandments" appears within the books of Moses, it is not a reference to the Ten Commandments but a general term for the broader law (Heb: *mitzvah*).

be rejected by an atheist or nonbeliever. But for those who come to believe that a creation demands a creator, the commandments are inherently sound. It makes perfect sense that a being of such genius and majesty capable of creating this universe should be humbly revered with the highest respect and awe. And the fourth commandment, a weekly day of rest, is again a sound provision for an individual and society to help keep life in perspective.

Consistent from Genesis

The Ten Commandments were the formal presentation of the moral standards that God had taught humankind since creation. They were not standards confined to the nation of Israel or Abraham's family. As discussed earlier, God is rational, and the laws he gave to Israel had to reflect the reality of life—otherwise, they would be arbitrary and inherently meaningless. The Ten Commandments could not be a random set of decreed laws given to Israel that could later be repealed—otherwise, morals would be transient and relative rather than universal.

The Ten Commandments were the formal presentation of the moral standards that God had taught humankind since creation.

There is also no biblical support for the idea that the fundamental standards of right and wrong appeared for the first time at Sinai. We see a basic moral code in place from the earliest chapters of Genesis.[2] Therefore, it makes sense based on the evidence, that the giving of the Ten Commandments at Sinai was a formal restatement of the laws given from creation—most of which can be described as natural laws built into the reality of the universe God created for man. They represent truth from a God of truth.

Even the Sabbath day commandment starts with an instruction to "remember," implying former knowledge. The Sabbath day had very old origins and was specifically noted by God to reflect the events of creation week (Exod. 20:11). We also note that the Israelites were keeping the Sabbath before the decalogue was formally given at Sinai (Exod. 16:28–29).

Today we continue to see the value of the moral standards of the Ten Commandments in the reality of life. When people kill, commit adultery, steal, lie, and covet, the consequences echo negatively through life. Sexual licentiousness does not produce happy families. Lying does not create strong

---

[2] Refer to Appendix "Laws before Moses."

interpersonal bonds. Pride and arrogance do not produce loving relationships. This is reality. God generally doesn't have to intervene for these negative side effects to result—people and societies simply reap the consequences of the natural laws God has put in place.

Inherently Obvious?

Some have suggested that the Ten Commandments contain moral principles that are "obvious" to any enlightened society. But history would directly challenge that viewpoint. Many culturally advanced societies in history have "loved" their god in all sorts of vile ways, including child sacrifice, religious prostitution, torture, murder, slavery, etc. There is no end to the atrocities done in the name of "love" for a god. Even in our modern world, there are those who are convinced that the murdering of innocent people is some sort of delight to their god. Even basic moral virtues have not always been accepted. Consider the following:

> *Many culturally advanced societies throughout history have "loved" their god in all sorts of vile ways.*

- *Murder* has been deemed acceptable when killing babies, slaves, or deformed children in some societies. Honor killings were often esteemed. Abortion and euthanasia are seen as a right in a large number of western cultures today.
- *Lying* has been a crafted and admired "skill" in some cultures.
- *Adultery* (prostitution) has been acceptable when done so for "religious reasons" in many ancient cultures. Wife-sharing and wife-swapping was not uncommon in history. Today in our own Western culture, having an affair is deemed "healthy" by many counselors.
- *Stealing* has been justified against someone hated or deemed oppressive.
- *Coveting* is particularly criticized today, striking many people as being outrageous. "It's none of anyone else's business what I think!"

As for the first four commandments, they are also non-intuitive:

- Pluralistic societies scoffed at the idea that there was only one god. Today, Christianity is similarly accused of being narrow-minded and bigoted for promoting Jesus as the only way to salvation.

- The idea that there would be no graven images of a god or gods would seem ridiculous to most religions in history. How can a person worship an invisible god?
- The taking of the name of a god in a vain oath has been standard practice in many cultures, done to reinforce someone's promise to perform.
- Losing a work day each week would make no sense to most societies.

This is why God had to reveal his standards to Israel. They were a *revelation*. They were *not* the natural way of man (Isa. 55:8–9). This was the issue that God had to address with Israel after their long sojourn in Egypt. God needed to set his people straight with a clear, easy-to-understand set of basic moral laws and standards. Israel had to be taught what the love of God and the love of man looked like in practice.

Characteristics of the Commandments

Several key characteristics of the Ten Commandments stand out as noteworthy:

God Is Central

Unlike other law codes that are generally secular, God is foremost and center in the Ten Commandments. They don't just assume he exists; they declare that he is supreme and utterly unique. The first commandment provides the key reason why the remaining commandments should be carefully observed. Without acknowledging the first commandment, a society will eventually devalue and abandon the remaining commandments.

The Commandments Are Personal

As noted earlier, the Ten Commandments are specifically directed to the individual. Each is addressed to "you" (e.g., "*You* shall not covet.") This personal focus built into the nation's most important document is highly significant and reinforces God's consistent desire to connect to the hearts of individuals. It is a recognition that the nation's strength started with the individual citizen.

The Commandments Are Simple to Understand

The Commandments are not abstract or complex. They are simple in their concise wording and fundamental meaning. They can be easily understood by young and old, educated and uneducated, and across all ages and cultures.

The Commandments Are Liberating

In his opening preamble to the Commandments, God confirmed to the people that he had brought them out of bondage (Exod. 20:2). They would no longer be oppressed but truly free people. The Ten Commandments that immediately follow that introduction are logically part of that liberation. Being obedient to these commandments would be how they would experience the new freedom on offer.

The Commandments Reflect Relationships

In line with the two great laws of loving God and loving man, each of the Ten Commandments reflects an aspect of a relationship, either with God or with fellow man.

The Commandments Can Be Broadly Applied

The Ten Commandments are easy to understand, while at the same time, they have wider and deeper applications. Jesus demonstrated this in the Sermon on the Mount with his examples of murder and adultery. In that sense, the commandments are categories of principles with broad application.

Key Aspects of the Ten Commandments

There are many fine commentaries on the Ten Commandments, and it is not the intention to go into depth here. But some key points of each commandment are worth noting:

1: *I am the LORD your God ... you shall have no other gods before me.*

The first commandment starts with a call to believe and trust in the God of Israel. It is based on the reality that there is one Creator God who is supreme and unique (Isa. 45:6). This commandment presents a standing challenge for a person to prove whether God is who he says he is or whether there is another explanation for our existence. Whether a person accepts that or not does not change the fact that God exists and is supreme.

2: *You shall not make idols.*

The true God is too holy to be demeaned by manmade images. This commandment also reinforces God's desire to have a relationship of the heart and mind, not one driven by the senses.

3: *You shall not take the name of the LORD your God in vain.*

God does not want his name used disrespectfully or falsely. God's reputation is important to him, and his word is true. He does not want to be misrepresented.

4: *Remember the Sabbath day by keeping it holy.*

The Sabbath commandment reinforces the value of work, and at the same time stresses the importance of life balance and perspective. Having the entire society rest on the same day would keep the people unified and focused on the creator who had given them life.

5: *Honor your father and your mother.*

This commandment puts a high value on the family as the core social structure. It works to build a strong caring society as children follow and respect the example of their parents. It confirms the equality of both mother and father.

6: *You shall not murder.*

The Hebrew word here is "murder," not "killing," which might occur in self-defense, war, or capital punishment. Murder is the taking of a life unlawfully. This commandment against murder implies a right to life because humans are made in the image of God. It includes taking the life of an unborn child (Exod. 21:22–25).

7: *You shall not commit adultery.*

This commandment again reinforces the integrity of the family as the backbone of God's design for society. God ordained the lifetime marriage between one man and one woman right at the outset of creation. Adultery was a serious offense because its impact extends beyond the two consenting adults to spouses, children, and the community.

8: *You shall not steal.*

A directive not to steal reinforces the right to private property ownership. Multiple secondary Mosaic laws are based on this principle, including the laws relating to weights, measures, boundary markers, etc. Respecting another's property is not restricted to goods. Kidnapping, stealing someone's reputation, etc. all flow from this commandment.

9: *You shall not bear false witness against your neighbor.*

This commandment puts truth and truthfulness as core values of society. It emphasizes the importance of respecting the reputation of others, especially in a legal context.

10: *You shall not covet.*

This commandment is unique in historical law codes and is a directive for a person to govern themselves from within, starting with thoughts of the mind. It confirms the importance God has always put on the inner person and teaches that sin starts long before external action. Coveting leads to breaking all the other commandments.

Could ancient Israel have understood the deeper meaning behind each of the commandments? Absolutely! God wanted them to deeply meditate on these ten principles as a starting guide to a relationship with God and a successful life.

Why Negative Law Is Positive

One criticism of the Ten Commandments is their negative "you shall not" style. It's a negativism that grates on people in today's world, coming across like a stern taskmaster. Even the positive "observe the Sabbath day" commandment is immediately followed by the negative "thou shall not do any work." The only entirely positive commandment of the ten is the fifth, "Honor your father and your mother."

> *Negative law is one of the great hallmarks of freedom and reinforces the liberty God wanted for his chosen nation.*

People have questioned why God didn't present such important laws in a more positive style of "thou shall." There is at least one book where the author attempts to rewrite the commandments in a positive way.[3]

Such an idea might sound great at a simplistic level, but it misses the key reason why God expressed these laws as he did. The positive God of Israel knew exactly what he was doing. His supposed "negative" style has nothing to do with controlling people and everything to do with *empowering* people.

---

[3] Bibliog: (Lebbert 2015)

Negative law is one of the great hallmarks of freedom and reinforces the liberty God wanted for his chosen nation.

The term "negative law" needs to be explained. Broadly speaking, there are two sorts of laws in society: laws that tell you what you *can't* do and laws that tell you what you *must* do. Simplistically they can be called negative and positive laws. For example, telling a small child "Don't touch that stove" is a negative law. Telling a child to "clean up your room" is a positive law. Notice the key difference in the two styles of law:

- Negative laws are a warning against certain actions.
- Positive laws confer a duty or an obligation and compel people to behave in a certain way.

There lies the difference. The great benefits of negative laws are that they are simple to understand, limited, and *passive*. Simply refrain from doing these negative things, and you are free to live your life. It's an empowering concept. As the author of *The Institutes of Biblical Law* writes:

> A negative concept of law ensures liberty: except for the prohibited areas, all of man's life is beyond the law, and the law is of necessity indifferent to it. If the commandment says, "Thou shalt not steal," it means that the law can only govern theft: it cannot govern or control honestly acquired property. When the law prohibits blasphemy and false witness, it guarantees that all other forms of speech have their liberty. The negativity of the law is the preservation of the positive life and freedom of man.[4]

It is the negative law that creates the freest societies. Economist Mark Hendrikson writes:

> Negative law has a long and hallowed history in Western civilization. The Hebrew Decalogue is primarily negative, commanding us NOT to kill, NOT to steal, covet, etc. This is the essence of justice. Justice, like law, is a negative concept. In his 1759 book *The Theory of Moral Sentiments*, Adam Smith said that "justice … is but a negative virtue, and only hinders us from hurting our neighbor. The man who barely abstains from violating either the person or the estate, or the reputation, of his neighbors … fulfills … all the rules of what is

---

[4] Bibliog: (Rushdooney 1973, 102)

peculiarly called justice ... We may often fulfill all the rules of justice by sitting still and doing nothing."[5] (Author's emphasis)

Similarly, a person can minimally keep nearly all the Ten Commandments by simply refraining from doing evil. Of course, there are positive laws in the law of Moses, and God wanted the children of Israel to go beyond the basics and learn to love him deeply—and love their neighbors with voluntary positive acts of care and service. But the starting point of love, the Ten Commandments, is simple to understand—*stop wrong behavior*. The individual is then free without coercion to express outgoing love to their neighbor.

Over recent decades we have seen a major shift away from negative law as the governments of Western democracies increasingly presume to compel individuals to speak and behave in certain ways to align with the "morality" of the day. Instead of being passive, such laws seek to *control* the individual. This was not God's intent for a free society. Positive laws have a role, but if carried too far and in the wrong hands, they can be intrusive and oppressive.

The negative style of law of the Ten Commandments aligns with God's desire for light governance of his people. They are noncoercive and noncontrolling, just as God is himself. There is a vast difference between a society where a government tries to control individual lives and a government that simply tells its citizens not to do evil things. Had Israel followed the Ten Commandments alone, their society would have been God-centered, safe, trustworthy, peaceful, and stable, providing the perfect environment for individual expression.

---

[5] Bibliog: (Hendrickson 2013)

The Application of the Judgments

Is it oxen God is concerned about? Or does He say it altogether for our sakes?
—1 Corinthians 9:9–10

The law of Moses contains judgments, which are somewhat like modern-day precedents or case law. Just as judges today deliberate on previous interpretations of law and how they might apply to a current situation, God gave judgments to teach foundational principles that can be applied to many situations in life.

But unlike modern judicial precedents, which are more narrowly interpreted in legal environments, biblical judgments were broad and intended for use both in the official judiciary and by individual citizens. The people of Israel were encouraged to personally study and meditate on the judgments and apply them as guides to their lives (Deut. 4:14; 6:1–2).

Judgments Are Not Commandments

People perusing the law of Moses sometimes dismiss the judgments as trivial, irrelevant, outdated, or even nonsensical. But God has never been small-minded or confused. He is deep and sensible and the source of truth and wisdom. If a judgment appears trivial on first reading, it needs deeper consideration.

The way in which Scripture presents judgments enables them to transition across different times and cultures.

The key mistake people make with judgments is treating them as commandments instead of judgments. Judgments were legal decisions based on particular situational contexts. They were not narrow, legalistic rules the way rabbinical Judaism often interpreted them. God designed judgments to teach wisdom for those prepared to explore and meditate on the underlying principles.

Not surprisingly, Jesus used a similar teaching technique in his ministry. Jesus spoke in parables, which were simple stories with profound meaning. And just like the law of Moses, many people did not understand the deeper meaning of Jesus' parables because they simply took the stories at face value (Luke 8:10).

The way in which Scripture presents judgments enables them to transition across different times and cultures. The fact that Paul applied these judgments in an entirely different culture over a thousand years after Moses proves their timelessness.

Paul's Use of the Judgments

The apostle Paul directly referenced several Mosaic judgments in his epistles. The way he understands and interprets them is insightful. Consider one specific judgment out of the law of Moses:

> You shall not muzzle an ox while it treads out the grain. (Deut. 25:4)

At first reading we would dismiss such a law as irrelevant today. Few people own an ox, and even if they did, it would be highly unlikely they would use it to thresh grain. "I don't have an ox, and I don't have a farm, so this law does not apply to me" would be the natural response.

But even in ancient Israel, not everyone owned an ox. For those who did, we might think that this law is all about animal welfare. After all, an ox walking round and round threshing the grain would become hungry. However, it has also been observed that unrestrained feeding may not be the kindest approach. An unmuzzled animal left free to devour raw grain could easily end up with severe bloat and die.

So why would God establish a law like this when common sense suggests leaving it to the farmer to decide? If it were simply a way of telling the Israelites to be kind to their animals, why not just say that?

Jewish rabbis discussed this particular law extensively in the Talmud, considering such esoteric questions as:

- What is the significance of the word "while"? Can an ox be muzzled outside before it starts treading out the grain, or only *while* actually treading the grain?
- Is this a prohibition against ever muzzling an ox, considering they are animals that can theoretically thresh grain?
- What if the grain is to be offered at the temple? Surely such grain should not be walked on by an animal.
- What is the significance of the ox having all four legs doing the work of threshing?[1]

Some rabbis concluded that it was far better to thresh the grain by hand and

---

[1] Bibliog: (Sefaria. 2023, Deut. 25:4)

avoid using an animal at all because of the potential conflicts with this law!

But is this the sort of arcane way of thinking God had in mind when he gave this law about muzzling an ox? Prior to his calling, Paul may have also spent time pondering such tedious questions. But after his conversion, he had an entirely different perspective—one that was both practical and wise.

Is It Oxen God Is Really Concerned About?

We can learn a great deal how God designed the judgments to be used by how Paul applies this specific law about muzzling oxen in his letter to the gentile Corinthians. Paul puts the judgment in its proper context and explains its true intent.

In his epistle Paul writes that some in the Corinthian church were critical of him for living off church donations rather than paying his own way on his travels (1 Cor. 9:1–2). Paul explains that he indeed has a *right* to live from the donations of believers. He first appeals to sound reason:

> *My defense to those who examine me is this:* Do we have no right to eat and drink? Do we have no right to take along a believing wife, as do also the other apostles, the brothers of the Lord, and Cephas? Or is it only Barnabas and I who have no right to refrain from working? Who ever goes to war at his own expense? Who plants a vineyard and does not eat of its fruit? Or who tends a flock and does not drink of the milk of the flock? (1 Cor. 9:3–7)

Surprisingly, Paul then goes further and *appeals to the law of Moses* as his principle authority to live off the gospel. In doing so he makes some surprising statements that teach us that the law was not primarily about oxen at all:

> Do I say these things as a mere man? *Or does not the law say the same also?* For it is written in the law of Moses, "You shall not muzzle an ox while it treads out the grain." *Is it oxen God is concerned about? Or does He say it altogether for our sakes?* (1 Cor. 9:8–10)

Notice Paul's pointed question: "Is it oxen God is concerned about?" Paul was a master of the law, and now as a deeply converted man, he understood that oxen had never been the main focus of this law. God established this law for the benefit of *people*, not animals. Paul continues:

> *For our sakes, no doubt, this is written*, that he who plows should plow in hope, and he who threshes in hope should be partaker of his hope.

... Even so *the Lord has commanded* that those who preach the gospel should live from the gospel. (1 Cor. 9:10, 14)

People sacrificed thousands of oxen in the tabernacle each year. Whether some oxen were allowed to eat some of the grain while threshing was a minor issue in the scheme of things. God's focus for this law was on far deeper matters.

Paul reveals the meaning of what otherwise seems to be an irrelevant and trivial law.

Note the weight Paul gives to the judgment—calling it a *command* that supports his right to live off the gospel.

Paul later reaffirmed this important principle in a letter to Timothy:

> Let the elders who rule well be counted worthy of double honor, especially those who labor in the word and doctrine. For the Scripture says, "You shall not muzzle an ox while it treads out the grain," and, "The laborer is worthy of his wages." (1 Tim. 5:17–18)

Paul put this judgment about oxen into its correct perspective, revealing the underlying depth and meaning of what otherwise seems to be an irrelevant and trivial law. He affirmed that the law of Moses was not about rules and regulations and trivia, and neither is God narrow-minded and petty.

At its simplest level, this law did teach the principle that animals should be treated humanely. But *far more significantly*, it offers a guide to life for organizations, families, employers, employees, and the church. It makes a strong statement about ensuring employees are properly cared for and remunerated and workers not exploited. It is a broad law relevant to all people and across all times.

Unequally Yoked

In another example of how to apply the law of Moses, Paul referred to a law that seems bizarre at face value. It's a law from which the Pharisees derived all sorts of rules and petty regulations:

> You shall not sow your vineyard with different kinds of seed, lest the yield of the seed which you have sown and the fruit of your vineyard be defiled. You shall not plow with an ox and a donkey together. You shall not wear a garment of different sorts, such as wool and linen mixed together. (Deut. 22:9–11)

At first reading, these laws appear to have no sense in the real world. Would a farmer spoil a vineyard by intermixing it with other types of seeds? Would someone really attempt to plow with two unlike animals? *Would any landowner do such illogical things?* And what could be wrong with wearing a garment of mixed materials?

At face value the average person would dismiss such things as nonsense and see no relevance to life in today's world. But we again need to be reminded that God is not irrational. When considering the earlier statement "Is it oxen that God is concerned about?" we can equally question: "Is it wool or linen or donkeys or fabrics (or many other such things in the law) that God is really concerned about?" Or does he have more important principles in mind?

Once again we can thank the apostle Paul for teaching us the deeper application of this law. In his second letter to the Corinthians, he references this law in a way that reveals its true intent:

> Do not be *unequally yoked* together with unbelievers. For what fellowship has righteousness with lawlessness? And what communion has light with darkness? And what accord has Christ with Belial? Or what part has a believer with an unbeliever? (2 Cor. 6:14–15)

Paul's use of the term "unequally yoked" is a direct reference to the judgment of not plowing with two mismatched animals (Deut. 22:10). It helps us understand that the original judgments were not ultimately about oxen and donkeys or linen and wool—they were about people and relationships. Being equally yoked is an important principle for a successful life. So many marriages, partnerships, and businesses have come to grief because they were unequally yoked. Just as a fabric made from mismatched materials can become distorted, they failed to weigh up the impact different backgrounds, beliefs, cultures, etc. could have on a relationship. Not being "unequally yoked" is a powerful principle that everyone should consider in life. It is timeless, wise advice from the law of Moses expressed in a memorable format.[2]

Cursing the Deaf

Consider another judgment, which again seems strange at first reading:

> You shall not curse the deaf, nor put a stumbling block before the blind, but shall fear your God: I am the LORD. (Lev. 19:14)

Images come to mind of someone mocking a deaf person behind their back,

---

[2] The command to not wear garments made of wool and linen may be related to reinforcing God's holiness by not copying the fabrics used in the holy ephod (Exod. 39:4–5). Whatever the intent of this judgment, it had meaning and relevance in the context of the time.

and of a blind man tapping his way down the street while unruly teenagers put a trap in front of him, causing him to fall.

But it would take a heartless sort of person even to consider such base behavior. Were the ancient Israelites such mean-spirited people that they needed to be counseled against such conduct as some commentaries state? No, this judgment was again teaching a deeper principle. Paul uses this judgment in his epistle to the Romans as a directive to the church:

> Therefore let us not judge one another anymore, but rather resolve this, not to put a stumbling block or a cause to fall in our brother's way. (Rom. 14:13)

In context, Paul was teaching the church an important principle: to be considerate and nonjudgmental in their dealings with others who did not see as clearly as they did and sincerely held other beliefs. He uses the same judgment in his letter to the Corinthians (1 Cor. 8:9–13), teaching that believers should even restrict their own freedoms at times to not make a weaker brother stumble.

The same principle applies to cursing the deaf. Jesus noted that there were spiritually blind and deaf people in his day (Matt. 13:14–15). Mocking such people, talking down to them, or despising those who don't understand did not show the love for a neighbor that the law required.

Blue Tassels

The use of tassels is another criticized judgment:

> The LORD spoke to Moses, saying, "Speak to the children of Israel: Tell them to make tassels on the corners of their garments throughout their generations, and to put a blue thread in the tassels of the corners." (Num. 15:37–38)

The Pharisees had again analyzed this law to the extreme, discussing such esoteric questions as:

- What did the corners of a garment refer to?
- Did this apply to night garments?
- What was the shape and length of the tassel?
- What was the shade of blue?[3]

---

[3] Bibliog: (Sefaria. 2023, Num. 15:37)

We can again ask Paul's question: "Is it tassels on clothing that God is really concerned about?" Is the color and size of the tassel the primary focus of this law? The law of Moses explains the deeper intent, and the explanation makes good sense:

> And you shall have the tassel, *that you may look upon it and remember* all the commandments of the LORD and do them, and that you may not follow the harlotry to which your own heart and your own eyes are inclined, and that *you may remember* and do all My commandments, and be holy for your God. (Num. 15:39–40)

The tassel itself was merely a symbol. God knew Israel would be tempted to drift away, so he proposed a simple reminder system as an aid. It was an important principle, not a petty law.[4] The principle is just as valid for someone today as it was for ancient Israel. Believers of all ages need to include reminders in their lives to keep God first and foremost, or they, too, might drift away.

Cultural Context

When judgments are interpreted to the letter instead of within their cultural context, bizarre regulations can result. As an example, consider the following judgment:

> You shall not boil a young goat in its mother's milk. (Exod. 23:19)

This judgment has led to rabbinic Judaism installing a highly complex regime of separating dairy and meat products. Their primary concern is the meat of a kid and the milk of its exact mother might unknowingly be used in the same meal. To counter this incredibly remote (but theoretically possible) situation, costly duplicate kitchens and parallel kitchenware sets are often installed in Jewish homes. Was this God's intention when he gave this judgment?

The understanding that God is rational, sensible, practical, and the source of wisdom, must be our starting point.

The understanding that God is rational, sensible, practical, and the source of wisdom, must be our starting point. God did not give Israel random rules. A far better understanding, and one supported by many scholars and

---

[4] Jesus criticized the Pharisees for turning this personal reminder system into an external status symbol (Matt. 23:5).

commentaries, is the probable association of boiling a young goat in its mother's milk with the pagan cultic practices.[5] The judgment then makes perfect sense. It was not a prescriptive rule to be blindly kept for all time. God, at that time, did not want Israel to copy the pagan religious superstitions that were such a snare to them.

In a similar vein, there are judgments in relation to hair, beards, and tattoos that have again been narrowly interpreted to the letter instead of to the original intent:

> You shall not shave around the sides of your head, nor shall you disfigure the edges of your beard. (Lev. 19:27)

The law itself explains that such practices related to pagan cultic rituals for the dead, and that is why they were forbidden[6]:

> You are the children of the LORD your God; you shall not cut yourselves nor shave the front of your head *for the dead*. (Deut. 14:1)

> You shall not make any cuttings in your flesh *for the dead*, nor tattoo any marks on you: I am the LORD. (Lev. 19:28)

> They shall not make any bald place on their heads, nor shall they shave the edges of their beards nor make any cuttings in their flesh. (Lev. 21:5)

The prophet Ezekiel later wrote that it was God's wish that priestly hair be trimmed and not unkempt, confirming that the issue being addressed in the judgment was related to pagan religious practices, not general appearance:

> They shall neither shave their heads, nor let their hair grow long, *but they shall keep their hair well trimmed*. (Ezek. 44:20)

To interpret and apply the judgments about hair, beards, tattoos etc. narrowly to the letter of the law and out of context totally misses the underlying intent. God is holy and separate and was instructing Israel not to intermix pagan symbols and concepts with his worship.

Could Israel Have Understood?

It has been suggested that ancient Israel could not have understood the deeper

---

[5] Bibliog: (Bakers 2013, 1149 Milk)
[6] Ugaritic tablets from Ras Shamra, Syria, suggest that such practices were a part of the cult of the dead and fertility rituals. Bibliog: (Bakers 2012, Deut. 14:1 p162)

principles underlying the judgments—that only a more sophisticated people could have grasped their true intent. And while it does seem that most of Israel didn't rise above a basic level of understanding, this was primarily due to their refusal to hold to the covenant. Only a small minority of individuals sought the Lord and took the law into their hearts. But that aside, there are sound reasons why such understanding was not beyond the people of that day.

Firstly, archaeology and history have shown contemporary ancient cultures (e.g. Egyptian, Babylonian, Assyrian) to be advanced in literacy and learning.

Secondly, God wanted Israel to be an intelligent and educated people standing tall among the nations. He specifically instructed the law to be taught at all levels of society, starting in the home, then via the priests, through the judicial system, and right up to the king. The importance of understanding the law was paramount to the success of the nation, and God desired everyone to have the opportunity to learn and comprehend his law as he intended. Had they followed this injunction, even young children could have understood the deeper meaning of the judgments.

Thirdly, these underlying principles are not complex. Just like Jesus' parables, they are easy to understand once expounded by sound teachers.

In his day, Jesus castigated the religious leaders multiple times for not understanding the deeper matters of the law. As teachers of the law, they were supposed to teach the weightier matters. Yet they focused on trivia and minutiae and missed the point so many times. But Jesus was clear: they *should have understood these things*! They were blind, but it was a self-induced blindness fed by their own pride and hypocrisy.

Exceedingly Broad

Understanding how judgments were to be applied was foundational to the success of the law of Moses. Many other practical guidelines related to life, relationships, personal success, business, treatment of employees, health, safety, the environment, etc. are referenced in the law. Many of these laws, which are so often narrowly interpreted, take on great meaning when a person meditates and seeks to understand the underlying principles God had in mind.

By using simple principles, God has ingeniously made his law relevant across times and cultures. As the psalmist wrote: "Your commandment is exceedingly broad" (Ps. 119:96).

Key Principles of Justice

Let justice run down like water, and righteousness like a mighty stream.
—Amos 5:24

Justice was a core value that underpinned the entire law of Moses, a point Jesus strongly confirmed (Matt. 23:23; Luke 11:42). God wanted Israel to be a just and fair society where people could count on just outcomes and feel confident and secure.

The system of justice God outlined was outstanding for its time and stood apart from the law codes of other ancient nations. The system included important legal principles we esteem highly today, including the rule of law, equality under the law, impartiality of the judiciary, the need for evidence and witnesses in judgment, laws against bribery and perjury, easy access to the judiciary, the proportionality of justice, and much more. These foundational concepts were an extension of God's own values.

We will touch on key principles here and expand on them in later chapters.

The Rule of Law

God's plan was for Israel to be governed not by the whims of leaders, not by "oral" traditions, but by the *rule of law* (Deut. 4:1; 5:1; 8:1). Early American President John Adams famously described such a system as "a government of laws, not of men,"[1] where a sound legal system, and a respect for that system, would allow a society to function with minimal need for people of authority.

The rule of law underlies all modern democracies and is recognized as one of the foundational principles of good government.[2] The rule of law is thought of as a modern concept having its foundations in the Magna Carta in the thirteenth century. For the ancient law of Moses to have so strongly presented the rule of law is again quite astonishing.

The rule of law includes the following fundamental principles:

1) A defined just and fair standard of law
2) An accessible and impartial judiciary
3) Everyone (including rulers) being subject to the law
4) An educated populace who understand the law they are subject to

---

[1] Bibliog: (J. Adams 1780)
[2] Bibliog: (The Rule of Law Education Centre 2022)

The rule of law was enormously significant to the civil administration of Israel. It provided the ability for the average citizen to verify whether a matter was in accordance with the law or not. It also worked to create an educated population with confidence in God, who was their king. Such a system aimed to empower people at the grassroots level.

For the ancient law of Moses to have so strongly presented the rule of law is quite astonishing.

God's reason for wanting such a deep and widespread knowledge of the law was the nature of the law itself. It wasn't only about an individual "knowing their rights" as our world might express it today. God wanted the average Israelite to understand that the strength of their society started with their own morality and their personal relationship with him.

One Standard of Law

One of the most enlightened standards of justice in the Mosaic system was God's decree there would be *one standard of law* for everyone in the country, including for foreigners and visitors:

> You shall have the same law for the stranger and for one from your own country; for I am the LORD your God. (Lev. 24:22)

> One law shall be for the native-born and for the stranger who dwells among you. (Exod. 12:49)

One standard of law has been rare throughout history. It further confirms the divine origins of the law. It is common historically to find different sets of rules for people of different class levels and for citizens versus non-citizens. Kings, pharaohs, and emperors were often above the law.

God, on the other hand, directed that all leaders (including future kings) be fully subject to the same law as everyone else in the land. A king was directed to write a personal copy of the law for himself and follow it carefully all his days so that his "heart was not lifted above his brethren" (Deut. 17:18–20).

Impartiality and Equality Under Law

The rule of law was further strengthened by the directive that everyone was to be equal under the law regardless of wealth, race, ethnicity, or status. The judiciary was directed to be impartial in all their judgments:

> You shall not pervert justice; *you shall not show partiality* …You shall follow what is altogether just, that you may live and inherit the land which the LORD your God is giving you. (Deut. 16:19–20)

Impartiality is one of God's key values:

> For the LORD your God *is* God of gods and Lord of lords, the great God, mighty and awesome, *who shows no partiality* nor takes a bribe. (Deut. 10:17)

This emphasis on impartiality again affirms God's hand because it is not at all intuitive. For much of history, the wealthy in most nations saw it as a right to be favored in judgment and to receive better outcomes in a court of law. In ancient Athens for example, under the law code of Draco, it was deemed just for rich landowners to be favored over the poor.[3] The legal code of Hammurabi also had biases against those in lower social ranks. Many of its gruesome penalties were based on the identity and gender of the perpetrator and the victim and whether they were property owners, free men, or slaves.[4] Under Roman law a defendant's social status was weighed heavily along with the evidence, and a privileged citizen of Rome could nearly always defeat someone from the lower social ranks. Even in the Modern Era of seventeenth and eighteenth-century Europe, there was a strong bias against the poor, and terrible, harsh punishments were regularly meted out in the name of "justice."

> *Everyone was to be equal under the law regardless of wealth, race, ethnicity, or status.*

In contrast, the law of Moses specifically directed that there be no partiality toward a rich or poor person in a dispute. There would be a natural tendency for a judge to favor a rich person or person of influence. Or alternatively, some judges might tend to rule in favor of a poor person simply because of their situation. *God says do neither*. Do what is just, regardless of the status of the individuals concerned:

> You shall do no injustice in judgment. You shall *not be partial to the poor, nor honor the person of the mighty*. In *righteousness* you shall judge your neighbor. (Lev. 19:15)

---

[3] Bibliog: (Loizides 2015, Draco)
[4] Bibliog: (King 2012)

> You shall not show partiality to a poor man in his dispute. (Exod. 23:3)

Anti-Racist

The law of Moses went further in its impartiality directives. It instructed individuals and judges to *love* and *respect* the stranger as one of their own:

> And if a stranger dwells with you in your land, you shall not mistreat him.[34] The stranger who dwells among you *shall be to you as one born among you, and you shall love him as yourself*; for you were strangers in the land of Egypt: I am the LORD your God. (Lev. 19:33–34)

God encouraged Israel to remember how badly they were mistreated as strangers in the land of Egypt, and to do the opposite:

> Therefore love the stranger, for you were strangers in the land of Egypt. (Deut. 10:19)

There could be no greater statements against racism than these. This law was, again, modeled on God's own love:

> He administers justice for the fatherless and the widow, *and loves the stranger*, giving him food and clothing. (Deut. 10:18)

The care and concern directed toward foreigners under the umbrella of the nation of Israel would have added greatly to their confidence that they had chosen a welcoming and just country to live in or visit. These laws alone show that the prejudice and partiality against foreigners practiced in Judaism at the time of Jesus had no basis at all in the law of Moses.

> *There could be no greater statements against racism than these.*

Educated in the Law

To add strength to the rule of law, God wanted everyone, both young and old, to be educated in the law. Understanding the law was not to be the exclusive domain of the religious or judicial hierarchy. All Israelites, both men and women, were strongly encouraged (even commanded!) to know the law well and to memorize it in their hearts (Deut. 5:1; 6:6). Parents were directed to diligently teach the law to their children so that they understood it from a young age (Deut. 6:6–20). Judges were not only to give judgments in line with the law, but they were also to explain the sense and meaning so that people would learn the application of the law (Lev. 10:11; Deut. 17:11; Neh. 8:8).

Law against Bribery

Bribery has been a common way of ensuring outcomes of legal cases for most of history across a broad range of civilizations. It was seen as a normal way of doing business, even necessary in some cultures.[5] One biblical example is the Roman Governor Felix hoping for money from Paul to pay for his release (Acts 24:26).

The law of Moses warned the judiciary against bribery:

> And you shall take no bribe, for a bribe blinds the discerning and perverts the words of the righteous. (Exod. 23:8)

This law against bribery is once again based on God's own values (Deut. 10:17). Bribery is a moral issue, and our modern judicial systems are no less susceptible to bribery and corruption than the ancient world. According to the United Nations, corruption, bribery, and lapses in the impartial rule of law continue to be a global scourge, directly affecting the lives of millions and impeding economic growth.[6]

Witnesses and Evidence

The need for witnesses and evidence might again seem an obvious principle needed to underpin a justice system, but history again has shown otherwise. The partiality of many historical justice systems meant that the word of one wealthy individual was often enough to convict some of a lower status without evidence.

In contrast, in all criminal or civil cases, the law of Moses required multiple witnesses for the matter to be determined:

> One witness shall not rise against a man concerning any iniquity or any sin that he commits; by the mouth of two or three witnesses the matter shall be established. (Deut. 19:15)

Witnesses were to be carefully cross-examined to ensure they were telling the truth:

> And the *judges shall make careful inquiry*, and indeed, if the witness *is* a false witness, who has testified falsely against his brother, then you shall do to him as he thought to have done to his brother. (vv. 18–19)

---

[5] Bibliog: (New World Encyclopedia 2022, Bribery)
[6] Bibliog: (United Nations 2018)

As expected in a court of law today, an accusation would need to be properly examined and supported before a final judgment given.

Personal Accountability

Another key principle of justice in the Mosaic law was personal accountability. Punishing family members of accused criminals has been a practice rife throughout history from the earliest to modern times. People have been legally harassed, held in prison, tortured, and executed despite their innocence—simply because they were related to the offender. Such practices are called *kin punishment* or *collective punishment* and were common throughout the ancient world.

The law of Moses, on the other hand, forbade such practices:

> Fathers shall not be put to death for their children, nor shall children be put to death for their fathers; *a person shall be put to death for his own sin*. (Deut. 24:16)

People were to be held accountable for their own wrongdoings only and could not be punished for another person's actions.[7] This is a recognized principle of law in our Western world today.

Understanding "Equality"

Because of today's confusion as to what "equality" means in relation to law, biblical equality needs to be explained. Equality under the Mosaic justice system was an expectation to be treated impartially, and of receiving a fair and just hearing. It was not aligned to modern social justice goals of wealth redistribution and trying to achieve equality of outcomes for all.

Equality also did not mean that every role and every opportunity was open to every person. For example, a future king of Israel could not be a foreigner (Deut. 17:15). This made perfect sense. Even today's western societies have rules to ensure leaders and judges are citizens. There are also rules for controlling foreign investment, which God also included. Farmland could not be sold permanently and would always revert to an Israelite family (Lev. 25:13, 23). These types of rules were not discrimination; they reflected sound judgment, without which the distinction of the nation's culture and heritage would be at risk.

Equal opportunity was also not open to everyone within certain areas of the

---

[7] For further discussion on this topic, refer to the chapter *Sins of the Fathers*.

worship system. For example, God made it clear that only those of the tribe of Levi and of Aaron's lineage could be priests (Exod. 29:9; Num. 18:8). The Passover ceremony was to be celebrated only by those who were circumcised (Exod. 12:48). These were not arbitrary rules. God gave them to teach important key aspects of God's great plan for humanity. The typology was very important to God and carried great meaning.

It's the same with the different roles God had in mind for men, women, elders, etc. in society. These roles were to be distinctly different, each honored in their own special way as they came together to form a unified nation under one God.

Today's Western societies are increasingly confused on the topic of equality, to our detriment. Natural God-given differences of gender, race, color, etc. are approached competitively instead of being appreciated for the unique value each bring. Wealth is criticized simply because others are poor. Ironically, societies that attempt to force "equality" upon their citizens in the name of social justice themselves become increasingly oppressive and unjust, as the twentieth-century experiment into communism clearly demonstrated.

A Just System

The key principles of Mosaic justice formed the basis of a just and fair judicial system. They were outstanding for their time and would have given confidence to both citizens and visitors that they would be treated fairly and receive just outcomes in law.

We will expand on many other enlightened aspects of the Mosaic system of justice in the chapters that follow.

Eye for Eye, Tooth for Tooth

You shall not take vengeance nor bear any grudge against the children of your people. —Leviticus 19:18

For many people the Mosaic system of justice is synonymous with "an eye for an eye" and "a tooth for tooth," bringing to mind thoughts of harsh and unforgiving retaliation. It sounds reminiscent of the old European blood-feuds between clans that dragged on for generations. "You hurt me, and I hurt you." In the Modern Era we might think of the Hatfields and McCoys of the American Midwest in the 1800s.

It was Mahatma Gandhi who is credited with the saying: "An eye for an eye and a tooth for a tooth and the whole world would soon be blind and toothless." But "An eye for an eye and tooth for a tooth" is not just an old saying; it was an instruction given by God himself:

> Whoever kills any man shall surely be put to death. Whoever kills an animal shall make it good, animal for animal. If a man causes disfigurement of his neighbor, as he has done, so shall it be done to him—fracture for fracture, eye for eye, tooth for tooth; as he has caused disfigurement of a man, so shall it be done to him. And whoever kills an animal shall restore it; but whoever kills a man shall be put to death. You shall have the same law for the stranger and for one from your own country; *for I am the* LORD *your God.*" (Lev. 24:17–22)

This was not just some trivial law that can be dismissed. Described in legal terms as *lex talionis*,[1] eye for an eye was a key principle of the justice system of the law of Moses.

Some commentators have written that to live under such a system would lead to a vengeful society of people continually feuding and trying to get even with each other. Yet Israel lived under this law (albeit imperfectly) for centuries, and there is no evidence to support such a stance.

Justice Should Be Proportional

The problem lies in a misunderstanding of both the law's application and responsibility. The eye for an eye principle was not given as a directive to

---

[1] Latin: *Law of retribution in kind.*

individuals for personal vengeance. The law of Moses specifically *forbade* people from taking matters into their own hands:

> You shall *not take vengeance* nor bear any grudge against the children of your people, but you shall love your neighbor as yourself: I am the LORD. (Lev. 19:18)

Eye for an eye was a principle reserved for the courts, not for individuals. The principle is mentioned three times in Old Testament law, and each time it is presented, it relates to a formal or judicial situation where a judge or magistrate was involved (Exod. 21:22–23; Lev. 24:12–20; Deut. 19:16–21). It is an instruction to a judge to ensure that a *punishment must fit the crime*. Eye for an eye was in fact an enlightened aspect of the justice system of the law of Moses, a principle that modern nations follow today in their judicial systems. In our modern democracies, we refer to this as the *proportionality of justice*. It is a bedrock legal principle that states that the punishment meted out by a judge must be fair and proportional to the loss incurred.

> *The eye for an eye principle was not given as a directive to individuals for personal vengeance.*

Today we rightly expect criminals and offenders to be punished according to the crime committed. When that doesn't happen, people are rightly upset. Occasionally in the news, we will see a violent rapist released from jail after a short term, and there is a huge outcry. Likewise, we see a similar uproar if a harsh sentence is delivered when there are obvious mitigating circumstances. Why? Because the punishment was not proportionate to the crime committed.

The law of Moses established the principle of proportionality of justice as central to the justice system. It protected a person from being punished out of proportion for what they did, which has been common for most of history. Even in cultures with the *lex talionis* principle, it usually applied only among class equals. Kill a rich man's horse, and you might lose your life in many societies in history. But under God's law, social status had no bearing. Whoever killed an animal shall make it good, "animal for animal" (Lev. 24:18, 21).

Historical Perspective

Today we take the protection we receive from the proportionality of justice for granted, but it has not always been like this even in our recent history. Consider the harsh system of justice that existed in England in the eighteenth century that led to the founding of the nation of Australia. The vast majority of those transported as convicts had committed petty crimes. People were transported for terms of seven or fourteen years, or even life, for stealing such items as string, cheese, meat, or even a handkerchief. There were no concessions or considerations for age. Poor or needy children were deemed a nuisance in the 1800s, so ships full of children aged nine to sixteen were sent to the colonies.

One boy, Robert Abel, was fifteen when he was arrested in 1783 for stealing five shillings, even though he claimed he was not involved. Because he could not provide a character reference, he was sentenced to death. Later his sentence was changed to seven years transportation. Another young woman, Catherine Makesay, aged eighteen, was sentenced to seven years transportation for homelessness.[2] By 1800, in England, there were over 200 *capital* crimes.[3] A person could be hung for shoplifting, stealing food, drunkenness, or even cutting down trees for firewood. Like most European nations of the day, the English had lost track of the proportionality of justice. The rich and powerful had rights and privileges. The weak and poor had little to none.

The enlightened law of Moses protected the vulnerable from such abuse.

Not Interpreted Literally

It is a mistake to read the eye for an eye principle in a strictly literal sense as if the law of Moses *demanded* a punishment that *exactly* matched the harm caused and that no alternate punishment or retribution be allowed. Some read the law in this way, assuming if an eye was damaged, the eye of the other person *must* also be damaged. But a strictly literal reading is not how judgments were to be understood. As we saw earlier, judgments were designed to teach principles of justice using the symbolism of various scenarios. Jesus himself spoke of symbolically "plucking out eyes" and "cutting off hands" in a similar manner to teach key principles (Matt. 5:29–30).[4] There are also other reasons to approach the eye for an eye law in this way.

> *It is a mistake to read the eye for an eye principle in a strictly literal sense.*

---

[2] Bibliog: (Convict Records 2023)
[3] Bibliog: (National Justice Museum 2023, Bloody Code)
[4] The Jewish Talmud supports the idea that the eye for an eye phrase was not to be taken literally. Bibliog: (Chabad. Yehuda Shurpin. 2022).

Firstly, the written penalty of the law was never mandatory. It was a guide to be considered by a righteous judge according to the circumstances. A judge had the authority to mercifully adjust the penalty or dismiss the complaint altogether.

Secondly, inflicting a physical punishment that exactly matched the hurt caused would not always be practical, desirable, or even possible.[5]

Thirdly, and most importantly, inflicting physical harm on the perpetrator provides *no compensation* for the victim. We note that for the loss of an animal, a replacement animal must be provided as compensation (Lev. 24:18). It is also logical to assume that for physical loss, some compensation be provided to help the victim.

Fourthly, the law implies that financial or other payment could be made in place of the harm caused. It was something that could be agreed on with the judge. One example in Scripture is the hypothetical situation of a man whose ox has been known to cause harm, being given the death penalty if his ox kills a person (Exod. 21:29). But the ox owner was able to redeem his life by paying a sum of money imposed by the judge (v. 30). In other serious life-threatening situations, we also note that judges could determine a monetary compensation (Exod. 21:22–27).

Finally, we note that the law specifically forbade a *ransom* (or monetary compensation) being paid in the case of first-degree murder. The clear implication is that for other situations a ransom *could* be paid:

> Moreover you shall take no ransom for the life of a murderer who is guilty of death, but he shall be surely put to death. (Num. 35:31)

If you took a life in first-degree murder, you could not buy your way out of it, but for most other situations causing harm, you could come to an arrangement either to pay a monetary sum or to become a servant of that other person until recompense was made.

Your Eye Shall Not Pity

Another criticism of the eye for an eye principle is a directive to the judge to "not pity":

> *Your eye shall not pity;* but life shall be for life, eye for eye, tooth for

---

[5] There may be rare cases of evil intent where directly inflicting a punishment to match a perpetrator's actions is a just outcome. We see such an example in Judges 1:5–7.

tooth, hand for hand, foot for foot. (Deut. 19:21)

Not pitying sounds harsh and hard, but again, consider the context. Realizing we are talking about a court of law, the word "pity" takes on a whole different meaning. For justice to be done, a judge should *not* arrive at their judgment based on pitying either the perpetrator or the victim. Justice must be done dispassionately, without emotion.

This is the true and proper standard recognized in all courts of law. As an example, the Supreme Court of the State of Queensland, Australia, provides the following direction to juries:

> You must reach your verdict on the evidence, and only on the evidence. *You should dismiss all feelings of sympathy* or prejudice, whether it be sympathy for or prejudice against the defendant or anyone else. *No such emotion has any part to play in your decision.* You must approach your duty dispassionately, deciding the facts upon the whole of the evidence.[6]

Understanding the importance of *legal impartiality* (which was strong in the law of Moses) helps us understand why it was important to "not pity." It has nothing to do with meanness or harshness but has everything to do with making a clear-headed decision—one not swayed by emotion or feeling sorry for one of the parties but a decision that is just and right.

> *A judge should not arrive at their judgment based on pitying either the perpetrator or the victim.*

It is good for a judge to show appropriate mercy in sentencing, but that is a separate matter to having a distorted judgment because of pity. Today we have seen a rise in judges feeling sorry for the perpetrators of crime and losing their impartiality.

Scripture is clear that God *did* expect the formal authorities to execute vengeance on evildoers, and he became angry when the weak of the society were not protected and justice not done (Zech. 7:10–12; Isa. 1:23–24; Jer. 5:28–29).

---

[6] Bibliog: (Queensland Supreme Court 2022, Direction 23.1)

New Testament Position

The Mosaic standard of prohibiting personal vengeance and empowering the courts to execute justice is fully supported in the New Testament. In the book of Romans, Paul confirms the right of the state to execute judgment on evildoers. He distinguishes between the dispassionate court system and the personal standard to which individuals must aspire. Quoting from Old Testament Scripture, Paul reminds his readers not to take personal vengeance:

> *Repay no one evil for evil.* Have regard for good things in the sight of all men. If it is possible, as much as depends on you, live peaceably with all men. *Beloved, do not avenge yourselves,* but rather give place to wrath; for it is written, "Vengeance is Mine, I will repay," says the Lord. Therefore "If your enemy is hungry, feed him; if he is thirsty, give him a drink; for in so doing you will heap coals of fire on his head." Do not be overcome by evil, but overcome evil with good. (Rom. 12:17–21)

Paul then immediately proceeds to explain that the executive government (in this case Rome) did have the right to execute vengeance on evildoers, confirming they operate with God's authority:

> Let every soul be *subject to the governing authorities.* For there is no authority except from God, and the authorities that exist are appointed by God. Therefore whoever resists the authority resists the ordinance of God, and those who resist will bring judgment on themselves. For rulers are not a terror to good works, but to evil. Do you want to be unafraid of the authority? Do what is good, and you will have praise from the same. For he is God's minister to you for good. But if you do evil, be afraid; *for he does not bear the sword in vain; for he is God's minister, an avenger to execute wrath on him who practices evil.* (Rom. 13:1–4)

Retribution does need to be taken out on evil people; otherwise, we would have anarchy in our societies. God has given our governments today the authority to establish judicial systems that can enforce justice in the same way he gave the authority to the leaders of Israel. It is right and proper for our nations in the twenty-first century to seek to protect their citizens against criminals and those who are out to harm or terrorize our people. The government's role is to take balanced vengeance against people who do such things with the executive power that God has vested on them. When we individually call on our court system for justice, that's exactly what we are asking a judge to do.

Jesus and Eye for an Eye

What about Jesus' position? At first reading of his Sermon on the Mount, Jesus seems to distance himself from the eye for an eye law, but we must look at the context.

Jesus was not criticizing the right of the executive civil government to execute justice against evildoers. God is a God of justice, and governments must maintain law and order to protect the weak and vulnerable in society. Nor was Jesus talking about serious matters that a judge must deal with.

Jesus was talking to the *individual* and addressing the misuse of the eye for an eye law by the hypocritical Pharisees of his day, who were practicing eye for an eye on a *personal* basis for *personal* vengeance:

> You have heard that it was said, "An eye for an eye and a tooth for a tooth." *But I tell you not to resist an evil person*. But whoever slaps you on your right cheek, turn the other to him also. If anyone wants to sue you and take away your tunic, let him have your cloak also. And whoever compels you to go one mile, go with him two. Give to him who asks you, and from him who wants to borrow from you do not turn away. (Matt. 5:38–42).

Notice that Jesus says, "You have heard that it was said." He was not referring to what is *written* in law but rather directly counteracting the oral misuse of the law by the Jewish religious leaders. The written law of Moses forbade people from taking the law into their own hands (Lev. 19:18). The Pharisees were breaking the law of Moses by harboring hatred in their hearts, holding grudges, and personally seeking vengeance on people who wronged them. Their hatred extended to Jesus himself.

There is no conflict between the law of Moses and Jesus' teaching.

Jesus was putting the law into its correct perspective. For most minor matters in life, like the examples Jesus used in his Sermon on the Mount, we should not fight back. We should do good in return for evil, allow ourselves to be wronged, and just move on. As it says in the Old Testament, to do so heaps coals of fire on the person's conscience (Prov. 25:21–22). This is what mercy and forgiveness is all about. It has been God's way from the start.

On the other hand, Jesus confirmed the importance of justice (Matt. 23:23). And for the serious issues of life, it is right and proper to seek justice through the appropriate legal channels in a non-vindictive way.

The Expositor's Bible Commentary sums up Jesus' eye for an eye instruction in Matthew this way:

> The principles of justice outlined here build on the sacred value of all people as created in God's image and anticipate modern justice systems where personal power or privilege has no claim in the court. Jesus' reference to this command is not to deny its validity but to affirm a spirit of grace and forgiveness in personal dealings between members of God's kingdom.[7]

There is no conflict between the law of Moses and Jesus' teaching, just as there is no conflict between Jesus and the teachings of Paul.

---

[7] Bibliog: (Hess 2008, p798 Matt 5:38)

Mercy and the Written Law

But if you had known what this means, "I desire mercy and not sacrifice," you would not have condemned the guiltless. —Matthew 12:7

Jesus strongly emphasized mercy throughout his ministry and called it a "weightier matter" of the law of Moses (Matt. 23:23). Yet often people's impression of the law of Moses is one of very little mercy. They point to specific sections of the Old Testament law with harsh penalties as proof of a lack of mercy. They assume therefore that Jesus came with a new understanding of mercy, compassion, and forgiveness that the Old Testament law did not reflect.

Yet we have clear evidence that mercy was well understood under the old covenant. Its importance is reflected extensively in the Hebrew Scriptures, including the writings of David, Jeremiah, Isaiah, Daniel, Ezra, Nehemiah, Joel, Zechariah, Micah, and Hosea. Jesus directly quoted from some of these to confirm the importance of mercy (Matt. 9:13; 12:7).

But here's the problem: a quick look through the relevant sections of law in the books of Exodus, Leviticus, Numbers, and Deuteronomy reveals little mention of mercy in the actual codified laws. If mercy was such a "weightier" matter of the law, why was it something that the Pharisees, and even people today, have difficulty finding in the Mosaic law?

People's impression of the law of Moses is one of very little mercy.

Understanding the Role of Law

To understand the perceived lack of mercy in the law, we must first address a fundamental misunderstanding about law. It was a point the Pharisees failed to understand and one that still confuses people today. It has to do with the purpose of law.

The Pharisees did not find the weightier matter of mercy in the law because that's not the purpose of law. Mercy has to do with *how a law is administered* and is outside the written law itself.

This is easily demonstrated by looking at how law codes are written. Most societies document their laws in a broadly similar style. Usually the law is presented in either a positive or negative sense and followed by a range of penalties for noncompliance. As an example, here are a sampling of codified laws related to murder:

Code of Hammurabi:

> 22. If any one is committing a robbery and is caught, then he shall be put to death.[1]

Law of Moses:

> Whoever kills a person, the murderer shall be put to death on the testimony of witnesses. (Num. 35:30)

King Alfred the Great English Law Code

> 13. The man who intentionally slays another man let him suffer death.[2]

18 United States Law Code § 1111 – Murder:

> Whoever is guilty of murder in the first degree shall be punished by death or by imprisonment for life.[3]

State of Queensland, Australia. Criminal Law Code:

> 305 Punishment of murder (1) Any person who commits the crime of murder is liable to imprisonment for life, which cannot be mitigated or varied under this Code or any other law or is liable to an indefinite sentence under part 10 of the Penalties and Sentences Act 1992.[4]

Mercy has to do with how a law is administered and is outside the written law itself.

Even though more could be included from each law code, the core idea is the same: 1) The law is presented, followed by 2) the potential penalties for noncompliance. Broadly speaking, this is how all laws are defined. Note the lack of any directives for a judge to be merciful.

Mercy is not included because mercy is beyond the scope of the written law itself. Written laws define acceptable or agreed societal behavior. *How* that law

---
[1] Bibliog: (King 2012, Sec. 22)
[2] Bibliog: (Dammery 1991)
[3] Bibliog: (United States Govt 2023, Ch 51. Sec 1111)
[4] Bibliog: (Queensland Government 2023, Ch 28. 305)

will be administered is a separate matter. Whether a judge is harsh or merciful in the application of the law will depend on the values of the society they represent, and to a lesser degree, the values they personally hold.

A study of the massive United States Law Code, for example, outlines thousands of pages of detailed legislation and penalties under various jurisdictions. To determine how mercifully a particular law should be applied in practice, one would need to look *outside* the written law to the expectations and values of the American people.

In a democracy, the ultimate lawgiver is the people. Judges and officials in America are expected to uphold the standards of justice and mercy that the people (the lawgiver) expect. Judges have been granted the discretion to enforce laws either to the prescribed penalty or to mercifully reduce the penalty based on the circumstances of the situation. We occasionally see an outcry when judges are too harsh or too lenient relative to community expectations.

The key point to restate is this: the law exists to tell a person what they can or cannot do. It has no mercy within itself. This is why law of itself is harsh and hard. This is something Paul wrote about in his epistles. He explained that the law is how we know right and wrong, but of itself, it is a harsh judge (Rom. 3:19–20; 7:7–12). If we are relying on the letter of the law to save us, we have no hope. Shakespeare beautifully expressed this thought in his play *The Merchant of Venice*:

> *Whether a judge is harsh or merciful in the administration of the law will depend on the values of the society.*

> In the course of justice none of us should see salvation.
> We do pray for mercy. [5]

Understanding this simple principle is at the heart of the Christian message of redemption. The law has never, and never will, save anyone. To negate a penalty of the law requires the intervention of a merciful judge. This is why Jesus called mercy a *weightier* (more important) matter. This is where Pharisees went wrong with their understanding of the law of Moses. They lost sight of the values of the Lawgiver and focused solely on the written words. And anyone today reading the law of Moses without seeking to know the heart and mind of the Lawgiver will also lose perspective. It is why the first great

---

[5] Bibliog: (Shakespeare 2015, *Merchant of Venice* Act 4. Scene 1.)

commandment of the law is to know and love God deeply (Deut. 6:5–6). Only then can the correct application of the law be understood.

God's Mercy Clearly Evident

Administrators of the law of Moses were supposed to emulate the merciful example of God, the supreme authority of the nation. And God's mercy is noted hundreds of times throughout the Hebrew Scriptures and is presented as one of his most important attributes. His mercy is an extension to his loving nature and is described in remarkable terms such as "abundant," "from everlasting to everlasting," "as far as east is from west," and "reaching to the heavens" (Ps. 103:8, 11, 17; 57:10). God's mercy is not given begrudgingly or reluctantly because he delights in the opportunity to be merciful:

God's mercy is noted hundreds of times throughout the Hebrew Scriptures.

> Who is a God like You, pardoning iniquity and passing over the transgression of the remnant of His heritage? He does not retain His anger forever, because *He delights in mercy.* (Mic. 7:18)

His mercy toward the people of Israel was evident from Egypt and all through the wilderness years:

> For the LORD your God is a merciful God, He will not forsake you nor destroy you, nor forget the covenant of your fathers which He swore to them. (Deut. 4:31)

In line with Jesus' principle of forgiving "seventy times seven" (Matt. 18:21–22), God forgave Israel repeatedly throughout their long history:

> He, being full of compassion, forgave their iniquity, and did not destroy them. *Yes, many a time He turned His anger away,* and did not stir up all His wrath; for He remembered that they were but flesh, a breath that passes away and does not come again. (Ps. 78:38–39)

God's willingness to forgive the worst of Israel's sins was extraordinary. Even as the prophets warned the nation of the disastrous road they were on, God continued to express his great desire for them to turn around:

> "Come now, and let us reason together," says the LORD, "Though your sins are like scarlet, they shall be as white as snow; though they are red like crimson, they shall be as wool." (Isa. 1:18)

Not only would he forgive if they changed their course, but he also promised to erase their sins from his memory:

> I, even I, am He who blots out your transgressions for My own sake; and *I will not remember your sins*. (Isa. 43:25)

Even in their dying days as a nation, after centuries of rejecting him and becoming morally bankrupt, God still held out the offer of mercy to his people if they would only turn around:

> Go and proclaim these words toward the north, and say: "Return, backsliding Israel," says the LORD; "I will not cause My anger to fall on you. *For I am merciful,*" *says the LORD; "I will not remain angry forever.*" (Jer. 3:12)

It was only because of God's great mercy that the nation survived what would otherwise have been its total destruction:

> Through the LORD'S mercies we are not consumed, because His compassions fail not. (Lam. 3:22)

This is the way God has always operated, *"showing mercy to thousands"* who have sinned (Exod. 20:6). The Israelites were told to *walk in all the ways* of their merciful and gracious God and lawgiver and be like him:

> And now, Israel, what does the LORD your God require of you, but to fear the LORD your God, *to walk in all His ways* and to love Him, to serve the LORD your God with all your heart and with all your soul. (Deut. 10:12)

God's merciful character was the standard that was supposed to guide leaders and judges in their administration of the law. The ceremonial system confirmed the central importance of mercy, with atonement and forgiveness at the heart of the worship system. Israelites, both individually and collectively, were able to come to the tabernacle and call on God's mercy.

Unfortunately, righteous leaders in Israel were few and far between, and even some of the "heroes of faith" were far from perfect in their administration of the law. This is again why we must refer to the Lawgiver (God) himself, to understand his intent.

Jesus' Mercy in Action

One incident in Jesus' ministry is often presented as contrasting old and new standards of mercy. It concerned the woman accused of adultery. The

Pharisees brought the woman before Jesus intending to accuse him of breaking the law. Here's what they said:

> "Teacher, this woman was caught in adultery, in the very act. Now *Moses, in the law, commanded us that such should be stoned.* But what do You say?" This they said, testing Him, that they might have *something of which to accuse Him.* (John 8:4–6)

The situation was clearly a setup with the guilty man nowhere in sight. Their complaint wasn't really about the woman—their target was Jesus (John 8:3–6). This situation is sometimes presented as Jesus countermanding the unforgiving Mosaic laws of stoning, but there is much more to be understood here.

Firstly, if we simply look at the matter of judgment, the Pharisees were out of line. As Jesus said elsewhere, he was not a judge (Luke 12:14). Capital punishment under the law of Moses could only be authorized by a court of law where due process was followed with multiple witnesses. And at that time under Roman law the Pharisees had no authority to put people to death, something they later acknowledged (John 18:31).

Secondly it is often assumed that the mercy Jesus showed to the woman was some sort of new idea not allowed for in the law of Moses. But this is incorrect. Jesus rebuked the Pharisees multiple times for not understanding the central importance of mercy in the law (e.g., Matt. 9:13; 23:23). It was a blind spot in their understanding. Immediately after the incident with the woman, Jesus said to them:

> You know neither Me nor My Father. If you had known Me, you would have known My Father also. (John 8:19)

Thirdly, there was a fundamental flaw in the Pharisee's statement when they said: "Moses in the law *commanded* that such should be stoned." They were clearly implying that the penalty of the law had to be enforced at all times. In their way of reasoning a judge who was merciful would be breaking the law. This is a *totally false premise* on their part.

The Penalty of a Law Is Not a Law

The Pharisees saw the prescribed penalty for adultery written in the law and took it as a *mandatory penalty* that must be enforced to the letter. Note that the Pharisees were going to accuse Jesus of breaking the law if he didn't *command* the woman to be stoned. Their premise was false. A perspective like that will make any law, not just the law of Moses, sound harsh. The Pharisees wrongly confused the *penalty* of the law with the law itself. They thought that *not* stoning the woman was to break the law of Moses. But whether a prescribed maximum penalty of the law is enforced or not has nothing to do with breaking the law. Note the law in question:

> The man who commits adultery with another man's wife, he who commits adultery with his neighbor's wife, the adulterer and the adulteress, shall surely be put to death. (Lev. 20:10)

The law against adultery is one of the ten commandments, and while this strong penalty is a *guideline* for a judge as to the serious nature of the offense, it is not a law unto itself.[6] The law specifically allowed for divorce in the case of sexual impropriety (Deut. 24:1). A spouse didn't have to make the matter public in the first place—it could be sorted out privately.

The Pharisees wrongly confused the penalty of the law with the law itself.

If the matter did come to court, the judge had the authority to apply wisdom and discernment to all such matters—and the matter could only be settled after due process was followed. This required a prosecutor to present charges, witnesses to be called, and the judge to verify the facts of the case. The judge then had to determine what penalty to apply. Justice is *righteous judgment*. Sometimes it was right and proper to apply the full penalty of the law to high-handed sinners. At other times justice required mercy.

We have God's own example of King David. Despite David committing adultery and premeditated murder (sins clearly defined as deserving the death penalty), God saw David's repentant heart and said through Nathan that "The LORD has also put away your sin and you shall not die" (2 Sam. 12:13). Bathsheba was also spared. The intent of the law is a changed heart, and it is a judge's prerogative to be merciful and not exact the highest penalty.

Sometimes the full force of the law was applied, but there are also many examples in Scripture where God did not enforce the penalty of the law. Those who take the time to read the entire Old Testament thoroughly will find an overwhelming impression of his mercy, compassion, patience, and kindness. When God saw the heart of a person or the people had changed, he so often

---

[6] In some translations of the Torah, an emphatic "surely" or "must" is used in relation to penalties. It can give the impression that the penalties were mandatory. It is better understood that the emphasis in Hebrew is simply confirming the serious nature of the offence.

relented from the punishment that he rightly and justly was going to dispense. As David acknowledged:

> The Lord *is* merciful and gracious, Slow to anger, and abounding in mercy. ...He has *not dealt with us according to our sins, Nor punished us according to our iniquities*. (Ps. 103:8-10)

God's application of mercy was supposed to set the example for righteous judges to follow.

Example of Joseph and Mary

Contrast how the Pharisees thought about the law with the attitude of righteous Joseph—Jesus' earthly father who lived under the old covenant. When Mary was found pregnant, it must have come as a terrible shock to Joseph. Yet his reaction was not to drag Mary before the religious leaders as some public spectacle:

> After His mother Mary was betrothed to Joseph, before they came together, she was found with child of the Holy Spirit. Then Joseph her husband, *being a just man*, and not wanting to make her a public example, was minded to *put her away secretly*. (Matt. 1:18–19)

Notice that Joseph, a man *living under the law of Moses*, is called a *just* man. Justice under the law of Moses didn't always require punishment. Justice is doing what is *right*. At times a just outcome was to offer mercy to someone who was not high-handedly breaking the law. Joseph may have been shocked, even angry, but he also knew Mary's humble demeanor. He knew she was no high-handed sinner. As a just man, Joseph rightly understood that there was a time when discreetly dealing with a matter was the right thing to do.

> *Justice under the law of Moses didn't always require punishment. Justice is doing what is right.*

God wanted mercy to be one of the foundational pillars of the law of Moses. The Pharisees missed the weightier matter of mercy because they failed to look beyond the law to the righteous standards of the Lawgiver and his overall purpose and intent for the law. God has always been primarily interested in exacting repentance and a changed heart, not punishment.

The Importance of Faith

Trust in Him at all times, you people; pour out your heart before Him; God is a refuge for us. —Psalm 62:8

Jesus identified faith as a weightier or foundational matter of the law of Moses (Matt. 23:23). It is important to understand what Jesus meant by that statement because there is confusion concerning faith and its relationship to the law.

Faith in itself is not a difficult concept to understand. Faith in simple terms has to do with trusting and believing. The writer of Hebrews emphasizes how important faith is to God:

> ***Without faith it is impossible to please Him***, for he who comes to God must believe that He is, and that He is a rewarder of those who *diligently* seek Him. (Heb. 11:6)

The faith God is looking for goes beyond simply acknowledging his existence. As it states, God wants believers to *diligently* seek him, trusting in him for their ultimate reward. Faith is *action oriented*. It is not a feeling; it is a choice—a choice to put our trust totally in him.

God has never changed. Faith was foundational to his relationship with ancient Israel just as it is with a believer today.

God has never changed. Faith was foundational to his relationship with ancient Israel just as it is with a believer today. Without Israel putting their faith in God and demonstrating that trust by their actions as their father Abraham had done, it was impossible to have a successful relationship with him.

Why Faith Is Foundational

Faith in biblical terms is *trust*. Trust and love go hand in hand. There can be no depth in any relationship that lacks trust. Love by itself does not always build relationships. We can show love to our enemies, but we would never trust them. We can show love to another person even when they are unaware of that love. But when trust is present, a deep, two-way loving relationship can develop and flourish. This is what God was looking for from Israel.

From the outset, trusting in God was Israel's biggest hurdle. God had proven himself trustworthy, and he wanted Israel's confidence and loyalty in return. Yet despite overwhelming evidence of his faithfulness, they refused to believe him and continually doubted his ability to protect them.

From their perspective, the question was never "Does God exist?" as people query today, because his existence was patently obvious. No one in early Israel who witnessed the series of incredible miracles and interventions, as they did, could doubt God's existence. Even the pagan nations knew the God of Israel existed and feared him (Josh. 2:11). Israel's problem was believing and acting on what God said.

The first generation out of Egypt so distrusted God that they missed out on the promised land and died in the wilderness. God could have made their journey through the wilderness easier, but he wanted the people to learn to trust him and acknowledge that he alone was the true source of life:

> So He humbled you, allowed you to hunger, and fed you with manna which you did not know nor did your fathers know, *that He might make you know that man shall not live by bread alone*; but man lives by every word that proceeds from the mouth of the LORD. (Deut. 8:3)

This was not a one-time-only lesson. Even after entering the promised land, God wanted Israel to be permanently reminded of the importance of relying on him. The land he had chosen was a good land but required God's providence to be viable:

> For the land which you go to possess is *not* like the land of Egypt from which you have come, where you sowed your seed and watered it by foot, as a vegetable garden; but the land which you cross over to possess is a land of hills and valleys, which drinks water from the rain of heaven ... And it shall be that if you earnestly obey My commandments which I command you today ... then I will give you the rain for your land in its season, the early rain and the latter rain, that you may gather in your grain, your new wine, and your oil. (Deut. 11:10–11, 13–14)

God wanted to bless these people greatly, but they had to make the decision to put their confidence in him. The proof that they trusted him would be their *obedience* to the way of life he had outlined in his law. They would be a special treasure to him above all other people—but *only if* they did what he asked:

> Now therefore, *if* you will indeed obey My voice and keep My covenant, then you shall be a special treasure to Me above all people. (Exod. 19:5)

Israel's obedience was never about proving how righteous they were. On the contrary, it was an acknowledgment that without God, they were nothing.

Keeping the Law Required Faith

The strong connection between faith and the law of Moses is evident in many other provisions of the law.

The first commandment required that Israel put God first and exclude all other gods (Exod. 20:2–3). This would have been a daunting proposition for the Israelites. They had grown up with multiple gods in Egypt, and they would later be tempted by the many gods of Canaan. Trusting in only one God was at odds with the other cultures of the day and would require much faith.

> *The strong connection between faith and the law of Moses is evident in many provisions of the law.*

God also wanted Israel to trust him as their invisible king instead of a human king (Deut. 17:14). This again was a big ask. All the nations around them had a visible king who established the army and led them into battle. God, on the other hand, wanted Israel to rely on him to fight their battles (Deut. 20:4).

Faith was at the heart of other key aspects of the law. Resting on the Sabbath would require confidence in God that losing a day's work would not be disadvantageous. In the same way, resting the land from harvest every seven years, forgiving debts, freeing servants, tithing, etc. would all rely heavily on God's providence and directly test their faith in God.

Just as they had to do in the wilderness, God wanted them to live by faith and he promised great rewards if they did so:

> Now it shall come to pass, *if you diligently obey the voice of the LORD your God*, to observe carefully all His commandments which I command you today, that the LORD your God will set you high above all nations of the earth. And all these blessings shall come upon you and overtake you, because you obey the voice of the LORD your God. (Deut. 28:1–2)

These promised blessings would include preeminence above other nations, blessed cities and farms, healthy children, bumper crops, livestock, protection from enemies, bountiful harvests, prosperity, leadership among nations etc. (Deut. 28:1-14; Lev. 26:1-13). Such incredible outcomes would not be possible without God's intervention. Yet God confidently said, "put your *trust in me*" and great things will happen.

Keeping the law was not a demonstration of "trusting in themselves" as it is sometimes presented. Quite the opposite, keeping the law was a demonstration of trusting in God. Even if they had somehow kept the law perfectly, the promised blessings could only come from a great God who had the ability to bestow such blessings.

> *Even if they had somehow kept the law perfectly, promised blessings could only come from a great God who had the ability to bestow such blessings.*

Faithfulness was Possible

It is often said that Israel had no hope of living up to God's high ideals. If that statement implies Israel had to be perfect in law-keeping, then it is correct. But God was not expecting perfection from these people. He has never expected perfection from any human being. But he did expect Israel to be faithful to him as their One True God, and when they sinned (which they surely would), he would forgive them when they turned humbly back to him.

The lives of Abraham, Isaac, and Jacob demonstrate this well. The fathers of the faithful were far from perfect, but never wavered in their commitment to God. These men, and many other imperfect people, are a part of that great cloud of witnesses listed in Hebrews that demonstrate what faith in God looks like in practice (Heb. 11; 12:1). It was not an impossible goal.

Even without the Holy Spirit being widely available under the old covenant, the Old Testament record shows that thousands did indeed maintain a loyal heart that was pleasing to God. Nothing prevented them from doing so. While they were a minority, people like Abel, Enoch, Job, Noah, Joseph, Rahab, Ruth, Hannah, Nehemiah, and many others decided to trust in God and were greatly rewarded. Several kings of Judah made the same decision to be faithful. David, Asa, Jehoshaphat, Hezekiah, and Josiah trusted in God and received his blessing. None of these were perfect. Evil King Manasseh turned to God in deep remorse late in his life, and God respected his repentance.

Even at the time when most of northern Israel was turned over to paganism, God told Elijah that a remnant of seven thousand people was still loyal and reserved to him (1 Kings 19:18). Many thousands of others under the reigns of the god-fearing judges and kings also turned to God. From the time of Joshua through to the return from exile, thousands, if not tens of thousands, of unnamed people had a humble heart that was loyal to God. So clearly, it was possible to be faithful and receive God's favor under the old covenant.

The Just Shall Live by Faith

We come back to the starting point. Trusting God is not a feeling—it's a choice. It was a choice for ancient Israel just as it is a choice for a person today. A believer *must* have faith to please God. Such faith is not blind or mindless. By definition, faith is based on *substance* and *evidence*:

> *Trusting God is not a feeling—it's a choice.*

> Now faith is the *substance* of things hoped for, the *evidence* of things not seen. (Heb. 11:1)

The evidence of God's faithfulness was right in front of Israel, and it's still visible for those who have eyes to see today. Israel ignored the evidence before them, hardened their hearts against God, and grieved him:

> *Do not harden your hearts*, as in the rebellion, as in the day of trial in the wilderness, when your fathers tested Me; they tried Me, though they saw My work. For forty years I was grieved with that generation, and said, "It is a people *who go astray in their hearts*, and they do not know My ways." (Ps. 95:8–10)

There will never be enough proof for a hard or skeptical heart. That is why a soft and childlike heart is so important to God. Faith is a matter of deciding to trust in God based on the evidence of creation, his intervention in history, the testimony of others, and God's personal involvement in a person's life. Faithfulness is staying the course when the going gets tough and during times of doubt. Quoting from the Old Testament prophet Habakkuk, the writer of Hebrews writes:

> *Now the just shall live by faith; but if anyone draws back, My soul has no pleasure in him.* (Heb. 10:38)

It takes courage and determination to hold fast to God, but the reward on offer is truly great.

The Centrality of the Family

You are the children of the LORD your God ... and the LORD has chosen you to be a people for Himself, a special treasure above all the peoples who are on the face of the earth. —Deuteronomy 14:1–2

God's plan was for the family, not the state, to be the central organizing unit of Israelite society. To emphasize the importance of family, God included familial laws at the heart of the Ten Commandments. The family-oriented directives to *honor your father and mother, not to commit adultery*, and *not to covet another's spouse* were key commandments designed to protect and strengthen marriage and the family unit. The Mosaic judgments then went further, with extensive moral guidelines and principles reinforcing family values.

But God had a far bigger picture in mind for family, one that went beyond the physical into the spiritual realm. Even in Moses' day the family structure was understood to be a type of greater reality that God had in the making. Understanding the great spiritual significance God places on family helps explain why the law was so strong in its focus on family values.

> *Even in Moses' day, the family structure was understood to be a type of greater reality that God had in the making.*

God's Intent for Family

Throughout all of history and across all cultures, no greater social bond has existed between people than that of family. The origins of the family go back long before Israel to the garden of Eden when God first ordained marriage and the family structure (Gen. 2:18–24; Matt. 19:4–6).

God wanted man to lead and protect his family in a loving and respectful relationship with his wife and lifelong partner. Men and women were designed to be complementary in their makeup, and together as "one flesh," provide the perfect environment for children to feel secure and grow to their God-given potential. Children were to honor, obey, and love both parents in return.

God wanted the family unit to be a bastion of love where the husband, wife, and children all flourished under his guiding hand. God's own example of faithful love was the benchmark for all husbands in ancient Israel (Deut. 4:37; Jer. 31:3; Hosea 11:4). As the nation's spiritual father, God had shown Israel extraordinary love, mercy, care, and patience (Deut. 1:31; 10:15). Israel also had the example of their founding fathers. Although Abraham, Isaac and Jacob had their failings, their love for their wives and families was beyond dispute. Consider Abraham's great love for Sarah, Isaac's love for Rebekah, and Jacob's love for Rachel, where he worked fourteen years for her hand in marriage (Gen. 29:18, 20).

The consistent focus on family throughout Scripture confirms God's unchanging view of the importance of the family structure.[1]

Family in Ancient Israel

God's plan for family in ancient Israel went beyond the immediate nuclear family and blood relatives. Family was built into the social structure at every level. Each Israelite knew their wider family clan and the specific tribe they belonged to (Num. 1; 2:2; 4:46). Fellow Israelites were generally referred to as "brethren," and the familial term "elders" described the leaders of the clans and tribes (Num. 11:16; Lev. 25:25; Deut. 1:16). This structure was not new at Sinai. Elders were the respected tribal leaders long before Israel left Egypt (Exod. 3:16).

Respect of the elders started with the commandment for children to honor their parents:

> Honor your father and your mother, that your days may be long upon the land which the LORD your God is giving you. (Exod. 20:12)

Building on this commandment, the law of Moses directed that all the elderly were to be honored and respected:

> You shall rise before the gray-headed and honor the presence of an old man, and fear your God: I am the LORD. (Lev. 19:32)

Just like the command to *love one's neighbor as oneself*, honoring parents and respecting the elderly was not to be subject to a person's emotions. God wanted them honored whether they were "worthy" of honor or not. A society that honors and respects its elders will be a more caring and stable society and bring God's blessing on the nation.

---

[1] Some critics highlight the lack of marriage ceremony specifics in the law of Moses as an oversight. But marriage had been a part of society since creation, and there was no need to include such details. Like many other aspects of life, God let the ceremonial format be determined by the culture of the day. As an example, long before Moses, Laban held a weeklong feast celebrating Jacob's marriage to his daughters (Gen. 29:22).

The importance of family in God's eyes continued into the New Testament era. Jesus reemphasized the command to honor parents and strengthened the commands against adultery and sexual immorality (Matt. 15:4; Luke 18:20; Matt. 5:27–28; 19:8–9). The role of elders continued within the church, as did the use of the term "brethren" among believers (Titus 1:5; 1 Cor. 1:10). Paul later reminded the church that the fifth commandment was the first with a promise (Eph. 6:1–3).

God's Design for Marriage

Through the prophet Malachi, God confirmed how seriously he viewed marriage. He saw it as the place where children would learn of him and the means by which he would gain godly offspring:

> But did He not make them one, having a remnant of the Spirit? And why one? *He seeks godly offspring*. Therefore take heed to your spirit, and let none deal treacherously with the wife of his youth. (Mal. 2:15)

Jesus made it clear that it was always God's design for marriage that *one* man and *one* woman would become one flesh for life (Matt. 19:4–6). Divorce and polygamy were never God's ideal at any time in history. But sin had entered the world and compromises were made. The Mosaic law therefore regulated, but did not encourage, such practices.

The divorce provisions included in the law were aimed at protecting a broken family from further damage. If someone was divorced and took another spouse, the law prohibited them from returning to their original partner (Deut. 24:1–4). This would make a couple think seriously before a breakup, realizing it was permanent. It also prevented people from using divorce and remarriage as a "legal" facade for sexual escapades.

Often people point to the polygamous behavior of the Old Testament patriarchs and assume that such behavior was approved by God. But as highlighted earlier, that is a false inference. The Bible is an honest record of the history of Israel and portrays many negative distortions and interpretations of the Old Testament law. We also consistently see in Scripture the negative consequences in the lives of those who practiced polygamous relationships.[2]

---

[2] Polygamous behavior included the practice of acquiring concubines. A concubine's main role was to provide a man with progeny without carrying the full status of wife. While the practice of taking concubines was copied from the nations around them, it was not encouraged in the law of Moses. The law made no allowance for a second-class level of wife. From the law's perspective a concubine was a wife.

While a case is made by some that the law does specifically forbid polygamy,[3] there was one scenario in the law where it seems to be presented in a positive light. But in this case the circumstances are dramatically different. It is called a levirate marriage. A levirate marriage was not driven by a man's desire for more wives—it was included for the preservation of family and protection of a vulnerable woman (Deut. 25:5–10). If a woman was left a widow and had no surviving sons to preserve her husband's name and inheritance, she had the right to call on her husbands near kinsman to take her as his wife. It was her decision, not the man's, to do so.[4]

> *Divorce and polygamy were never God's ideal at any time in history.*

Spiritual Typology

The family structure also reflected how the God of Israel wanted to be understood in a spiritual sense. Although he was not formally called the "Father" under the old covenant, the God of Israel was still understood to be the father of the nation. In Egypt, God described the nation of Israel as his firstborn son:

> Thus says the Lord: "Israel *is* My son, My firstborn." (Exod. 4:22)

Moses later reminded the people that the God of Israel was their father, and they were his children:

> You are the children of the LORD your God. (Deut. 14:1)

> Do you thus deal with the LORD, O foolish and unwise people? Is He not your Father, who bought you? Has He not made you and established you? (Deut. 32:6)

The later prophets also emphasized God's fatherly role over the nation (1 Chron. 29:10; Jer. 31:9; Isa. 64:8):

> Doubtless You are our Father, though Abraham was ignorant of us, and Israel does not acknowledge us. You, O LORD, are our Father; our Redeemer from Everlasting is Your name. (Isa. 63:16)

---

[3] It has been argued that the law does specifically forbid polygamy (Lev. 18:18). Most interpret this verse to be a directive against a man marrying 2 literal sisters. But the case is made that the Hebrew may be referring to women in general. Bibliog: (Wilbur 2016-2022)

[4] Discussed further in the chapter *The Redeeming Kinsman*.

The God of Israel was also described in marriage terms as a 'husband' to an unfaithful nation (Jer. 31:32). A husband who was faithful and loving, willing to forgive—even when his wife had gone astray (Jer. 3:14).

Loving and Fearing God

Understanding God as a loving parent puts the fear of God into the proper perspective. A major difference between the God of Israel and the pagan religions of the day is that God wanted his relationship based on love, not fear. Unlike the pagan gods who were to be feared and appeased, God wanted to love and to be loved. This has enormous ramifications. A strong leader who loves his people and is loved in return creates a confident, bold, and secure people. Leaders who operate on these principles inspire their people to do great things. They motivate and empower their people to surpass anything a controlling relationship can ever attain. As the apostle John wrote, "There is no fear in love" (1 John 4:18).

Understanding God as a loving parent put the fear of God into the proper perspective.

Unhealthy fear in any group of people—whether a nation, a corporation, or a religious institution—points to something deeply wrong in the hierarchy. People who know they are loved and who love in return are, by nature, secure and bold. They are confident because they know where they stand. There is enormous resilience in a strong relationship based on love. It is liberating.

Many people have questioned how a person can both love and fear God at the same time. Moses saw no contradiction to this idea and mentioned the fear of God *right alongside* the requirement to love God with all the heart:

> And now, Israel, what does the LORD your God require of you, but to *fear the LORD your God*, to walk in all His ways *and to love Him*, to serve the LORD your God with all your heart and with all your soul, and to keep the commandments of the LORD and His statutes which I command you today for your good? (Deut. 10:12–13)

This sort of fear was a positive fear—an awe and respect for the great God who had done so much for them and was offering them a great future. Moses contrasts a negative fear of God (dread) with the correct fear of God (reverence) in a statement he makes at Mount Sinai, telling Israel *not to fear* but at the same time to have the *right* positive fear:

> And Moses said to the people, "*Do not fear*; for God has come to test you, and *that His fear may be before you*, so that you may not sin." (Exod. 20:20)

The perfect place to demonstrate positive fear working with love is within a family. How many tall, strong sons have stood in fear of their diminutive mother because they've done something wrong? A respectful fear of disappointing a parent is a healthy thing in a loving family. Such a family has no difficulty understanding that the disciplining of a son or daughter is an expression of love for the child's good. A parent takes no delight in such correction. Neither did God express delight in having to correct Israel. It was, in fact, an expression of God's love when he corrected the children of Israel whom he loved:

> You should know in your heart that as a man chastens his son, so the LORD your God chastens you. (Deut. 8:5)

> For whom the LORD loves He corrects, just as a father the son in whom he delights. (Prov. 3:12)

The family structure is critical to a correct understanding of the sort of relationship God was desiring. The proper fear of God as a Father is the beginning of wisdom and a great enabler (Ps. 111:10). As the saying goes, "Fear God, and you'll need fear nothing else."

Family Shadows God's Greater Purpose

Family has always been important to God because it shadows the great spiritual purpose he has for human beings. When God decreed in Genesis that he was making male and female in his own image, he clearly had something extraordinary in mind. And while the Hebrew Scriptures hint as to what this actually meant, the deeper understanding of God's purpose was a mystery for those of old, only revealed by the later New Testament writers. They show that God's ultimate desire all along has been to have a family of his own and to bring many children to spiritual glory:

Family shadows the great spiritual purpose God has for human beings.

> For the earnest expectation of the creation eagerly waits for the revealing of the sons of God ... into the glorious liberty of the children of God. (Rom. 8:19, 21)

> But as many as received Him, to them He gave the right to become children of God, to those who believe in His name. (John 1:12)

Jesus wanted believers to understand that they are being invited to be children in a spiritual family (Matt. 5:9)—God the Father, as the head of the family, and Jesus as the firstborn son and elder brother (Matt. 28:10; Heb. 2:11).

There is a tendency to read these statements as mere analogies, but a deeper look shows that it is *our family structures that are the analogy of a far greater reality*. God gave the family structure right at the outset of creation so that humans could come to understand the nature of the relationship that he desires between us and him as our father.

It is highly significant that the great God in heaven desires to be called "Father" by those who turn to him (Matt. 6:9; John 14). He could have selected a title of the kind used by great kings and conquerors in history, but he instead chose the familial term "father." And not "father" in a formal sense, but one denoting warm intimacy, as in *my personal* father. This is reflected in the affectionate term *abba* that Jesus used when addressing his Father (Mark 14:36; Rom. 8:15; Gal. 4:6). Believers are invited to the same intimacy:

> And because you are sons, God has sent forth the Spirit of His Son into your hearts, crying out, "Abba, Father!" Therefore you are no longer a slave but a son, and if a son, then an heir of God through Christ. (Gal. 4:6–7)

This is the deeper explanation of God's original desire to make man "in his own image"—to create a family of like-minded individuals sharing common values and bound by a deep and unshakeable love.

> Behold what manner of love the Father has bestowed on us, that we should be called children of God! Therefore the world does not know us, because it did not know Him. (1 John 3:1)

Paul goes further and explains the selfless love a husband should have for his wife as a type of how Christ loved the church and gave himself for her (Eph. 5:22–33). He calls marriage a great mystery explained by the spiritual plan of God:

> For we are members of His body, of His flesh and of His bones. "For this reason a man shall leave his father and mother and be joined to his wife, and the two shall become one flesh." This is a great mystery, but I speak concerning Christ and the church. Nevertheless let each

one of you in particular so love his own wife as himself, and let the wife see that she respects her husband. (Eph. 5:30–33)

The final fruition of this relationship is the future great marriage supper of the Lamb with the purified church as the bride of Christ (the church) being formally married into the spiritual family of God (Rev. 19:9–10).

Even though the full ramification of the meaning of marriage and the family was not understood by the people of old, God had his master plan in mind right from the outset of creation. For this reason, marriage between a man and a woman has always been a sacred institution.

Family Is Foundational

There is no more fundamental structure for society than the family. The law of Moses makes it eminently clear just how important family was. It's a structure that retains its importance to this day. Far from being outdated or retired, Scripture from Genesis to Revelation supports the traditional family structure as God's intent for the core social structure of humankind.

The idea that a family should be based on the marriage of a man and woman who becomes a father and mother does not align well with the "progressive" view of today's society. The requirement for a monogamous, heterosexual relationship is seen as out of step with a modern world that supports family variants and various gender lifestyles and rejects any society where men and women don't have equal opportunities in all roles.

But the rejection of the traditional family structure is not new. Karl Marx and his offsider, Friedrich Engels, spoke strongly against the family in the 1848 *Communist Manifesto*, blaming it as the source of the evil of capitalism. Karl Marx strongly presented his negative views of the family in his manifesto.[5] With socialism and Marxism on the rise today, many are naively unaware of the direct opposition the family structure presents to many modern social justice goals. We are now seeing the state becoming more important than the family and the authority of parents being increasingly challenged. The only way to properly determine what is structurally the best for society is to seek the truth from a God of truth. Anything else is simply a social experiment.

---

[5] Bibliog: (Marx 1848, Ch II 1848)

Women and the Law of Moses

God created man in His own image; in the image of God He created him; male and female. —Genesis 1:27

There is often criticism directed at the law of Moses in relation to women. Some assume that it was God's design for women to be second-class citizens under the Old Testament patriarchal system—that women were to be suppressed and treated as property. Jesus, on the other hand, is seen as a champion for women after centuries of suppression, bringing in a new standard of social behavior that the old law of Moses did not support.

Scripture does not support this contrasting view of the God of Israel and Jesus. The consistent, gracious, and loving God of Israel, the Creator of women, is not, and never has been, a misogynist. And neither did Jesus bring in a new standard of social behavior with the idea of overthrowing a previously bad Mosaic system of law which harmed women. The Creator God has never changed his values or standards.

> *The consistent, gracious, and loving God of Israel, the Creator of women, is not, and never has been, a misogynist.*

Jesus instead came to restore the *law's original intent*, including how women were to be respected and treated. Society had gone off the rails—not just in Israel but in an entire world that had rejected the earlier revelation of God. As has been emphasized multiple times, what we have in the Old Testament is an honest record of the history of humankind and the nation of Israel. But it does not represent the ideal. It contains some shocking stories of failure and abuse by all sorts of people, including by some notables of the Bible. None of this was God's will or desire. From the outset, humans have always pushed against God with tragic results.

When properly understood, the law of Moses was a strong advocate for women at a time in history when women were vulnerable and often mistreated. Those who criticize specific aspects of the law relating to women often fail to understand the social and cultural contexts in which these laws were given. But it is not valid to project our current modern standards on the ancient world and demand that their society conform to ours. It was an entirely different time and place.

Equal in the Eyes of God

God's overall perspective of women was made clear at creation when he stated that *both* male and female equally bore his image, and *both* were to have dominion over the earth (Gen. 1:27–28).[1] From the beginning, men and women have always been of equal value in his sight. His ultimate goal is to have both men and women be part of his spiritual family (John 1:12; 2 Cor. 6:18; 1 John 3:1).

When God created woman, he made her as a helper to man, not as man's property (Gen. 2:18). Nothing in the Hebrew word "helper" (*ezer*) implies inferiority. When husband and wife come together, it is to be as *one flesh*—not as unbalanced partners but two individuals complementing each other to become one whole (Gen. 2:24). As Paul later explained in a direct reference to Genesis, the original concept of becoming one flesh confirmed

> *From the beginning, men and women have always been of equal value in his sight.*

marriage was designed from the outset to be a close and loving relationship (Eph. 5:31–33). When a man and woman married, the man was to leave his father and mother and establish his own household. His first obligation was now to his wife above all others, even above his parents and family—not a man dominating or lording over the woman but nourishing and cherishing his wife as his own flesh:

> So husbands ought to love their own wives as their own bodies; he who loves his wife loves himself. (Eph. 5:28)

God has never changed. This is the type of relationship between a man and a woman God envisaged at creation and what he desired for marriages in both ancient Israel and today.

God's Respect for Women

The Hebrew Scriptures present a God who was as respectful of women as Jesus

---

[1] The Hebrew words translated "man" in English Bibles is often an inclusive reference to both male and female. As an example, God created "man" in his own image and then notes that this includes both male and female (Gen. 1:27). In the phrase "When a man shall have" in Leviticus 13:2, "man" is a reference to any person. The term was not meant to be sexist. The context generally makes it clear. English has also had a similar usage of the word man (e.g., "mankind," "manmade," etc.), although it is now being phased out in favor of gender-neutral words. *Vines Expository of Old Testament Words* offers a further explanation of the use of the Hebrew words translated "man". Bibliog: (Vine, 146 Man)

was. And we have many examples and interactions to study.

Even before they left Egypt, God singled out the Hebrew midwives for their faith and specifically provided for them (Exod. 1:15–21). The story of Rahab also demonstrates God's respect for a woman of faith (Josh. 2). When Rahab courageously protected the spies, the men made an agreement with her that her entire household would be protected, including her parents and siblings. Despite Rahab being a Canaanite living in a doomed city, God upheld the spies' arrangement and miraculously ensured that Rahab and her family were protected. God has never been a respecter of persons. He has always taken notice of any person who turned to him, whether male, female, child, foreigner, or Israelite. Rahab's inclusion in the lineage of Jesus says it all (Matt. 1:5).

God's appointment of Deborah as a judge and prophetess of Israel is particularly noteworthy (Judg. 4:4–5). God fully supported Deborah in that role by the events that occurred during her tenure. God gave Deborah the gift of wisdom and insight and revealed to her a prophecy that Israel would be successful if they warred against the Canaanites. Deborah had enough status in the community to be able to summon the leading army commander, Barak. Barak was no coward, but he refused to go to battle without Deborah coming with them (v. 8). Because of Deborah's faith and leadership, God delivered a great victory (Judg. 5).

Scripture notes other prophetesses, Miriam being the first (Exod. 15:20). Later, King Josiah consulted Huldah the prophetess, and God spoke through her (2 Kings 22:14).

There are other interactions of God with women worth noting. God didn't just promise a lineage through Abraham but made it clear that Sarah would be equally a part of that promise (Gen. 17:19). Hannah cried out to God to hear her prayer and made a vow that God heard and graciously responded to (1 Sam. 1:11). And God had no problem when the daughters of Zelophehad strongly complained to him about their inheritance. He graciously admitted they were correct (Num. 27:1–6). Esther became queen and was honored for using her wisdom and courage to save the Jews from annihilation (Esther 4:16).

The last chapter of the book of Proverbs outlines the attributes of a theoretical faithful Israelite woman of the times, and it says a lot about the role of women. Here is a woman who is well respected in the community, is wise, can buy and sell property, organizes business transactions, and is industrious and strong

(Prov. 31:10–31). This picture again counteracts the negative stereotypes so often presented about the ancient world and aligns with how Jesus viewed women in his day.

Women and the Law of Moses

The law includes some key principles related to women that we take for granted today but were unusual for the ancient world.

Firstly, the law makes no distinction between the value of a life of a woman or that of a man (or a child). All people were equal under the law and had the same legal protection. God emphasized multiple times the high importance of the value of *all* human life (e.g., Gen. 9:6; Num. 35:30–34; Deut. 21:1–9). Men and women were also equally held accountable for adultery, which was not the case in many ancient societies (Deut. 22:22).

Secondly, there is no concept in the law of women being second-class citizens. Women were full participants in the civil society. As we saw earlier, women were well respected and could hold important offices in the nation such as judge and prophetess. Women had the right to bring a case directly to the judges and be heard (Num. 27:1–2; 2 Sam. 14:4). Women could buy and sell property (Prov. 31:16).[2]

Thirdly, women were invited to fully participate in the worship system. The old covenant itself was made with all Israel, not just the men (Exod. 24:3; see also Deut. 29:10–12). Women had equal opportunity to assemble with the men at the tabernacle and bring offerings to God (Lev. 5).[3] Women could make Nazarite vows in special dedication to God (Num. 6:2). When the law was taught, it was taught to all—men, women, and children (Deut. 31:12). It was not exclusive to males.[4] All citizens were encouraged to use the law as a guide to life.

Fourthly, within the family, mothers had considerable authority and were to be highly respected. The fifth commandment directed children to equally honor *both* father and mother (Exod. 20:12). This is in contrast to some ancient

---

[2] Note that Naomi became the owner of her husband's land after Elimelech died (Ruth 4:3). The land was to stay within the tribe and family, but it was under Naomi's control to determine how that would be applied.
[3] There is no scriptural indication that the tabernacle or Solomon's Temple separated men and women as later occurred in the Second Temple.
[4] Centuries later under Judaism, men created laws that segregated men and women and diminished women's rights to study the law. Such man-made ideas did not come from the law of Moses. Bibliog: (Keren, Torah Study)

cultures where the eldest son could have authority over his mother.[5] In the same vein, a rebellious child could be punished for disrespecting either parent (Deut. 21:18). The later writer of Proverbs directs a child *not to forsake the law of their mother* (Prov. 1:8; 6:20).

The tenth commandment is sometimes criticized for highlighting the coveting of a woman and not a man (Exod. 20:17). Some draw a long bow and imply that the wife must, therefore, be the chattel of a man to be listed along with other items that are not to be coveted. But the tenth commandment is simply reflecting the reality of life—namely that it is men who have been the main problem when it comes to sexual lust. Men's coveting of women has caused enormous harm throughout history, including being the main drivers behind the pornography industry that so demeans and harms women.

Different Roles for Men and Women

While the equal value of women and men is evident in the law of Moses, God did not intend for women and men to fulfill the same role within the family.

> *God had specific societal structures in mind and wanted a distinction maintained between the sexes.*

God had specific societal structures in mind and wanted a distinction maintained between the sexes. As covered previously, God highly prioritized the family structure as his foundational design for society. This included his design for man to be in the position of leadership in the family and society. We see this reflected in several of the provisions of the law, including in the inheritance laws, and the male role as elders and priests. Paul later confirmed an implied male leadership role in marriage and the family right from the outset of creation (1 Cor. 11:7–12).

As with everything God does, this was done for a greater purpose. God's design was not about power and control. He was not trying to limit or suppress women; *he was putting order into his creation*. A husband and father as the head of the family had great spiritual parallels and he wanted this to be understood.

Our modern culture pushes back at any thought that men and women can't be equal in every role, but such a stance opposes the reality of God's design. Women and men are physically and emotionally different and have strengths that complement each other. Such differences are meant to be celebrated, not

---

[5] The *paterfamilias* law of Rome gave autocratic authority over the entire family to the eldest male.

blurred. It was God's plan that when the two come together in marriage, these differences create a complementary union that was stronger and more complete than the individual male and female involved.

Having differences in roles and jurisdiction does not diminish the value of a person. It has always been God's prerogative to select individuals, groups, and nations for various roles as he has seen fit for his own purpose. A case in point being God's exclusive choice of the tribe of Levi for the priesthood. Levi's selection did not diminish the value of the other tribes; each had their own purpose.

While the biblical position concerning male and female roles within the family is unpopular today, forcing Scripture to align with our current social values is fraught with danger. Scripture is not subservient to culture and it's far more important to align our values with our Creator, and to seek to understand his purpose and intent.

The "Curse" of Eve

While both men and women have participated in the immoral and corrupt behavior of humanity, there is no doubt that women have suffered disproportionally at the hands of man. Some interpret this being the result of God bringing down a "punishment" on women for Eve's involvement in the events of the garden of Eden:

> To the woman He said: "I will greatly multiply your sorrow and your conception; in pain you shall bring forth children; your desire shall be for your husband, and he shall rule over you." (Gen. 3:16)

God's prediction has certainly come true. But the last part of God's curse is not a directive or approval for men to behave domineeringly, nor is it an expression of God's will. God was simply declaring the fruits that will naturally follow from man's rejection of him and the consequences of sin spreading into the world. Adam and Eve were *both* culpable and put under a curse, and the resulting negative effects would be evident from that time forward (Gen. 3:17–19). Pain would come into the world, and life would be much harder for humanity as a whole because of their decision to reject God. The curse for the woman was not the husband's leadership per se; it was a prediction of strife, as men would tend to rule and dominate women instead of treating them as the partner they were designed to be.

The effects of this curse have been evident in all cultures (including ancient Israel) right up to our present day. Even in our modern world, despite education and legislation designed to protect women, women are still abused by men in all sorts of ways including domestic violence, cultural bias, religious suppression, and pornography. This proves that the denigration of women is, and always has been a moral problem. The law of Moses had selfless love as its central value, clearly proving that negative treatment of women has never been God's plan. He has always desired for men to fight against the natural tendency to be domineering, and respectfully treat women the way in which he originally intended.

God's Plan for Society

Ancient Israel is often described as a patriarchal society, but that definition is not strictly correct. A patriarchal society is generally understood to be one where women are excluded from any positions of leadership, and men have total control. As we saw earlier, that's not the society God had in mind. God chose women for key positions of leadership at various times. We also note that in a marriage, the husband had jurisdiction as the head of his family, but this did not extend to other women in the society. Women had no obligation to submit to the general directives of men other than their own husband.

> *The family hierarchy was given to educate humankind on the mind of God and his ultimate plan for humanity.*

God's design for the family hierarchy should not be understood as legalistic "rules" to blindly follow, but as key principles of life given to educate humankind on the mind of God and his ultimate plan for humanity.

The most important overarching principle of all was for each person to put God first above all others (Deut. 6:5). This put the onus on a woman to obey God rather than her husband if the two were in conflict.

Women can and should step up if necessary. The Bible praises those bold and courageous women who rose to the challenge when righteous leadership was required. Rahab was praised for doing what was right and taking command of her entire household; Jael bravely killed Sisera, the Canaanite army commander (Judg. 4:21; 5:24–27); Abigail saw her husband acting foolishly and took command of the situation to avert disaster (1 Sam. 25:2–18). The wise woman of Abel Beth Maachah saved her city from destruction (2 Sam. 20:14–22). God respected these and other courageous women.

Unfortunately, whenever authority is involved, it always has the potential for abuse. But this was never God's idea for marriage and family. God wanted men to model their lives after the caring and serving attitude he expressed as husband to the nation of Israel (Jer. 31:32)—the same loving authority that Jesus modeled for the church (Eph. 5:25).

Firstborn and Firstfruits

You are the children of the LORD your God ... and the LORD has chosen you to be a people for Himself, a special treasure above all the peoples who are on the face of the earth. —Deuteronomy 14:1–2

The concepts of firstborn and firstfruits had important civil and ceremonial significance and were threaded throughout the law of Moses. The firstborn system impacted families, tribes, the management of flocks and herds, and the ceremonial law. The firstfruits of crops were highly significant in agriculture and were reflected in holy day celebrations and rituals.

As with all the social structures God gave Israel, the firstborn/firstfruits system carried a deeper purpose and meaning. This becomes abundantly clear in the New Testament, with extensive references to the firstborn and firstfruits and the role of the church in God's great plan for humanity.

An Ancient Concept

The concept of firstborn significance has ancient origins. As far back as the time of Adam and Eve, we see Abel offering the firstborn of his flock, indicating God must have outlined some understanding of the concept from the beginning (Gen. 4:4).[1]

Later we see great significance of the role of the firstborn in the lives of the patriarchs Abraham, Isaac, and Jacob. Firstborn were entitled to a birthright—a special blessing—along with the inheritance of patriarchal authority. These were matters that the patriarchs (and God) took very seriously. The firstborn/birthright system was not supposed to be about favoritism, which some patriarchs exhibited and paid a penalty for (Deut. 21:15–16).

The firstborn/firstfruits system carried a deeper purpose and meaning.

The birthright was a leadership role designed to strengthen and protect the wider family. God was clearly behind the firstborn system, ensuring the special prophetic birthright blessings were fulfilled.

The firstborn birthright could be lost and transferred to another sibling. This happened in the case of Ishmael, Esau, and Reuben. Esau infamously "sold"

---

[1] Scholars have noted a focus on firstborn in other ancient Near East cultures, and some have implied Israel borrowed the concept. A biblical worldview holds the position that other cultures learned the concept from God's original revelation to man.

his birthright to Jacob, and Isaac "trembled exceedingly" when he realized he had blessed the wrong son (Gen. 27:33). Esau was later greatly distraught over his loss (Gen. 27:34). Reuben lost his birthright, which was later given to Joseph (Gen. 49:3–4; 1 Chron. 5:1). Years later, Joseph tried to correct his father Jacob when he prioritized Joseph's younger son Ephraim over Manasseh, despite Manasseh being the firstborn (Gen. 48:18).

These were not insignificant events for those involved. Esau is later strongly criticized for treating his birthright with such contempt (Heb. 12:16).

Israel and the Firstborn

The firstborn birthright system continued into the Mosaic era. Within the nation of Israel, the firstborn son was deemed special. He was the inheritor of the family birthright and continued to receive a special blessing and a double portion of the inheritance (Deut. 21:17).

At this time God also expanded the concept of firstborn. At a national level, God identified the entirety of Israel as his firstborn nation:

> Then you shall say to Pharaoh, "Thus says the LORD: '*Israel is My son, My firstborn*. So I say to you, let My son go that he may serve Me. But if you refuse to let him go, indeed I will kill your son, your firstborn.'" (Exod. 4:22–23)

As God's firstborn of the nations, Israel would be a special treasure, receive a special blessing, and be a leading light to other nations.

God went further and set apart all the firstborn within the nation of Israel for himself:

> Then the LORD spoke to Moses, saying, "Consecrate to Me all the firstborn, whatever opens the womb among the children of Israel, *both of man and beast; it is Mine*." (Exod. 13:1–2)

The consecration of each firstborn was done in a special ceremony at the tabernacle where the infant son was redeemed by a special offering. Joseph and Mary were careful to follow these statutes with baby Jesus: [2]

> Now when the days of her purification according to the law of Moses were completed, they brought Him to Jerusalem to present *Him* to the Lord (as it is written in the law of the Lord, "*Every male who opens the*

---

[2] Being poor, Joseph and Mary's offering was less than the usually required lamb (Lev. 12:8).

womb shall be called holy to the Lord"), and to offer a sacrifice according to what is said in the law of the Lord, "*A pair of turtledoves or two young pigeons.*" (Luke 2:22–24)

The firstborn system extended beyond humans to farm animals. The firstborn of cows, sheep, and goats (clean animals) were offered as a sacrifice to the Lord, but the firstborn of other animals were redeemed with an offering (Num. 18:15–18). The firstfruits of crops were also dedicated to God and were given to the priests (Deut. 18:4).

Firstborn and the Priesthood

The Levitical priesthood was inherently linked to the firstborn system. At Mount Sinai, God had described the entire nation of Israel as a kingdom of priests:

> Now therefore, if you will indeed obey My voice and keep My covenant, then you shall be a special treasure to Me above all people; for all the earth *is* Mine. And *you shall be to Me a kingdom of priests* and a holy nation. (Exod. 19:5–6)

Israel was a nation of priests in God's eyes because they were his firstborn son, a special treasure among the nations (Exod. 4:22). Later in the wilderness, God outlined the establishment of the formal priesthood within Israel. This would have meant consecrating the firstborn of each family in special service to God. But in exchange for setting apart all the individual firstborn of each household, God selected the tribe of Levi:

> Now behold, I Myself have taken the Levites from among the children of Israel instead of every firstborn who opens the womb among the children of Israel. *Therefore the Levites shall be Mine, because all the firstborn are Mine.* On the day that I struck all the firstborn in the land of Egypt, I sanctified to Myself all the firstborn in Israel, both man and beast. They shall be Mine: I am the LORD. (Num. 3:12–13)

Again, God took this matter seriously. Moses calculated the total number of firstborn in Israel, and it was more than the number of Levites. A redemption payment of five shekels each was required to be paid for each firstborn in excess of the Levites.

After their consecration, the Levites became the representative firstborn of the nation, uniquely carrying the special priestly role. Priests were mediators between God and man and would be responsible for managing the worship system at the tabernacle. As firstborn, their special blessing was the Lord. They would receive no inheritance in the land like the other tribes (Num. 18:23–24).

Because of the high levels of respect and trust that accompanied their priestly status, God intended the firstborn Levites to fulfill major leadership roles in the community.

The Levitical priesthood was inherently linked to the firstborn system.

Foreshadowing a Greater Plan

The concepts of the firstborn and firstfruits were foundational to the social fabric of Israel and intertwined extensively throughout the ceremonial system.

These concepts are also foundational to understanding the role of Jesus and the New Testament church of the firstborn and priesthood of believers. They will be expanded on in later chapters on the worship system.

5

PART 5: The Law and the Nation

The law of Moses included a comprehensive range of social, civil, and judicial laws needed to establish the new nation of Israel in the promised land. For a relatively small law code, its breadth and depth is remarkable.

Although the laws were simpler than a complex society would require today, they were groundbreaking for the time and included far-reaching principles by which the nation could prosper and grow.

The Unique Structure of Government

I will walk among you and be your God, and you shall be My people.
—Leviticus 26:12

It was Ronald Reagan who said: "Government is not the solution to our problem; government is the problem."[1] It seems the God of Israel had a similar perspective, but he went much, much further. God wanted Israel to understand that *he* was the solution to their problems, not the rule of men. To reinforce the point, God outlined a system of civil government for Israel unlike any nation in history.

God's design for Israel was a government without a human ruler and virtually no concept of a central administration. It was to be a decentralized civil government managed from the ground up locally by the individuals, families, and tribes, not from a central national bureaucracy down. God would be their invisible, incorruptible king. God wanted to be close to the people, to bless and protect them, and for the people to be free from the oppression of flawed human rulers.

> *It would have been the most minimal and nonintrusive system of national governance in history.*

There would be a central worship system centered around the national tabernacle, but civil administration was to be a localized affair, spread across the towns and tribes. The human monarchy, which came later in Israel's history, was not a part of God's original plan.

It would have been the most minimal and nonintrusive system of national governance in history. It confirms God's supernatural involvement in the law of Moses because no man would ever propose such a system.

Some immediate questions come to mind: How would law and order be maintained? How would the country remain homogeneous? How would the country defend itself from enemies? How could such a nation even survive?

Surprisingly, the nation operated and survived under this structure for centuries before the first king (Saul) was appointed. Although Israel's application of the law during this period of Judges was far from the ideal God had in mind, there is still much we can learn from the directives God gave on

---

[1] Bibliog: (Reagan 1981)

how the people were to be governed.

The Period of the Judges

The period of the Judges in Israel started after Moses and Joshua. In his old age, Joshua did not appoint a successor as Moses had done but confirmed that the regional elders and judges of the day would collectively be the new leaders (Josh. 23:1–2; 24:1). From then on, the nation was to be governed by local judges appointed by the elders of the individual tribes.

The period of the Judges is often wrongly viewed as a time of chaos in Israel. And it's true that the last chapters of the book of Judges contain some disturbing chapters in Israel's history: moral depravity, violence, religious confusion, infighting, and everyone "doing what was right in their own eyes" (Judg. 21:25). Some assume that this was the natural result of the unusual system of government, which was later corrected by the installation of a monarchy. But this is incorrect.

What is often overlooked is that the twenty-one chapters of Judges cover an enormous period of over 400 years (Acts 13:20). This was roughly equivalent to the period of the later monarchy covered in the books of Samuel, Kings, and Chronicles. And although this period was an ongoing cycle of rejecting God and returning to him, it wasn't all negative—at times periods of peace and tranquility existed in the land (Judg. 3:11, 30; 5:31; 8:28). And to the point, even centuries later, and despite all their problems, God had not changed his view on Israel's system of government. He still did not want them to have a human king (1 Sam. 8:4–8).

The reason is clear: Israel's problems were not a result of their system of government, and neither would their problems be solved by a human king. Their problems came from turning away from God:

> So the people served the LORD all the days of Joshua, and all the days of the elders who outlived Joshua. ... When all that generation had been gathered to their fathers, *another generation arose after them who did not know the LORD nor the work which He had done for Israel.* Then the children of Israel did evil in the sight of the LORD, *and served the Baals* (Judg. 2:7, 10–11)

Just as God had predicted and warned against many years previously, the people had disobeyed his command not to intermingle with the Canaanites. Because of their negative influence, Israel kept losing sight of the true God (Exod. 34:12). They reaped the consequences of their own actions. Despite this,

God rescued them multiple times by sending leaders who would rally the nation to fight off the oppressors and turn the people back to him (Judg. 2:11–19).

And the nation survived. By the time of judge Samuel all those years later, and despite all their ups and downs, the nation was still united as a people, and judges like Samuel were widely respected. This alone proves that the unique system of government could have worked indefinitely if Israel had just remained loyal to God.

God's Plan for Government

Some have assumed that without a strong central government, Israel would have been somewhat scattered and powerless like other loosely coupled ethnic tribal groups have been in history. But God did not want Israel to be a scattered group of tribes each doing their own thing. He wanted Israel to be a distinct and unified nation admired by other nations, a light to the world (Deut. 4:5–8).

> *He wanted Israel to be a distinct and unified nation admired by other nations, a light to the world*

His plan to achieve that was based on five key fundamentals:

1. Acknowledgement that the God of Israel was the one and only true God
2. The establishment of a national rule of law
3. A unifying central system of worship that brought the nation together for deeply meaningful national holy days and celebrations
4. A recognition of local tribal elders' authority
5. A judicial system involving Levites that operated across tribal boundaries

The key to the nation's success was the first point: maintaining a focus on God. Had Israel trusted in God, acceptance of his law would have logically followed. The nation would have been tightly unified without the need for force or coercion from a central human authority. Israel's idolatrous nature was the real problem. This was a moral failure that continued into the later period of the centralized monarchy and eventually led to Israel's downfall.

An Unusual Theocracy

Israel's system of government can be technically described as a theocracy because God himself was to be their king (1 Sam. 8:7; 12:12). But the theocracy

God had in mind was unlike how theocracies have normally been implemented in history. Theocracies normally require human religious leaders to be the head of their nation (e.g., the Vatican, Iran, Afghanistan).

Significantly, God did *not* appoint the high priest and the supporting Levites to be civil administrators. Executive power would *not* lie with a ruling religious class. Civil authority was to be separate from the religious hierarchy. Therefore Israel was not a theocracy as we understand the term today.

> *Executive power would not lie with a ruling religious class.*

God knew that having the high priest as leader of the nation would have created even more problems than a human king. We learn this lesson from other theocracies in history where ruling religious leaders weaponize religion to achieve their civil objectives: claiming a "divine right" or a "divine channel" to God's will to keep people under control. Theocracies of men have always had the potential to turn the voluntary, heart-felt worship of God into a religion of fear and coercion.

In our Western world today, democracy is presented as the gold standard, and that may be true in a world that rejects God. But from a Christian perspective, the inherent weaknesses of democracy should be obvious. Democracies rely on the people's collective "wisdom," and over time people will generally take the path of least resistance. Democracies left to run their course will decay morally and eventually collapse from within.

God's design was for Israel to be permanently sustainable, and that could only occur with an unchanging standard of law and leadership. That standard could only come from an unchanging God. Today a theocracy is presented on the opposite spectrum to democracy and the rule of law. Yet God's plan was to have both a theocracy *and* a rule of law, with fully empowered and involved citizens.[2]

Checks and Balances

In our Western democracies, we refer to the three branches of government: the legislative, the executive, and the judicial. This 'separation of powers (as it is called) exists to provide checks and balances so that no part of government

---

[2] In some ways God's original design for government could be described as a *republic*. There would be a spiritual monarch (God), but otherwise, the power of government was to be broadly spread among the people.

becomes too powerful. Although such checks and balances were not as clearly defined under the Mosaic system, God did limit the powers available to any one individual or group.

Legislative

The legislative branch of government was God himself. God was the Lawgiver, not man. There would be a need for new administrative laws as society developed, but the moral and statutory laws were designed to be timeless and were not to be altered (Deut. 4:2).

Executive

God did not want Israel to have one all-powerful executive ruler like other nations. The executive power of the society would lie with the people through their local elders and God as their king. This was God's original plan. Elders would administer towns and regions along tribal lines (Deut. 1:13). If matters arose between people that could not be settled locally by the elders, they could be taken to the appointed judges of the land for a decision (Deut. 17:8–9). Even under the later monarchy, elders continued to play a leading role in the society (e.g. 2 Sam. 5:3; 1 Kings 12:6; 2 Chron. 34:29).

Judicial

The priests and Levites had an important role to play in the judicial system and were located throughout the nation. They were to be the teachers and interpreters of the law and were to be sought out as judges for legal decisions when more complex cases arose (Deut. 17:8–12). This is somewhat like modern democracies, where the judiciary is independent of the executive government.

Executive Judges

Before the monarchy, God at times raised up specific leaders to help the people in times of crisis. These leaders were called "judges." The job description of "judge" should not be understood narrowly as we use the term today. Sometimes it did refer to a judicial role, and other times, the term is used to denote a regional military leader who was raised up to break the stranglehold of an oppressor (Judg. 2:16–17). After the people were liberated, the judge stayed on as a judge and administrator in that area. Usually the people remained faithful to God while the judge was alive.

In all cases, the people accepted these judges as their go-to person for advice, mediation, and judgment on serious matters. Deborah was recognized as both a prophetess and a judge among the people (Judg. 4:4). Deborah is an example of the people recognizing the obvious gifts God had given her; therefore, people went to her for judgments. The same happened to the judge Samuel. From a child it was known that God had given him special understanding (1 Sam. 3:19).

It is significant that these rulers of Israel were called "judges." That was their primary role. They were not to rule as de facto kings. When the elders tried to appoint Gideon to rule over them, he reminded them that God alone was their king (Judg. 8:22–23).

Executive Monarchy

The separation of powers continued under the later monarchy. A king was still subject to the rule of law (Deut. 17:18–19) and would be advised and corrected by the prophets that God sent from time to time. Kings had authority to organize the Levites (1 Chron. 23:6; 2 Chron. 8:14; 31:2, etc.) but were strictly excluded from religious duties, as both Saul and Uzziah found out, to their dismay (1 Sam. 13:7–13; 2 Chron. 26:18).[3]

In Times of War

God did not want Israel to have a standing professional army like the surrounding nations. Neither would there be taxation or levy to support or equip such an army. If they kept their trust in God, he would fight for them (Deut. 20:1–4). This did not mean the people were not required to be involved. When the time came for battle, the relevant judge at the time would send word to the nearby tribes and call for volunteers. When the fighting was finished the army would disband, and the judge would revert to judging.

> *God did not want Israel to have a standing professional army like the surrounding nations.*

When the army was called and the men gathered, God's directives on preparing the army were surprising. A priest of the Lord was to be called to motivate and encourage the troops (Deut. 20:1–4). He was to remind the men that God would be with them regardless of the size or shape of the enemy

---

[3] David is noted as offering burnt offerings on occasion, but we must assume officiating priests were present (2 Sam. 6:18; 1 Chron. 21:26).

army. The officers were then to cull the army down to a core unit of men who were truly ready and willing. Men who had not finished building their houses were to leave, those who were in the process of establishing a new farm were to leave, and men who were engaged to be married and the newly married were to leave (Deut. 20:5–9).

Most astonishing of all, those who were fearful were told to go home (Deut. 20:8)! What national army, professional or otherwise, would ever decree such a thing?

These laws emphasized an important point to the people. Numerical superiority in battle meant nothing with God on their side (Lev. 26:7–8). God had demonstrated his great power from the outset in Egypt through the battles for Canaan. They had defeated much bigger and better-equipped armies than their own. But this all depended on maintaining their trust in him. The story of Gideon is particularly striking (Judg. 6–8). The armies of Israel were significantly outnumbered, and Gideon was worried that his army of 32,000 wasn't nearly enough against the massive army of the Midianites. God's response? You have too many men! And he whittled them down to 300 (Judg. 7)! God wanted Israel to know that the battle was won because of God, not because of their own might.

Considering how much of a nation's national budget goes toward military expenditure, what an incredible blessing God's protection and help would have been had Israel put their trust in him as their king:

> The LORD will cause your enemies who rise against you to be defeated before your face; they shall come out against you one way and flee before you seven ways. (Deut. 28:7)

The Period of the Monarchy

Despite his desire otherwise, God knew that the people would have difficulty maintaining their confidence in an invisible leader and would one day ask for a human king (1 Sam. 8:5, 19). When the elders originally came to Samuel, they asked for a king to be "like all the other nations," and they mentioned two specific things: 1) for the king to be the supreme judge in the land, and 2) for the king to be the head of the military (1 Sam. 8:20). Prior to this, military leaders were either appointed by the elders or raised up by God as needed.

Knowing the hearts of these people, hundreds of years earlier God had given Moses laws that a future king would need to follow if the nation was to be successful. The heart of God's message to a future king was this: Don't be like the kings of other nations. Instead, come to know the true God by studying and applying his law and put your trust in him:

> But he (a king) shall not multiply horses for himself, nor cause the people to return to Egypt to multiply horses, for the LORD has said to you, "You shall not return that way again." Neither shall he multiply wives for himself, lest his heart turn away; nor shall he greatly multiply silver and gold for himself. Also it shall be, when he sits on the throne of his kingdom, that he shall write for himself a copy of this law in a book, from the one before the priests, the Levites. And it shall be with him, and he shall read it all the days of his life, *that he may learn to fear the LORD his God* and be careful to observe all the words of this law and these statutes, *that his heart may not be lifted above his brethren*, that he may not turn aside from the commandment to the right hand or to the left, and that he may prolong his days in his kingdom, he and his children in the midst of Israel. (Deut. 17:16–20)

The king was not to be above the law—he would be subject to the rule of law like any other citizen. God wanted any future king to serve his people in the same way that God himself served Israel. Having a humble king, whose heart was not lifted above his fellow Israelites, would be unlike the surrounding nations. If such a king did as he was directed and read the law all his days, he would understand how to properly govern and have a successful nation.

> *The king was not to be above the law—he would be subject to the rule of law like any other citizen.*

As the supreme judge, he would need to understand the importance of respecting the rule of law and following due process. If he lost sight of God and the law, he would be held to account by God, who would correct him through the prophets.

Unfortunately, there is little evidence that any king followed these directions fully. Even King David, who seemed to follow the admonition to read the Book of the Law regularly, had multiple wives and established a standing army. His son Solomon went to further extremes and put a heavy taxation burden on the people. When the people asked for a king "like all the other nations"— that's exactly what they ended up with. The government of Israel (and later Judah) became like all the other nations, something God did not want for his people.

A Realistic System

God's idea of decentralized government has been criticized as unrealistic and impractical. But God wasn't being unrealistic. He was well aware of the imperfect nature of human beings, particularly the hard-hearted Israelites. It was for this reason that he did not want an imperfect human king who would hold sway over the entire nation. A decentralized government would protect the people with multiple checks and balances.

Even with a king, Israel could have been a success in God's eyes. The nation could have prospered and been a light to the world. But the success of the nation would now depend on an individual, fallible human. A king who forgot God would lead the entire nation astray, and that's exactly what happened.

Civil Rights and Freedom

I have set before you life and death, blessing and cursing; therefore choose life, that both you and your descendants may live. —Deuteronomy 30:19

How much freedom would the average Israelite have living under the system of law God gave to Moses? Many assume it would have been the opposite of the liberty offered by our modern democracies—that it was a controlling, legalistic environment, restricting and suppressing its citizens. This unfortunate misrepresentation has been at the heart of many people's perspective of the law of Moses.

As we saw in earlier chapters, God highly values personal freedom and wanted the people of Israel to live with minimal interference from government and religious authorities. His stated goal was for the individual to learn to love him deeply with all their heart, so clearly people had to be able to freely come to know him without coercion.

But how did the freedom God had in mind compare to the liberties we value so highly in our modern democracies?

Two of our most precious freedoms are *freedom of speech* and *freedom of religion*. How would they work in ancient Israel?

In the United States, *freedom of religion* is also a constitutional right specifically protected by the First Amendment and is one of the founding principles that led to the rise of the nation.

> *God wanted the people of Israel to live with minimal interference from government and religious authorities.*

In contrast, God made it clear to Israel that he was the One True God and expected the entire nation to worship him. Those who worshipped other gods were to be punished. The separation of church and state is also a big issue today. In contrast, the law of Moses outlined what was essentially a "state religion."

Without freedom of religion, could the Israelites be truly free?

To answer these questions, we must look in more detail at God's ideal for human governance and what he was trying to achieve with these people.

Modern Big Governments

We live at a time in history when people generally expect governments to provide for all their essential needs and protect them from calamity. The modest demands for assistance from citizens a century ago have now exploded to social security and welfare support on a massive scale, pushing economies and national debts to unsustainable levels. There is an insatiable appetite for such support because it is inherent in people to want to be cared for. As the Rational Bible commentary rightfully notes:

> It is a myth that people yearn most for freedom. ... Many, if not most people prefer to be taken care of—even at the price of a loss of freedom—rather than to have to take care of themselves. That is why most people almost everywhere in the world prefer a big state to a limited one, even though, by definition, the bigger the state, the less the individual's freedom.[1]

There are major problems with massive state bureaucracies. They become unsustainable in the long term and have the negative effect of reducing individual rights and freedoms. Although there are benefits for those on the receiving end of state assistance, they often come with the proviso that the state has the right to impose its values on citizens. "Unalienable rights" can quickly disappear when the secular state is given jurisdiction over individual lives—and it is difficult to reclaim such rights when they are gone.

History is against those who consider it possible for human governments to contain their authority and bureaucratic reach. Nations have always tended toward increasing the power and status of the central government, especially when they achieve military and/or economic success. This occurs under all types of man's governments—democracy, dictatorship, monarchy, communism etc. It is an issue that stems from human nature and is directly opposed to God's ideal for society.

Centuries after Moses, when the Israelite people came to Samuel asking for a king like all the other nations, God warned them of the natural consequences of centralized human power:

> And he said, "This will be the behavior of the king who will reign over you: He will take your sons and appoint them for his own chariots and to be his horsemen, and some will run before his chariots. He will appoint captains over his thousands and captains over his fifties, will

---
[1] Bibliog: (Prager 2018, Exodus 182)

set some to plow his ground and reap his harvest, and some to make his weapons of war and equipment for his chariots. He will take your daughters to be perfumers, cooks, and bakers. And he will take the best of your fields, your vineyards, and your olive groves, and give them to his servants. He will take a tenth of your grain and your vintage, and give it to his officers and servants. And he will take your male servants, your female servants, your finest young men, and your donkeys, and put them to his work. He will take a tenth of your sheep. And you will be his servants. And you will cry out in that day because of your king whom you have chosen for yourselves, and the LORD will not hear you in that day." (1 Sam. 8:11–18)

God's prediction for Israel under a human king came to pass just as he had forecast.[2] God understood the inevitable overreach of all centralized forms of human government.

God's Plan for a Free Society

In contrast to man's idea of government, God wanted Israel to rely on him, not on the state. God alone would be their incorruptible king and the source of all truth. If they trusted him, he would provide for them, protect them from their enemies, and ensure that their basic needs were met.

Furthermore, he wanted *individual responsibility* to be central to the functioning of society, not big state. The law of Moses put the primary focus of responsibility on the individual and the local community. Other than antisocial behavior and matters that needed judicial involvement, the Israelites were free to live their lives under a system of light governance. Rephrasing President Lincoln's description, Israel was designed to be a "government of God, by the people, for the people."[3] God wanted it to be a society where individuals cared for one another. Abrogating personal responsibility to the state comes at an enormous social cost—where faceless bureaucracy replaces the personalized benefits of local family and community support.

The light system of governance God outlined is a striking confirmation of how free and open he wanted the society to be.

---

[2] The people cried out for relief in the days of Rehoboam (1 Kings 12:4).
[3] Bibliog: (Lincoln 1863)

The light system of governance God outlined to Israel is a striking confirmation of how free and open he wanted the society to be. But having such freedom was unsettling to the people. God wanted them to govern themselves, but they were unable to do so consistently. When the people finally came forward and formally asked for a human king, God made it clear that the request was a rejection of himself as their king (1 Sam. 8:5–8).

Some have assumed the people were asking for an escape from God's "tight control," but it was the exact opposite. The problem was they felt *too vulnerable* not having a human king or an army. They didn't appreciate the incredible freedoms they had been given. Because of their lack of confidence in God and their desire to be "like the nations around them," their freedoms would be diminished, not enhanced by their new king.

Freedom of Religion

But could the Israelites be truly free if there was no "freedom of religion," as we call it today?

We first must understand what is meant by the term. Regardless of how a person interprets the term today, "freedom of religion" in our society has never meant that individuals or institutions were allowed to practice every religious ideology they believe. Many religious practices of past advanced societies are rejected in no uncertain terms today as being totally "immoral": polygamy, pedophilia, underage marriage of children, bestiality, female mutilation, honor killing of women, the list goes on. Such behavior is *not* protected in our society under the right to "freedom of religion." Yet many previous (even current) cultures in the world have legally allowed some or all of these practices. In the ancient world, religious prostitution was seen as favorable to the gods and forced on many young women and children. Even human sacrifice was acceptable in some ancient societies.

So who defines whether these or any of a long list of other "religious" practices are acceptable within society?

Why don't people have the "religious freedom" to do such things today? Clearly, there must be a moral standard of some sort if there is going to be a homogeneous society. But where does that standard of morality come from? Abortion, considered murder at one stage, is now called "choice." Euthanasia is on the rise. Underage children are now allowed to change their gender. What else might change in the future? Is morality simply defined by social agreement and the "feelings" of the majority people of the time? Considering what has been acceptable in many former highly educated societies, such a scenario presents a frightening perspective of the future.

Regardless of what an individual believes, or on whatever end of the spectrum their morals reside, to presume that everyone in the future will somehow align to one standard of "goodness" is delusional. When a society rejects the principle of a God of truth, anything is possible, as the depravities of so many former nations of history demonstrate.

Freedom of religion, therefore, can never be the right to accept any standard of morality and any corrupt form of "religious" behavior. If society is to survive, there must be a standard of morality that is not a moving target but is secured in truth—and objective moral truth can only come from the divine law of a supreme God.

> *Freedom of religion can never be the right to accept any standard of morality and any corrupt form of behavior.*

Religion without Coercion

Properly understood, true freedom of religion *is the right to seek the true God without threat or persecution*. This is what God wanted for Israel—a moral society that provided leeway for people to gradually grow in understanding and knowledge of the Lord *without coercion*. Nonbelieving foreigners would need to be able to visit Israel and coexist without persecution as they came to learn about the true God.

This is the beauty of the negative system of law God gave. Most of the Ten Commandments are directives to *not* behave a certain way. Although the spirit and intent of the law has far greater ramifications, a person can nominally follow the first commandment by simply not promoting other gods and or speaking against the God of Israel. None of the commandments require enforced participation in religious ceremony. Likewise, the Sabbath puts no positive impost on anyone. A visiting nonbeliever to Israel could simply refrain from work on that day. Believing Israelites would go to the holy day celebrations three times a year. But again, there was no enforcement and no punishment for non-believers if they didn't.

This is something a traveler today can relate to when they visit a foreign country. It is not hard, for example, for a visitor to modern democratic Israel to refrain from working on the holy day of Yom Kippur. Similarly, visitors to the Christian nation of Tonga are expected to respect Sunday rest day laws.

Tourists to Islamic nations are required to dress modestly and refrain from publicly consuming offensive food and drink.

Even in a religiously free country like America, up until the mid-twentieth century people were required to respect the Christian roots of the society, even if they weren't a Christian. Modesty laws existed in most states. Sunday closing laws were in place from colonial times to modern times. Some are still in force in some areas.[4] All these are examples of negative laws that are not hard to keep. Even though such laws may be considered "religious" in nature, those who publicly and deliberately push against them would rightfully expect punishment from the civil government.

This is similar to how life was to work in ancient Israel. God's plan for Israel was for each person to come to love him personally. But at the same time, there had to be standards of public morality and societal behavior. God knew that the greatest threat to the nation was the false religions of the surrounding people. So there had to be penalties for those who promoted false gods and publicly pushed against the God of Israel. But that left a lot of room for an individual to personally work out their own relationship with the true God without interference.

> *That left a lot of room for an individual to work out their own relationship with God without interference.*

Separation of Church and State

The concept of the separation of church and state is a relatively recent interpretation of American law, which has further confused the topic of freedom of religion. For some, the term "separation of church and state" has resulted in a reinterpretation of the First Amendment from "freedom *of* religion" into "freedom *from* religion." This has changed the idea of religious freedom in ways that the founding fathers would never have imagined.

That there should be separation of the state from *religious institutions* or *specific denominations* makes perfect sense in a democracy. But the idea that the state can be "separate" from *religion* has always been a fantasy. All nation states, whether intentionally or unintentionally, teach and promote "religion." The definition of the word "religion" is open to some interpretation, but for all intents and purposes, "religion" is simply a set of beliefs, values, and practices

---

[4] Bibliog: (Zeigler 2017, Blue Laws)

that extend from the worldview of its adherents. "Religion" includes the teaching of origins, and defines the standards of morality for its followers. This is exactly what we find in secular states today. The theory of evolution, social justice ideals, Critical Race Theory, etc. are all examples of belief systems that are "religiously" held by their adherents.

A state *must* teach values if there is going to be any semblance of a homogenous society. As previously noted, law by its nature is structured around value systems. The communist regime of the USSR was a perfect demonstration of a supposedly "nonreligious" state, teaching a "religion." The state preached a dogma on the origins of man and the values that one should have in their life. An article in the *Journal for the Scientific Study of Religion* notes that the Soviet Union: "Introduced a 'belief system called "scientific atheism," complete with atheist rituals, proselytizers, and a promise of worldly salvation.'" [5]

The idea that the state can be "separate" from religion has always been a fantasy.

The issue is not whether a state promotes moral standards and beliefs but what those moral standards and beliefs are, and where the values came from.

Benefits of a Homogeneous Society

If we divorce ourselves from the thinking of our time and look at the topic dispassionately, there are enormous benefits to a homogenous society with a common standard of morality and alignment to a national purpose.

The idea has risen in recent times that it is somehow positive to have a multicultural society with different languages, cultures, holiday seasons, and widely varying views on morality, justice, and social structures. Common sense should tell us that such a stance will lead to a fractured and divided society. This is not referring to racial or regional differences in the form of local traditions, foods, dress etc., which *do* add zest to a nation. The problem arises when there is a difference in the *core values* and *national standards*. As Angela Merkel of Germany said in recent years, "Multiculturalism leads to parallel societies, and therefore, multiculturalism remains a grand delusion. This (multicultural) approach has failed, utterly failed."[6]

Ms. Merkel is not someone disparaging of people of other races. In 2015 she welcomed a massive number of migrants to the country against the objections

---

[5] Bibliog: (Froese 2004)
[6] Bibliog: (The Guardian 2015)

of many of her countrymen. What she is saying is simply common sense: "Those who seek refuge with us, also have to respect our laws and traditions and learn to speak German" she went on to say.

A nation will be at its strongest when its core values are agreed on by the majority, when they are espoused by the leaders of the nation, and when immigrants and visitors know that they must respect those values. This was God's desire for Israel. To borrow the ideal of the American Pledge of Allegiance, he wanted it to be: *"one nation under God, indivisible, with liberty and justice for all."*

> *Some cultures are superior to others and build strong, prosperous communities of truly happy people.*

God had given them an enlightened "constitution" that defined a way of life for the individual and the nation that would have led to greatness. A standard that other nations would admire, be attracted to, and learn from.

Regardless of modern radical idealisms that say otherwise, some cultures *are* superior to others and build strong, prosperous communities of contented people. So many cultures of the past—even the present—suppress the natural rights of individuals, teaching and promoting falsehoods in the name of "religion," or set unattainable "ideals" with terrible outcomes for their people. The decline of cultural confidence in Western countries like America has been in direct proportion to the rejection of the God of the Bible and the moral values that originally underpinned the entire fabric of national law.

Freedom of Speech and Assembly

Freedom of speech and the right to peaceful assembly are also regarded as vital to a free society. The American First Amendment exists to protect those rights.

But even with constitutional protection there have always been boundaries. The First Amendment affirmed the right of people to assemble *peaceably*. It did not grant any rights for people to assemble for the purposes of rioting or to cause harm in some way.

It was also understood that even with freedom of speech, it was not acceptable to slander, to publicly promote immorality, or to incite rebellion against the nation. American law correctly put guidelines on such behavior.

The freedom to assemble *peaceably* and speak what is *right and true* should never be curtailed—and this is what the First Amendment was primarily addressing. The problem we see today with new laws against such things as "hate speech" and "racism" is that these laws are not based on divine values but on the transient values of a materialistic society. When a society allows a secular state to define morals, the result will be a *loss* of free speech as the state increasingly disallows criticism of immoral behavior as defined by Scripture.

The way in which the law of Moses addressed freedom of speech and freedom of assembly was similar to the original American ideal. The law of Moses put no general restraints on freedom of speech nor on the right to assemble peaceably. We see ample evidence of people assembling freely and people openly speaking their mind in the time of Moses and throughout Old Testament times. It is also worth noting the large number of times that people were blunt (even rude) to leaders of Israel and to God himself without fear. Cain, Moses, Joshua, David, Jeremiah, Elijah, and Jonah were just some of the many who spoke their mind in frustration or anger to God without fear of retaliation. Being a person of truth, God has always accepted candid honesty over pretense.

The law of Moses put no general restraints on freedom of speech nor the right to assemble peaceably.

At the same time, the law of Moses empowered the governing authorities with the right and appropriate boundaries on freedom of speech when such teaching would threaten the nation, such as blaspheming the God of Israel, promoting other gods, or promoting immorality. God made it clear that this sort of teaching would surely destroy the nation more than foreign armies.

Freedom Despite Doubts

How importantly God values freedom is evident in his statements at the end of the book of Deuteronomy. These words were written just before the nation entered the promised land. God had been dealing with these people for forty years, and neither he nor Moses were under any illusions that the heart of these people had changed for the positive. He knew they would eventually forsake him. In speaking to Moses he says:

> Behold, you (Moses) will rest with your fathers; and this people will rise and play the harlot with the gods of the foreigners of the land, where they go to be among them, and they will forsake Me and break My covenant which I have made with them. (Deut. 31:16)

Moses knew what God said was correct. He further told the people:

> For I know that after my death you will become utterly corrupt, and turn aside from the way which I have commanded you. And evil will befall you in the latter days, because you will do evil in the sight of the LORD, to provoke Him to anger through the work of your hands." (Deut. 31:29)

Yet even knowing that these people would eventually reject him, God *still* gave them freedom of choice—showing just how important free will was to him:

> I call heaven and earth as witnesses today against you, that *I have set before you life and death*, blessing and cursing; *therefore choose life*, that both you and your descendants may live; that you may love the LORD your God, that you may obey His voice, and that you may cling to Him, for He is your life and the length of your days. (Deut. 30:19–20)

A Truly Free Society

God's plan for Israel was positive and far-reaching. God outlined to Israel a system of government, a culture, and values superior to all other nations at the time. And he didn't just impose it on them—it was an agreement he made directly with all the people, not just the leadership (Exod. 24:3; Deut. 29:10–12).

The system God gave them was based on truth and virtue. He wanted them to be a free, culturally confident, and prosperous people united under the One True God—a "shining light on the hill" to the nations around them. With so many laws about caring for strangers and foreigners, it would be a free and welcoming society—a nation that espoused standards so positive that other people would find it attractive (Deut. 4:5–8).

This is where the Pharisees later went wrong. They felt it was their role to police the behavior of individuals, to micromanage, and exclude people they deemed inferior, when the law commanded no such thing. Under his governance, God wanted people to be themselves, free to follow their dreams and aspirations. He wanted them to be free to make choices, be successful, fail, and learn. James later calls the system a "law of liberty" (James 2:8–12). This is what the law was designed to be when correctly administered.

> *God realized that such a free and open society needed to be protected.*

At the same time, God realized that such a free and open society needed to be protected. If someone was actively out to destroy the underlying standards of the society that came from God himself, they were to be dealt with. This must be the case in any society if it is to survive. God told Israel multiple times what would happen if they adopted the false gods and destructive ideas of the cultures around them, but they ignored him. Their society eroded and was finally destroyed from within—just as we see in the Western world today, with the loss of the values that made the nations strong.

One thing is obvious. The people of Israel *were* free to reject God because that is exactly what they did—repeatedly. Their destiny was always in their own hands.

What It Meant to Be a Citizen of Israel

The LORD your God has chosen you to be a people for Himself, a special treasure above all the peoples on the face of the earth. —Deuteronomy 7:6

Citizenship today is a prized possession, particularly in countries that offer superior benefits for those who hold the privilege. Citizenship can offer security, stability, protection from extreme poverty, and endows the holder the right to participate more fully in a nation's affairs. Citizenship also comes with obligations on the bearer and, in some countries, may even require participation in the military or other public service roles.

Citizenship as we understand it today did not exist in the ancient world. Most ancient nations were ruled by dictatorial authoritarian leaders, with the masses having little, if any, rights. There were some bright spots in history, but these were generally short-lived and rights narrowly restricted. Athens, for example, often called the birthplace of democracy, invited the participation of its citizens, but this did not include women, men who had not served in the military, slaves, or foreign residents.[1] Therefore, only a percentage of the population was involved. Rome later created a system of citizenship, which became highly sought after and could be purchased for a high price. But it was a citizenship with various class levels that were deeply intertwined in the justice system.[2] Note, for example, how differently Paul was treated when he was found to be a Roman citizen (Acts 22:25–29). This type of class distinction was common in the empires of history.

Ancient Israel had a concept of citizenship, and though there were advantages, they did not extend into preferential treatment in a court of law. Under the law of Moses, all people, native-born and foreigners, were equal in the sight of the law (Lev. 19:33–34; Num. 15:16).

Foreigners Could Become Citizens

While being the chosen people was a special offer to Abraham's family, it was not exclusive. Even before the children of Israel had left Egypt, God made it clear that a foreigner was welcome to enter into a relationship with him by following the same rites required of an Israelite. In God's eyes, this made them no different from a native of the land:

> And when a stranger dwells with you and *wants* to keep the Passover

---

[1] Bibliog: (National Geographic 2022, Democracy in Ancient Greece)
[2] Bibliog: (Bakers 2013, Roman Law. Roman Citizenship. p 1439)

to the LORD, let all his males be circumcised, and then let him come near and keep it; *and he shall be as a native of the land.* For no uncircumcised person shall eat it. (Exod. 12:48)

Keeping the Passover demonstrated a person's voluntary commitment to the God of Israel, a commitment sealed by the circumcision of the males of the family. Passover was the only holy day ceremony requiring such a commitment to participate.[3]

Through the prophet Isaiah, God confirms just how welcome foreigners were to come into his fellowship. He has never been partial to race or ethnicity:

> *While being the chosen people was a special offer to Abraham's family, it was not exclusive.*

> Do not let the son of the foreigner who has joined himself to the LORD speak, saying, "The LORD has utterly separated me from His people" … Also the sons of the foreigner who join themselves to the LORD, to serve Him, and to love the name of the LORD, to be His servants—everyone who keeps from defiling the Sabbath, and holds fast My covenant—even them I will bring to My holy mountain, and make them joyful in My house of prayer. Their burnt offerings and their sacrifices will be accepted on My altar; for My house shall be called a house of prayer for all nations. (Isa. 56:3, 6–7)

Many individuals of different ethnicities did precisely this. When Israel left Egypt, a "mixed multitude" also left with them (Exod. 12:38). These former "foreigners" who had accepted the God of Israel were not put in a separate category by themselves. Instead, they were individually assimilated into one of the tribes of Israel, the only exception being the priestly tribe of Levi.

One example is Caleb, who is called a Kenizzite (Num. 32:12). Scholars generally associate Kenizzites with the Edomites. Despite his Kenizzite heritage, Caleb was chosen to represent the tribe of Judah in the exploration of the land (Num. 13:3–6). Caleb was granted land in Israel and is included in the genealogical listing of Judah (1 Chron. 4:15).

Another example is the story of Obed-Edom, a Gittite. When David failed in his attempt to move the ark of the covenant to Jerusalem, he took it to Obed-Edom's home, where it remained for three months (2 Sam. 6:10–11).

---

[3] It is significant how partaking of the Old Testament Passover foreshadowed the New Testament covenantal relationship expressed in the symbols of the Lord's Supper (1 Cor. 10:16–17).

Obed-Edom was someone who had accepted the God of Israel. David was clearly not concerned with Obed-Edom's race or heritage, even though Obed-Edom would be caring for the most holy of objects. God certainly didn't mind either; he blessed the man's household during that time.

Or consider the ready acceptance of foreign women as citizens when they put their trust in the God of Israel—Rahab and Ruth being the most well-known examples.

One interesting example is that of the Israelite leader Sheshan who had daughters but no sons. To keep tribes and their inheritance distinct, daughters were to marry within the tribe (Num. 36:6–9). But in this case, Sheshan gave his daughter to his Egyptian servant, Jarha, and Jarha became part of Sheshan's lineage (1 Chron. 2:34–35). It is significant that Jarha was a foreigner but was accepted into the tribe and lineage, confirming again that a foreigner could choose to become a full citizen.

Categories of Foreigners

Although foreigners and strangers are regularly referenced in the books of Moses, not all foreigners were of the same kind. Three different categories of foreigners existed at the time:

1. People of other ethnic heritages (e.g. Caleb, Ruth) who were living in Israel and had accepted the God of Israel and become full citizens of the country (Exod. 12:48). They kept their heritage but became associated with a specific tribe.
2. Foreigners who lived in other nations outside of Israel (Lev. 25:44).
3. Foreigners in Israel who lived in their own enclaves who were culturally and religiously different, worshipping their own gods (Num. 33:55).

It was this last category of foreigner that posed a *serious threat* to the nation. God warned Israel of the dangers of these people. The issue was not race or ethnicity but *religion*:

> Nor shall you make marriages with them. You shall not give your daughter to their son, nor take their daughter for your son. For they will turn your sons away from following Me, to serve other gods; so the anger of the LORD will be aroused against you and destroy you suddenly. (Deut. 7:3–4)

Israel was to be an open and free society but was not pluralistic regarding religious worship. God had warned Israel of the dangers of having people with different gods living among them and knew they would be a thorn in their side (Num. 33:55). Moses and Joshua both reinforced God's warning of the potential calamity (Deut. 7:16; Josh. 23:13). Such people were a threat to the nation because they undermined the God of Israel. Even wise Solomon was later brought down by his foreign wives and their foreign gods (1 Kings 11:8).

> *Israel was to be an open and free society but was not pluralistic regarding religious worship.*

Foreigners Versus Citizens

A distinction was made between a citizen and foreigners who had *not* accepted the God of Israel in some of the ceremonial and civil laws. Such foreigners:

- Could be charged interest by citizens (Deut. 23:20)
- Could not permanently own rural farmland in Israel (Lev. 25:23)
- Were not subject to the debt cancellation provisions in a year of release (Deut. 15:1–3)
- Could be held in servitude permanently (Lev. 25:45–47)
- Could be sold an animal that died of itself, that would otherwise defile an Israelite (Deut. 14:21).

In relation to leadership in Israel:

- No foreigner could be king (Deut. 17:14–15)—a king had to be a "brother," implying he was to be a native-born Israelite.
- Certain categories of foreigners could not hold office (Deut. 23:3–8).[4]

At the same time such foreigners:

- Could lease land from Israelites and hold servants (Lev. 25:47–55)
- Could buy houses permanently (Lev. 25:29–30)
- Could become wealthy in the society (Lev. 25:47)

Regardless of whether a foreigner had accepted the God of Israel, they still had to respect the ceremonial laws of the land. During the feast of Unleavened Bread, for example, they had to respect the command to avoid leaven just like

---

[4] There are differing opinions as to the interpretation of these verses. Refer to the chapter *Hard-to-Understand Mosaic laws*.

everyone else:

> For seven days no leaven shall be found in your houses, since whoever eats what is leavened, that same person shall be cut off from the congregation of Israel, whether he is a stranger or a native of the land. (Exod. 12:19)

Foreigners were equally liable to show respect to the God of Israel in all their actions:

> The person who does anything presumptuously, whether he is native-born or a stranger, that one brings reproach on the LORD, and he shall be cut off from among his people. (Num. 15:30)

Citizenship did have its advantages, but they were relatively few. The main emphasis from God's perspective was to protect the nation from the decadent and destructive false religions of the nations around them.

New Testament Citizenship

The New Testament presents the coming together of Jews and gentiles in a unified fellowship in Christ without division (Gal. 3:28; Eph. 2:19; Col. 3:11). Those who do not take the time to examine the Mosaic law and the supporting narrative of ancient Israel will assume that this is a new concept arriving in the new covenant—that the God of Israel was previously exclusive or even "racist" as some would label today.

But all along God welcomed believing gentiles into his fellowship. The old covenant was primarily focused on Israel, but gentiles who turned to God were always welcome. Gentiles who wished to sacrifice to the God of Israel were welcome to do so (Lev. 17:8; 22:18; Num. 15:14–16). When Paul later wrote about gentiles being "grafted" to spiritual Israel, it was not a new idea, but one which God had expressed to ancient Israel right from the outset (Rom. 11:13–19; see also Exod. 12:48; Num. 9:14).

The old covenant was primarily focused on Israel, but gentiles who turned to God were always welcome.

Had the religious leaders of Israel who returned from the Babylonian captivity followed God's original directives, the great division that developed between Jew and gentile in the Second Temple period would not have existed. It was always God's intent for Abraham's descendants to be a blessing to *all* nations not a stumbling block (Gen. 18:18).

Consider the beautiful words God spoke through the prophet Ezekiel of a future time—one that demonstrates the unchanging gracious mind of God:

> "Thus you shall divide this land among yourselves according to the tribes of Israel. It shall be that you will divide it by lot as an inheritance for yourselves, and for the strangers who dwell among you and who bear children among you. They shall be to you as native-born among the children of Israel; they shall have an inheritance with you among the tribes of Israel. And it shall be that in whatever tribe the stranger dwells, there you shall give him his inheritance," says the LORD God. (Ezek. 47:21–23)

The Structure of the Judicial System

You shall not show partiality in judgment; you shall hear the small as well as the great; you shall not be afraid in any man's presence. —Deuteronomy 1:17

As George Washington considered his appointments to his new nation's judiciary in 1789, he wrote:

> The Due Administration of Justice is the Firmest Pillar of Good Government ... hence the selection of the fittest characters to expound the laws, and dispense justice, has been an invariable object of my anxious concern.[1]

Washington understood that a nation aspiring to greatness must have a system of justice administered by qualified people of character. Citizens needed to know they would receive a fair hearing before a competent and impartial judiciary.

God also took the establishment of the judiciary in ancient Israel very seriously. He wanted the judges to reflect his own standards because they would be making judgments *in his name* (Deut. 1:17; 16:18; 2 Chron. 19:6). God desired *righteous judgment*, which, by definition, must align with God's values (Lev. 19:15). Therefore, first and foremost, the judicial system for ancient Israel would require individuals of character who were knowledgeable in the law and had an appropriate level of godly wisdom and discernment.

> *God wanted the judges to reflect his own standards because they would be making judgments in his name.*

The judicial system of Israel also needed to be practical, efficient, and timely. Judges had to be accessible by all citizens in the land. There also needed to be a way to escalate more complex or serious cases that required a deeper understanding of the law.

In addition to the authorized judiciary, an effective justice system had to provide for the roles of prosecutor and defender for those unable to pursue justice for themselves. Finally, the system required designating a person or persons who could ensure that the court's judgment was upheld and a the sentence duly executed.

---

[1] Bibliog: (Washington 1789)

The law of Moses addressed these matters in practical ways suitable to the culture of the day.

Selection Criteria of Judges

The law of Moses outlined the general selection criteria for all those in positions of judgment. Being a judge was not a position a person could purchase or achieve by bribery. Judges were to be individuals of experience who were knowledgeable in the law and known to be people of godly character and integrity:

> Choose wise, understanding, and knowledgeable men from among your tribes, and I will make them heads over you. (Deut. 1:13)

> Moreover you shall select from all the people able men, such as fear God, men of truth, hating covetousness ... And let them judge the people at all times. (Exod. 18:21–22)

Judges would need to be courageous, not intimidated by people of wealth or fame and not susceptible to bribes:

> You shall not show partiality in judgment; you shall hear the small as well as the great; you shall not be afraid in any man's presence. (Deut. 1:17)

> You shall not pervert justice; you shall not show partiality, *nor take a bribe*, for a bribe blinds the eyes of the wise and twists the words of the righteous. (Deut. 16:19)

As Israel drifted away from God, the character of judges declined accordingly. Like the nations around them, bribery, partiality, and corruption became key issues that brought down the nation (1 Sam. 8:3; Isa. 1:23; Amos 5:12).

The Role of Elders

The starting point of the formal judicial system was aligned with the tribal culture of the day. From their earliest time in Egypt, the nation of Israel was governed by elders. Elders were the respected leaders of the family clans who had gained their position by virtue of their age, wisdom, and experience. The people looked to the elders for their collective leadership. God showed respect to the elder system from the outset (Exod. 3:16).

It was from the elders that God told Moses to select the initial seventy judges of Israel when in the wilderness (Num. 11:16). When settled in the land, judges would continue to be selected from the elders, who would administer justice at the local level in each of the towns and cities:

> You shall appoint judges and officers *in all your gates*, which the LORD your God gives you, according to your tribes, and they shall judge the people with just judgment. (Deut. 16:18)

The availability of elders in each town gave people easy access to the judicial system for day-to-day matters. Elders would sit at the gates of the city at certain times of the day so people knew where to go to receive advice or have a matter resolved (Deut. 21:19; 22:15; 25:7; Ruth 4:1–11). City elders would handle most minor disputes and civil matters. Being local, the elders were connected to the people and issues involved. False witnesses would be generally less likely to get away with fabricated events. Elders generally operated as a group in such matters, which reduced the vulnerability of having just one judicial perspective.

> *Elders in each town gave people easy access to the judicial system for day-to-day matters.*

Levitical Judges

For more difficult or serious cases, the Levitical priesthood provided a higher level of judicial authority to call upon in the land. Individual Levites may have been appointed to their judicial role by the high priest or by Levitical elders. The Levitical judges were not an appeals court as such but were available to handle more complex cases:

> If a matter arises which is too hard for you to judge, between degrees of guilt for bloodshed, between one judgment or another, or between one punishment or another, matters of controversy within your gates, then you shall arise and go up to the place which the LORD your God chooses. And you shall come to the priests, the Levites, and to the judge there in those days, and inquire of them; they shall pronounce upon you the sentence of judgment. (Deut. 17:8–9)

The Levites were both judges and teachers of the law (Mal. 2:7). When the nation was close to God, their role carried enormous respect. The option to take a matter before the Levites would have given people confidence that their case would be properly considered. When judgments were delivered, their word was final:

> Then the priests, the sons of Levi, shall come near, for the LORD your God has chosen them to minister to Him and to bless in the name of the LORD; *by their word every controversy and every assault shall be settled*. (Deut. 21:5)

Their judgments were not to be taken lightly:

> You shall do according to the sentence which they pronounce upon you in that place which the LORD chooses. And you shall be careful to do according to all that they order you. ... Now the man who acts presumptuously and will not heed the priest who stands to minister there before the LORD your God, or the judge, that man shall die. So you shall put away the evil from Israel. And all the people shall hear and fear, and no longer act presumptuously. (Deut. 17:10, 12–13)

Decisions of the court were not legal precedents as we understand the concept today, but they were supposed to teach the principles underpinning the law. For this reason, judges were specifically directed to explain how they came to their decision:

> According to the sentence of the law in which *they instruct you*, according to the *judgment which they tell you*, you shall do. (Deut. 17:11)

To provide easy access to the Levites for more complex judgments, 48 special status Levitical cities were spread throughout the land (Num. 35:1–7; Josh. 21:1–42). These were cities owned and overseen by Levites. Out of the 48 cities, 6 were designated as sanctuary cities. Sanctuary cities were to provide a safe haven for any individual who had accidentally killed another person until the case came to trial.

For more complex judgments, 48 special status Levitical cities were spread throughout the land.

Later we see Samuel following a circuit court similar to the circuit judges of old. Samuel was a serving Levitical priest and a prophet (1 Sam. 2:18; 3:20).

> And Samuel judged Israel all the days of his life. He went from year to year on a *circuit* to Bethel, Gilgal, and Mizpah, and judged Israel in all those places. But he always returned to Ramah, for his home was there. There he judged Israel, and there he built an altar to the LORD. (1 Sam. 7:15–17)

This overreliance on Samuel at the time may have reflected the people's lack of confidence in some of the other judges. The previous high priest, Eli, and his sons were corrupt. Even Samuel's own sons he appointed as judges became corrupt (1 Sam. 8:1–3).

Specially Appointed Judges

At times, specific leaders of Israel from various tribes were also appointed as judges. The Hebrew word translated "judge" in the Old Testament has a broader connotation than just a judicial authority. As we see in the book of Judges, many of the "judges" of Israel were military leaders God sent to rescue the nation from foreign oppression (e.g., Othniel, Jephthah, Barak, Samson, Gideon, Elon, etc.). They became governors and rulers in their regions. Scripture tells us that they "judged" Israel, but this seems to primarily refer to their role in governing.

Not a lot is written about the formal involvement of these judges in the judicial process. Deborah is specifically noted as judging those who came to her, and she had the respect of the leaders of the day (Judg. 4:4–6). Later when the elders came to Samuel asking for a king, they specifically noted they wanted a king to "judge" them like the other nations:

> We will have a king over us, that we also may be like all the nations, and that our king may *judge* us and go out before us and fight our battles. (1 Sam. 8:19–20)

This again is using the term *judge* in reference to Israel's desire for a human leader rather than relying on an invisible God. It was not specifically a request for a king to act as a higher judicial authority, even though the king would fulfill that role as well.

Later we see David both judging people and appointing a substantial number of judges throughout the land (1 Chron. 23:4). People came to both David and Solomon for complex judgments, the most famous being the case of the two women before Solomon (1 Kings 3:16–28). The option to come before the king for judgment seems to have resulted in bottlenecks in the judicial system, which was not God's original intent (2 Sam. 15:2–4). God's original plan for the Levites to be the higher-level judiciary would have resulted in a far more efficient judicial system.

Prosecutors and Enforcers

The Mosaic system also defined other roles necessary for a working justice system. Today we have public defenders and prosecutors employed by the state whose role it is to either defend or bring criminal matters to trial. The role of prosecutor is particularly important for those who cannot bring their plea for justice to court, including those who are deceased. In ancient Israel, with minimal state bureaucracy, matters were, by necessity, handled differently. An individual would usually bring a matter before the judge themselves. But if they could not do so, a specially authorized near family member, variously called the redeeming kinsman or avenger, could prosecute justice on their behalf.[2]

Our modern legal system also has police officers, officers of the court, prison wardens, and various other authorized roles to arrest lawbreakers and enforce court decisions. Many of these roles are relatively recent inventions. Professional police forces as we know them today appeared in the eighteenth century. Prior to that, nations and leaders generally used armies or private militia to maintain law and order.

In ancient Israel, it was generally the individual plaintiff or their redeeming kinsman who would bring a matter before a judge. This was not a lawless vigilante system as it might have been in some other nations. In Israel, only the individual or their appointed kinsman could act in that role.

Once the elders or judges had made a decision, it was the accuser or redeeming kinsman's duty to enforce the punishment. In the case of capital punishment, the witnesses who testified against the guilty party and the relevant community would also be involved in executing the sentence (Num. 35:19; Deut. 13:9; 17:6–7; 21:21).

No doubt we would recoil at such a system today. As a society we have detached ourselves from such roles. We employ professional executioners in prisons for capital punishment situations. The ancient world was much more "in your face," so to speak. Being so personally involved would make an accuser balk at bringing a false charge. It would also send a message to other offenders to "hear and fear" (Deut. 13:11).

Had Israel lived in line with the law God gave, it would have been a safe and secure society (and at times, it was) with little need for enforcers and executioners. But when serious issues arose, it had to be clear who took responsibility. Later, under the monarchy, kings at various times used military enforcers to execute judgment (e.g., 1 Kings 2:25; 46).

---

[2] For more details, refer to the chapter *The Redeeming Kinsman*.

The Judicial Process

The actual process of judging a matter was legally sound and included key elements we expect today in a fair trial.

> *The process of judging a matter was legally sound and included key elements we expect today in a fair trial.*

Equality under the law meant that all citizens could access the judiciary. We see this principle in action several times in the historical narrative, where widows, single women, and even prostitutes had the right to come before a judge for a judgment (Num. 27:1–2; 2 Sam. 14:4; 1 Kings 3:16). Their voice was not too small to be heard.

The court was an open environment, and a matter brought before the relevant judges had to have supporting witnesses for it to be heard:

> One witness shall not rise against a man concerning any iniquity or any sin that he commits; by the mouth of two or three witnesses the matter shall be established. (Deut. 19:15)

Witnesses were particularly important in the case of murder. The ramifications of their words carried a heavy weight of responsibility:

> Whoever is deserving of death shall be put to death on the testimony of two or three witnesses; he shall not be put to death on the testimony of one witness. The hands of the witnesses shall be the first against him to put him to death, and afterward the hands of all the people. (Deut. 17:6–7)

False witnesses were to be punished with the full force of the law:

> If a false witness rises against any man to testify against him of wrongdoing, then both men in the controversy shall stand before the Lord, before the priests and the judges who serve in those days. And the judges shall make careful inquiry, and indeed, if the witness is a false witness, who has testified falsely against his brother, then you shall do to him as he thought to have done to his brother; so you shall put away the evil from among you. (Deut. 19:16–19)

There was also liability for a witness who was later found to have withheld information:

> If a person sins in hearing the utterance of an oath, and is a witness, whether he has seen or known of the matter—if he does not tell it, he bears guilt. (Lev. 5:1).

As previously noted, if a matter was too complex for the local judges to handle, they could escalate the matter to a more qualified judge.

Comparison to the Modern World

There are obviously major differences between the ancient world and the more complex way our modern society pursues justice. One fundamental difference compared to our modern system is the role that the judges' wisdom and discernment was to play in the judgment. God desired judges to be people of high character with godly discernment. This is not always the way the system works in our world today.

Today, our Western world places a heavy emphasis on legislation and legal precedents, and cases can be lost on technicalities even when an individual is obviously guilty. Jurors and judges are often required to listen to minute details of a crime, even to the point of being traumatized. This is all part of our legalistic adversarial system, which often requires complex, long, and expensive trials even when the case is essentially open and shut.

Ancient Israel was a far simpler culture, but we should avoid thinking of it as primitive. God's plan for Israel was for the nation to be a leading light among the nations with a justice system that protected the society and individuals in a way that was fair, just, timely, and reflected God's own values.

Sentencing and Penalties

Thus says the LORD of hosts: "Execute true justice, show mercy and compassion everyone to his brother." —Zechariah 7:9

All societies must provide for the restraint and punishment of antisocial and criminal behavior to protect their citizens. The forms and degrees of the sentences meted out reflect the values of that society. In the ancient world, punishments for antisocial behavior included financial penalties, imprisonment, servitude, banishment, and physical punishments extending to torture and death. The Romans perfected the terrible death by crucifixion, but later European practices exceeded them in terms of cruelty. One must only visit one of the many "torture museums" in Western Europe to realize how debase the human mind can be. Excruciating public and private tortures were often administered in the name of "justice" right up to the Modern Era in "civilized" countries. Aside from the inhumane barbarity of these punishments, there was often the total lack of proportionality of the punishment to the crime.

How the world has changed! Capital punishment has been abolished in most Western countries, and people generally look with disdain at any form of corporal punishment. Today our main forms of punishment are either a prison sentence or financial penalties for those who can afford it.

We view much of history through the eyes of the society in which we live and automatically assume that our ways are more enlightened. But ask anyone who has spent time in the prison system, and they will explain just how imperfect our modern systems are. Incarceration is a major cost to society and has a track record of poor rehabilitation and long-term mental health issues—and ultimately does not satisfy the wronged party.

Even considering the failures of our own system, most people will think it superior to the "harsh and cruel" law of Moses. But this view is again skewed by perception more than reality. While the ancient world was a tougher and more brutal world to live in, God did not intend for there to be cruelty or lack of proportionality in his justice system. As we have amply seen, godly justice was supposed to go hand in hand with mercy and grace (Ps. 89:14). Long before Jesus, the prophets castigated the leaders of their nation for not understanding these most basic of principles in the way the law was supposed to be administered (Isa. 1:17; Jer. 22:3; Hosea 10:12; Mic. 6:8; Zech. 7:9–11).

The law of Moses had no qualms about capital or corporal punishment, but it rejected any idea of torture or humiliation. Punishment was meant to be swift, humane, and proportional to the crime committed. In many crimes there can be no positive outcomes, but the law of Moses provided more options to restore and rehabilitate than many Western systems today.

God did not intend for there to be cruelty or lack of proportionality in his justice system.

The Sanctity of Life

One major difference between our society and ancient Israel has to do with the understanding of the "sanctity" of life. While the term "sanctity" is no longer used in our secular society, there is still a latent belief that life has a specialness that must be preserved at all costs. Ironically, the atheist/agnostic stance against capital punishment is often stronger in this regard than the Christian worldview.

Although rejected in our legal system today, the true perspective of the specialness of life can only come from our Creator, who made man in his own image. God made it clear early in man's history that *because* humans were made in his image, an account must be made for a life wrongly taken:

> Surely for your lifeblood I will demand a reckoning; from the hand of every beast I will require it, and from the hand of man. From the hand of every man's brother I will require the life of man. Whoever sheds man's blood, by man his blood shall be shed; for in the image of God He made man. (Gen. 9:5–6)

In the same vein, when Cain committed the first murder, God said the *blood of Abel was crying out to him from the ground* (Gen. 4:10).

This same standard was incorporated into the justice system of the law of Moses. God did not support the idea that taking the life of a murderer is barbaric and not worthy of a "civilized" people. In God's eyes, it was "uncivilized" (so to speak) to not remove a murderer from the land. Spilled blood demanded justice. God, as the ultimate avenger of blood, authorized the civil authorities of ancient Israel to deal with such matters on his behalf. God described the land as polluted when a murderer was not brought to account:

> So you shall not pollute the land where you are; for blood defiles the land, and no atonement can be made for the land, for the blood that is shed on it, except by the blood of him who shed it. Therefore do not

defile the land which you inhabit, in the midst of which I dwell; for I the LORD dwell among the children of Israel. (Num. 35:33–34)

In God's eyes, it was not *just* to have a murderer pointlessly spend the remainder of their life in the safety of a prison. It diminished the value of the life lost. The big difference between God and secular man is that God is the giver of life and has the prerogative to "take life and to wound and to heal" (Deut. 32:39). He has the ultimate power over death and the ability to raise all people to a future judgment.

Types of Punishment

A range of different types of punishments are noted in the law of Moses, including capital punishment, corporal punishment, financial penalty, servitude, and being "cut-off" from society. Imprisonment was not an option in early Israel other than holding a person in custody pending a trial.

Capital punishments noted in the text include stoning, being shot by an arrow, and death by sword (Exod. 19:13; 32:27). The law notes burning in two instances (Lev. 20:14; 21:9). But considering the law's overarching emphasis on humane punishment, this seems to be a reference to the burning of a dead body *after* capital punishment is first inflicted. Achan's trial supports this position: Achan was stoned and his corpse was later burned (Josh. 7:15, 25). Hanging is also referenced, but again, this seems to have only occurred after the person was executed (Deut. 21:22).

Critics highlight the punishment of *stoning* as barbaric. But the intention of stoning was not to torture but to bring the offender to a *quick* end. Death in such instances would have been swift. And neither was stoning a mandatory method of punishment. When this law was introduced, Israel was in the wilderness, where rocks were plentiful. We also note that there are very few examples in Scripture of people receiving such a punishment.

What Punishment Was Not to Do

In many ancient cultures (Assyria, Rome, etc.), enslaved people, criminals, and dissidents could be abused as the state saw fit—even tortured and executed as a public spectacle. Israel was to be different. The character of God set the overall tone in how punishment was to be understood by judges in ancient Israel. God is not vindictive and took no delight in the death of any wicked person (Gen. 6:6; Ezek. 33:11; 18:32). Judges were to dispassionately mete out sentences that were proportional to the crime committed (Deut. 19:21).

Cruelty was not condoned. When corporal punishment was necessary, limits were in place so that the individual was not degraded.

> If the wicked man deserves to be beaten, that the judge will cause him to lie down and be beaten in his presence, according to his guilt, with a certain number of blows. Forty blows he may give him and no more, lest he should exceed this and beat him with many blows above these, *and your brother be humiliated in your sight.* (Deut. 25:2–3)

When capital punishment was called for, death was to be swift and the body buried at the end of the day.

> If a man has committed a sin deserving of death, and he is put to death, and you hang him on a tree, *his body shall not remain overnight on the tree, but you shall surely bury him that day,* so that you do not defile the land which the LORD your God is giving you as an inheritance; for he who is hanged is accursed of God. (Deut. 21:22–23)

Joshua followed this directive, even when dealing with cruel and evil kings of Canaan (Josh. 8:29; 10:27). Unfortunately, these laws, like many others, were not always followed.

The judge's sentence was to take into account the offense, the offender, the victim, and the society.

Purpose of Punishment

Under the law of Moses, the judge's sentence was to take into account the offense, the offender, the victim, and the society. The law noted several outcomes a sentence would variously aim to achieve.

To Teach God's Justice

God is a God of justice, and evil must be accounted for and not be ignored (Deut. 32:4). A sentence was to teach Israel God's perspective of evil so the community would learn and understand that certain behavior was unacceptable.

Deterrence

A sentence was to be a deterrence to others. People would "hear and fear" and be deterred from following in the same path (Deut. 13:11; 17:13; 19:20). Deterrence works when sentencing is swift, the judgment without fear or favor, and the punishment fair and in the public domain. As a further deterrence, any persons bearing false witness were also dealt with the same judgment they thought to bring upon another (Deut. 19:18–21).

Protection of Society

To protect society from serious offenders, capital punishment permanently removed the offender from the society. This was to "put away the evil from among you" (Deut. 17:7; 19:19; 22:21).

Restoration

In the case of loss or theft, the offender was to either repay the loss plus a penalty or indenture themselves and work off the value of the loss. The one who suffered loss received the compensation (Exod. 22:1–3; Lev. 6:1–5). Once the offender had fulfilled their obligations, their civil rights were restored.

Rehabilitation

The offender could redeem themselves by being indentured to the one harmed. This provided the opportunity for rehabilitation.[1]

Examples of Harsh Justice?

Two stoning incidents at the time of Moses are sometimes referred to as examples of harsh justice. The first concerns the breaking of the Sabbath:

> Now while the children of Israel were in the wilderness, they found a man gathering sticks on the Sabbath day. And those who found him gathering sticks brought him to Moses and Aaron, and to all the congregation. They put him under guard, because it had not been explained what should be done to him. (Num. 15:32–34)

The reason Scripture highlights this story is because it *was* unusual. It was included by Moses because it was an exception. In all the history of Israel over hundreds of years, it is the *only* such example concerning the Sabbath. To understand why the judgment was given, we must look at the context. This event is noted immediately after God had explained the difference between unintentional and deliberate sins. He explained that forgiveness was available when a person sins unintentionally (Num. 15:27–29). But the individual who deliberately and publicly rejected the God of Israel was to be punished:

> But the person who *does anything presumptuously*, whether he is native-born or a stranger, that one brings reproach on the LORD, and he shall

---

[1] This topic will be discussed further in the chapter *The Issue of Slavery*.

be cut off from among his people. Because he has despised the word of the LORD, and has broken His commandment, that person shall be completely cut off; his guilt shall be upon him. (Num. 15:30–31)

This is the context of the man working on the Sabbath. The matter was brought before God, and he decreed that the man should be put to death (vv. 35–36). God, who sees the heart, knew that this man's actions were not accidental or an emergency, but outright defiance against him, and so the man received the maximum penalty of the law (Exod. 31:15).

In the second nonrelated incident, a man publicly blasphemed God:

And the Israelite woman's son blasphemed the name of the LORD and cursed; and so they brought him to Moses. ... Then they put him in custody, that the mind of the LORD might be shown to them. (Lev. 24:11–12)

The man's crime was similar to the previous incident: it was a rejection of the God of Israel. Again, God judged that the man should be put to death. What the man did was again not an accident, but a product of his hatred of God. God was teaching Israel the importance of understanding his holiness and that society would be harmed when a person's crime went unpunished. The judgments in both cases were just.

To use these two exceptional incidents as proof of God's harshness is unreasonable. All societies come down hard on high-handed, "in-your-face" lawbreakers at times, both as an example to others and to remove the evil from society. In the same way, anyone who publicly promoted idolatry and worshipped false gods would be liable for severe punishment because to do so sowed seeds of destruction for the nation. (Exod. 22:20; Deut. 13:1–5; 17:2–5)

And let's be reminded that there were no religious police to enforce such things as we might find in some Islamic countries today. When a person publicly acted against the God of Israel, the community had to approach the individual and, if necessary, bring a serious public matter before a judge. People were not to take the law into their own hands.

Being Cut Off

One noted penalty for various offenses is to be "cut off from his people." God noted this penalty across a wide range of offenses, including ignoring food and purity laws, breaking the Sabbath, and failing to respect the ceremonial system (e.g., Exod. 31:14; Lev. 7:21, 25, 27; 23:29). Being "cut off" is also used for serious offenses, including sacrificing to pagan deities, prostitution, and incest (e.g., Lev. 20:3–6; 20:17).

In practice, the meaning of the expression "cut off" has been the subject of scholarly debate. In most instances, it seems to refer to being put out of the fellowship of Israel (Num. 19:20). But it can also refer to being barred from various roles (Num. 4:18), being excluded from the sanctuary (Lev. 22:3), and even death for serious intentional sins (Lev. 20:1–3). The term is also in the context of the blotting out of a family name from the nation (Ruth 4:10).

Considering the multiple ways the term is used, it appears that being "cut off" is not a specific punishment but an expression of the day that must be understood from the context. In many ways the expression is similar to the concept of a *curse*, where God pronounces the negative future that will come upon an individual because of their actions (Deut. 27:15).[2] Many of the applicable sins would be private and take God's intervention for the "cutting off" to take effect.

Overall, the thought of potentially being cut off from the fellowship of their countrymen and of their God would be a serious matter in such a tight-knit community. A person's family name and heritage were an important part of who they were.

---

[2] This subject will be considered in more detail in the chapter *Sins of the Fathers*.

The Redeeming Kinsman

The LORD redeems the soul of His servants, and none of those who trust in Him shall be condemned. —Psalm 34:22

Under the law of Moses, it was God's plan for caring neighbors to rally around and support an individual or family in need. But when serious disaster struck, such as the untimely death of a family member, the loss of the family property, a family member caught in debt servitude, or a widow left potentially destitute, it was the role of a specifically designated family member to take charge of the situation on behalf of the family or the individual involved. This person was called the *near kinsman* but had other descriptive titles depending on the duties they were called on to fulfill.

The Hebrew word for the near kinsman is *go'el*, which is variously translated as "redeemer," "near relative," "redeeming kinsman," "guardian-redeemer," and "family-redeemer." The *go'el* carried the serious responsibility of protecting, redeeming, and preserving the family name and its assets. In cases of serious crimes of manslaughter or murder, it was the near kinsman's duty to fulfill the role of prosecutor, enforcer, and even executioner if necessary. In this role they became the *redeemer* (or *avenger*) *of blood* (as it is often translated) and were a key aspect of the justice system.

> *The redeeming kinsman carried the serious responsibility of protecting, redeeming, and preserving the family name and its assets.*

The Duties of the Redeemer

The concept of a redeemer is deeply rooted in the Mosaic system. The redeemer kinsman was appointed according to their family relationship to the relevant individual, starting first with brothers, then uncles, cousins, etc. (Lev. 25:48–49). A person in need could call upon their near kinsman for help, and the kinsman was obliged to act. Not fulfilling the role could also potentially bring shame to the individual (Deut. 25:9–10).

The scope of the redeeming kinsman's duties included:

Bringing a manslayer to justice.

In this role as the avenger of blood, the redeeming kinsman was to seek justice for the family on behalf of a murdered relative (Num. 35:12–27).

Buying back family property:

When family property had to be sold because of debt or family tragedy, a redeeming kinsman (if he had the means) had the option to buy back and reclaim the property for the family (Lev. 25:25).

Buying back a relative in servitude.

If, in conjunction with the loss of land, an individual was in bonded servitude to another, the redeeming kinsman could free them by buying out the value of their service (Lev. 25:47–48). In biblical terms, this was termed paying a *ransom*—a word with a different meaning today.

Receiving restitution on behalf of the family.

If restitution was required for a crime of some sort, and the individual to whom the restitution was due was deceased, restitution was paid to the near kinsman on their behalf, and it was his responsibility to distribute the proceeds accordingly (Num. 5:5–8).

Preserving a family name by levirate marriage.

When a husband died and left a widow without sons, the woman had the right to call on a near kinsman to marry her and provide an heir to the dead husband so that her husband's name and land inheritance were not lost (Deut. 25:5–10; Ruth 3:13). This was more than just protecting the dead husband's name; it was a way of giving the widow security in a world where she would be more at risk without sons to defend and support her. The near kinsman was obligated to look after a widow in this way. Of course, the widow could always choose to marry someone else if that option was available. It was the woman's choice, as the story of Ruth demonstrates (Ruth 3:10). But if she married outside the tribe, the land inheritance would be lost (Num. 36:2–9).

Why the Need for a Redeemer

In a close-knit society with minimal state resources, the role of the near kinsman made perfect sense. Who else could a vulnerable person call on to help their cause or prosecute their case for compensation or justice? Even in our modern society, if the state doesn't choose to prosecute a case, justice may require a person to go it alone or engage a private law firm at great expense. A near kinsmen

> *In a close-knit society with minimal state resources, the role of the near kinsman made perfect sense.*

would have a far greater interest in supporting the family than a detached state official or hired legal firm. They would have personal relationships with family members and ideally act in the best interests of the individual concerned.

The primary purpose of the role of *go'el* can therefore be best described by the term *redeeming kinsman*, because redemption (i.e., release, restoration, rescue, deliverance) was at the heart of the role. Even when fulfilling the role of an *avenger of blood*, the specific task for the near kinsman was not vindictive retaliation (which was prohibited) but justice for the family in the sight of God.

Boaz the Redeemer

The most well-known biblical example of a redeeming kinsman system is described in the book of Ruth. It's a beautiful story demonstrating the positive benefits of the near kinsman system in the ancient world. Naomi and Ruth were essentially destitute after the loss of their husbands. They relied on the social welfare system (gleaning) to survive. As the widow of Elimelech, Naomi was the owner of the family property. To preserve the lineage of her deceased husband and retain the property in the family, either she or her daughter-in-law, Ruth, needed to marry a kinsman who accepted the levirate marriage conditions. Naomi was past childbearing age and needed Ruth to agree. If Ruth had just married whom she wished, it would have left Naomi with no guarantee of protection from Ruth's new husband, a point Boaz well understood (Ruth 3:10).

It was Ruth's loyalty and her agreeance to marry Naomi's kinsman Boaz, as well as Boaz's willingness to accept the duties of a near kinsman, even at the expense of his own heritage, that led to such a positive outcome for all. The result of Boaz and Ruth's actions was the preservation of the family line, the protection and honor of Naomi, a beautiful marriage, and Ruth becoming the great-grandmother of King David.

The Avenger of Blood

The kinsmen's role as an *avenger of blood* was a heavy responsibility but an important one in the justice system of the day. The near kinsman was responsible for ensuring that justice was upheld for a relative who had been murdered or killed under suspicious circumstances. The law prohibited personal vengeance, but that did not negate the right of duly appointed authorities to prosecute manslayers. All this aligned with the high value God placed on human life (Gen. 9:6). Murder or manslaughter was not to be ignored. God symbolically describes the blood of the victim as polluting the land and needing atonement (Num. 35:33–34; Deut. 21:1–9).

Someone reading the parts of the law referring to the *avenger* can gain a wrong impression of a crazed, angry relative out for blood, hunting for the one who had done their family harm. But keep in mind the principles of justice, which underpinned the entire law of Moses, *especially* when it came to murder or manslaughter.

> *Someone reading the parts of the law referring to the avenger can gain a wrong impression of a crazed, angry relative out for blood.*

The law was clear on the need for judicial process, impartiality, and the necessity for multiple witnesses, especially when capital punishment was a possibility (Num. 35:29–30). These principles could not be simply discarded by someone in a fit of anger. An avenging kinsman would be held liable for his own actions if he ignored these principles and took the law into his own hands.[1]

The role of the avenger provided another protection for all concerned. Only the designated redeeming kinsman was allowed to prosecute and execute justice. Other members of the family were not allowed to take matters into their own hands. This minimized the potential for retaliatory feuds to develop. Once the matter had been settled by the avenger, it was legally over, with no further recourse on either side.

Manslaughter and the Avenger

Six cities were nominated as sanctuary cities for someone committing manslaughter (Num. 35:9–15). Three cities were located on the east of the Jordan River and three on the west (Josh. 20:1–9). There a manslayer would receive a fair and impartial hearing from the Levitical judges while being in the protected custody of the city. Again, we must consider the culture at that time. There was no police force or jails to provide personal protection for a manslayer pending a trial. These cities were provided for just that purpose. A redeeming kinsman could not act against an individual while they were in one of these cities.

When a manslayer arrived in a city of refuge, an inquiry was to be made by the

---

[1] Joab abused the role of avenger by murdering Abner who had acted in self-defence (2 Sam. 2:21-23; 3:27–30). David directed Solomon to execute Joab for his actions (1 Kings 2:5–6).

elders and judges of the city (Josh. 20:4; Num. 35:30). If the matter was judged to be a case of *murder*, the murderer was turned over to the avenging kinsman to be executed (Num. 35:16–21; Deut. 19:11–12). This sounds harsh to our modern minds, but again, there were no state executioners. It was the avenger's God-given responsibility to deal with the matter according to the judgment given.

In the case of manslaughter, the matter was more complex, just as it is under modern law codes.[2] Much would depend on the circumstances of the case, including the response of the near kinsman to the tragedy. An angry kinsman may have caused an innocent person to flee in haste to the nearest city of refuge for his own protection, even when he was not deserving of death (Deut. 19:6).

There is some ambiguity in the process as written, but natural justice would dictate that someone judged innocent of the matter would be free to go. If there was minor culpability or if it was a proven case of self-defense, it would generally be hoped that an avenging kinsman would either forgive and/or come to a financial settlement on behalf of the victim's family as allowed for in non-murder situations (Exod. 21:29–30). Otherwise, the law stipulated that a person guilty of manslaughter stay in the city of refuge for their own protection until the death of the serving high priest (Num. 35:25–28). If they left before that, their life was in their own hands. An avenger who found the person outside the protection of the sanctuary city could execute the person without legal regress.

All this sounds somewhat strange to our ears but is perfectly consistent with God's standard that the death of another human must be atoned for and cannot be ignored (Gen. 9:5–6). Even when there was no intention to kill, there is still a penalty to be paid. The symbolic atonement, in this case, was for the manslayer to remain in the city under the protection of the high priest.

Significantly, the manslayer was redeemed and free to go upon the high priest's death, with the avenger of blood having no further claim. Christians will see shadows of the future atoning role of Jesus Christ as the spiritual High Priest in this process (Heb. 7:26–27).

Israel's Faithful Kinsman Redeemer

The Old Testament concept of the redeemer kinsman also shadows God's plan of redemption and restoration for humanity. God himself is described as the

---

[2] A charge of involuntary manslaughter continues to be a serious charge today, and a guilty verdict can result in jail time, regardless of whether there was deliberate intent to harm.

faithful *go'el* throughout Scripture. He is described as the redeemer of Israel, rescuing the nation from Egypt in a great judgment:

> Therefore say to the children of Israel: "I am the LORD; I will bring you out from under the burdens of the Egyptians, I will rescue you from their bondage, and *I will redeem (go'el) you with an outstretched arm and with great judgments."* (Exod. 6:6)

Later prophets referred to the God of Israel as their *go'el*:

> You, O LORD, are our Father; our Redeemer (*go'el*) from Everlasting is Your name. (Isa. 63:16)

Christ Our Redeemer

The typology of the redeeming kinsmen finds its ultimate fulfilment in the role Jesus would play for all humanity. The concept of redemption is foundational to the understanding of the gospel. Jesus was our kinsman redeemer who came to redeem humankind from the slavery of sin (John 8:34–36). He came to give his life as a ransom (a payment) so that others could be free (Matt. 20:28).

The concept of redemption is foundational to the understanding of the gospel.

> For there is one God and one Mediator between God and men, the Man Christ Jesus, who *gave Himself a ransom for all*, to be testified in due time. (1 Tim. 2:5–6)

> Our great God and Savior Jesus Christ, who gave Himself for us, *that He might redeem us* from every lawless deed and purify for Himself His own special people, zealous for good works. (Titus 2:13–14)

Jesus redeemed us from the penalty of our own sins by paying the penalty for us (Gal. 3:13–14). This was a payment—not of gold or silver but of his own precious blood (1 Pet. 1:18–19). Recall the previously mentioned typology of the high priest in the sanctuary city, who "covers" for the sins of the offender (Heb. 2:17). All this shows how deeply and thoughtfully God's guiding hand was involved in the design of the Mosaic law system.

Even outside the spiritual typology of the Messiah, the general principle of a faithful kinsman who rescues, looks after, and provides for their wider family is continued into the New Testament as an admonition for all Christians:

But if anyone does not provide for his own, and *especially for those of his household,* he has denied the faith and is worse than an unbeliever. (1 Tim. 5:8)

Tort Laws

If fire breaks out and catches in thorns, so that stacked grain, standing grain, or the field is consumed, he who kindled the fire shall surely make restitution.
—Exodus 22:6

The rights and obligations of citizens under the law of Moses surprisingly align with what one might expect in a modern society. They include most major concepts that define our modern tort law. Tort laws are civil laws that seek to redress and compensate for harm or damage done to another person. Similar to our law systems today, the law of Moses identified liabilities arising in various situations and prescribed how an individual was to be compensated for accidental loss, carelessness, or willful negligence.

These laws were expressed in the form of judgments, or case law examples, that outlined principles or precepts that could be adapted and applied in various situations. They could be used both by individuals for problem resolution and by judges in a more formal court situation. They included law addressing property rights, health and safety, consumer protection issues, and defamation, among other topics. All these laws were designed to teach Israel how to love their neighbor in a practical sense.

> *It is unrealistic to think that a former slave nation would derive such sophisticated legal judgments on its own.*

Considering the ancient times in which these laws were given, these laws are extraordinary, and again show God's hand. It is simply unrealistic to think that a former slave nation would derive such sophisticated legal judgments on its own.

Liability and Duty of Care

As an extension of the foundational principle to love one's neighbor as oneself, the law of Moses put a duty of care on citizens to consider the potential harm their actions or carelessness may cause to another. The law included a range of judgments outlining various liability scenarios, and provided guidelines on where liabilities lay and how compensation was to be addressed:

> And if a man opens a pit, or if a man digs a pit and does not cover it, and an ox or a donkey falls in it, the owner of the pit shall make it good; he shall give money to their owner, but the dead animal shall be his. (Exod. 21:33–34)

> If fire breaks out and catches in thorns, so that stacked grain, standing grain, or the field is consumed, he who kindled the fire shall surely make restitution. (Exod. 22:6)

> If a man causes a field or vineyard to be grazed, and lets loose his animal, and it feeds in another man's field, he shall make restitution from the best of his own field and the best of his own vineyard. (Exod. 22:5)

The law specifically differentiated between a person borrowing an item from their neighbor and, on the other hand, asking their neighbor to mind their goods. These judgments are quite sophisticated in their allocation of liability and are similar to modern tort laws. When borrowing something from another person, the borrower became fully responsible for the item while it was in their custody, regardless of whether the borrower directly caused the damage.

> If a man borrows anything from his neighbor, and it becomes injured or dies, the owner of it not being with it, he shall surely make it good. (Exod. 22:14)

But if the owner was with the item, the liability changed because the relationship changed into a contractor-for-hire situation:

> If its owner was with it, he shall not make it good; if it was hired, it came for its hire. (v. 15)

In another scenario where a person had their neighbor mind their goods, the liability changed depending on what occurred to the goods:

> If a man delivers to his neighbor a donkey, an ox, a sheep, or any animal to keep, and it dies, is hurt, or driven away, no one seeing it, then an oath of the LORD shall be between them both, that he has not put his hand into his neighbor's goods; and the owner of it shall accept that, and he shall not make it good. But if, in fact, it is stolen from him, he shall make restitution to the owner of it. If it is torn to pieces by a beast, then he shall bring it as evidence, and he shall not make good what was torn. (Exod. 22:10–13)

The law also addressed the resulting liability when personal injury resulted. The person causing the harm had to pay for the loss of the victim's time and his medical costs:

> If men contend with each other, and one strikes the other with a stone or with his fist, and he does not die but is confined to his bed, if he rises again and walks about outside with his staff, then he who struck him shall be acquitted. He shall only pay for the loss of his time, and shall provide for him to be thoroughly healed. (Exod. 21:18–19)

In all these scenarios, the liability was limited to making good that which was lost, which was so unlike other class-structured societies of the ancient world. The remedy was to restore the goods or the person to their previous condition. We can appreciate the nuances of these Mosaic laws today. They are right, fair, and just. But to see such sound and thoughtful differentiations in the ancient world is quite extraordinary.

Negligence and Compensation

The law of Moses also differentiated between an unforeseen accident and inconsiderate negligence. In the case of an unforeseen accident, a shared compensation was specified:

> If one man's ox hurts another's, so that it dies, then they shall sell the live ox and divide the money from it; and the dead ox they shall also divide. (Exod. 21:35)

But if the incident was a result of negligence, the individual concerned had to fully recompense the harmed party:

> Or if it was known that the ox tended to thrust in time past, and its owner has not kept it confined, he shall surely pay ox for ox, and the dead animal shall be his own. (Exod. 21:36)

All these judgments provided guidelines for the affected parties to reach a compensation settlement.

The consequences became more severe when the negligence resulted in human injury or death. A case of manslaughter might be triggered:

> If an ox gores a man or a woman to death, then the ox shall surely be stoned, and its flesh shall not be eaten; but the owner of the ox shall be acquitted. But if the ox tended to thrust with its horn in times past, and it has been made known to his owner, and he has not kept it confined, so that it has killed a man or a woman, the ox shall be stoned and its owner also shall be put to death. If there is imposed on him a sum of money, then he shall pay to redeem his life, whatever is imposed on him. (Exod. 21:28–30)

Another judgment presents the scenario of a thief harmed while breaking in. Interestingly, even though the victim was breaking the law, that did not give the homeowner the automatic right to harm the individual. If it was dark, the homeowner may be excused, but otherwise, the homeowner had to account for the harm done to the thief:

> If the thief is found breaking in, and he is struck so that he dies, there shall be no guilt for his bloodshed. If the sun has risen on him, there shall be guilt for his bloodshed. (Exod. 22:2–3)

Other situations where individuals could be harmed became more complicated and required a judge to determine where the fault lay and for an appropriate remedy to be applied. But the principle of proportional justice always remained:

> If men fight, and hurt a woman with child, so that she gives birth prematurely, yet no harm follows, he shall surely be punished accordingly as the woman's husband imposes on him; and he shall pay as the judges determine. But if any harm follows, then you shall give life for life, eye for eye, tooth for tooth, hand for hand, foot for foot, burn for burn, wound for wound, stripe for stripe. (Exod. 21:22–25)

Health and Safety Liability

Our modern law codes are broken into a myriad of distinct legislative categories and include extensive case histories to guide a judge. The Mosaic law was far less complex but still touched on most principles of modern tort law. The beauty of these laws was their simplicity, which outlined principles that could be applied to a wide variety of situations.

One particular Mosaic judgment is closely aligned to our modern workplace safety laws. It puts the onus on the relevant persons to look ahead and foresee potential accidents and negligence claims that may arise from their workmanship:

The Mosaic law was far less complex but still touched on most principles of modern tort law.

> When you build a new house, then you shall make a parapet for your roof, that you may not bring guilt of bloodshed on your household if anyone falls from it. (Deut. 22:8)

The deeper intent is for this law to be taken as a broad principle. It was a general directive for all responsible persons to consider the safety of their products and services and the consequences that could ensue from thoughtless actions.

Slander and Defamation

Caring for a neighbor also included protecting their reputation:

> You shall not circulate a false report. Do not put your hand with the wicked to be an unrighteous witness. (Exod. 23:1)

> Keep yourself far from a false matter. (Exod. 23:7)

The penalty for bearing false witness in a court situation was severe (Deut. 19:18–19). These laws were an extension of the nineth commandment to *not bear false witness against your neighbor*.

But the Mosaic law went further by prohibiting slander, even if the story was factually true. In modern society a test of truthfulness is usually applied in cases of slander, allowing a true story to be spread even if it is damaging to the individual. A person who has otherwise changed their life and moved on can have their past actions widely spread without having any recourse to privacy. The law of Moses prohibits talebearing and slander, whether true or not:

> You shall not go about as a talebearer among your people; nor shall you take a stand against the life of your neighbor: I am the LORD. (Lev. 19:16)

There is a time to address the actions of an unrepentant evil person in society, but there is also a time to forgive and put a person's past behind, just as God himself does (Isa. 43:25).

Consumer Protection Laws

Having standards that a consumer can have confidence in was also important. It has been common in history for merchants and vendors to swindle consumers with varying weights and measures and for coins to be trimmed to maximize profit. God wanted Israel to reflect the highest standard of honesty:

> You shall do no injustice in judgment, in measurement of length, weight, or volume. You shall have honest scales, honest weights, an honest ephah, and an honest hin: I am the LORD your God, who brought you out of the land of Egypt. (Lev. 19:35–36)

God was clear how important these matters were to him:

> You shall not have in your bag differing weights, a heavy and a light. You shall not have in your house differing measures, a large and a small. You shall have a perfect and just weight, a perfect and just measure, that your days may be lengthened in the land which the LORD your God is giving you. For all who do such things, all who behave unrighteously, are an abomination to the LORD your God. (Deut. 25:13–16)

A similar standard of integrity was required when it came to noting land boundaries:

> You shall not remove your neighbor's landmark, which the men of old have set, in your inheritance which you will inherit in the land that the LORD your God is giving you to possess. (Deut. 19:14)

> Cursed is the one who moves his neighbor's landmark. (Deut. 27:17)

These laws were designed to create an honest and just society that people could have confidence in. The commandments *not to steal* and *not to bear false witness* underpinned these ideals.

Extended Responsibilities

The foundation for all the above rights and obligations was the core principle of *loving one's neighbor as oneself* (Lev. 19:18). Because of that, the obligations described in the law toward neighbors went further than our own more detached societal laws today where we have no such command to love our neighbor. Today a person has no legal obligation to care for another's property not in their care. It would be seen as going above and beyond the call of duty for someone to do so.

> *The foundation for all the above rights and obligations was the core principle of loving one's neighbor as oneself.*

The Mosaic law, on the other hand, put the onus on the individual to proactively care for unclaimed or lost property until the owner was found:

> You shall not see your brother's ox or his sheep going astray, and hide yourself from them; you shall certainly bring them back to your brother. And if your brother is not near you, or if you do not know him, then you shall bring it to your own house, and it shall remain

> with you until your brother seeks it; then you shall restore it to him. You shall do the same with his donkey, and so shall you do with his garment; with any lost thing of your brother's, which he has lost and you have found, you shall do likewise; you must not hide yourself. (Deut. 22:1–3)

There was also the command to help someone in need. They should not ignore a distress situation:

> You shall not see your brother's donkey or his ox fall down along the road, and hide yourself from them; you shall surely help him lift them up again. (Deut. 22:4)

And the law was clear that a neighbor was anyone in need, even an adversary:

> If you meet your enemy's ox or his donkey going astray, you shall surely bring it back to him again. If you see the donkey of one who hates you lying under its burden, and you would refrain from helping it, you shall surely help him with it. (Exod. 23:4–5)

Jesus' famous parable of the Good Samaritan is based on these same principles (Luke 10:29–36). These are laws with broad application reflecting a caring society where people looked out for their neighbor. It was not simply a nice thought or a suggestion as it is today; it was a command from the God who does likewise:

> For the poor will never cease from the land; therefore *I command you*, saying, "You shall open your hand wide to your brother, to your poor and your needy, in your land." (Deut. 15:11)

In our world today, courts will generally evaluate a person's responsibility and liability in a particular situation according to what a theoretical "reasonable and prudent" person would do. The problem with this standard is it is benchmarked against a moving target of changing societal standards.

For Israel the standard was what a loving person would do—the ideal standard being God himself.

Sexual Morality

According to the doings of the land of Egypt, where you dwelt, you shall not do; and according to the doings of the land of Canaan, where I am bringing you, you shall not do. —Leviticus 18:3

Sex has been a powerful cultural driver since creation, with its influence evident in the historical records and artifacts of nearly all ancient cultures. Viewed as the ultimate source of physical pleasure, humans have experimented with every variant of sexual expression and lifestyle. Early in man's history, sex was intertwined with religion and conveniently became an expression of worship of the gods. Just as we are seeing today, when the true God is pushed out of the picture, society seeks to fill the spiritual void with hedonistic experiences.

But since creation, God's standards have never changed. God created sex as a gift to a married couple, designed to bring two people together as one flesh in a physical union that has great spiritual overtones. How seriously he took marriage and sex is reflected in the strong penalties outlined in the law for adultery, rape, prostitution, and degenerate sexual behavior (Deut. 22:22, 25; 23:17–18; Lev. 18).

Even for those civilizations that did not know the true God and did not understand the higher significance of his design, God still held people accountable to understand the fundamentals of morality by nature. Centuries before the law of Moses, God condemned misguided sexual behavior and lifestyles (Gen. 18:20; 19:4–13). The land of Canaan was similarly declared defiled because of their immorality long before Sinai (Gen. 15:16; Lev. 18:24–25).

God obviously understands how powerful sexual desire is: he created it.

In stark contrast to the nations around them, God made it clear to Israel that sex was to have no part in his worship system (Exod. 19:15; Lev. 15:16, 31). God wanted Israel to be a holy and special people who held marriage, sex, and family in high esteem. Sexual license and relationships opposed to the traditional family have always worked against God's plan for humankind to be imagers of himself.

Feelings Are Secondary to Truth

God obviously understands how powerful sexual desire is: he created it. In his kindness he also created other pleasures for humans to enjoy—food, drink, music, adrenalin highs, etc. But all these gifts were intended to be exercised with discipline and used within the context of God's design. A major tenet of the entire law of Moses was having the discipline to do what was right *regardless of feelings*. The *command* to love one's neighbor as oneself (and particularly to show love to one's enemies), requires feelings and innate chemical responses to be *subservient* to actions. This is the essence of the tenth commandment not to covet. Simply living a life according to feelings is opposite to God's plan for human beings.

Sometimes people will express the idea that all innate sexual desires and feelings are "God-given." But even though same-sex attraction and transgender dysphoria are certainly real for some people, such desires cannot be "God-given" because they are against God's ordained order for society. A God of truth does not put people in a double bind by giving such desires and then proclaiming them against his design.

> *Simply living a life according to feelings is the opposite to God's plan for human beings.*

Gay and lesbian lifestyles are out of sync with God's order for creation. They cannot create life and do not reflect God's design for family. Although a highly unpopular stance today, the Bible consistently teaches that those who are unmarried by choice, or because they don't find a suitable partner, or for physiological, psychological, or emotional reasons, must restrain their sexual passions and desires. Jesus reaffirmed this to his disciples (Matt. 19:10–12).

Notably, the Mosaic law did not condemn those who had homosexual attractions any more than it condemned a married or unmarried person who was naturally attracted to someone of the opposite sex. What the law did speak out against were those who lustfully harbored such thoughts and who eventually acted them out.

Maintaining Male and Female Distinctions

Scripture teaches us that male and female bodies have a God-given meaning and dignity. They carry the authority of the Creator's design and his unique purpose for each individual. The law of Moses affirmed the importance of maintaining the distinction between the sexes with a simple directive to do with outward appearance:

> A woman shall not wear anything that pertains to a man, nor shall a man put on a woman's garment, for all who do so are an abomination to the LORD your God. (Deut. 22:5)

This instruction was not meant to be understood at a trivial level of "pants versus dresses" as it has been interpreted in some eras. Neither does this law define the specifics of garment design which will change across cultures and locations. Just like the other judgments, this seemingly trivial law has broad ramifications. It was a reinforcement of God's fundamental order for society established at creation. This law makes God's intent clear—that regardless of a person's sexual feelings and desires, he wanted individuals to align their appearance and lifestyle to their God-given biological gender. To otherwise have a person's identity defined by their sexual desires is to give feelings a preeminence far above their intended purpose.

Male and female bodies have a God-given meaning and dignity.

The key issue ancient Israel faced is the same in our societies today. It is a question of authority. Who had authority over their lives? Was it them or God? Scripturally, there has never been any doubt. As Creator, it has always been God's prerogative to establish the order of society and to define the roles of male and female and family in line with his great purpose.

Basic Morality

The Ten Commandments established the foundational guidelines for sexual morality. The fifth, seventh, and tenth commandments addressed the importance of family and sexual fidelity. The commandments against coveting and adultery were not meant to be taken narrowly but were broad principles on which society could build strong families.

The tough penalties outlined for sexual misconduct can make the Mosaic law sound harsh to our modern ears. But God wanted the law administered justly, with mercy and grace. The penalties for sexual offenses were not mandatory sentences but guidelines for judges when serious matters came before them. Such penalties were primarily for those who high-handedly and publicly pushed against the God of Israel, as in the case of the man who unashamedly brought a Midianite prostitute into the camp after God specifically warned against such behavior (Num. 25:6–8). Public prostitution and involvement in pagan religious rites were also dealt with severely at times (Num. 25:1–5).

There is otherwise no historical evidence of capital punishment being widely applied for sexual misconduct in Israelite society.

There was also no state authority or morality police force to pry into the private affairs of individuals like we have witnessed in some regimes in history. If a charge of adultery or rape was to be brought against an individual, it would need to come before a judge with evidence and witnesses. For this reason, most matters of sexual infidelity would be handled privately by the individuals concerned. The law allowed for divorce for sexual misconduct with no requirement to make the details of the affair public (Deut. 24:1). Individuals and families could also come to settlements in the case of premarital sexual misconduct (Exod. 22:16–17).

> *There was no state authority or morality police force to pry into the private affairs of individuals.*

Some comment on the lack of a specific directive against premarital sex as surprising. This is explained by understanding God's view of sex. Two coming together as one in sexual union was inherently part of the marriage contract. Although there was still an option for parental intervention, if a couple engaged in premarital sex, it was assumed they were now married. In ancient Israel, a betrothal was considered a marriage contract. An affair with a betrothed person was treated as adultery (Deut. 22:23–24).

We also must understand the culture. Marriage was far more than just the union of two people; it was the joining of two families with wider tribal ramifications. Marriage ceremonies involved parental dowries and extensive celebrations lasting days. Premarital sex worked against these societal traditions.

Marry a Rapist?

Some criticize the law of Moses as implying that a victim of rape would be forced to marry her rapist. This idea is incorrect and out of line with God's character.

Throughout the law, God shows a great sensitivity to the mistreatment of the vulnerable, and he includes a wide range of legal protections for those most at risk. Furthermore, every situation of rape in the Old Testament is portrayed negatively. To then assume that God would condone or support violence against women is simply untenable. The misconception comes from reading specific judgments very narrowly.

Rape was considered a capital offense on the level of murder for the perpetrator:

> But if a man finds a betrothed young woman in the countryside, and the man *forces her* and lies with her, then only the man who lay with her shall die. But you shall do nothing to the young woman; there is in the young woman no sin deserving of death, *for just as when a man rises against his neighbor and kills him, even so is this matter.* For he found her in the countryside, and the betrothed young woman cried out, but there was no one to save her. (Deut. 22:25–27)

Some read the above judgment *narrowly* as if the woman had to be betrothed (essentially married) for the serious charge of rape to be applied. But God's stance against sexual violence did not change according to a technicality. God is not a legalist. Violence against a woman, whether adultery or rape, was a serious matter.

> *Rape was considered a capital offense on the level of murder for the perpetrator.*

The law also separately presents a scenario where there is an *enticement* of a virgin who is not betrothed. The wording implies a nonviolent consensual act:

> If a man *entices* a virgin who is not betrothed, and lies with her, he shall surely pay the bride-price for her to be his wife. If her father utterly refuses to give her to him, he shall pay money according to the bride-price of virgins. (Exod. 22:16–17)

God was clear in the law that sex outside marriage has consequences. In this case the couple should be married because they have essentially taken the step to become "one flesh." But even here, if the woman's father has serious misgivings about the man, he still had the right to block the marriage. No doubt, a father would also listen to his daughter's concerns if she had any. Regardless of the outcome, the man must pay the dowry to the family for what he has done. A dowry was held in trust for the future welfare of the daughter.

The passage most criticized in relation to forced marriage is Deuteronomy 22:28–29:

> If a man finds a young woman who is a virgin, who is not betrothed, and he seizes her and lies with her, and they are found out, then the man who lay with her shall give to the young woman's father fifty

shekels of silver, and she shall be his wife because he has humbled her; he shall not be permitted to divorce her all his days.

Rather than consider this a new law, it is logical to assume that this is an affirmation of the original law given in Exodus 22:16. Where the controversy lies is the use here of the Hebrew word translated "seize" in most translations. Some assume this involves violence. But scholars note that the Hebrew word here is different from the word translated "force" in the preceding verses (Deut. 22:25) and could be used to describe a seduction.[1] There is also no mention of the woman crying out; the couple are instead "found out." The selection of different verbs is intentional, highlighting a different scenario where both are complicit in some way. Again, to otherwise assume the law supports rape against women is completely at odds with other aspects of the law and the foundational principle of showing love to neighbors.

While we may push back today at any concept of a compulsory marriage, the intent of this law was to ensure that the now "humbled" woman is protected. In the culture of the day, her best security was marriage (albeit her father could refuse). Both the man and woman engaging in premarital sex had to understand the ramifications of their actions and how seriously God considered marriage.

Protection against False Accusation

There is one law related to a test for virginity that seems unfair and out of sync with our modern culture. It is another of the criticized sections of the Old Testament law code.

The law in question presents a case of a woman rightly or wrongly accused of deceiving a new husband that she was a virgin at the time of marriage. The woman's parents are required to present "proof" of her virginity in the form of a stained cloth from the wedding night:

> If any man takes a wife, and goes in to her, and detests her, and charges her with shameful conduct, and brings a bad name on her, and says, "I took this woman, and when I came to her I found she was not a virgin," then the father and mother of the young woman shall take and bring out the evidence of the young woman's virginity to the elders of the city at the gate. And the young woman's father shall say to the elders, "I gave my daughter to this man as wife, and he detests her. Now he has charged her with shameful conduct, saying, 'I found

---

[1] Bibliog: (Butt 2015, 9 Vol 35. No. 8)

your daughter was not a virgin,' and yet these are the evidences of my daughter's virginity." And they shall spread the cloth before the elders of the city. (Deut. 22:13–17)

The consequences for the young woman are potentially dire:

> Then the elders of that city shall take that man and punish him; and they shall fine him one hundred shekels of silver and give them to the father of the young woman, because he has brought a bad name on a virgin of Israel. And she shall be his wife; he cannot divorce her all his days. But if the thing is true, and evidences of virginity are not found for the young woman, then they shall bring out the young woman to the door of her father's house, and the men of her city shall stone her to death with stones, because she has done a disgraceful thing in Israel, to play the harlot in her father's house. So you shall put away the evil from among you. (Deut. 22:18–21)

On the face of it, this seems an unreliable and unfair way to prove anything. Why would God include such an unfair test in the law? How does it align with God's desire to see the vulnerable protected, and for the law to be just and merciful?

To understand this law, we must understand the culture and the reason for its inclusion. We've seen that the law already makes provision for families to address premarital sex: the couple could wed if the woman's father agreed, or in the case of rape, the man was punished (or if the woman was found to be a prostitute, she was punished).

The specific issue being dealt with here is what is stated at the outset: a matter of *slander*. A man accuses his wife of deceit. He paid a dowry and married her with the understanding she was a virgin and then later suspected she was not. Such an accusation would bring shame on the woman and her family and imply a fraudulent arrangement. His reasons for the accusation may be valid, but he might otherwise want to dissolve the marriage for his own reasons. Either way, it would be easy for the man to make such an accusation to the woman's detriment.

To ensure that the woman was not at a disadvantage in such a situation, the law noted two things: Firstly, it states that the matter "must be true" *and* (in addition) "evidences of virginity not found" (v. 20), implying that the matter had to be properly looked into according to law and witnesses brought forward. If there was no wedding sheet, a man would still have to present evidence of the woman's promiscuity. Secondly, the woman's parents were the custodians of the wedding sheet (v. 15), which put them in a distinctly advantageous position.

A man who attempted to slander his wife without hard evidence of other affairs would be on the back foot and be at risk of severe humiliation and punishment. He would think carefully before making such an accusation. He would realize that it would be easy for parents to "cover up" their daughter's previous indiscretions by ensuring that evidence of the wedding sheet was provided. [2]

In a culture where marriage, sex, and family were highly esteemed, it is understandable that virginity would be expected. If proof was found that the woman was indeed "playing the harlot" (v. 21), the consequences for her were potentially severe. At the same time, nothing prevented a woman who was not a virgin from being married. The prophet Hosea, for example, married a prostitute (Hosea 1:2). And a newly married woman who was found not to be a virgin did not have to suffer the maximum penalty of the law; she could be divorced (Deut. 24:1). The main point in this example was not to *deceive*.

Protection of Women in Times of War

The law of Moses also contained unique provisions for the protection of women in times of war when they would be particularly vulnerable. Throughout history it has been considered a right of conquerors to rape and subjugate women as part of the spoils of battle. But God did not want the soldiers of Israel behaving in such a way.

The law directed that if an Israelite soldier desired a foreign woman, he could not just have his way with her. He must first agree to marry her. But before he could do that, he had to go through a prescribed cooling-off procedure lasting a month. The woman was to be first taken back home, ritually cleaned, given new clothes, and given the respect of time to mourn her loss of family before the marriage:

> When you go out to war against your enemies, and the LORD your God delivers them into your hand, and you take them captive, and you see among the captives a beautiful woman, and desire her and would take her for your wife, then you shall bring her home to your

---

[2] The law of Moses does not decree that a wedding sheet be kept. It seems that God aligned this law with the customary practices of the day (as he did with other laws) to ensure that a woman was not disadvantaged.

> house, and she shall shave her head and trim her nails. She shall put off the clothes of her captivity, remain in your house, and mourn her father and her mother a full month; after that you may go in to her and be her husband, and she shall be your wife. (Deut. 21:10–13)

While we may criticize this ancient procedure today, we must consider the context of the time and culture. It was extraordinary to show such respect to a foreign woman in a time of war. Having to follow such a process would have made hot-blooded fighting men carefully consider their actions. Once she became the man's wife, she was afforded all the protection of an Israelite wife. If the marriage didn't work out, the man could not just discard her or sell her as a servant but had to essentially follow the standard divorce arrangements:

> And it shall be, if you have no delight in her, then you shall set her free, but you certainly shall not sell her for money; you shall not treat her brutally, because you have humbled her. (Deut. 21:14)

Timeless Principles

Although it is impossible from our modern perspective to perfectly understand the cultural context of all these laws, certain foundational principles about sexual morality come through strongly.

Firstly, sex was not simply a source of entertainment and pleasure as it was in some ancient nations (and now becoming in our society). Secondly, God-given male and female genders were to be honored and respected as the basis of a family-oriented society. Thirdly, becoming "one flesh" with another was a serious matter and part of a long-term committed relationship. Promiscuous behavior was not acceptable in the eyes of God. Fourthly, God wanted men and women to understand the great importance he holds toward the family structure and for them to be faithful to him, to their families, and to each other.

At the same time, God knew the propensity for both men and women to make mistakes, so he built mercy and forgiveness into the law and the worship system. Just as there were those in the New Testament who had made serious sexual misjudgments and were forgiven (1 Cor. 6:9–11), in the same way, many greats of old, like Tamar, Rahab, David, and Bathsheba, were also forgiven and later esteemed of God.

Sabbatical Cycles and the Jubilee

And you shall consecrate the fiftieth year, and proclaim liberty throughout all the land to all its inhabitants. —Leviticus 25:10

At the start of his ministry, Jesus read a passage from the book of Isaiah, which was to set the tone for his ministry in the years ahead:

> The Spirit of the LORD is upon Me, because He has anointed Me to preach the gospel to the poor; He has sent Me to heal the brokenhearted, to proclaim liberty to the captives and recovery of sight to the blind, to set at liberty those who are oppressed; to proclaim the acceptable year of the LORD. (Luke 4:18–19; Isa. 61:1–2)

These gracious words have their origin in the law of Moses. To "proclaim the acceptable year of the Lord" is an allusion to the year of Jubilee, which was to be proclaimed every fifty years throughout the land of Israel as the culmination of a cycle of seven annual Sabbath years (Lev. 25:10). God's intent for the Jubilee encapsulated the essence of Jesus' ministry. The Jubilee Year was designed to be an extraordinary time of rejuvenation, celebration, and great joy, particularly for the underprivileged and poor who would have a chance to start their life anew.

> *It is striking that there is nothing like the weekly Sabbath, the annual sabbaths, or the Jubilee Year historically in other cultures.*

Jesus' reading of these words on a Sabbath day was not coincidental. The weekly and annual Sabbaths were founded on the same core principles of release and freedom and God's grace. Had Israel fully embraced the sabbatical and Jubilee systems, the social, cultural, and economic effects on society would have been far-reaching and profound. The system would have helped preserve the nation's cultural identity, ensure wealth was properly disbursed, and provide a remarkable social support system for the most vulnerable. The sabbatical system was "a sign" of the special relationship between the nation and the God of Israel (Exod. 31:13).

It is striking that there is nothing like the weekly Sabbath, the annual sabbaths, or the Jubilee Year historically in other cultures. To assume, as some critics do, that the idea for such a system arose from the collective minds of men years later is simply fanciful. No group of leaders in leading positions of influence would propose caring for the poor and disadvantaged on such a scale to the detriment of their own wealth and power. The economic cost of the loss of a weekly day of work and the loss of an annual year's production combined with the other provisions of the years of release would be enormous. Such an unintuitive idea could only come from the mind of a great and merciful God who sees the world differently than men.

The fact that the entire world today continues to recognize a weekly cycle of seven days when there is no astronomical or observable reference to such a cycle in nature is an ongoing testimony of God's guiding hand in history.

> *Such an unintuitive idea could only come from the mind of a great and merciful God.*

The Weekly Sabbath

The Sabbath has its origins in creation week. At Mount Sinai, God told the people that the weekly Sabbath day was a memorial of his actions at creation week and a day to remember their Creator and all he had done for them:

> Remember the Sabbath day, to keep it holy. ... *For in six days the* LORD *made the heavens and the earth, the sea, and all that is in them, and rested the seventh day. Therefore* the LORD blessed the Sabbath day and hallowed it. (Exod. 20:8, 11)

The day was inherently linked with the concept of freedom and release from bondage:

> And *remember that you were a slave in the land of Egypt,* and the LORD your God brought you out from there by a mighty hand and by an outstretched arm; *therefore* the LORD your God commanded you to keep the Sabbath day. (Deut. 5:15)

The Sabbath was also a day when people were to assemble to worship God:

> Six days shall work be done, but the seventh day *is* a Sabbath of solemn rest, *a holy convocation*. (Lev. 23:3)

God intended the Sabbath as a day of *freedom*—freedom from normal work and a joyous time for the community to come together. A *convocation* in Hebrew implies reading and learning, a time for the people to grow in understanding of God and the way of life he had outlined to Moses.

This was Jesus' perspective of the Sabbath. He understood it as a day of release, designed for doing good and restoring and uplifting those in need

(Matt. 12:12). He challenged the misguided teachers of his day who had introduced a tedious list of man-made do's and don'ts for the day, which worked against God's intent for the law.[1] Their rules made the day a burden, directly opposite the original intent of the law:

> Then He said to them, *"Is it lawful on the Sabbath to do good or to do evil, to save life or to kill?"* But they kept silent. And when He had looked around at them with anger, being grieved by the hardness of their hearts, He said to the man, "Stretch out your hand." And he stretched it out, and his hand was restored as whole as the other. (Mark 3:4–5)

On another occasion Jesus intentionally healed a woman on the Sabbath to drive home the point to his audience and to put his adversaries to shame:

> So ought not this woman, being a daughter of Abraham, whom Satan has bound—think of it—for eighteen years, *be loosed from this bond on the Sabbath?* (Luke 13:16)

God intended the Sabbath as a day of freedom, a joyous time for the community to come together.

Jesus' actions had nothing to do with denigrating the Sabbath but had everything to do with restoring the day's rightful role as a day of liberation and caring for others. Considering this, it is surprising that there has been such pushback against a day of rest. God wanted the Sabbath to be a great blessing to both the individual and the nation, given as a day of freedom to a people who had been oppressed for centuries in Egypt (Deut. 5:15). It was a weekly reminder of God's grace to an undeserving people.

The Annual Sabbaths

Shadowing the weekly Sabbath was the annual sabbatical cycle. Every seventh year was to be a Sabbath of rest for the land and its inhabitants (Exod. 23:10–12; Lev. 25:1–7).

---

[1] Edersheim documents the wearisome Sabbath ordinances that existed in Jesus' time, none of which came from the law of Moses. Bibliog: (Edersheim 1993, 1046-1056) 39 categories of labor were forbidden on the Sabbath—broken down into such detail as wearing false teeth, looking in mirrors, killing insects, drying clothes, carrying a fig, plucking a blade of grass, etc. In the same vein, modern rabbinic decrees have banned such activities as switching electric lights, tracing lines, tying shoes with a double knot, tearing toilet paper a certain way, cutting a cake with writing etc Bibliog: (Chabad 2022). It shows a lack of understanding of the mind of God and his true intent for the day.

> Six years you shall sow your land and gather in its produce, but the seventh year you shall let it rest and lie fallow, that the poor of your people may eat; and what they leave, the beasts of the field may eat. In like manner you shall do with your vineyard and your olive grove. (Exod. 23:10–11)

Just like the weekly Sabbath rest, the annual Sabbath was a time for society to be refreshed and rejuvenated. In certain vocations the benefits of a "sabbatical year" is still recognized today.[2]

The sabbatical year was a time when noncommercial debts were to be forgiven and those under debt servitude released (Deut. 15:1–4, 12–15). It was a time for those who had fallen into bad times, either by their own choice or due to circumstances, to economically start their life afresh. The years of release would help the poor break the poverty cycle and support wealth disbursement in society. Later chapters will further explore the economic and social benefits that such a system would have provided for society.

> *The annual Sabbath was a time for society to be refreshed and rejuvenated.*

But a year without an annual harvest invites the obvious question: How would society survive? God provided the answer, but it would be of little comfort to a faithless people:

> And if you say, "What shall we eat in the seventh year, since we shall not sow nor gather in our produce?" Then I will command My blessing on you in the sixth year, and it will bring forth produce enough for three years. And you shall sow in the eighth year, and eat old produce until the ninth year; until its produce comes in, you shall eat of the old harvest. (Lev. 25:20–22)

Even with these years of rest God promised they would be blessed above all the surrounding nations (Deut. 7:14). But they would have to trust him. Faith in God was central to the entire sabbatical system and explains why they struggled with its implementation.

---

[2] The term "sabbatical" in today's usage means a general long break from a career or profession, but its origins lie in the biblical, seven-year annual sabbath system.

The Jubilee and Land Ownership

The sabbatical year system culminated with the Jubilee Year. After seven cycles of annual sabbaths (forty-nine years), the shofar was blown on the Day of Atonement to announce the coming fiftieth year as a special year of release (Lev. 25:8–9). Unlike the sabbatical year release from debt and servitude, this time, the focus was on land:

> And you shall consecrate the fiftieth year, and proclaim liberty throughout all the land to all its inhabitants. It shall be a Jubilee for you; and each of you shall return to his possession, and each of you shall return to his family. (Lev. 25:10)

These beautiful words calling for "liberty throughout all the land" have inspired many people, the most famous example being the leaders of the province of Pennsylvania, who had these words cast in bronze on what is now known as the American Liberty Bell. The bell represented fifty years of freedom for the fledgling colony and later became symbolic of American independence and freedom.

The Jubilee system was based on a unique concept of land ownership within the boundaries of the promised land. God had a special interest in the land:

> The land shall not be sold permanently, for the land is Mine; for you are strangers and sojourners with Me. And in all the land of your possession you shall grant redemption of the land. (Lev. 25:23–24)

The land of Canaan was allocated by lot to tribes and then to family clans at the time of settlement (Josh. 14:2; Josh. 18; Josh. 19). Each land allotment was to be permanently owned within each family and handed down through their generations (Num. 36:7). Control of the land might be sold or lost through bad management or misfortune, but in the Jubilee Year, the land was to be returned unencumbered to the rightful inheritors of the family land. The provisions for perpetual land ownership did not apply to houses in walled towns and villages. They could be bought and sold permanently (Lev. 25:29–31).

The Jubilee Year would create a once-in-a-lifetime major economic and social reset of society.

There were also specific provisions for property ownership by the priestly tribe of Levi who otherwise did not have an inheritance (Lev. 25:32–34). The Levites had forty-eight special cities where they owned houses that could not be permanently sold (Lev. 25:32–35). They also shared in the common land directly surrounding these cities (Num. 35:2–5).

The Jubilee Year, combined with the previous year's annual Sabbath, would create a once-in-a-lifetime major economic and social reset of society, an opportunity for all those who had lost their inheritance to settle in their family land once again. It would be a time when dignity could be restored, stigmas removed, and families brought back to together. Land is the fundamental resource of a state, and the reset of land holdings would have prevented an over-concentration of wealth in the hands of a few. It was also a reinforcement of God's desire that the family be the primary social unit of the nation.

It is common for countries to have laws related to foreign land ownership. Even in the modern world, foreign land ownership remains a contentious issue in nations with a strong desire to retain a unique cultural heritage and identity. The loss of agricultural and mining lands to foreigners can also be a sovereign risk to the nation. In the ancient world agricultural land was vital to a nation's survival.

From the outset, the biggest threat to the nation's future was the coexistence of Canaanite cultures among them. The restoration of lands to original family owners would have had a strong cultural impact, helping to preserve the heritage and identity of the nation.

Land Ownership and Redemption

The system God outlined provided an ability to buy and sell heritage land in the same way long-term leases can be bought and sold. The fundamental ownership of the land didn't change, but the owner of the lease could work the land for profit. A modern equivalent of such laws would be leasing crown land in British Commonwealth countries. But unlike a modern lease, which essentially guarantees rights of usage for the term of the lease, God provided a right for the landowner to redeem the property at any time, either personally or through a near relative:

> If one of your brethren becomes poor, and has sold some of his possession, and if his redeeming relative comes to redeem it, then he may redeem what his brother sold. Or if the man has no one to redeem it, but he himself becomes able to redeem it, then let him count the years since its sale, and restore the remainder to the man to whom he sold it, that he may return to his possession. But if he is not able to have it restored to himself, then what was sold shall remain in the

hand of him who bought it until the Year of Jubilee; and in the Jubilee it shall be released, and he shall return to his possession. (Lev. 25:25–28)

The price to redeem the land was negotiable and was to take into account the date of the sale and the number of years left until the Jubilee release (Lev. 25:50–52). It was a fair system that allowed a buyer and seller of the leased land to achieve an equitable outcome.

There were other provisions for landholding transactions within a family. According to the laws outlined to the daughters of Zelophehad, women could inherit the land, but to keep the inheritance, they had to marry within the same tribe so that the tribal boundaries were maintained (Num. 27:1–11; 36:2–9). In the book of Ruth, for example, Naomi became the landowner when her husband died, showing that the law recognized the widow as the rightful inheritor of the land. But for her husband Elimelech's name to continue through her daughter-in-law, Ruth, Naomi would have to find a redeemer who would also accept Ruth as his wife and acknowledge any offspring of the marriage as being of the widow's lineage (Ruth 4:1–6).

At the time of King Ahab of Israel, these land inheritance laws were still in place. When evil Ahab tried to buy the property of a man called Naboth, Naboth refused, citing that it would be wrong in the sight of God to sell his father's inheritance (1 Kings 21:1–3). Ahab's murder of Naboth and disregard of the law brought calamity to himself and his house (1 Kings 21:17–19).

Israel's Failure to Implement Sabbatical Laws

Like many other aspects of the law of Moses, no historical evidence exists to affirm the effects of these annual sabbatical and Jubilee laws on the society over time. Israel did not keep God's laws with any consistency, and there is no record of a Jubilee Year ever being celebrated. Ezekiel describes Israel as defiling and profaning God's Sabbaths (Ezek. 20:13, 21). God specifically notes to Jeremiah that Israel had ignored his annual Sabbaths from the outset (Jer. 34:13–15). God's decree of 70 years of captivity for Judah was in part a retribution for the ignored sabbatical years:

> And those who escaped from the sword he carried away to Babylon ... to fulfill the word of the LORD by the mouth of Jeremiah, until the

> land had enjoyed her Sabbaths. As long as she lay desolate she kept Sabbath, to fulfill seventy years. (2 Chron. 36:20–21)

Israel and Judah's reluctance to keep the sabbatical rests is not surprising. Firstly, as noted earlier, it was a system that entirely relied on God's providence. Without God, letting the land rest without production in the seventh year (and particularly in the Jubilee Year) could be economically disastrous. It required people to have total confidence in God's faithfulness to provide.

Secondly, the economic impact of the system would have been greatest on the wealthy. In the sabbatical year they would stand to lose both money and goods owed to them and their Hebrew servants working off debt servitude. This would be hard for the wealthy who didn't trust in God to accept. Later in the time of the prophet Jeremiah, we see just such a pushback. At the direction of King Zedekiah, the leading families had reluctantly agreed to order the liberation of Hebrew servants (Jer. 34:8–10). But afterward they changed their minds and made their servants return to servitude.

> This is the word that came to Jeremiah from the LORD, after King Zedekiah had made a covenant with all the people who were at Jerusalem to proclaim liberty to them: that every man should set free his male and female slave—a Hebrew man or woman—that no one should keep a Jewish brother in bondage. Now when all the princes and all the people, who had entered into the covenant, heard that everyone should set free his male and female slaves, that no one should keep them in bondage anymore, *they obeyed and let them go.* But afterward they *changed their minds* and made the male and female slaves return, whom they had set free, and brought them into subjection as male and female slaves. (Jer. 34:8–11)

God took this matter very seriously. He was greatly displeased and sent a warning to the king and the people that they would fall under his judgment because of their actions (vv. 12–17). The wealthy, in this case, obviously disliked the concept of losing their valuable assets and felt disadvantaged. But their mindset, developed over years of ignoring these laws, was wrong. The release was not an impost on the free-market system, and neither did they have any claim on something that wasn't theirs. The law was clear regarding Hebrew servants. They were engaged until the next year of release, for a maximum of six years, based on the value of their earning capacity. For the wealthy to force their servants to remain because they were vulnerable was, in fact, theft.[3]

The years of release, in that sense, would not interfere with free market operations because, just like a modern lease, all parties would know the terms of the arrangement in advance. It is the same with the Jubilee land reset. Just as a person today who acquires a leasehold property knows in advance that it is not a permanent freehold title sale and pays a price according to the remaining years of the lease, a person of old should have understood the same. There should have been no expectation beyond the stated terms of the sale.

The weekly Sabbath, the sabbatical years, and the Jubilee Year were God's gift to the nation. Like so many other aspects of the law, the people pushed against it because they refused to trust in the God of Israel despite his track record of providence.

---

[3] This will be explained more fully in the chapter *The Issue of Slavery*.

The Economic System

This Book of the Law shall not depart from your mouth, but you shall meditate in it day and night, that you may observe to do according to all that is written in it. For then you will make your way prosperous, and then you will have good success.
—Joshua 1:8

There were a variety of economic systems represented across the nations of the ancient Near East. They ranged from subsistence economies in the poorer nations to command or centrally planned economies like Egypt and the mixed economies of nations like Assyria and the Phoenicians.

Today the dominant economic systems in the world are capitalism and socialism, with varying degrees of each in place. Capitalism is generally defined as a system involving private individuals and private corporations, with the market as the dominant driver. Socialism, on the other hand, requires centralized planning, government controls, and public ownership.

Even though there is a tendency to try and classify the law of Moses into one of these two systems, modern definitions do not work well when compared to the less sophisticated ancient economies. But one thing is certain: God's plan for Israel was not as a central, government-controlled economy, simply because it was not God's desire for Israel to even have a central civil government. But neither was the system an unrestrained free market. The unique national laws God gave Israel were aimed at ensuring that life and work were kept in a godly balance while at the same time providing positive economic outcomes if the nation stayed the course God outlined for them.

> *God's plan for Israel was not as a central, government-controlled economy but neither was the system an unrestrained free market.*

Promise of Success

The Mosaic law has a lot to say about economics, but Israel's lack of any consistent application of the Mosaic law makes it historically difficult to see the effects of the law on their economy over any length of time. But we do have God's clear promises that Israel would have been an extraordinarily bountiful country if they had been obedient. The promised boons were to include blessings for the Israelites in the city as well as the country, with abundant food and goods for all (Deut. 28:3–6, 8, 11). This included mining and production of various metals, confirming that God's promises extended beyond a primitive barter and exchange agricultural economy. They would "lack nothing":

> For the LORD your God is bringing you into a good land, a land of brooks of water, of fountains and springs, that flow out of valleys and hills; a land of wheat and barley, of vines and fig trees and pomegranates, a land of olive oil and honey; a land in which you will eat bread without scarcity, *in which you will lack nothing; a land whose stones are iron and out of whose hills you can dig copper.* (Deut. 8:7–9)

God also promised that the nation would be set high above all other nations of the day, many of which we know historically were quite advanced:

> Now it shall come to pass, if you diligently obey the voice of the LORD your God, to observe carefully all His commandments which I command you today, that the LORD your God *will set you high above all nations of the earth.* (Deut. 28:1)

Clearly, God did not desire or expect Israel to remain an isolated, primitive, agrarian society—he envisaged his people to be lenders and leaders over the nations around them:

> For the LORD your God will bless you just as He promised you; *you shall lend to many nations, but you shall not borrow; you shall reign over many nations,* but they shall not reign over you. (Deut. 15:6)

There is no suggestion that the Mosaic system would have inhibited general wealth creation.

While the Mosaic system would have constrained the rich from becoming overly powerful, there is no suggestion that the system would have inhibited general wealth creation. God has no problem with wealth in principle, either with his people of old or for Christians today (3 John 2). He had blessed each of the founding fathers of Israel with enormous personal wealth (Gen. 13:2; 24:35; 26:13–14). He specifically directed the Israelites to "plunder" the Egyptians before leaving, encouraging them to ask for gold, silver, and valuables (Exod. 3:21–22). And the people gained more wealth from the various battles en route to Canaan (Num. 31:25–54). Later, after the initial conquering of the land, Joshua noted the extensive wealth the Israelites had gained from the conquest (Josh. 22:8). The location of the promised land was also significant. God chose Canaan, a central position among the leading nations of the day and located at the crossroads of major trade routes. It was a perfect location for trade and commerce to flourish and wealth to be created.

It was God's ideal for the Israelites to continue to prosper under his system of law if they remained faithful to him (Deut. 8:18; 29:9; Josh. 1:8). It was their failure to do as he asked which created their economic problems and subservience to others, not the system of law or any desire of God to see them suppressed.

The Pre-Monarchical Economy

Ancient Israel had two phases of economic order in its history: the time of the judges, and the later period of the kings.

God's original plan was to be Israel's invisible King, and the nation operated like this for hundreds of years. God warned his people of the tendency of human kings to overreach into the lives of individual citizens and that life would be economically tougher under a human king than under the system he initially envisaged (Deut. 17:14–17; 1 Sam. 8:10–18). But even though he warned them of the consequences, he would not prevent them from going down that road if they chose to do so (1 Sam. 8:21–22).

There is an automatic but false assumption that had Israel remained under the decentralized system of judges, its economy could never have been anything other than a vulnerable subsistence economy. But God's promises clearly said otherwise. As noted earlier, had they kept his initial covenant, he promised that they would be set high above other nations and be a wealthy and prosperous nation (Deut. 28:1). The negative perspective of the pre-monarchical time is reinforced in the minds of many by the negative events highlighted in the book of Judges. But the book of Judges mostly focuses on the failures of Israel, not their successes. The book covered an extensive period of around 300 years and included quiet years of rest about which we know little (Judg. 3:11, 30; 5:31).

Economic Success in the Monarchial Period

Just as God predicted, Israel's fortunes waxed and waned in line with its faithfulness to him. The pinnacle of Israel's economic clout came during David and Solomon's reigns. David conquered and took tribute from all the surrounding nations (2 Sam. 8:11–12). David's son Solomon reigned after him. Because of young Solomon's humble and loyal attitude, God promised him great riches and wealth in addition to wisdom (2 Chron. 1:12). God blessed King Solomon and the nation to an extraordinary degree before Solomon drifted from God (2 Chron. 9:20–22).

Under Solomon, Israel became a strong trading nation. As noted earlier, their central location in the Levant was ideally conducive to trade. Archaeology has shown that the contemporary ancient Near East civilizations were advanced with many attributes of complex mixed economies, including extensive international trade arrangements, wide ranges of products and services, monetary systems, and market pricing. The extensive record of the cuneiform tablets found at ancient Nineveh detail a complex society under the Assyrian Empire with sophisticated markets, trade, and accounting systems.[1]

> *Israel's fortunes waxed and waned in line with its faithfulness to God.*

Even back in the time of Abraham, his hometown of Ur was a great cosmopolitan city and the center of an extensive trading empire.[2] The nearby Phoenicians were an important and wide-ranging trading nation David and Solomon partnered with (2 Sam. 5:11; 1 Kings 5:1). The biblical record reveals Solomon had merchants traveling the known world, including a fleet of trading ships working with the Phoenicians, bringing an extensive range of goods back to Jerusalem (1 Kings 9:26–27). Solomon imported horses from Egypt and exported them to the Hittites and Syrians (1 Kings 10:14–29).

How much of this wealth filtered down to the average Israelite is uncertain, but a passing comment in 1 Kings 10:27 affirms that silver was as common as stones in Jerusalem during the time of Solomon. It is also noted that Solomon's servants were "happy" in the early years of his reign, although he later appeared to have oppressed some of the people by putting them into his labor gangs (1 Kings 10:8; 12:4). The excesses of Solomon seem to have resulted in such indebtedness that it was necessary to make massive payments and give away national territory (1 Kings 9:11–14). Israel seems to have specialized in certain commodities by this time, possibly as a command-type economy (1 Kings 5:11). The original warnings of God against a king had come to pass in a major way.

After Solomon, the divided kingdoms had only moderate economic success. There were some highlights: Hezekiah, a righteous king of Judah, was greatly blessed by God with wealth (2 Chron. 32:27). At one time he had the ability

---

[1] Bibliog: (Gojko Barjamovic 2019)
[2] Bibliog: (Lawler 2016)

to pay an enormous tribute payment to Assyria, reflecting an economy with far more than simple agrarian wealth (2 Kings 18:14).

Critical scholars often view these parts of the biblical record with skepticism. They consider the wealth and achievements of King Solomon to be an exaggerated fable. As stated at the outset, this book is written with the premise of the veracity of the Bible, the truth of which continues to be confirmed and strengthened in line with new archaeological discoveries. Even the historicity of King David was doubted by many until the finding of the Tel Dan Inscription in 1993.[3]

Israel's Economic Framework

To understand how the law of Moses could have worked for the financial betterment of the nation and of each Israelite, we must look at the law itself rather than the poor example of the nation.

Being made in the image of God brings the desire to create, build, achieve, and accomplish. These desires are built deeply into the human psyche. The system God gave ancient Israel was designed to align with these human aspirations, not suppress them. When we look at the law itself, the economic framework it outlined was a free-enterprise system that supported private property, personal initiative, and freedom of choice. It included many features today regarded as necessary to create a vibrant economy, including the previously covered rule of law. It was a system that encouraged work and personal responsibility. But even without a central management authority, the Mosaic economy was not designed to be a laissez-faire, "anything goes" free market. It included relief valves to ensure the economy remained fair and sustainable.

The system God gave was designed to align with human aspirations, not suppress them.

Key economic aspects of the law included:

Encouragement for entrepreneurs

- Wealth was seen as a positive blessing (Deut. 8:18; 28:1; Prov. 10:4; 13:4)
- Enterprising people could receive the fruit of their labor (Deut. 28:8; Isa. 3:10; Prov 13:11)

---

[3] Bibliog: (Biblical Archaeology 2023)

Respect for work

- The foundational law outlined a six-day work week (Exod. 20:9; Deut. 5:13)
- Diligence was rewarded, laziness was not (Prov. 6:6–11)

General private property ownership

- Laws against theft and coveting the private property of others (Exod. 20:15, 17).

Land ownership laws

- Special laws for families to retain heritage farmland (Lev. 25:23–28)
- City houses could be bought and sold (Lev. 25:29–30)
- Cooling off period for house purchases (Lev. 25:29)

Low taxation environment

- Tithing (10 percent) of profit (not gross) to support Levitical priesthood (Deut. 14:22).
- No government taxation under original pre-monarchical system

Contracts and agreements to be honored

- Not to bear false witness (Exod. 20:16)
- Defined process with witnesses for legal transactions (Ruth 4:1–9)

Fairness in economic transactions.

- Fair weights and measures (Lev. 19:35–36; Deut. 25:13–16).
- Respecting of land boundaries—rule of law (Deut. 19:14)

Fair wages

- Workers to be paid fair rate of pay (Lev. 19:13; Deut. 25:4; 1 Tim. 5:8)
- Low-paid workers to be paid daily (Deut. 24:15)

Quality of life kept in perspective

- A positive work-life balance with mandated day of rest (Exod. 34:21)
- Cyclical sabbatical week, sabbatical years, and Jubilee Years demonstrating that materialism was not the primary goal

Local focus

- No central government. Local people decided on local expenditure.

- Less opportunity for large scale corruption

Economic relief valves

- Seven-year cycles of rest, debt forgiveness and release
- Major society reset each fifty years (Jubilee Year)

Restraints to a Pure Market Economy

There were aspects of the law that were unique. Although the intent behind some laws was not primarily economic, the economic effect would have been dramatic. The cyclical weekly Sabbath rest, the sabbatical year rest, and Jubilee laws were designed to keep the society focused on God as their provider while also putting the brakes on unbridled materialism. The intent of these laws was not to constrain wealth creation but to ensure that the nation's unique identity and individual family heritage was not lost.

These economic relief valves gave each citizen a chance to restart their life afresh and break free from a cycle of poverty that ensnared so many people of the ancient world. Had they kept these laws, it would have had a long-term stabilizing effect on their society.

There are major benefits to this unique Mosaic system when compared to the Keynesian economic system practiced in most Western countries today. John Maynard Keynes' idea was to have the government intervene in the market to mitigate the negative cycles of economic recessions and depressions. The theory was for governments to spend and boost the economy when times are tough and repay the borrowings when times are good. But such thinking has long gone by the wayside. Deficits and debt keep rising. Driven by our insatiable desire for growth, governments borrow and spend in both good times and bad, living far beyond their means. There is no path out of the colossal debt most governments carry. While there is occasional talk of debt cancellation, the system provides no ability to reset or restart without a total economic collapse. The system we have in the world today is simply unsustainable.

> *There are major benefits to the Mosaic system when compared to the Keynesian economic system practiced today.*

The Mosaic system slowed the whole pace down. Economic growth and materialism were not the primary national goals. God wanted Israel to understand that the highest quality of life revolved around him and his providence.

The beauty of the Mosaic system was its predictability. People under financial stress could look forward to the designated years of release and reset. Entrepreneurs and the wealthy could plan for those special years of debt forgiveness and release. The negotiated (lease) price of agricultural land was to be measured by the number of years remaining before the transfer back to the original family owners (Lev. 25:14–17).

Commercial Lending and Interest

The sort of vibrant economy that God promised would be one that encouraged investment. He promised that if they stayed loyal to him, they would be a *gross lender nation*, not a nation in debt or under tribute to gentiles (Deut. 15:6). Being a lender nation demonstrates God's approval of commercial business loans both inside the nation and without.

In relation to charging interest, the law explicitly notes that interest could be charged on loans to foreigners (Deut. 23:20). This confirms there was nothing fundamentally immoral about charging interest. The law of Moses did forbid interest being charged on loans to the *poor* of the nation. Some commentators have concluded that interest was not allowed on any loans between Israelites, even commercial or business loans. They base their opinion on the wording of a later directive in Deuteronomy:

> You shall not charge interest to your brother—interest on money or food or anything that is lent out at interest. To a foreigner you may charge interest, but to your brother you shall not charge interest, that the LORD your God may bless you in all to which you set your hand in the land which you are entering to possess. (Deut. 23:19–20)

To read this verse as a blanket ban against all interest implies a broadening of the intent of the original directives in Exodus and Leviticus, which are clearly directed at not charging interest to the poor (Exod. 22:25; Lev. 25:35–36).

But it would make no sense to ban interest on loans that were for the purpose of wealth creation (i.e., trade opportunities, infrastructure investment, commercial lending, etc.). There would be no incentive for a lender to risk their wealth for no return, and capital would flow *outside* the country to foreigners where they could charge interest, rather than be used internally to improve the lot of the Israelites.

It makes sense, therefore, that the directive in Deuteronomy 23:19 was not a change to previous laws in Exodus and Leviticus but to be read in conjunction with them.[4] The entire point of not charging interest was to build a caring society where people did not seek to profit from another in need.[5] This was the issue Nehemiah faced after the return from exile, where the wealthier Jews were preying on the poor (Neh. 5:1–12). This was a totally separate matter to business investment loans that benefited both parties.

Jesus confirmed the appropriateness of expecting interest on business investments (Luke 19:23; Matt. 25:27). But there was to be no profit-taking from the poor and vulnerable in society.

Trapped in Poverty?

Several traditional and modern Bible commentaries either imply or directly express the negative idea that the law of Moses would have somehow trapped people in poverty. In his commentary, Adam Clark quotes a folk story from the Jewish Midrash about a poor widow who attempts to follow the directions of Moses and ends up in abject poverty and "overwhelmed with affliction." Clark sums up the story with the following comment: "This is a terrible picture of the requisitions of the Mosaic ritual; and, though exaggerated, it contains so many true features."[6]

Nothing in the law of Moses supports such a negative proposition. The law of Moses was specifically designed to keep people out of poverty, not to worsen their condition. For the average person, the law's financial imposts were extremely light, and there were few constraints to a person of entrepreneurial ability. Abraham was a successful entrepreneur who used his trading skills to become wealthy in gold and silver as well as livestock (Gen. 13:2). His son and grandson followed in his course (Gen. 26:13–14). These fathers of Israel were an example to the nation of God's willingness to bless those who followed his law. God promised Israel beautiful homes full of good things if they stayed focused on him (Deut. 6:10–11). The law implied that even a

> *The law of Moses was specifically designed to keep people out of poverty.*

---

[4] For more detailed commentary on interpreting Deuteronomy 23:19, refer to the following: Bibliog: (Issler 2017) Bibliog: (Holman 2015, Interest. p 811-812).
[5] This topic will be further discussed in the chapter *The Social Welfare System*.
[6] Bibliog: (Clarke 1810, Acts 15:10)

foreigner living in the land could become wealthy (Lev. 25:47).

Erroneous and negative perspectives of the Mosaic law are unsupported assumptions, presumably based on the hardships Israel experienced because of disobedience. For others, negative ideas come from confusing the law of Moses with the more oppressive religion of Judaism, which developed after the return of the Jews from Babylon. But even under this more repressive system, honest Jews could still become wealthy (e.g., Joseph of Arimathea, the rich young man, etc. Matt. 19:22; 27:57).

Tithing on the Increase

The simple facts of the law of Moses are as follows: God wanted the people to be as free as humanly possible, and freedom is the number one ingredient for economic prosperity. His tithing system required a tithe (or tenth) of the *increase* (not of the principal) of their wealth in any one year (Deut. 14:22). Tithing, by its design, could never send a person backward. If there was no profit or increase after subtracting expenses, there was no tithe payable. The tithing system was also not a "tax" that went into the central depository of a king. The tithe money was injected directly back into the economy. It was given to support the priestly Levites who otherwise would have limited income.

> *Tithing, by its design, could never send a person backwards.*

Tithing was managed on a personal honesty basis, where each individual would privately determine their own increase and give according to how God had blessed them. A second tithe was to be saved for *personal use* at the annual festivals (Deut. 14:22–25). There is simply no support for the idea that the system would suppress wealth creation. As David wrote:

> Praise the LORD! Blessed is the man who fears the LORD, who delights greatly in His commandments. His descendants will be mighty on earth; the generation of the upright will be blessed. Wealth and riches will be in his house. (Ps. 112:1–3)

Some have queried why there were so many provisions for the support of the poor if the system was so anti-poverty. A verse in Deuteronomy that states that "the poor will never cease from the land" is sometimes cited as evidence of a fundamental structural problem in the law (Deut. 15:11). But a reading of the context in Deuteronomy 15 shows that this was God simply being realistic. He promised to richly bless the nation, but it was conditional on their obedience (vs. 4–5). This was not setting an impossible benchmark; it was specifically referring to the implementation of the sabbatical cycle cancellation of debts, which we saw earlier that the nation did not follow. But even if Israel had been a model nation, there would always be individuals who made poor choices in life—and strangers and foreigners among them who would need support.

Morals and the Economy

God's system also included a vital ingredient for economic success that most modern economists overlook—morals. People try to divorce morals from theories of economics, but such separation is impossible. Economics, after all, is simply the study of how people interact with wealth. No matter how well the strengths and weaknesses of various economic systems are analyzed and presented, no system is sustainable in the long run if unbridled greed, selfishness, and corruption are not restrained.

Many people today think the answer is to move away from "selfish" capitalism to "sharing" socialism. But centralizing power in a socialistic system to an even smaller class of ruling elite, only compounds the tendency to corruption if morals are ignored. This has been amply demonstrated by the history of communism, where leaders lived in a class far above the average worker.

And the modern idea that centrally forced redistribution of wealth (aka social justice) will somehow solve what is fundamentally a moral problem is also misguided. The inefficiencies that come from bloated bureaucracies making arbitrary decisions as the agenda changes are a disincentive to economic success.

Prosperity requires individual freedom and private ownership to incentivize and encourage hard work and achievement. Modern communist China had to allow private capitalists and entrepreneurs to revive their economic fortunes, but then had to follow with an intrusive Social Credit System to ensure their citizens were maintaining their obedience to the state. Because if you don't have trust, you must have control.

In contrast, God designed his economic system to be based on the freedom and morality of the individual. The two were to go hand in hand. Freedom is necessary for economic prosperity, but it cannot be sustained in the long run without a people of virtue. American President and founding father James Madison expressed it well:

> To suppose that any form of government will secure liberty or

happiness without any virtue in the people, is a chimerical idea.[7]

When the individuals of a society are generally thankful, unselfish, generous, compassionate, and strive to love their neighbors as themselves, a free-market economy works extremely well. When morality is out of the picture the economy can only be held together by force. The United States and most western democracies today are going down the path of trying to solve moral problems in their societies through legislation, policing, and social engineering. By tackling the symptoms and not the true cause, the result will be a continued slow decline of both freedom and ultimate prosperity. This is why the law of Moses was so unique in history. God understood the heart of man and what was needed for truly sustainable prosperity across all levels of society.

> *Freedom is necessary for economic prosperity, but it cannot be sustained in the long run without a people of virtue.*

God's Providence

While most of the fundamental economic provisions of the Mosaic law make sense for any society to adopt, there were aspects of the law that relied entirely on God's intervention. This was by design. These included the land ownership laws, sabbatical laws of reset and release, charging no interest etc., all of which relied on God's blessings to work.

God wanted Israel to be free and successful, but along with their success, he wanted them to remember the source of their wealth. The natural tendency for anyone receiving great blessings is to assume they are the by-product of their own talent and hard work. For Israel this was definitely not the case. Israel was rescued from Egypt and received the promised land purely because of God's grace. As they struggled on the journey through the wilderness and saw God's intervention, he was hopeful that they would come to rely on him as their sustainer and provider (Deut. 8:3).

Moses warned them not to forget the true source of their wealth when they entered the land:

> Do not ... say in your heart, "My power and the might of my hand have gained me this wealth." And you shall remember the LORD your

---

[7] Bibliog: (Madison 1788)

God, for it is He who gives you power to get wealth. (Deut. 8:11, 17–18)

This is exactly what God wanted the Israelites to understand, that this was an economic system that would be reliant on God's providence and the virtue of the people. Trusting in him was the key to both individual and national economic success. Without this the system would, and in fact did, fail.

There are lessons in all this for Christians today. As Jesus said, quoting from Moses:

It is written, "Man shall not live by bread alone, but by every word that proceeds from the mouth of God." (Matt. 4:4; Deut. 8:3)

The Social Welfare System

He administers justice for the fatherless and the widow, and loves the stranger, giving him food and clothing. —Deuteronomy 10:18

It has been rightly said that a nation's greatness is measured by how it treats its weakest members.[1] But rarely in history has this measure been adopted. Our Western societies have made great progress in social welfare in the last 100 years or so, but for most of history, the poor and vulnerable were ignored and had few, if any, rights or privileges.

Yet thousands of years before social welfare arrived in developed countries, the law of Moses set a high standard for a caring society. It offered strong and wide-ranging provision for those most at risk, epitomized by the phrase "widows, orphans and foreigners." This support for the vulnerable came from the highest authority possible, the Creator God himself, who stated his position in no uncertain terms:

> You shall neither mistreat a stranger nor oppress him, for you were strangers in the land of Egypt. You shall not afflict any widow or fatherless child. If you afflict them in any way, and they cry at all to Me, I will surely hear their cry. (Exod. 22:21–23)

The inclusion of strangers and foreigners reinforces the supernatural origins of these laws. The natural human response to Israel's mistreatment in Egypt would be to strongly favor Israelites over foreigners. Yet multiple times, God told Israel to remember their negative experience in Egypt and do the opposite by caring for strangers (Exod. 22:21; 23:9; Lev. 19:34; Deut. 10:19; 24:22). This was the same caring mindset Jesus displayed during his ministry.

From the heart of the gracious God of Israel came a truly enlightened social welfare system that was far reaching in its scope.

From the heart of this gracious God of Israel came a truly enlightened social welfare system that was far reaching in its scope.

---

[1] This statement is generally attributed to Mahatma Gandhi.

No Interest to Be Charged

A foundational aspect of the social welfare system was God's instruction that no interest was be charged on loans to the poor. In our world today, it is the poor and most vulnerable who pay the highest rates of interest. Moneylenders and pawnbrokers are notorious for charging exorbitant rates to those who can least afford it. Under the Mosaic system, the poor were not to be charged any interest:

> If you lend money to any of My people *who are poor* among you, you shall not be like a moneylender to him; *you shall not charge him interest.* (Exod. 22:25)

> If one of your brethren becomes poor, and falls into poverty among you, then you shall help him, like a stranger or a sojourner, that he may live with you. *Take no usury or interest from him*; but fear your God, that your brother may live with you. *You shall not lend him your money for usury, nor lend him your food at a profit.* (Lev. 25:35–37)

These directives against charging interest to the poor were incredible for the ancient world. Mesopotamian history records high interest rates of 20–50 percent in place, with interest often required to be paid up front.[2] Israel was starkly different. People were directed to be softhearted to those in need and lend, even if it was doubtful the poor were able to repay:

> If there is among you a poor man of your brethren, within any of the gates in your land which the LORD your God is giving you, *you shall not harden your heart nor shut your hand from your poor brother*, but you shall open your hand wide to him and *willingly lend him sufficient for his need*, whatever he needs. (Deut. 15:7–8)

These were loans to a person for their necessities in times of need.[3] It was these same laws that Jesus related to when he encouraged lending without thought of return (Luke 6:34–35).

These were the same laws that Jesus related to when he encouraged lending without thought of return.

While God encouraged people to be generous, these laws related to loans, not gifts, and he

---

[2] Bibliog: (Holman 2015, Interest. p 812)
[3] This was not a reference to commercial business loans, which are needed for a successful economy but lending "sufficient for his needs." Refer to the chapter *The Economic System* for further comments on commercial lending.

allowed his people to hold loan guarantee pledges (Deut. 24:12–13). Loans would preserve the dignity of the borrower and encourage the person to work to overcome their difficult situation. Ideally, the recipient would regain their financial footing and be able to repay the principal. But if they could not repay, debt relief provisions were available in the law.

Respect for those in Need

God included many thoughtful and practical directives in the law to ensure the poor were treated respectfully. Consider the following:

The law directed an employer to pay their poor employees *daily* so that they didn't have to wait for their wages. This allowed their immediate subsistence needs to be provided for:

> You shall not oppress a hired servant who is poor and needy, whether one of your brethren or one of the aliens who is in your land within your gates. Each day you shall give him his wages, and not let the sun go down on it, for he is poor and has set his heart on it; lest he cry out against you to the LORD, and it be sin to you. (Deut. 24:14–15)

The law directed creditors to be sensitive to those under financial pressure. If some sort of collateral was due for a loan, the creditor had to respectfully stand outside the house and could not just barge in as an impatient lender might otherwise do:

> When you lend your brother anything, you shall not go into his house to get his pledge. You shall stand outside, and the man to whom you lend shall bring the pledge out to you. (Deut. 24:10–11).

Fundamental living necessities could not be taken as pledges or securities:

> If you ever take your neighbor's garment as a pledge, you shall return it to him before the sun goes down. For that is his only covering, it is his garment for his skin. What will he sleep in? And it will be that when he cries to Me, I will hear, for I am gracious. (Exod. 22:26–27)

Neither could tools of trade be taken from someone who needed them for work:

> No man shall take the lower or the upper millstone in pledge, for he takes one's living in pledge. (Deut. 24:6)

Historically across most cultures, the poor have been preyed on and abused, not respectfully treated in this manner. The outwardly "righteous" Pharisees "devoured widows' houses," prompting great criticism from Jesus (Mark 12:40). Even today, not all countries have laws for the protection of the poor.

Poor and the Festivals

God included commands to ensure the poor were included in the statutory holy day celebrations so that no one missed out. At the Feast of Weeks (Pentecost):

> You shall rejoice before the LORD your God, you and your son and your daughter, your male servant and your female servant, the Levite who is within your gates, *the stranger and the fatherless and the widow who are among you,* at the place where the LORD your God chooses to make His name abide. (Deut. 16:11).

Similar directives were given for the Feast of Tabernacles (Deut. 16:14–15). The weekly Sabbath day was also to be a blessing for the poor and the strangers (Exod. 23:12).

In the worship system, God included many allowances for the poor by reducing the offering requirements and making them affordable (e.g., Lev. 5:7; 14:21–22). At other times, they only had to give as they were able (Deut. 16:17). The poor could participate without feeling inferior. These small, thoughtful instructions in the law demonstrate the greatness of God.

Food for the Poor—Gleaning

God also outlined permanent programs to provide food for the poor. These were not centrally managed programs. They involved landowners taking personal responsibility to act to help those in need. It was between the landowner and God, with promises of blessings if they obeyed.

The first was a system called gleaning. Farmers were to leave a remnant of their crops for the poor. Gleaning was a self-help system that provided food for those willing to work:[4]

> When you reap your harvest in your field, and forget a sheaf in the field, you shall not go back to get it; it shall be for the stranger, the fatherless, and the widow, that the Lord your God may bless you in all the work of your hands. When you beat your olive trees, you shall not go over the boughs again; it shall be for the stranger, the fatherless, and the widow. When you gather the grapes of your vineyard, you

---

[4] Ruth, a poor foreigner from Moab, availed herself of this system in Boaz's field (Ruth 2).

shall not glean it afterward; it shall be for the stranger, the fatherless, and the widow. And you shall remember that you were a slave in the land of Egypt; therefore I command you to do this thing. (Deut. 24:19–22)

In addition to gleaning, there was a provision in the law for travelers and itinerants to eat as they passed through any field.

> When you come into your neighbor's vineyard, you may eat your fill of grapes at your pleasure, but you shall not put any in your container. When you come into your neighbor's standing grain, you may pluck the heads with your hand, but you shall not use a sickle on your neighbor's standing grain. (Deut. 23:24–25)

While they could not harvest, they could eat sufficient for their immediate needs.

Food for the Poor – Third Year

Even more significant was a food supply system where 10 percent (a tithe) of the harvest every third year was to be set aside for those who needed it most:

> So you shall rejoice in every good thing which the LORD your God has given to you and your house, you and the Levite and the stranger who is among you. When you have finished laying aside all the tithe of your increase in the third year—the year of tithing—and have given it to the Levite, the stranger, the fatherless, and the widow, so that they may eat within your gates and be filled. (Deut. 26:11–12)

Then in the seventh year (the sabbatical rest year), the land was left unworked, but its produce was available to the poor and vulnerable:

> But the seventh year you shall let it rest and lie fallow, that the poor of your people may eat; and what they leave, the beasts of the field may eat. In like manner you shall do with your vineyard and your olive grove. (Exod. 23:11)

This was an incredible support system, where the produce of the land was to be shared and enjoyed by all the nation. It respected the rights of ownership while at the same time providing restricted access to those who were in need.

Debt Relief

To provide a way out of poverty, God further directed that debts be canceled at the end of the seventh year of release, providing the opportunity for individuals and families to be released from crushing debt and to start over:[5]

> At the end of every seven years you shall grant a release of debts. And this is the form of the release: Every creditor who has lent anything to his neighbor shall release it; he shall not require it of his neighbor or his brother, because it is called the LORD's release. Of a foreigner you may require it; but you shall give up your claim to what is owed by your brother, except when there may be no poor among you; for the LORD will greatly bless you in the land which the LORD your God is giving you to possess as an inheritance. (Deut. 15:1–4)

Debt cancellation laws were specifically aimed at helping the poor. The comment that "you shall give up your claim to what is owed by your brother, "except when there may be no poor among you" (vv. 3–4) confirms that this law was not a release of commercial debts, nor were loans to foreigners outside the nation included.[6]

Debt cancellation laws were specifically aimed at helping the poor.

Lenders were specifically told to not harden their hearts against lending as the year of release came near:

> If there is among you a poor man of your brethren, within any of the gates in your land which the LORD your God is giving you, you shall not harden your heart nor shut your hand from your poor brother, but you shall open your hand wide to him and willingly lend him sufficient for his need, whatever he needs. Beware lest there be a wicked thought in your heart, saying, "The seventh year, the year of release, is at hand," and your eye be evil against your poor brother and you give him nothing, and he cry out to the LORD against you, and it become sin among you. You shall surely give to him, and your heart should not be grieved when you give to him, because for this thing the LORD your God will bless you in all your works and in all to which you put your hand. (Deut. 15:7–10)

The seventh year was also a time for the release of those in servitude, those who had become involuntarily indentured (Deut. 15:12–18).[7] It provided

---

[5] The Mosaic debt cancellation laws influenced the introduction of English bankruptcy laws by Queen Anne in 1706 and eventually found their way into our modern world Bibliog: (Chesnutt 2009).

[6] Obviously, an unbelieving foreigner would not reciprocate and cancel their loans to Israelites.

[7] Refer to the chapter *The Issue of Slavery*.

them the opportunity to start life anew.

Following on from the cycle of seven sabbatical years was the Jubilee Year. Every fifty years, family lands that had been sold or lost because of misfortune or bad management would be returned to the family. The Jubilee system was the capstone of a truly outstanding social welfare system.

Big Government Not Involved

We must again be reminded of a critical key point: this was not a welfare system run by big government. There was no coercion or policing involved. It was God's plan that all these caring laws were to be executed and managed locally by those with the means to do so.

> *This was not a welfare system run by big government. The state was not involved. It was neighbors supporting neighbors.*

This was the second great law that Jesus identified in action—*loving your neighbor as yourself*. The state was not involved. It was about people dealing with people. Neighbors supporting neighbors. This is the way a society becomes strong.

Today we think: *Why should I help my neighbor? The government will.* But the state doesn't build relationships the way individuals can. God designed his law to create interactions between people that would build strong, caring communities, something a government-managed system can never do.

A Light to Other Nations

How positively God's social welfare system would have presented itself to the vulnerable in Israel! It was a system designed to break the poverty cycle. Imagine how the poor would have felt to be treated so respectfully and with such kindness.

And most unusual of all—it was not just for their own people. It welcomed and included strangers! A foreigner who was treated with such respect and with such generosity would praise the God of Israel.

> *The state doesn't build relationships the way individuals can.*

There was nothing like this in history. Whether we study the ancient Hittites, Babylonians, Egyptians, Romans—even modern European history—we do not see such care for the poor and vulnerable as God outlined for Israel. Had Israel done these things, she would have been a light and attraction to the people of all other nations.

We are reminded of those inspiring words written by Emma Lazarus for the Statue of Liberty. Emma Lazarus was a young Jewish poet who would have known the words of Moses well:

The New Colossus

> Not like the brazen giant of Greek fame,
> With conquering limbs astride from land to land;
> Here at our sea-washed, sunset gates shall stand
> A mighty woman with a torch, whose flame
> Is the imprisoned lightning, and her name
> MOTHER OF EXILES. From her beacon-hand
> Glows world-wide welcome; her mild eyes command
> The air-bridged harbor that twin cities frame.
>
> "Keep, ancient lands, your storied pomp!" cries she
> With silent lips. "Give me your tired, your poor,
> Your huddled masses yearning to breathe free,
> The wretched refuse of your teeming shore.
> Send these, the homeless, tempest-tossed to me,
> I lift my lamp beside the golden door!"
>
> Emma Lazarus. 1883.

Such beautiful words could have equally been written by a poet in ancient Israel if they had only chosen to trust God and follow the system he outlined to them.[8]

---

[8] It's not hard to see the influence of the Mosaic narrative in Bartholdi's design of the Statue of Liberty. Consider Liberty's tablet of stone, her head shining like Moses, her feet breaking the shackles of bondage, and the invitation to a land of promise.

The Importance of Education

For the LORD gives wisdom; from His mouth come knowledge and understanding.
—Proverbs 2:6

God's intent was for Israel to be an educated and literate people who stood against the religious superstition and ignorance of the day. God desired to be worshipped—not blindly as other gods but with the *mind* (Deut. 6:5; Matt. 22:37).

Throughout the law of Moses, education at all levels was encouraged, from the young to the old. God wanted Israel to develop into a people of understanding. Leaders and judges were to be chosen because of their wisdom, understanding and knowledge (Deut. 1:13). He wanted everyone, male and female, rich and poor, taught the law from childhood (Deut. 6:7). An educated people could never be a threat to a God of truth.

As noted earlier, the word Torah means *instruction* or *teaching*. The law was far more than a prescriptive list of rules and regulations, it was designed to teach the principles of true success. God gave the law as a lamp to shine a light on the reality of life (Ps. 19:8; 119:105; Prov. 6:23). It was a system based on wisdom and truth. Had Israel followed God's instructions, they would have become an enlightened and educated people who attracted the attention of the nations around them (Deut. 4:6).

An educated people could never be a threat to a God of truth.

And although ancient Israel chose the darkness of religious superstition for much of their history, we see evidence of that potential greatness under the reign of David and Solomon. Showing how much he prized understanding, God blessed the young Solomon with wisdom greater than any sage of the time (1 Kings 3:9–14). Rulers came from distant nations to hear Solomon's words (1 Kings 4:34). This golden age of Israel demonstrates what Israel could have been had its people stayed the course.

Israel's failures aside, the Old Testament record retains a powerful testimony of an enlightened and educated way of life:

- The far-reaching scope of the Mosaic law
- The timeless beauty of the prose and poetry of the psalms of David
- The wisdom of Solomon

- The rich tapestry of the writings of the prophets
- The impact on world history of leaders like Joseph, Moses, David, Mordecai, and Daniel
- The inspiring record of many godly individuals

The words of the Hebrew Scriptures have been used throughout history and across nations to inspire, teach, and motivate people out of ignorance.

Ancient World Not So Primitive

There is a tendency to look back on the ancient Near East as a primitive and uneducated time in history. But archaeological evidence has uncovered cultures that were rich in literature and artistic expression with complex market economies. There was certainly religious superstition, moral confusion, and ignorance in certain branches of science (particularly health and medicine), but in many other fields of endeavor, the knowledge and achievements of ancient Near East cultures were astonishing. Take, for example, the 30,000 cuneiform tablets found in the ruins of the royal library at Nineveh, showing an advanced, educated society discussing medicine, astronomy, literature, and science. The ancient Egyptian understanding of astronomy, mathematics, irrigation, shipbuilding, construction, and many other fields was very advanced. Their engineering feats and precision of construction still puzzle the world.

Israel was witness to the greatness of Egypt, and Israelites would have been involved in many of the associated trades. The biblical record reveals skilled craftspeople existed among the Israelites who left Egypt, including metal workers, weavers, tailors, jewelers, and artisans of all types. The Israelites would have been a skilled and intelligent people, with their leader Moses educated in "all the wisdom of the Egyptians" (Acts 7:22). God called on many of these people for the skilled work he had in mind for his tabernacle (Exod. 28:4–6). He then enhanced their skills to an advanced level (Exod. 35:25–26, 30–35). The workmanship of these inspired master craftspeople would have been outstanding.

God wanted his people to excel in skills and knowledge. But most importantly, it was his desire for the people to come to know him personally and be educated in godly standards of right and wrong. This was God's measure of greatness.

Educated in the Law

For a nation to become great, all citizens must be educated in the nation's laws and values. Each household then becomes a defense against misguided leaders who try to take the nation off course.[1]

God knew the background of these people, and he knew the flawed standards of the surrounding nations, so he instructed parents to teach the law as a priority in every home. The laws were to be put deeply into their minds (the "frontlets" between their eyes) and mounted on the walls of their houses (Deut. 6:8–9):

> *God wanted everyone in the nation to have the opportunity to learn his law.*

> Therefore you shall lay up these words of mine in your heart and in your soul, and bind them as a sign on your hand, and they shall be as frontlets between your eyes. You shall teach them to your children, speaking of them when you sit in your house, when you walk by the way, when you lie down, and when you rise up. And you shall write them on the doorposts of your house and on your gates, that your days and the days of your children may be multiplied in the land of which the LORD swore to your fathers. (Deut. 11:18–21)

God wanted everyone in the nation to have the opportunity to learn his law. Priests were to be the teachers of the law to the people (Lev. 10:11; Mal. 2:7; 2 Chron. 17:8–9). The law was to be taught at every opportunity, including a public hearing every seven years (Deut. 31:11). These occasions were to be more than just a reading—they were intended to teach the *sense* and *meaning* behind the law (Neh. 8:8).

When judges (or priests acting in that capacity), gave determinations in law, they were to include both a judgment and an instruction on the law so that people could understand and learn the reasoning behind the ruling:

> According to the sentence of the law in which *they instruct you*, according to the *judgment which they tell you*, you shall do; you shall not turn aside to the right hand or to the left from the sentence which they pronounce upon you. (Deut. 17:11)

Moses had previously set a similar example of not just passing judgments, but *teaching* people to know and interpret the law:

---

[1] Thomas Jefferson commented that the safest depository of the ultimate powers of a society are in an educated populace Bibliog: (Jefferson 1820).

> When they have a difficulty, they come to me, and I judge between one and another; *and I make known the statutes of God and His laws*. (Exod. 18:16)

Any future king was also to write his own copy of the law and read it daily so that he also would learn the true intent of these laws (Deut. 17:18–19). As king, he would be the highest judge in the nation, and he had to know the law well.

Educated in the History of Their Nation

It has been said, "A nation that forgets its past has no future." In essence, this is exactly what God, Moses, and Joshua said to the Israelites consistently for years. In addition to the laws of the nation, God wanted each citizen to know and understand the *history* of their nation. It is a thread that runs through the entire law system, warning the people to remember the incredible works God had done for them. Civic education was to be a core subject taught in every home:

> *God wanted each citizen to know and understand the history of their nation.*

> And *teach* [God's statues and judgments] *to your children and your grandchildren, especially concerning the day you stood before the* LORD *your God in Horeb,* when the LORD said to me, "Gather the people to Me, and I will let them hear My words, that they may learn to fear Me all the days they live on the earth, and that they may teach their children." (Deut. 4:9–10)

God asked Moses to specifically write down the record of their journey for posterity (Num. 33:2). He wanted the history of the nation to be taught to the young children by their parents at every opportunity so that each generation would understand their origins and not forget their God and redeemer:

> When your son asks you in time to come, saying, *"What is the meaning of the testimonies, the statutes, and the judgments which the* LORD *our God has commanded you?"* then you shall say to your son: *"We were slaves of Pharaoh in Egypt, and the* LORD *brought us out of Egypt with a mighty hand;* and the LORD showed signs and wonders before our eyes, great and severe, against Egypt, Pharaoh, and all his household. Then He brought us out from there, that He might bring us in, to give us the land of which He swore to our fathers. (Deut. 6:20–23)

God encouraged the use of music and song to teach Israel of his providence:

> Now therefore, write down this song for yourselves, and teach it to the children of Israel; put it in their mouths, that this song may be a witness for Me against the children of Israel. ... Therefore Moses wrote this song the same day, and taught it to the children of Israel. (Deut. 31:19, 22)[2]

God also gave Israel holy days so that successive generations would not lose sight of their heritage. The Passover and days of unleavened bread were reminders of the pivotal event of Israel's history:

> You shall eat no leavened bread with it; seven days you shall eat unleavened bread with it, that is, the bread of affliction (for you came out of the land of Egypt in haste), *that you may remember the day* in which you came out of the land of Egypt all the days of your life. (Deut. 16:3)

The Sabbath day was a weekly reminder of the exodus:

> And *remember* that you were a slave in the land of Egypt, and the LORD your God brought you out from there by a mighty hand and by an outstretched arm; *therefore the LORD your God commanded you to keep the Sabbath day.* (Deut. 5:15)

The Sabbath was also a memorial of the history of creation—a reminder to honor God as the Creator of all things. (Exod. 20:8–11)

Literacy in Israel

If the people were to be well educated, they would need to be literate and not just rely on oral traditions, which would vary over time. Widespread literacy is only possible through a phonetic alphabet system, which opens the door for average people to quickly learn how to read and write concisely. The benefit of an alphabet is its simplicity, allowing complex words of a language to be written with only a small set of phonetic symbols. A complex symbol system like those used in Egyptian hieroglyphics and Mesopotamian cuneiform would involve highly trained scholars and could not be expected to be learned by the average person.

We find internal biblical evidence of writing early in Israel's history. By the time of Moses, the Bible presents writing as generally extant in the nation. Moses received the Ten Commandments in written form, and before his death, he wrote both the expanded law and the narrative of Israel into a *Book*

---

[2] The "Song of Moses" will be sung in heaven in the end times (Rev. 15:3).

of the Law and instructed that it was to be carried with the ark as a testimony (Deut. 31:24–26).

Further confirming widespread literacy, Moses commanded each Israelite to write parts of the law on the doorposts of their future houses and gates as reminders (Deut. 6:9; 11:20–21). He instructed the people to make a written record of the law on large, whitewashed stones after they crossed the Jordan (Deut. 27:1–3, 8). After Moses, Joshua affirmed the covenant with the people and added his own written record to the book (Josh. 24:25–26).

There are other passing references to general literacy, such as certificates of divorce to be written by husbands (Deut. 24:1–3). The book of Joshua records that men who were sent in advance to survey the land were required to write a description of what they found (Josh. 18:8–9). In the book of Judges, we note a passing comment that even a random youth could write (Judg. 8:13–14). All this points to early Israel being an educated people with widespread literacy.

Doubts have been expressed over the accuracy of these biblical notations, questioning whether the average person at that time could read and write. However, recent archaeological finds have reinforced biblical claims and identified the development of the alphabet at the very time of the founding of the nation of Israel in the region of Egypt. The Semitic alphabet is believed to be the forerunner of all modern alphabets. Its origins have been traced to a script that represented the language of the Semitic-speaking workers in the Levant in the second millennium BCE.[3]

> *The timing and location of the rise of the alphabet is more than coincidental.*

The timing and location of the rise of the alphabet is more than coincidental. God wanted his word accurately written and transmitted, and he ensured that the capabilities to do so were available when needed.[4]

The Influence of Scripture

God always intended for his people to be educated and wise. It's a theme that recurs throughout the words of the Mosaic law. Because early Israel failed to teach their upcoming generations, they quickly forgot God and lost their way as a nation (Judg. 2:17; 3:7). Most of the ten tribes of northern Israel who went

---

[3] Bibliog: (Herrman 2023)
[4] The *Patterns of Evidence* series by Tim Mahoney explores evidence that demonstrates the extent of writing throughout the Levant area in all levels of society Bibliog: (Mahoney 2020).

into captivity became largely lost to history because they forgot their God and lost their identity.

The southern kingdom of Judah was different. The Jews also went into captivity, but while in Babylon, they started taking seriously the directive to write down and teach their children the Torah. Although their interpretation of the law and added oral traditions increasingly diverged from God's original intent, it nevertheless resulted in a highly educated people. Over the centuries, the Jewish people survived their diaspora against all the odds because they taught their children and kept their traditions. Never in the history of the world had a nation survived culturally intact without a homeland. It is also thanks to the Jews taking education so seriously that we have the Hebrew Scriptures available in such accuracy today. The Jews may have gone astray in their understanding of Scripture, but we have them to thank for its preservation (Rom. 3:1–2).

From the time of Jesus to now, the truth and inspiration of these ancient writings have helped shape the course of history. The power of Scripture to enlighten was clearly evident at the time of the Reformation. Access to the Bible had been suppressed for centuries, but once lifted, and Scripture available in the vernacular, knowledge in all areas exploded. Arts, culture, and music—so often influenced by the power of Scripture—developed in extraordinary ways.

Some scholars have credited the explosion in scientific knowledge to the religious reformation. People came to understand that the Creator God was rational, and therefore they would find a rational universe. Martin Luther, called the father of the Reformation, summed up the power of God's Word to educate:

> Would that this one book were in every language, in every hand, before the eyes, and in the ears and hearts of all men! Scripture without comment is the sun whence all teachers receive their light.[5]

This was God's original intent for ancient Israel—for the nations of the world to see and learn from their enlightened way of life and say, "Surely this great nation is a wise and understanding people." (Deut. 4:6)

---

[5] Bibliog: (D'Aubigne 2012, Ch V)

The Issue of Slavery

I am the LORD your God, who brought you out of the land of Egypt, that you should not be their slaves; I have broken the bands of your yoke and made you walk upright. —Leviticus 26:13

For most people, the fact that slavery of any sort is mentioned in the laws of the Old Testament is troubling. Slavery is a highly emotive word and conjures up images of terrible conditions of times gone by. Those in the Western world will most likely think of the harsh antebellum American slave plantations epitomized by the book *Uncle Tom's Cabin* or the appalling slave ships full of kidnapped people as depicted in the movie *Amistad*.

But these sorts of images do not align with the law of Moses, and they definitely don't align with the loving and gracious character of the Lawgiver. God is not double-minded. He had rescued his people from slavery in Egypt and wanted them to be free, not oppressed (Lev. 26:13). He didn't want the nation of Israel to enslave their own people or anyone else—rather he wanted Israel to be a light to the world, a nation that would be attractive to people of other nations, a blessing to the world. Slavery, as we understand it from history, could never fit that picture. It would have been a blight on the nation, just as it was in nineteenth-century America.

What we will find is that the law of Moses did not support slavery as people imagine slavery today, but it did include guidelines for voluntary and involuntary servitude. Servitude was a system designed to deal impartially, fairly, and sensibly with the realities of life at that time. Had Israel followed God's guidelines, it would have had positive outcomes for the individuals concerned—and for society overall.

The law of Moses did not support slavery as people imagine slavery today.

Why Servitude at All?

There is a simple question Christians and critics alike ask: "If God is God, and he is who he says he is, why didn't he just decree that there would be no slavery of any sort?" A question like this sounds reasonable but comes with several implied assumptions:

1. It assumes a negative definition of the word "slavery," which the law of Moses does not support.

2. It does not consider social alternatives that may have to be implemented when people break laws or get into financial trouble, which they will most certainly do.
3. It assumes that no good can come from any system where people are restrained or managed by others.

The question is also similar to the one Jesus was asked about divorce laws: "Why didn't Moses simply command that there would be no divorce?" (Matt. 19:3–7). Jesus explained that God enacted divorce laws because of the hardness of people's hearts, but they were never God's ideal. God hates divorce, yet he gave divorce laws to set boundaries when divorces did occur.[1]

The simple fact is that people are not perfect, and laws will always be needed to manage negative situations that arise in families and societies. The laws God gave were not given to encourage slavery any more than they were to encourage divorce. Neither does their existence imply that servitude was a positive thing. They were there to solve a problem and *regulate* and *protect* the vulnerable who otherwise would be at risk.

We still have involuntary servitude with us today in modern countries.

People who state that slavery should not exist in any form often forget that we still have involuntary servitude with us today in modern countries. It's called *prison*. The American Constitution states:

> Neither slavery nor involuntary servitude, *except* as a punishment for crime whereof the party shall have been duly convicted, shall exist within the United States, or any place subject to their jurisdiction. (Thirteenth Amendment)[2]

No one today equates a prison sentence for a duly convicted felon with the dreadful conditions of a slave ship full of mistreated and stolen people. Neither should a person make the same invalid link of tying together historical slavery with the laws of servitude under the law of Moses.

Other forms of servitude (both voluntary and involuntary) are also an acceptable part of Western societies today. Consider the following:

---

[1] Discussed in the chapter *In Touch with the Reality of Life*.
[2] Bibliog: (National Constitution Center 2023)

Involuntary Servitude Examples:

- Military draft is involuntary servitude practiced in times of war.
- Compulsory military service is mandated in many Western democratic countries for all able-bodied people of a certain age.[3] If a person refuses to serve, serious jail terms can apply.
- Community service for petty crimes is involuntary servitude. If individuals do not comply, harsher punishments apply.

Voluntary Servitude Examples:

- Choosing to voluntarily enlist in the military contractually indentures a person's life to the government for several years. They become a servant of the state with little control over their own life.
- When a person signs a major league sporting contract, they lose control over their life (more in some sports than others). They can be traded and transferred as their club sees fit.
- Many nations bring in large numbers of migrant workers for their building projects or seasonal work. These migration schemes often come with bonded employment arrangements. Such experiences are often deemed beneficial for all parties concerned. Employees often see these indentured arrangements as an opportunity for themselves and their families to get ahead.
- Apprenticeships and internship arrangements also restrict the working freedom of the individual to some degree, as do various types of employment contracts.

The laws of servitude in the Mosaic law are far closer to these sorts of legal employment agreements than the degrading "slavery" most people envisage today.

The Word "Slave"

Much of the negative sentiment toward biblical slavery arises from the translation of the Hebrew word *ebed*.

The word *ebed* appears over 800 times in the Old Testament, and depending on the context, is translated as either *servant* or *slave*.

---

[3] Countries with compulsory military service include Denmark, Finland, Switzerland, Israel, Norway, Austria, Singapore, etc.

Note the historical disparity in the way *ebed* has been translated. In the original 1611 King James Version the word *slave* appeared only *once* in the Old Testament, but newer translations have increased the use of the term:

Translation		No. times "slave(s)" appears in OT
KJV	King James Version	1
NKJV	New King James Version	40+
NIV	New International Version	100+
ESV	English Standard Version	100+
YLT	Young's Literal Translation	0

Clearly, translators either did not agree with the contemporary meaning of the word "slave" or with the specific textual context. As biblical scholar Dr. Peter J. Williams notes:

> Translating *ebed* as "slave" is problematic because of its negative connotations, which were not originally there, but we associate from other historical contexts. This generally leads to inconsistency in translation, and it becomes hard for readers not to read into the word ideas from subsequent, very different systems of slavery (e.g., in Greece, Rome and North America).[4]

Williams then explains:

> (*Ebed*) is not an inherently negative term and is related to work. The term shows the person is subservient to another. All subjects of Israel are servants of the king. The king himself is a servant of their God. So in the time of the Old Testament, no-one is free—everyone is subservient to (an "ebed" of) someone else.

The term *ebed* is also used to describe Israel's relationship with God—they are his servants (Lev. 25:55). This is not intended to be a negative statement but one describing a positive relationship with a caring master.

The only way therefore for us to understand God's laws of servitude in the Old Testament is to remove preconceived notions and look at both the *intent* of

---

[4] Bibliog: (Williams 2015)

the Lawgiver and how servitude in the law was to be implemented. And when we examine what the Bible says on the subject, we find that the brutal slavery that men and women (and children) have suffered throughout history is nothing at all like the servitude that God outlined in the law of Moses.

Love Toward Strangers

To understand the Mosaic system of servitude, we must first be reminded of the foundational directive to *love*. The guiding principle underpinning the entire law code is: *"you shall love your neighbor as yourself: I am the LORD."* (Lev. 19:18). All the laws relating to servitude were to be understood and applied in light of this underlying principle.

And if there was any doubt as to who the definition of neighbor includes, God specifically clarified that this love must be applied to the foreigners who lived among them:

> And if a stranger dwells with you in your land, you shall not mistreat him. *34 The stranger who dwells among you shall be to you as one born among you, and you shall love him as yourself;* for you were strangers in the land of Egypt: I am the LORD your God. (Lev. 19:33–34)

Kidnapping—a Capital Offense

Historical slavery usually began with the kidnapping of people against their will. To prevent such behavior, Mosaic law stipulated that kidnapping a person was a *capital offense*:

> He who kidnaps a man and sells him, or if he is found in his hand, shall surely be put to death. (Exod. 21:16)

No person could be taken into servitude against their free will or without a legal judgment of wrongdoing from a court of law. Note the capital punishment applied not just to the kidnapper, but also those found in receipt of the kidnapped persons.

Mosaic law stipulated that kidnapping a person was a capital offense.

This law alone dramatically distinguishes the Mosaic laws of servitude from most of the slavery in history. The kidnapping and enslavement of Africans by other Africans and by Europeans during the sixteenth to nineteenth centuries were directly against Scripture, a point among many others that William Wilberforce used to prosecute the case for the abolition of slavery in Britain.

Reasons for Servitude

Scripture provides us with the common reasons why someone in Israel might have ended up in a servitude arrangement—the main ones being poverty, debt, liability, and theft. These are social problems that still exist in our world today. The difference lies in how we address the issues. Let's see the Mosaic solution.

Poverty: Voluntary Servitude

We noted earlier how the law of Moses was designed to keep people *out* of debt. Extensive support provisions for the poor and needy were built into the law code. But life in the ancient world was much tougher than our world today. Crop failure, the loss of a spouse or family member, the loss of a valuable work animal, an accident, or other personal disaster situations could quickly lead to poverty for a family with minimal resources. *Voluntarily* indenturing oneself for a period of time was a way of providing security through tough times (Lev. 25:39). It was an option that provided the security and legal protection of an employer.

Debt: Involuntary Servitude

Society has always had to deal with debt situations. Harsh debtor prisons were extant throughout history.[5] Even up until the mid-nineteenth century, debtor prisons existed in Western Europe and America. Today most countries have bankruptcy provisions, which can still make it difficult for someone to reset their life because of the stigma and bad credit rating. Bankruptcy also means the lender loses out.

The law of Moses addressed these issues humanely and fairly for all parties. A person who stole another's property or accidentally caused another's loss could be sold into servitude to pay for reparations if they didn't have the means to settle the matter (Exod. 22:1–3). A determination like this would need to be a judgment from a court of law (Deut. 19:15). The length of servitude was proportional to the debt incurred.

Servitude could also result from actions by a creditor who needed to recover their investment by selling the value of the person's labor. (2 Kings 4:1; Matt. 18:25). Such a person would be required to work in servitude either until the debt was repaid, the debt was redeemed (paid out) by themselves or another

---

[5] Bibliog: (Univ. of Maryland. Francis King Carey School of Law 2016, p494-496)

person, or when the statutory maximum term of six years (for Hebrews) was complete.

Significantly, in the entire law of Moses, there is no mention of the use of prisons, yet prisons were in use from the earliest times in other cultures. Prisons appeared much later in Israel's history but were not a part of the legal structure God gave to Moses. People could be held in custody pending a trial (e.g., Lev. 24:12), but beyond that, if found guilty, they were either punished, fined, or directed to indentured work.

Servitude by Vocation

As if to reinforce the positive way in which a servant was to be treated, the law of Moses anticipated that a servant may wish to remain permanently indentured to their master:

> But if the servant plainly says, "I love my master, my wife, and my children; I will not go out free," then his master shall bring him to the judges. He shall also bring him to the door, or to the doorpost, and his master shall pierce his ear with an awl; and he shall serve him forever. (Exod. 21:5–6)

Permanent indenture was not an unusual situation. Masters often entrusted their servants with important responsibilities. Being permanently associated with a family could be attractive for many, giving them and their own family protection, security, and status. We have modern examples of similar arrangements from such places as England, where servants often felt privileged and honored to be a permanent part of a family's heritage. But permanent servitude in Israel was not something a master could impose. The servant had to publicly declare his love for his master before the courts and go through a prescribed ceremony (Exod. 21:5–6). The ring in the ear was a symbol of that relationship. It was a big decision. Of course, a considerate employer could always agree to release a servant at a future time if circumstances changed.

The relationship was sometimes so strong that a permanently indentured servant could become a part of the family inheritance line, as seen in the relationship between Abraham and his chief servant, Eliezer. Before Ishmael was born, Eliezer was the heir of Abraham's house, ahead even of Lot (Gen. 15:2–3). Although this was before the law of Moses, the practice may have continued. The later example of Sheshan and his Egyptian servant, Jarha, demonstrates how a highly esteemed servant could become part of the family lineage (1 Chron. 2:34–35).

Working Conditions under Servitude

The working conditions God decreed for all servants, both Hebrew and foreigners, were generous and humane. There were no exceptions. God did not want servants treated like the slaves of other nations. The law stresses the importance of treating servants with respect and with love.

> *The working conditions God decreed for all servants were generous and humane.*

Sabbath Rest

The Sabbath was a mandated day of rest for everyone, including servants (Exod. 20:8–10). Moses particularly noted that one reason God gave the Sabbath was to remind everyone that the whole nation was once under bondage and was now free (Deut. 5:15).

Festivals

Servants were to be involved in the annual festivals (Deut. 16:11–12). This included traveling with their hosts to the chosen festival site and fully partaking and rejoicing in the celebrations.

Statutory Limit of Term for Hebrew Servants

There was a maximum of six years of servitude for Israelite servants, after which time they were free to go if they so chose (Exod. 21:2; Deut. 15:12). Foreign servants could be held permanently. (Discussed later in this chapter).

Bonus upon Release

At the end of their term of service, servants were to be given generous provisions to ensure that they could get off to a good start on their own:

> And when you send him away free from you, you shall not let him go away empty-handed; you shall supply him liberally from your flock, from your threshing floor, and from your winepress. From what the LORD has blessed you with, you shall give to him. (Deut. 15:13–14)

This general principle of generosity paralleled the earlier exodus from Egypt. God moved the Egyptians to give liberally to the Israelites when they left (Exod. 3:21–22).

Wages

Some assume that those in servitude in the Mosaic system were not paid. This idea arises from an invalid association with historical slavery. The whole idea of debt servitude (or retribution for a crime) in the Mosaic system was for the person to pay off the associated debt with their labor:

> He should make full restitution; if he has nothing, then he shall be *sold for his theft*. (Exod. 22:3).

Being "sold" *for his theft* directly implies a term that is commensurate with what is owed. This logically means a servant's time of service was credited as value against the balance owing. In that sense, they were being "paid." This is further supported by the law's fundamental requirement that punishment or retribution must be *proportionate* (as in *eye for an eye*). The length of the period of servitude would be determined at the outset by agreement or by a judge. Some in debt servitude may have been contracted for a full six years, others much shorter, depending on their indebtedness.

Scripture does not indicate how compensation was calculated, but it does indicate an indentured servant was a lower cost to the master than a hired hand:

> It shall not seem hard to you when you send him away free from you; for he has been worth a double hired servant in serving you six years. (Deut. 15:18)

This verse seems to be a general statement of the greater value of having a full-time servant rather than paying a hired hand by the day.

A person who *voluntarily* indentures themselves because of financial hardship would certainly expect wages in some form. Arrangements may have also varied depending on whether the master provided room and board for the family etc. Regardless of the arrangement, a foundational principle of the law is clear: a laborer is worthy of his wages (1 Tim. 5:18; Deut 25:4). The law states that servants could even "prosper" in a servitude relationship (Deut. 15:16).

Legal Protection

A person in servitude under the law of Moses also had the strength of legal protection. And it was a strong protection, unlike the chattel slavery of other nations.

If a master so much as knocked out a tooth of a servant, the servant was to be set free:

> If a man strikes the eye of his male or female servant, and destroys it, he shall let him go free for the sake of his eye. And if he knocks out the tooth of his male or female servant, he shall let him go free for the sake of his tooth. (Exod. 21:26–27)

The mention of a tooth and eye was not meant to be prescriptive but simply to represent a certain level of infraction. This law would certainly make any master think twice before violence. To lose a servant was to lose a valuable resource. This directive also confirms that a servant could not be branded or permanently scarred somehow, as was common in other nations.[6]

> *A person in servitude had the strength of legal protection.*

Furthermore, if the master killed his servant, the murder had to be accounted for under the law. There was no devaluing of human life—everyone was equal under the law (Lev. 24:22). The punishment for murdering a servant was the same as killing a free person:

> And if a man beats his male or female servant with a rod, so that he dies under his hand, *he shall surely be punished* (Exod. 21:20)

The word translated "punished" is "avenged" (Heb. *naqam*), implying the servant's life must be accounted for.

Runaways

One law that drives home the major difference between Israelite servitude and slavery is the law concerning runaways. Servants who fled from oppressive masters were not to be given back:

> You shall *not give back to his master the slave who has escaped from his master* to you. He may dwell with you in your midst, in the place which he chooses within one of your gates, where it seems best to him; *you shall not oppress him.* (Deut. 23:15–16)

Some commentaries suggest that this law is specifically for foreign servants who escape from foreign masters into Israel because it emphasizes the runaway now "dwelling with you" in the land. Regardless of whether this command

---

[6] The voluntary awl through the ear for permanent servants did not brand the servant but was how they externally acknowledged their role and lifetime commitment.

references local or foreign servants, the emphasis is on *not oppressing* the servant involved. For this reason, the context here most likely supports a servant running from oppression, not justice. We must assume that a servant running from the law, or running to avoid repaying their debt would be treated differently.

Violence Against Servants?

One section of the law in Exodus is criticized for implying that a master could beat a servant, and as long as the servant didn't die, he was free to go—as if violence against a servant was condoned (Exod. 21:20–21). But this reads a wrong implication into the law. We saw earlier that masters were to treat their servants well and not abuse them. Even at the level of the loss of a tooth, a master could lose a valuable servant. A beating could have far worse outcomes than a lost tooth.

The law in question does not condone violence. It simply acknowledges that squabbles and fights were bound to happen in society and gives a guideline on where the relevant liabilities lay. Two separate scenarios involving violence are referred to in these verses.

First, the law addresses the liability arising from a physical conflict between two individuals.[7] In this scenario, if the victim does not die, the perpetrator is liable to cover the victim's medical costs and loss of income:

> If men contend with each other, and one strikes the other with a stone or with his fist, and he does not die but is confined to his bed, if he rises again and walks about outside with his staff, then he who struck him shall be acquitted. *He shall only pay for the loss of his time, and shall provide for him to be thoroughly healed.* (Exod. 21:18–19)

The second scenario is the liability that arises when the conflict is between a master and a servant. The judgment is compatible with the first scenario. The difference being that the master does not have to compensate the servant because his servant's injuries and loss of time are a *cost to the master:*

> And if a man beats his male or female servant with a rod, so that he dies under his hand, he shall surely be punished. *Notwithstanding, if he remains alive a day or two, he shall not be punished; for he is his property.* (Exod. 21:20–21)

The verse reads harshly from our modern perspective but does not give any

---

[7] Discussed in the chapter *Tort Laws*.

sanction for violence. It simply outlines where the cost of compensation lies in such a scenario. A master who harms a servant will have to pay for the cost of his servant's recovery since he works for him, and the master will also lose the potential income generated from the servant while he heals. So the cost to the perpetrator of the violence is the same in both scenarios.

In both cases, if the victim did die, the perpetrator could be liable for murder as noted earlier.

"Selling" a Daughter?

One section of servitude law deserves an explanation:

> If a man sells his daughter to be a female slave, she shall not go out as the male slaves do. (Exod. 21:7)

A man selling his daughter to be a slave rightly sounds both appalling and culturally foreign to us. However, if we rephrase the verse in less emotive terms, the intent becomes clearer:

> If a man accepts money for his daughter to be a maidservant, she shall not go out as the male servants do.

This law was not given to encourage fathers to "sell" their daughters but to protect females in a world culturally different from ours. Historically it was not uncommon for a father to agree to indenture his daughter in a servitude arrangement, but with that came the potential for the new master to simply treat her as chattel and do as he pleases with her. God was clear in this law this was not to be the case. The verses following explain the context:

> If she does not please her master, who has betrothed her to himself, then he shall let her be redeemed. He shall have no right to sell her to a foreign people, since he has dealt deceitfully with her. And if he has betrothed her to his son, he shall deal with her according to the custom of daughters. If he takes another wife, he shall not diminish her food, her clothing, and her marriage rights. And if he does not do these three for her, then she shall go out free, without paying money. (Exod. 21:8–11)

The terms of such an arrangement were laid out: if the new master was unhappy with her, her father could redeem her and return the monies (bride price/dowry). The master couldn't just sell the servitude arrangement to another party. If the master wished to take her as a wife for his son, then she must be treated with the full respect of a daughter-in-law with the full rights and privileges of a wife. She was not to be treated as a second-class citizen. If she was not treated properly, she was free to leave the arrangement without penalty. Such legal rights and protection for women, particularly maidservants, were in stark contrast to other cultures in the ancient world.

Wife Left in Servitude?

Another servitude scenario is often criticized for separating a family, but that is not the context at all:

> If you buy a Hebrew servant, he shall serve six years; and in the seventh he shall go out free and pay nothing. If he comes in by himself, he shall go out by himself; if he comes in married, then his wife shall go out with him. If his master has given him a wife, and she has borne him sons or daughters, the wife and her children shall be her master's, and he shall go out by himself. (Exod. 21:2–4)

This law exists to clarify the contractual arrangement. If a man came into the arrangement married, his wife and children were also released at the end of the contractual period. If his master had provided a wife (which was probably a common scenario), then the wife had to complete her contracted term of employment (six years max) before she was released. The children logically stayed with her as the husband potentially sought new work elsewhere. Nothing implies the family was separated. We assume that they would still live together. The judgment simply clarified that the master would suffer no financial loss for providing his servant with a wife. She would remain employed by him.

Foreign Servants

Additional criticism of the laws of servitude is sometimes given to the "slavery" of foreigners who could be held for life (unlike Israelite servants with their maximum term of service of six years). Again, we must first replace the emotive word "slavery," which puts a negative bias on the context:

> And as for your male and female [servants] whom you may have—from the nations that are around you, from them you may buy male and female [servants]. Moreover you may buy the children of the strangers who dwell among you, and their families who are with you, which they beget in your land; and they shall become your property. And you may take them as an inheritance for your children after you, to inherit them as a possession; they shall be your permanent [servants]. (Lev. 25:44–46)

Lifetime servitude was not at all unusual in other nations—it was standard. Why the different treatment in Israel between Hebrews and foreigners? The answer lies in understanding who this group called "strangers" refers to. "Strangers" here refers to foreigners who lived in the surrounding nations or lived in their own enclaves within Israel. These were people who retained their own gods and cultural practices. From the outset, God had made it eminently clear that such people were a threat to the nation. And while they were equally protected under the law and to be treated fairly, they did not have the full rights as someone who had chosen to accept the God of Israel.

We must also be reminded of the context of this law concerning foreign servants:

- Kidnapping or stealing people was forbidden (Exod. 21:16). So for a foreigner to be permanently indentured meant they must already have been a genuine indentured servant of someone else, or they had to voluntarily agree to indenture themselves to the new Hebrew master permanently. They could not just be "taken." (Wartime situations were different; see below.)
- God provided a way for "strangers" to accept the God of Israel and become full citizens.[8] Once they were citizens who accepted the God of Israel, the laws pertaining to Hebrews would apply to them (Exod. 12:48).
- Not all foreigners in Israel were servants. Foreigners who lived inside the nation's boundaries could become wealthy and even have Hebrew servants of their own (Lev. 25:47).

Interestingly, despite this law concerning foreigners, no scriptural or historical evidence exists that Israel ever imported foreign workers on any scale, despite the option being available to them—and despite permanent slavery being extant in the nations around Israel. Where we do see this law in practice is in relation to the Canaanites who remained in the land after the conquest. On occasion, Israel put these people into servitude:

> And it happened, when the children of Israel grew strong, that they put the Canaanites to forced labor, but did not utterly drive them out. (Josh. 17:13)

Solomon raised a workforce from such people:

---

[8] Refer to the chapter *What It Meant to Be a Citizen of Israel*.

All the people who were left of the Hittites, Amorites, Perizzites, Hivites, and Jebusites, who were not of Israel—that is, their descendants who were left in the land after them, whom the children of Israel did not destroy—from these Solomon raised forced labor, as it is to this day. But Solomon did not make the children of Israel servants for his work. (2 Chron. 8:7–9)

The story of the Gibeonites demonstrates what the servitude of foreigners looked like in practice. The story can be found in Joshua 9. The Gibeonites deceived Israel and, as a consequence, were made servants to the nation. The Gibeonites readily agreed, knowing the alternative was to lose their lives. But this, again, was not the slavery we see in other nations of the day. Joshua decreed they would be "woodcutters and water carriers" to the tabernacle (Josh. 9:27). It was respectful work. Years later we see Gibeonites becoming fully part of the nation. One Gibeonite became a mighty man of David, and after the captivity, another helped in the reconstruction of Jerusalem (1 Chron. 12:4; Neh. 3:7).

Servitude in Time of War

For general wartime situations against distant cities and nations, the law included provisions for subjugating those who were enemies of the nation. Israel was to first make an offer of peace:

> When you go near a city to fight against it, then proclaim *an offer of peace to it*. And it shall be that if they accept your offer of peace, and open to you, then all the people who are found in it shall be placed under tribute to you, and serve you. (Deut. 20:10–11)

If such a city chose not to accept the offer of peace, normal wartime scenarios applied. The men would die in battle, and the remaining women, children, livestock, etc. could be taken as spoils of war—a logical outcome. Without enough men in the city, it would be vulnerable to future attack and famine:

> Now if the city will not make peace with you, but war against you, then you shall besiege it. And when the LORD your God delivers it into your hands, you shall strike every male in it with the edge of the sword. But the women, the little ones, the livestock, and all that is in the city, all its spoil, you shall plunder for yourself; and you shall eat the enemies' plunder which the LORD your God gives you. Thus you shall do to all the cities which are very far from you, which are not of the cities of these nations. (Deut. 20:12–15)

There is no suggestion here that the women could be raped or mistreated. Taking them as "plunder" simply means the women and children could be taken back as servants, which would be preferable to being left in a ruined city to potentially starve.

Again, it must be stressed that regardless of how a person came to be in servitude, all servants, including foreigners in wartime situations, were afforded protection under the law.

Rejecting the Negative Stereotype

As stated at the outset, servitude is not a simple matter of right and wrong, as some naively present it. There is a whole range of scenarios involving servitude in the narrative of the Old Testament, some positive and others negative where they ignored the laws of Moses. Some were compromise situations.

But what is clear, as this brief synopsis has hopefully demonstrated, is that the negative, oppressive stereotype of slavery that so often comes to mind was categorically disallowed in the law of Moses. The loving and gracious God of Israel did not want anyone living under the umbrella of his enlightened system of law to feel oppressed. Yes, there was a time when people had to work off debts, compensate for another's loss, or be corrected for bad behavior. But done properly with a "master" who held godly values, lessons could be learned and positive results achieved. In other indentured scenarios, the employer/employee relationship could be a way to get ahead or ensure that a family was protected.

> *The negative, oppressive stereotype of slavery that so often comes to mind was categorically disallowed in the law of Moses.*

The big picture to keep in mind is the loving nature of God who gave these laws, and the merciful, just way he wanted them administered. Emotive statements in use today, such as "It is immoral to own another person," simply confuse the discussion. If "owning" means having the right to totally control and mistreat another person, then yes, it is immoral. But if "owning" means having *limited* authority to care for and protect another (as in our *own* children, our *own* employees, our *own* servants), then it has the potential to be a very positive relationship.

The Public Health System

If you diligently heed the voice of the LORD your God ... I will put none of the diseases on you which I have brought on the Egyptians. For I am the LORD who heals you. —Exodus 15:26

It is astonishing how little most civilizations knew of the basic concepts of hygiene and disease control, even up to relatively modern times. Venice introduced quarantining in the 1300s in an effort to protect the city from the Black Death. But even after enacting those laws, the reasons why quarantining had positive results were not understood. Unhygienic practices continued for centuries in European cities with excrement and filth often dumped into the streets and clean drinking water a scarce commodity. The rise of the industrial age and the mass migrations to cities compounded public health issues.

As late as the nineteenth century, there continued to be a frighteningly limited understanding of how disease spread. Some doctors considered their soiled operating gowns as badges of honor and resented the idea of washing their hands. "Laudable" (good) pus was thought to promote healing and was spread intentionally.[1] The now greatly respected Hungarian Josef Semmelweis, described as the "father of hand hygiene" and "savior of mothers," found a link between deaths in hospitals and cleanliness but was ignored and died a discredited man in 1865. Before the twentieth century, the massive death tolls in wars were primarily from infection and disease. In the American Civil War two-thirds of combatants died from non-life-threatening wounds and infection.[2] It was only in the latter half of the nineteenth century that awareness started to grow of the importance of sanitation.

> *The health laws God gave to ancient Israel are remarkable. They were thousands of years ahead of their time.*

Considering how late in history it was before people properly understood the concepts of infection and disease control, the health laws God gave to ancient Israel through Moses are remarkable. They were thousands of years ahead of their time.

---

[1] Bibliog: (National Library of Medicine 2017)
[2] Bibliog: (National Library of Medicine 1993)

In this chapter, we will look at the enlightened health and hygiene principles that God included in the laws of Moses. In a later chapter we will review the ceremonial aspect of these laws and what God was also aiming to achieve from a spiritual perspective.[3]

Diseases of Egypt

Just how far ahead of its time the Mosaic law was is evident when we compare its teachings with the contemporary medical knowledge of Egypt. Egypt was a powerful and advanced civilization at that time. The Ebers Papyrus, written circa 1500 BCE, is the most extensive and best-preserved record of ancient Egyptian medicine.[4] It contains hundreds of formulas and prescribed remedies. The papyrus demonstrates Egypt's ignorance of fundamental health and medicine. Medical doctors Stern and McMillan comment:

> The Ebers Papyrus lists hundreds of prescriptions with an amazing array of ingredients: statue dust, beetle shells, mouse tails, cat hair, pig eyes, dog toes, breast milk, human semen, eel eyes, and goose guts. ... To splinters, the ancient Egyptian doctors applied a salve of worm blood and donkey dung. Since dung is loaded with tetanus spores, a simple splinter often resulted in a gruesome death from lockjaw.[5]

The papyrus outlines hundreds of similar bizarre and unhealthy practices involving such substances as urine, animal blood, manure, beer, etc. Stern and McMillan make the valid observation that Moses would have been taught these medical procedures since he was educated in all the "wisdom of Egypt" (Acts 7:22). Yet not a single Egyptian practice can be found in the law of Moses! Instead, we find health and hygiene practices in the Mosaic law that only came to be understood in the nineteenth century. There is no way Moses could have independently understood these things without divine revelation. It further confirms the law of Moses was not a human invention.

> *The papyrus demonstrates Egypt's ignorance of fundamental health and medicine.*

We might naturally assume that the ancient Near East world would be "purer" and more disease-free than some later civilizations, but recent advances in biomedical techniques have also shown otherwise. Modern medical

---

[3] Refer to the chapter *Ceremonial Uncleanness*.
[4] Bibliog: (University of Leipzig 2023)
[5] Bibliog: (McMillen 2000, 10)

engineering provides the ability to analyze ancient remains for both the cause of death and the presence of disease. What it has revealed is surprising. Diseases such as malaria, tuberculosis, cancer, polio, parasitic diseases, and plague are now understood to have affected large numbers in ancient Egypt.[6] Only the wealthy could afford to be mummified, so the analysis provides a perspective of the lives of the high strata of Egyptian society. Surprisingly, what is often called *modern lifestyle diseases* have also been detected in Egyptian mummies, including coronary disease (atherosclerosis) and kidney stones.[7] Sexually transmitted diseases (STDs) were also recorded by ancient writers and were rampant in many ancient Near East nations.[8]

The Bible record confirms these modern findings and notes that the diseases of Egypt were well-known in ancient times and something the Israelites were concerned about:

> Moreover He will bring back on you all the *diseases of Egypt, of which you were afraid*, and they shall cling to you. (Deut. 28:60)

> The LORD will strike you with the boils of Egypt, with tumors, with the scab, and with the itch, from which you cannot be healed. (Deut. 28:27)

God promised that if the people of Israel followed his law, they would be free of these scourges (Deut. 7:15). Although it is expressed in a way that sounds as if God is taking a personal involvement in inflicting disease, what occurs in most cases are natural outcomes. If a society breaks the fundamental health, sanitation, and moral laws God has put in place, disease will follow. These natural cause and effects built into creation have been evident throughout history. As a corollary, most of the health blessings God promised for following his laws would be a by-product of following his laws of sanitation, quarantine, health, and moral behavior.

Personal Cleanliness and Hygiene Laws

God wanted his chosen nation to be a clean and hygienic people, healthy in mind, body, and spirit.

To achieve this, the law of Moses included an extensive list of cleanliness laws for both personal and communal application.

---

[6] Bibliog: (Hays 2018)
[7] Bibliog: (Columbia Heart Surgery 2016)
[8] Bibliog: (Franjo Gruber 2015)

Basic hygienic principles given in the law included:

- Wash after handling a dead body (Num. 19:11–12)
- Wash one's body and clothes after handling animal carcasses (Lev. 11:27–28, 40)
- Wash after coming into contact with vermin (Lev. 11:29–32)
- Restrain from sex during a woman's menstrual cycle (Lev. 18:19)
- Clean (or destroy if lower cost value) kitchen items that have had vermin contact (Lev. 11:32–34)
- Deep clean stoves that have had vermin contact (Lev. 11:35)
- Recognize that containers without a tight lid are prone to contamination (Num. 19:15)

Other laws were given for the management of bodily discharges and infections (Lev. 15):[9]

- Carefully monitor infections and weeping sores (vv. 2–3, 19)
- Wash to prevent cross-infections (vv. 4–10)
- Wash hands after coming into contact with contaminated areas (v. 11)
- Destroy contaminated items that can't be cleaned (v. 12)
- Wait a week to ensure an infection is gone (v. 13)
- Cleanse body after sex (vv. 16–18)

Priests were also given strict instructions concerning personal cleanliness when serving in the tabernacle. They were required to wash their bodies and their hands and feet upon entering and leaving the tabernacle (Exod. 29:4; 30:17–21; Lev. 16:4). A large bronze laver for washing was a key part of the temple items (Exod. 40:30).

> *God wanted his chosen nation to be a clean and hygienic people, healthy in mind, body, and spirit.*

Most of these principles align with what we follow today as a matter of course. Many Mosaic sanitation and cleanliness directives had both a practical and a ceremonial aspect. They would serve as a reminder for all the people to maintain daily levels of cleanliness and be hygienic people.

God's instructions even include basic toileting hygiene, indicating people were probably careless in such matters. They were to maintain hygienic

---

[9] Scholars suggest that some of these symptoms may relate to STD's Bibliog: (Hess 2008, V1 p710) Bibliog: (Harrison 1980, V3 p162-163)

standards even when camping out during wartime when it would be easy to be lax:

> Also you shall have a place outside the camp, where you may go out; and you shall have an implement among your equipment, and when you sit down outside, you shall dig with it and turn and cover your refuse. For the LORD your God walks in the midst of your camp, to deliver you and give your enemies over to you; therefore your camp shall be holy, that He may see no unclean thing among you, and turn away from you. (Deut. 23:12–14)

Interestingly, the stated reason for this law was not disease control, which may or may not have been understood, but the Lord not wanting to see uncleanness in the camp. This may have carried more weight with the mindset of the day.

Public Health Management

For the protection of society at large, the Levitical priests were given the role of medical workers and health inspectors who could order the inspection and quarantining of potential infections (Lev. 13–14). While people would generally rely on their family or tribal expertise in dealing with most sickness and injury, when it came to diagnosing more uncommon ailments and infections, they were required to go to the priestly authorities. Their oversight would help protect society from potential contagions and outbreaks. Taking public health so seriously was unique at that time.[10]

As medical officials the role of the priests was to:

- Diagnose unusual and undetermined ailments in the people (Lev. 13)
- Isolate patients to reduce chances of further infection (Lev. 13:4–5, 21, 26, 31, 33, 50, 54)
- Direct those with infectious diseases to cover their mouths (Lev. 13:45)
- Permanently quarantine those with infectious diseases until they are healed (Lev. 13:46)
- Inspect garments and direct the disinfecting or burning of contaminated clothing (Lev. 13:47–59)
- Diagnose those who show improvement (Lev. 14:2–3)
- Direct severely infected patients to wash their clothes, shave the hair of the head, beard, and even the eyebrows (Lev. 14:8–9)

---

[10] Jesus supported this system when he advised the healed lepers to show themselves to the priests (Mark 1:44; Luke 5:14; 17:14).

- Declare a disease-free person clean (Lev. 14:11)

The generic term "leprosy" used throughout the Bible refers to a broad range of infectious diseases, not just the most severe form of leprosy (Hansen's disease) as we call it today. The term "leprosy" is also used to refer to severe mold and mildew in buildings, and rot and bacteria on fabrics and clothing.

As health inspectors, the priests were to do such things as:

- Inspect for mold and bacteria in houses (Lev. 14:34–52)
- Order either the cleaning or removal of parts of infected homes or the demolition of buildings beyond repair (Lev. 14:40–48)
- Direct the affected occupants to wash (Lev. 14:47)

Today mold and mildew in buildings are known to create severe health problems. The housing and living standards in the ancient world were nothing like our modern homes. They were often built with stone, and with poor ventilation may have been more prone to mold and mildew issues.

Some other health-related laws given to Israel included:

- In times of war, booty was to be sterilized and cleansed before general use. Metal objects were to be sterilized in fire and other valuables washed in water (Num. 31:20–23)
- Soldiers were to wash themselves and their clothes before returning home (Num. 31:24)
- The dead bodies of executed offenders were not to be left in the open but were to be buried on the same day (Deut. 21:22–23)

Putting aside some ceremonial rituals that went with all these laws, our modern world recognizes the benefits of these practices God taught ancient Israel. The World Health Organization continues its battle to educate people in some third-world countries on many fundamental principles of hygiene that God made evident such a long time ago.

> *Our modern world recognizes the benefits of these practices God taught ancient Israel.*

Interestingly, God charged Moses to use hyssop oil as a purifying agent in many procedures (e.g., Num. 19:18; Ps. 51:7). Although there is some question over exactly what plant or plants the biblical *hyssop* is referring to, we now know that many of aromatic plants of the Mediterranean region are beneficial as antiseptics and as healing agents. The plant traditionally identified as hyssop (*hyssopus* genus) is noted to kill bacteria and reduce inflammation.[11]

Foreign to Our Culture

One understandable criticism is the way in which many of these laws are written. Instead of a stated emphasis on health or hygiene, they are mostly presented as part of a system of ceremonial and ritual cleanness. To our modern mind, these make the otherwise sensible hygiene practices sound somewhat bizarre in their application.

To understand why God might have done things this way, it is worth considering the context and what he was aiming to achieve with the Israelites.

Firstly, God intertwined health and hygiene standards with the ceremonial system to emphasize the importance of such practices in the eyes of the people. Israel would not naturally have appreciated the benefits of cleanliness that we understand today.

They had come out of slavery from a nation whose medical knowledge ranged from the rudimentary, to the misguided, to the superstitious. Having lived under slave conditions for a long period of time, their homes and villages in Egypt would have been substandard. No doubt with their fast-growing population, there would have been overcrowding and the potential for many health problems. Scripture indicates they had experienced the diseases of Egypt (Deut. 7:15). Changing the mindset of such a people and teaching them a new high standard of health and hygiene would not be easy. The way God chose to teach them was ideal.

> *God intertwined health and hygiene standards with the ceremonial system to emphasize the importance of such practices.*

Secondly, God wanted Israel to understand his holiness. He wanted Israel to know the reality of who he was and to understand just how special it was for them to be close to him. God wanted Israel to be a physically, morally, and spiritually clean people as a reflection of their status as his special people. Some of these laws will be laughed at today because of the style of language with which they are written, but they would have helped establish a clean and healthy society.

---

[11] Bibliog: (National Library of Medicine 2022, Hyssop)

Certification Ceremonies

The purification rituals that *accompanied* the laws of cleanliness are particularly foreign to our culture. These rituals involved items like clean birds, blood, wood, scarlet cloth, etc. (Lev. 14:1–6, 48–53). Rituals like this are rejected by the modern mind as superstitious nonsense and proof of the ignorance of the times.

But such criticism assumes that these rituals were a part of the cleansing process, which Scripture does *not* support.

A reading of Leviticus 14 for example, shows that only *after* a person or a habitat is inspected and *found to be already clean* are the rituals invoked. The rituals, therefore, played no part in correcting the problem. There was no claim along those lines. The rituals were simply the formal sign-off or certification process that the problem was gone. A ceremonial ritual like this would have been important to those concerned, confirming to others that they had been declared free of disease.

Dietary Laws

In Leviticus 11 God presents a list of animals acceptable for food and those not acceptable for food.[12] There is a modern tendency to be critical of the clean and unclean animal classification, thinking it was a purely ceremonial categorization without any scientific basis. But looking at the dietary laws purely as ritual misses the dual intent of the laws.

Firstly, there are objectively identified health benefits in avoiding many of the animals and creatures listed as unclean. These benefits have been well documented. Even today, many health practitioners warn of the heightened potential for allergic reactions to pork and shellfish. And the meat of many scavenger animals and certain seafoods must be carefully prepared to avoid illness. There clearly was a physical benefit for the people with these laws, particularly in a time without refrigeration.

But God had a bigger perspective in mind. After presenting the list of what was clean and unclean, he summarized his intent with the following:

---

[12] The simple list of clean and unclean foods in the Mosaic law should not be confused with the extensive Kosher laws developed by rabbinic Judaism. As they did with much of the law, Jewish religious leaders expanded God's simple dietary laws into a highly complex set of rules for food storage and preparation—an example being the separation of milk and meat products, which is not according to Scripture.

> For I am the LORD your God. You shall therefore consecrate yourselves, and you shall be holy; for I am holy. Neither shall you defile yourselves with any creeping thing that creeps on the earth. For I am the LORD who brings you up out of the land of Egypt, to be your God. *You shall therefore be holy, for I am holy.* This is the law of the animals and the birds and every living creature that moves in the waters, and of every creature that creeps on the earth. (Lev. 11:44–46)

God wanted Israel to be holy as he was holy, a people who represented God's own excellence.

There is an increasing tendency in our Western world to consider anything that moves as food. We see this on reality television survival shows, people eating all sorts of creepy crawlies, and even high-end restaurants that create dishes out of insects, animals, and sea creatures that previously would not have been considered acceptable for human consumption. Yet history confirms that civilized peoples have always accepted that certain creatures are not considered food, regardless of whether they might technically keep a person from starving to death. Rodents, snakes, dogs, foxes, cats, crows, lizards, horses, and vultures are just a few of a long list of animals that people in the West have historically rejected as food. Regardless of how well rat or dog is prepared and cooked, presenting such dishes to a guest would generally be regarded as repugnant and demeaning. The simple fact is that all cultures classify some animals as unfit for food, and we continue to make such distinctions in our own society.

God's list of clean and unclean animals presents God's perspective of his creation. He wanted Israel to reflect his high standard of holiness. God, who made all the animals, made a distinction that some animals were not acceptable as food or as an offering to him. Just because the consumption of unclean animals would not kill a person was not the point. God was not talking about the bare minimum but doing what was best. God's way is a way of excellence—in mind, body, and spirit.

Circumcision

Male circumcision is another example of God intermixing ceremony and positive health directives (Lev. 12:3). The circumcision God directed for Israelite males had physical benefits that would have been especially evident in ancient times when personal cleanliness was more difficult. Even today around one-third of the world is circumcised, and the percentage of those circumcised in the United States is still over 70 percent.[13] Circumcision was standard practice in many Western countries in the twentieth century.

Despite growing opposition to the practice in some quarters, the World Health Organization recognizes the practical benefits of male circumcision in hygiene and disease prevention.

Such knowledge would have been impossible for the ancients to determine and could only have come from divine revelation.

Interestingly, God directed that a male child be circumcised on the eighth day. Medical science now recognizes that the eighth day is the ideal time for circumcision, when vitamin K and prothrombin levels are at their peak.[14] Such knowledge would have been impossible for the ancients to determine and could only have come from divine revelation.

Morality and Health

A final point to note concerning health is the protection from STDs Israel would have received had they obeyed God's instruction and rejected the sexual practices of the surrounding nations.

Egyptian religion was steeped in sexual themes and practices. The Ebers Papyrus (previously noted) describes multiple cures for various STD symptoms, showing how real the problem was in ancient Egypt. STDs were also rampant in the Canaanite cultures due to their lax morals and the integration of sex acts into their religious worship.

Because of Israel's ongoing attraction to these surrounding pagan cultures and their gods, STDs would have infiltrated the nation. Had Israel obeyed God's moral directives in the law, they would have been kept largely free of these ailments which were so prevalent in the ancient world.

---

[13] Bibliog: (National Library of Medicine 2016, Circumcision)
[14] Bibliog: (McMillen 2000, Ch 9)

Caring for the Environment

The land which you cross over to possess is ... a land for which the LORD your God cares; the eyes of the LORD your God are always on it, from the beginning of the year to the very end of the year. —Deuteronomy 11:11–12

The environment and sustainability are big issues in our modern world. People are rightly concerned with man's impact on our planet with our increasing urbanization, rising consumerism, and exponential population growth. Most of the environmental issues we face today started with the rise of the industrial age of the eighteenth century. Over the last 200 or more years, the impact on our planet has been massive.

But preindustrial civilizations also left their scars, including the complete loss of some animals and plant species, as well as soil degradation. The massive deforestation around the Mediterranean by the Romans and earlier Greeks caused permanent environmental damage. Even though they didn't have modern machinery, the impact of destructive policies and massive use of slave labor over centuries had a huge impact.[1]

The Creator God of this earth, the God of Israel, had a different idea. In Genesis, he confirmed that this earth *was* created as a resource for man:

> And God said to them, "Be fruitful and multiply; *fill the earth* and *subdue it*; *have dominion* over the fish of the sea, over the birds of the air, and over every living thing that moves on the earth." (Gen. 1:28)

But the earth was a resource to be used and cared for in a sustainable way, not raped and pillaged for all its worth. Humans are merely stewards of this earth—it ultimately belongs to God (Exod. 19:5). When he placed Adam and Eve in the garden of Eden, he directed them to both *tend* and *keep* it (Gen. 2:15)—in other words, use it but

> *Humans are merely stewards of this earth—it ultimately belongs to God.*

maintain its beauty in a sustainable way. This type of stewardship reflected how God wanted man to approach the earth.

When he later gave his system of law to Moses, God included moral and civil directives, which, had they been followed, would have created an

---
[1] Bibliog: (J. D. Hughes 2014)

Land Care

From the outset of his interactions with Abraham, God told him that the land of Canaan would be for his descendants (Gen. 17:8). For this reason, Canaan was a land God was going to take a special and permanent interest in:

> The land which you cross over to possess is ... *a land for which the LORD your God cares*; the eyes of the LORD your God *are* always on it, from the beginning of the year to the very end of the year. (Deut. 11:11–12)

God's perspective was reflected in the laws of land management he gave to Moses. As we saw earlier, the laws of farmland ownership were to teach Israel to trust in God and keep their eyes on him for their prosperity. But these laws also had positive environmental ramifications and implications. Every seventh year was to be a year of no cultivation, allowing the land to rest and recover from human activity.

> Six years you shall sow your land and gather in its produce, but the seventh year you shall let it rest and lie fallow, that the poor of your people may eat; and what they leave, the beasts of the field may eat. In like manner you shall do with your vineyard and your olive grove. (Exod. 23:10–11)

In the Jubilee (fiftieth) year, God set an additional year of rest and a time of economic reset (Lev. 25:11).

Mosaic land ownership laws would have also had long-term benefits on the management and sustainability of the land. The law stated that the farmland (and their associated village houses) outside cities were to remain in the hands of families. Even if they lost control of the land, it was to revert to the family in the fiftieth year (Lev. 25). Agricultural land was not to be sold permanently, meaning wealthy individuals or groups could not amass large-scale land holdings (Lev. 25:23).

While it is possible in today's world for an individual or family to mistreat their land, most major environmental issues that arise are caused by larger bodies, whether it be governments, corporations, or military activity. The development of the corporation in the Modern Era radically changed the nature of the world. For the first time, wealth could exist outside families and governments, allowing corporations to amass enormous wealth and hold ownership beyond the life of individual shareholders. Corporations have accelerated the pressure humans put on the natural environment.

Managing the Environment

The law of Moses included a range of other key principles covering many aspects of life, including management of the environment, and the need to do so positively and sustainably. These principles are again in the form of simple judgments that carry deeper meanings. One such judgment is as follows:

> If a bird's nest happens to be before you along the way, in any tree or on the ground, with young ones or eggs, with the mother sitting on the young or on the eggs, you shall not take the mother with the young; you shall surely let the mother go, and take the young for yourself, *that it may be well with you and that you may prolong your days.* (Deut. 22:6–7)

The concluding phrase "that it may be well with you and prolong your days" implies God was teaching a deeper principle beyond simple birds and eggs. This judgment is an instruction in conservation that has a broad application. Generally speaking, the ancient world showed little interest in any sort of conservation. If a resource could be used, it was taken. Yet here we see an approach to environmental

The law of Moses included principles on the management of the environment, and the need to do so positively and sustainably.

management where the law instructed people to stop and consider the ramifications of taking everything: take the eggs and young for food but release the mother to sustain the long-term food source.

The law's inclusion of such minor and seemingly unimportant directives is a major contrast to other contemporary law codes. It confirms the supernatural involvement in the law. Our modern world has realized that the sustainability of species and our environment starts with a similar attention-to-detail mindset. Jesus reflected the same mindset, noting that even sparrows were under God's eye (Matt. 6:26; Luke 12:6).

Another law told Israel that care of the environment applied even in times of war when such thoughts were rarely entertained:

> When you besiege a city for a long time, while making war against it to take it, you shall not destroy its trees by wielding an ax against them;

> if you can eat of them, do not cut them down to use in the siege, for the tree of the field is man's food. Only the trees which you know are not trees for food you may destroy and cut down, to build siegeworks against the city that makes war with you, until it is subdued. (Deut. 20:19-20)

The principle here again was to avoid the careless or wanton destruction of the environment which has long-term negative effects.

God wanted Israel to meditate on all these underlying principles, take them to heart, and teach them to their children (Deut. 6:6-7).

Animal Welfare

The law also included principles for the care and humane treatment of animals. In the laws of the Sabbath it specifically notes that working animals were also to rest:

> Six days you shall do your work, and on the seventh day you shall rest, *that your ox and your donkey may rest*, and the son of your female servant and the stranger may be refreshed. (Exod. 23:12)

It is also noted that the annual Sabbath (every seven years) was also a year of rest and provision for animals, both domesticated and wild. This is a strong statement of support for environmental sustainability:

> It is a year of rest for the land ... for your livestock and the beasts that are in your land—all its produce shall be for food. (Lev. 25:5, 7)

As noted earlier, the law against muzzling an ox had a deeper relevance beyond oxen, but at its face value, it also taught a person to show consideration to their animals. In a similar vein, the higher principle of loving your neighbor was also taught by referring to the caring way in which animals under stress should be treated:

> You shall not see your brother's ox or his sheep going astray, and hide yourself from them; you shall certainly bring them back to your brother. ...
>
> You shall not see your brother's donkey or his ox fall down along the road, and hide yourself from them; you shall surely help him lift them up again. (Deut. 22:1, 4)

Later Old Testament writers specifically understood that a righteous person would care for their animals:

> A righteous man regards the life of his animal, but the tender mercies of the wicked are cruel. (Prov. 12:10)

Consider David's furious response when Nathan brought the story of the rich man taking a pet lamb (2 Sam. 12:1–6). While the story was not ultimately about animals, it reflects the understanding that a person could deeply love their pet.

There are other Mosaic laws where we don't understand the full cultural background, but they have anti-cruelty implications. While animals were given for food, they were to be killed humanely:

> When a bull or a sheep or a goat is born, it shall be seven days with its mother; and from the eighth day and thereafter it shall be accepted as an offering made by fire to the LORD. (Lev. 22:27)

> Whether it is a cow or ewe, do not kill both her and her young on the same day. (Lev. 22:28)

Regardless of the specific reasons behind these laws, they positively reflect the heart of the God of Israel the people were to emulate.

The Creation Praises the Creator

The law of Moses pushed against the reckless pursuit of materialism in so many of its constructs, by reminding the people to consider God first in all their doings. From the very outset of creation, when God declared everything he had made to be "very good" (Gen. 1:31), there has been an implied directive for humans to manage this earth for the glory of the creator and ultimate owner.

For those who have eyes to see, Psalm 148 is a beautiful reminder of how the heavens and the earth, and all creation, continues to praise and glorify God (Ps. 148). It's a message that has just as much relevance today as it did all those many years ago.

PART 6: The Worship System

God was very particular with the details of the system of worship he gave Israel. It was both a teaching device and a revelatory system, rich in symbolism, purpose, and meaning that looked forward far into the future.

This section will review aspects of the tabernacle, the priesthood, the sacrificial system, the holy days, and other ceremonial rituals that were a shadow of God's great master plan to reconcile humanity to himself.

The Key: God's Holiness

For thus says the High and Lofty One who inhabits eternity, whose name is Holy.
—Isaiah 57:15

The ceremonial system of the law of Moses revolved around a simple but important understanding: *the God of Israel is holy*. And if the children of Israel were to be God's special people and take advantage of the special opportunity being offered, they would need to respect God's holiness, both in the worship system and how they lived their lives (Lev. 19:2; Deut. 7:6).

The Hebrew word for "holy" carries the meaning of being special and distinct. Describing God as holy means recognizing the reality of his unique status as the supreme eternal being above all. It is a simple description of an indescribable being. God alone is intrinsically righteous and holy (Rev. 15:4). He is "the high and lofty one who inhabits eternity, whose name is holy" (Isa. 57:15). He is the Creator God, supreme in every way. He is perfect, the essence of truth and righteousness, a being of immense and awe-inspiring power. It is how he has always been. The entire heavenly host of vast numbers of mighty beings attest to this fact, saying, "Holy, holy, holy Lord God almighty, who was, and is, and is to come" (Rev. 4:8; Isa. 6:3).

> *Describing God as holy means recognizing the reality of his unique status as the supreme eternal being above all.*

Holiness is not a concept people generally give any thought to today. It's viewed as an archaic and esoteric idea confined to the world of religion. But the holiness of God has never changed. It is just as real today as it was back in ancient times.

The Greatness of God

A simple way to grasp the reality of God's holiness is to look at the response of those who came near to his presence. When Moses first met God at the burning bush, he fell on his face trembling (Acts 7:32). When God later came down to Mount Sinai, the people also trembled at the nearness of God and were warned to stay clear of the mountain (Exod. 19:16, 21–23). Moses was given a mere glimpse of the back of his Creator and fell to the ground in awe (Exod. 34:8). Even when God wanted to show his glory to Moses, he said, "You cannot see My face ... and live" (Exod. 33:20). His glory would have consumed

Moses in an instant. When Moses came down from the mountain, his face was radiating light (Exod. 34:29).

Later, the prophet Isaiah was taken to heaven in vision, and his immediate reaction was to cry, "Woe is me!" He knew he could not possibly live in God's presence (Isa. 6:1–5). Ezekiel, also in a vision, fell on his face at the glory revealed before him (Ezek. 1:28). Job became speechless when God revealed himself to him (Job 42). Others like Daniel fell to the ground shaking in the presence of the mere messengers of this great being (Dan. 10:7–10).

The New Testament affirms the same reaction to holiness. John is called the disciple whom Jesus loved, and it was to him that Jesus gave a special revelation. That revelation opens with a vision of Jesus in all his glory, "like the sun shining in its strength" (Rev. 1:16). John's response to the vision was quick and automatic: "And when I saw Him, I fell at His feet as dead." (v. 17). Even though this was his beloved friend and master, John collapsed at the brilliant sight before him. Even in vision, the sheer glory of Jesus' presence was overwhelming.

This was not God trying to prove something. It is simply who he is. All this is exactly what we would expect from a being able to command a universe into existence. The energy in the cosmos is beyond measure, yet it is all the creation of his hands.

Any connection of man to God can only originate from God's unmerited kindness.

To fear God is simply common sense. In reality, an enormous, unfathomable gulf exists between us and our God. His holiness is a terrifying thing indeed unless accompanied by his grace (Heb. 10:31). No works of man, no matter how impressive, could ever span such a chasm. Any connection of man to God can only originate from God's unmerited kindness—a lesson undeserving Israel needed to learn through the ceremonial system.

The Fear of God Is the Beginning of Wisdom

God's desire to dwell with Israel and be close to them was an incredible privilege and enormous blessing to the nation, but they first had to understand who they were dealing with. Despite multiple warnings, some in Israel had to learn the hard way about the holiness of God. The first tragic incident occurred early in the operation of the tabernacle:

> Then Nadab and Abihu, the sons of Aaron, each took his censer and

put fire in it, put incense on it, and offered profane fire before the LORD, which He had not commanded them. So fire went out from the LORD and devoured them, and they died before the LORD. (Lev. 10:1–2).

This seems a harsh judgment from our perspective, but these sons of Aaron had no excuse for their careless and disrespectful behavior. They had been in the presence of God on the mountain, they had seen his great works and had been carefully trained and consecrated (Exod. 24:9–10; Lev. 8:30). After the incident, Moses explained why their example as priests was vitally important to the nation:

> And Moses said to Aaron, "This is what the LORD spoke, saying: '*By those who come near Me I must be regarded as holy; and before all the people I must be glorified.*'" (Lev. 10:3)

In another major crisis, a man called Korah and some other Levites who were not of the family of Aaron demanded that they be allowed to perform the full priestly duties. They criticized Moses for taking too much on himself (Num. 16:3). They felt that they had a right to serve God as they saw fit, regardless of God's clear directive that the officiating priests were only from Aaron's family. They again failed to fear and respect God's holiness with tragic results.

Later in Israel's history, we have other incidents where God's holiness was ignored with disastrous consequences, including the captured ark episode (1 Sam. 5–6), the Uzza incident of David's day (1 Chron. 13), and the events of King Uzziah's leprosy (2 Chron. 26:16–21). When these events occurred, they put fear into the people. Even David was afraid of God when Uzza was struck down (1 Chron. 13:12).

The correct kind of fear of God is a great enabler and opens the door to true understanding.

Interestingly, after Uzza was struck for touching the ark, the ark was looked on in terror and temporarily located in the nearby house of Obed-Edom. But during the ark's stay in his home, God blessed Obed-Edom's family greatly (1 Chron. 13:14). The lesson was clear: when proper respect is shown to God, there is *nothing to fear*. And when David later followed the correct protocol for moving the ark, it was a joyous occasion (1 Chron. 15).

The fear God wanted Israel to learn was not the dread or terror of a capricious God but of great respect in the presence of his holiness. The correct kind of fear of God is a great enabler and opens the door to true understanding. David wrote that "the fear of the LORD is the beginning of wisdom" (Ps. 111:10). Even Jesus, who was at one with his Father in spirit, was still prophesied to be empowered and uplifted by the *fear* of God when he was on this earth:

> There shall come forth a Rod from the stem of Jesse, and a Branch shall grow out of his roots. The Spirit of the LORD shall rest upon Him, the Spirit of wisdom and understanding, the Spirit of counsel and might, *the Spirit of knowledge and of the fear of the LORD. His delight is in the fear of the LORD.* (Isa. 11:1–3)

Mosaic Holiness Code

When we understand God's holiness, the ceremonial system and holiness code he gave Israel makes perfect sense. God had chosen Israel from the nations and wanted them to be separate and holy in their conduct. It was a standard distinctly different from the surrounding nations:

> And you shall be holy to Me, for I the LORD am holy, and have separated you from the peoples, that you should be Mine. (Lev. 20:26)

> Consecrate yourselves therefore, and be holy, for I am the LORD your God. (Lev. 20:7)

Because he had chosen to dwell among them, he also wanted to teach them the importance of understanding his holiness, especially when they came near him in the tabernacle. The tabernacle was the symbolic location of God's presence. It was the earthly representation of God's heavenly throne, and strict guidelines were in place for those who came near, particularly for the priests and Levites who were rostered on for work (Lev. 10:3).

When we understand God's holiness, the ceremonial system and holiness code he gave Israel makes perfect sense.

God established the Mosaic holiness code to ensure his people understood the incredible privilege of being chosen by him. The system was not meant to be a burden on daily life. It was instead a teaching device and a reminder of the greatness of God when they came before him at the tabernacle. For the priests and the Levites serving in the tabernacle, God's holiness was of paramount consideration.

The misunderstanding that the ceremonial law was an impost on normal life comes from reading the book of Leviticus out of context. The book of Leviticus was written primarily as a directive to the priestly Levites and outlines the relevant procedures to be followed by them in the management of the tabernacle.[1] The word *holy* occurs over 100 times in the book of Leviticus. Mostly these were not directives to the average Israelite—*except* when they came into God's presence at the tabernacle.

The later Pharisees distorted the understanding of "holiness." In a misguided attempt to achieve their own righteousness, the Pharisees took the holiness laws—meant to teach and remind the people of *God's* holiness (his specialness and purity)—and made them about their *own* "purity." They looked down on others who were not as strict as they were. Not only was their focus wrong, but they also extended the holiness code far beyond the original scope and intent. By the time of Jesus, they had developed a tedious, legalistic system of ritual purity that did not glorify God. They turned a practical system of cleansing and ceremonial preparedness for the tabernacle into a daily series of burdensome rites for which Jesus derided them (Mark 7:1–6).

> *We should not confuse the rituals God desired in the ceremonial system with pettiness or legalism.*

We should not confuse the rituals God desired in the ceremonial system with pettiness or legalism. God wanted Israel to be special and separate and learn of his greatness but in a way that attracted other people, not drove them away.

New Testament Holiness

God has not changed his character, nor his plan for humanity, and his holiness remains. The identical words used to describe the specialness of Israel are now reserved for the called-out ones in the New Testament church.

> But you are a chosen generation, a royal priesthood, a holy nation, His own special people, that you may proclaim the praises of Him who called you out of darkness into His marvelous light. (1 Pet. 2:9; Deut. 7:6)

---

[1] The Greek title for the book of Leviticus in the Septuagint is "That which pertains to the Levites."

Just like ancient Israel, our holiness does not come from ourselves but is imputed from God when we put our confidence in him.

> Jesus Christ, who gave Himself for us, that He might redeem us from every lawless deed and purify for Himself His own special people, zealous for good works. (Titus 2:13–14)

This same holy being wants to share his love, his mind, his life—everything he has—with undeserving humans. And just like ancient Israel, followers of Jesus today are to be holy in their conduct:

> Rest your hope fully upon the grace that is to be brought to you at the revelation of Jesus Christ; as obedient children, not conforming yourselves to the former lusts, as in your ignorance; but as He who called you is holy, you also be holy in all your conduct, because it is written, *"Be holy, for I am holy."* (1 Pet. 1:13–16; Lev. 19:2)

The ceremonial law was a teaching device, designed to teach the holiness and perfection of God and reinforce the need for the people to put their trust in him. The book of Hebrews explains the true meaning of those symbols and how the ceremonial law pointed to the coming of the Messiah. We will look at those in the chapters that follow.

The Tabernacle

For Christ has not entered the holy places made with hands, which are copies of the true, but into heaven itself. —Hebrews 9:24

The tabernacle was the central hub for Israel's system of worship. It was a high-quality, portable, tent-like structure used during the years of wandering and throughout the period of the judges. Scripture also refers to it as the sanctuary, the tent of meeting, or tabernacle of the testimony (Exod. 25:8; 38:21; 40:2). The tabernacle was later superseded by the temple of Solomon in Jerusalem.

The tabernacle was a structure rich in meaning on multiple levels, shadowing important concepts God wanted Israel to understand about himself, his plan for Israel, and the future of all humanity. It was highly significant for the nation and the individuals who worshipped there. While Israel could not have understood the deeper meaning of the typology relating to the future Messiah, the key principles of God's grace, mercy, and forgiveness were clearly evident to them in the ceremonial framework.

Important to God

The importance of the tabernacle was reflected in the detailed level of God's involvement in the design. This alone should capture our attention. For the Creator God to give such close attention to a manmade object is highly significant. He gave comprehensive plans to Moses on Mount Sinai, describing every aspect of the structure and internal artifacts (Exod. 25–27).

> *The importance of the tabernacle was reflected in the detailed level of God's involvement in the design.*

And he was meticulous, specifying such minutiae as the colors of the curtains, the number of curtain loops, the clasps, the choice of fabrics, and the specific formula for the incense and anointing oil (Exod. 26:1–14; 30:22–38). God further charged Moses to ensure his design instructions were followed *precisely* (Exod. 25:9; 25:40; 26:30). He then inspired the artisans with extra talent and skill to ensure the workmanship on these items was as perfect as humanly possible (Exod. 31). Clearly, the tabernacle and what it represented was important to God.

Centuries later, when David desired to construct a temple to replace the tabernacle, God told him that the job would be left to his son Solomon. But that did not stop David from preparing in great detail before his death. And at that time also, God took great interest in the project, outlining detailed plans to David through his spirit to ensure everything was designed according to his will (1 Chron. 28:12, 19).

In New Testament era, Jesus was also respectful of the temple and ceremonial system. Despite the Second Temple of his day being constructed by the evil Herod the Great, Jesus understood its great significance and zealously drove the money changers out of the temple. He called it "My Father's house" (John 2:16). He regularly taught there and went to the temple to keep the holy days outlined in the law of Moses (e.g., Matt. 26:17; Luke 2:42; John 2:23; 7:10, 14, 37; 12:12). He paid the temple tax (Matt. 17:24–25, 27).

Although the temple was destined to be phased out, no negativity was associated with its use from Jesus' perspective. It was deeply significant to him.

The Design

The original tabernacle had a relatively simple layout. A central tent (the tabernacle) was surrounded by an ornate perimeter privacy fence creating an outer courtyard (Exod. 27:9–18; 38:9–20). The tabernacle was constructed from exotic fabrics, timber paneling, gold, silver, and bronze (Exod. 26). Everything was made using the finest materials fashioned to the highest possible standards (Exod. 35–36).

The tabernacle tent itself was partitioned into two sections: the *Holy Place* and the *Most Holy Place* (Holy of Holies). Only priests could enter the Holy Place, but access to the Most Holy Place was further restricted to the high priest only, and then only once a year (Lev. 16).

The most holy object in the tabernacle was the ark of the covenant. The ark was a gold covered chest containing the stone tablets of the covenant. On top of the lid of the ark were two gold cherubim facing each other with their wings reaching over and covering the ark (Exod. 25:19–20).[1] This lid became known as the mercy seat or atonement cover. The ark was placed in the Holy of Holies behind a heavy opaque curtain. The ark could only be moved by a specific clan of the Levites, and had to be carried in a certain prescribed manner by authorized priests (Num. 4:4–6). Even the priests transporting the ark were

---

[1] The book of Hebrews notes that the ark also contained Aaron's rod that budded and a pot of manna (Heb. 9:4). But this should be interpreted as being beside the ark rather than inside. This is more consistent with Scripture (Num. 17:10; Deut. 10:2). Scripture specifically notes the ark only contained the tablets (1 Kings 8:9; 2 Chron. 5:10).

not to look upon the ark before it was covered (Num. 4:17–20).

Other significant items in the tabernacle complex were the table of the shewbread, golden lampstand, bronze laver, and altar. Priests performed sacrifices on the altar in the outer courtyard at the entrance of the Holy Place (Exod. 27:1–8). Those coming to the tabernacle with an offering could enter the outer courtyard, but access to the tabernacle itself was off-limits to everyone except the priesthood.

God's Dwelling Place

There were several reasons for God's meticulous involvement in the tabernacle design, the most obvious being the tabernacle was where he would symbolically dwell among his people:

> And let them make Me a sanctuary, that I may dwell among them. (Exod. 25:8)

While in the wilderness, the tabernacle was located at the center of camp, surrounded by the Levites, symbolically placing God at the heart of the nation (Num. 1:52–53; 2:2).

The Hebrew meaning of the word translated "tabernacle" is "dwelling place." This was not God agreeing to be contained within the tabernacle or the ark like a pagan deity, as some have interpreted the idea. Solomon later exclaimed that no physical structure, no matter how grand, could ever contain the God of Israel (2 Chron. 6:18–21). God was simply declaring that if the people remained faithful, his presence would be at the tabernacle, and he would be close to the people and abide with them (Lev. 26:11–12). Despite the tabernacle being somewhat unimpressive compared to the later temple of Solomon, God was quite content with his temporary dwelling place and everything it depicted (2 Sam. 7:5–7).

Once it was inaugurated, the glory of God descended to the tabernacle in the form of a cloud by day and fire by night, the same cloud that had led the children of Israel during the time of the exodus (Exod. 13:21). It would rise and move as a sign for the people to break camp. This visible sign of the presence of God stayed with the nation throughout the forty years of wandering (Exod. 40:34–38; Num. 9:15–17). It seems the cloud disappeared once the people arrived in the promised land, but its fading may have to do with the people's unfaithfulness. It later briefly appeared at the time of the inauguration of Solomon's Temple (2 Chron. 7:1).

Because of God's holy presence, the tabernacle complex was to be regarded as sacred space and was therefore not to be taken lightly. Just as the people were warned to stay away when God came down to Mount Sinai, the average Israelite, even when ceremonially clean, could not enter the main tabernacle tent. It was off limits under pain of death.

Because of God's holy presence, the tabernacle complex was to be regarded as sacred space.

Before the tabernacle was complete, Moses met with God in a tent of meeting outside the camp (Exod. 33:7–11). Once complete, God told Moses their meeting place would be at the ark and he would speak to him from between the cherubim:

> You shall put the mercy seat on top of the ark, and in the ark you shall put the Testimony that I will give you. *And there I will meet with you*, and I will speak with you from above the mercy seat, from *between the two cherubim* which are on the ark of the Testimony. (Exod. 25:21–22)

The eventual fate of the ark has been the source of great intrigue. It is last noted in history at the time of King Josiah of Judah when he ordered the caretakers of the ark to return it to the temple in Jerusalem (2 Chron. 35:3). After this it disappeared from biblical history, although speculation on its whereabouts continues to abound.[2]

No Wall of Separation

As noted in an earlier chapter, there were no restrictions for foreigners wishing to sacrifice to the God of Israel (Num. 15:14–15; Lev. 17:8; 22:18). Neither did the tabernacle design include an outer court of the gentiles like the one Herod added to the Second Temple at the request of the Jewish religious leaders.

There were no restrictions for foreigners wishing to sacrifice to the God of Israel.

Solomon even *encouraged* foreigners to come to the original temple:

> Moreover, concerning a foreigner, who is not of Your people Israel, but has come from a far country for the sake of Your great name and Your mighty hand and Your outstretched arm, when they come and

---

[2] In a prophecy of the future kingdom of God, Jeremiah writes that the ark will not be made again, possibly implying it had been previously destroyed (Jer. 3:16).

> pray in this temple; then hear from heaven Your dwelling place, and do according to all for which the foreigner calls to You, that all peoples of the earth may know Your name and fear You. (2 Chron. 6:32–33)

The later Jewish religious leaders created a "wall of separation" between Jews and gentiles, directly *against* the law of Moses. Not only had they developed rules of segregation to keep gentiles at a distance, they also had installed a *physical wall* around the Second Temple and prevented gentiles from entering upon pain of death.[3] Despite its magnificence, Herod's temple became a symbol of the great divide between Jew and Greek. These "ordinances" that caused so much division between Jew and gentile were not from God. They were the commandments of men.[4]

Shadows of the Heavenly

Our modern world looks at the ancient tabernacle as a relic of a bygone era, but the symbolism of the tabernacle is timeless and of great significance for Christians.

The writer of the book of Hebrews tells us that the tabernacle and artifacts God outlined to Moses were copies and shadows of the permanent and true heavenly realm of God:

> We have such a High Priest, who is seated at the right hand of the throne of the Majesty in the heavens, a Minister of the sanctuary and of the true tabernacle which the Lord erected, and not man. ... There are priests ... who serve the copy and shadow of the heavenly things, as Moses was divinely instructed when he was about to make the tabernacle. For He said, *"See that you make all things according to the pattern shown you on the mountain."* (Heb. 8:1–2, 4–5)

> For Christ has not entered the holy places made with hands, which are *copies of the true*, but into heaven itself, now to appear in the presence of God for us. (Heb. 9:24)

Elsewhere in Scripture, we are given glimpses of the fabulous *real* dwelling place of God in his heavenly abode. These visions confirm how the ark in the

---

[3] Bibliog: (Whiston 1989, Josephus, Jewish Antiquities 15.417))
[4] In all the very detailed instructions God gave to Moses concerning the tabernacle, there is no mention of constructing a barrier to keep out gentiles. The idea to exclude gentiles arose in the Second Temple period.

Most Holy Place was indeed a representation of the throne of God (Ezek. 10:1–2; Rev. 5:6–14).

The typology and meaning of the tabernacle and the priesthood is solid proof of God's intense interest in man. God designed the tabernacle, the artifacts, and ceremonies to teach Israel about himself and invite them to be a part of his world. The layout of the tabernacle with the outer court, inner court, and the Most Holy Place highlighted the gulf between God and man, while at the same time, the ceremonies outlined God's plan for bridging that gap.

The entire structure was a shadow of the reality of God's realm and the good things still to come.

The typology and lessons to be learned from the tabernacle remain for Christians today. As the author of Hebrews describes, the entire structure was a shadow of the reality of God's realm and the good things *still to come* (Heb. 10:1). The tabernacle was a physical representation of God's great plan to one day "tabernacle" among men as he has always desired to do from the outset in the garden of Eden (Rev. 21:3).

What Israel Understood

There is some debate on how much ancient Israel could have understood of the symbols of the ark and tabernacle. At least some fundamental aspects of the typology would have been perfectly clear to them.

When God stated he would speak to Moses from between the cherubim (Exod. 25:21–22), Moses would have understood this as a representation of God's true heavenly dwelling place. He understood that cherubim were angelic beings close to God. Cherubim were known to have guarded Eden (Gen. 3:24). The leading elders of Israel had also been invited with Moses onto Mount Sinai to see the God of Israel in vision. They saw God depicted in his glory with a sea of sapphire stone under his feet. They may have also seen the covering cherubs as Ezekiel later did (Exod. 24:9–11).

Solomon also understood that the physical temple was a representation of God's true dwelling place. When he built the temple, he added two large cherubim, one on each side of the room with their massive wings touching the walls on one side and touching together in the middle (1 Kings 6:19–28; 2 Chron. 3:10–14). And the ark with its smaller winged cherubim was placed underneath these larger cherubim, reinforcing the representation of God's dwelling place (2 Chron. 5:7–8).

Later kings spoke of God dwelling among the cherubim. For example, when King Hezekiah was imploring God for his mercy, he addressed him as the one who *dwells between the cherubim* (Isa. 37:15–16).

To think that Hezekiah was referring to the ark of the covenant does not hold to the context of God being above all the kingdoms of the earth and inhabiting the universe. Similarly, David, knew that God dwelt between the cherubim (Ps. 99:1; 2 Sam. 6:1–2). Ezekiel later had visions of the cherubim and God's throne (Ezek. 10:1–2).

Ancient Israel may not have understood the deeper New Testament typology related to the Messiah, and the points highlighted by the writer of Hebrews. But they did understand that the ark represented God's throne, God was holy, and the tabernacle was a place where the nation could come and call on God for mercy and forgiveness through the mediation of the priesthood and the high priest.

Each aspect of the design, the sacred items, and the worship ceremonies were a teaching device for ancient Israel and all future believers, educating them about the realm of God, his holiness and specialness, and his plan of redemption for all people.

The Priesthood

Christ came as High Priest of the good things to come, with the greater and more perfect tabernacle not made with hands, that is, not of this creation.
—*Hebrews 9:11*

Just as he was with the design of the tabernacle, God was meticulous with his plans for the establishment of the Levitical priesthood. As we saw earlier, in exchange for setting apart all the individual firstborn of each household, God selected the entire tribe of Levi.[1] The Levites became the representative firstborn of the nation, carrying the special priestly role (Num. 3:12–13).

From within the Levites, God then chose the family of Aaron for the formal officiating priesthood. They would be the custodians and officiators at the tabernacle, serving as mediators between the people and the God of Israel.

Because of stereotypical ideas of what it means to be a priest, we tend to think of the role of a Levitical priest as someone solely focused on religious rites and ceremonial duties. But God's plan for the priestly Levites was far broader than the tabernacle and ceremonial aspects of the worship system. Even in a practical sense, the central tabernacle could only involve a small percentage of the total number of Levites, and an even smaller portion could be rostered on at any one time.

> *God's plan for the priestly Levites was far broader than the tabernacle and ceremonial aspects of the worship system.*

God had a bigger role for Levites to play. His plan was for most Levites to live throughout the nation in forty-eight designated cities and serve the nation in key civic leadership roles. Their primary mission was to help the people maintain their focus on God and his standards.

Ancient Priesthoods

The idea of a priesthood is an ancient concept. Every major culture had its priests who were the conduit between the people and their gods. The Old Testament mentions the priests of several other cultures and deities, including

---

[1] Exodus 19:22 mentions the existence of priests before the selection of the Levites. Based on Numbers 3:12–13, the firstborn of families may have been fulfilling some priestly duties (e.g., sacrifices) before the tabernacle.

priests of Egypt, Dagon, Baal, Chemosh and Asherah. The first mention of a priest of God in Scripture is Melchizedek, whom Abraham offered a tenth of his spoils (Gen. 14:18–20). Jethro, Moses' father-in-law, is also noted as being a priest of Midian and, in the context of his interaction with Moses, seems to have been a priest of the true God (Exod. 3:1).

Some critical scholars assume that Israel copied many of the priestly concepts from the cultures around them, but the biblical record again contradicts that idea. God clearly wanted Israel to have nothing to do with either the practices of Egypt where they had come from, or the nations of the land where they were headed (Lev. 18:1–3).

Further reinforcing this position, God included specific directives within his priestly system that were directly opposed to the cultic practices of the nations around them, including such key points as:

- Statutory sacrifices could only be done at the central tabernacle (Deut. 12:13–14)
- All the high places, altars, and groves used by previous religions were to be destroyed (Deut. 12:2–4)
- Priests of God were not to have tattoos or body markings like priests of other nations (Lev. 19:28)
- Priests were not to shape their hair or beard as pagan priests did (Lev. 19:27)
- Priests were not to mourn as pagans did, cutting themselves for the dead (Lev. 19:28)
- Sex could play no part in worship practices (Exod. 19:15; Lev. 15)

Because they had been set apart for special service to God, priests of the God of Israel were to represent the highest standards of moral and physical behavior, unlike the powerful and corrupt priests of so many ancient nations.

The Levitical Priesthood

From within the tribe of Levi, Moses' brother, Aaron, and his sons were selected for the formal priesthood. This became known as the Levitical or Aaronic priesthood. Aaron would be the high priest, and his sons would be the official priests of the sanctuary (Num. 1:50–53; 3:1–4). Their consecration into the role was an elaborate weeklong process (Exod. 29:30, 35, 37). The dedication ceremony was a sign of their special role in God's service (Exod. 29:9). From then on, formal officiating priests could only come from Aaron's lineage (Exod. 29:44).

Because of the significance of the role they were to fulfill, God gave detailed instructions to Moses covering each aspect of the priesthood. This included their structure, practices, personal standards, rituals, and intricate dress (Exod. 28, 39). The priestly attire for the high priests and Aaron's sons was to be particularly special, designed for its "glory and beauty" (Exod. 28:2, 40). Just as he had done with the tabernacle, God called on Moses to appoint gifted artisans to create these priestly garments and accoutrements. These were male and female artisans with the sophisticated skills of fabric weaving, embroidery, jewelry manufacture, lapidary, metal work, and engraving (Exod. 28:3; 35:25–26; 39:1–31).

While the majority of Levites were not officiating priests and not permitted in the Holy Place or Most Holy Place of the sanctuary, all Levites were still regarded as priests in a general sense (Deut. 18:1). They would support the official priests on a rostered basis, helping supply, set up, transport, and manage the tabernacle's sacrificial system (Num. 3:5–10). Specific Levitical families were nominated to fulfill various priestly support roles (Num. 4). General service work in the tabernacle, which would have been quite strenuous at times, was for younger men aged 25 to 50 (Num. 8:23–25); other specific roles required the Levite to be at least 30 (Num. 4).

God's Detailed Involvement

We return to an earlier question posed about the tabernacle: Why would the Creator God show such a detailed interest in the priesthood of a relatively minor nation in the ancient Near East? Critical scholars will claim all this detail regarding priests in the books of Moses as the aggregate work of fabled priestly scribes[2] written centuries later than the nominated writing period. In doing so they negate the concept of a supernatural directive in the priestly establishment. But if they are correct and all this is a dreamed-up, fabricated reality written much later, what value does it carry? It can have no value other than as an esoteric analysis of historical religions.

The Bible, on the other hand, clearly states that it was the Creator God who outlined these and other detailed instructions to Moses. In line with his character, this implies truth and purpose, which should be evident in the details of the priestly system. Even if historical records and archaeological finds are scant, we should still be able to cross-check the veracity of these ancient writings by looking for long-term internal biblical consistency and meaning

---

[2] Priestly sources "P" of the JEDP Documentary Hypothesis theory

in what these priestly symbols represented.

And that's precisely what we do see: a consistent purpose and meaning in every aspect of the priesthood—the physical symbols, rituals, and ceremonial practices. It would not be possible for a group of men to invent historical figures and practices centuries later and maintain coherence in all areas. The book of Hebrews expounds on the ultimate meaning God had in mind for the priestly system, starting with ancient Melchizedek through the Levitical system to the New Testament church and on to the future kingdom of God. The consistency of the symbolism and typology throughout biblical history is clear proof of God's involvement from the outset.

> *We see a purpose and meaning in every aspect of the priesthood, including the physical symbols, rituals, and ceremonial practices.*

High Priestly Standards

The officiating Levitical priests were held to higher standards than the average Israelite because they would be serving in the Holy Place of the tabernacle. The priests were interfaces between the people and God, accepting the sacrifices of the people and presenting them on the altar to God. The high priest would go into the holy of holies once a year symbolizing being in the presence of God.

Because of their closeness in serving God in the tabernacle, God set high standards for the officiating priests:

- They could not be of illegitimate birth (Deut. 23:2).
- They could not marry a divorced woman (Lev. 21:7; Ezek. 44:22).
- They could not marry an immoral woman (Lev. 21:7).
- They could have no physical defects (Lev. 21:16–23).
- They could not be a eunuch (Lev. 21:20).

This was not God being a respecter of persons. Being a priest was by selection, not by right. God was reinforcing to both the Levites and the people the serious reality of his holiness and perfection. For a priest on duty in the tabernacle, attention to detail was also important. They were required to:

- be physically clean (Lev. 8:6)
- be ritually clean (Lev. 21:1–4; Ezek. 44:25)
- dress carefully and respectfully (Exod. 28:42–43)

- consume no alcohol while on duty (Lev. 10:9)
- even manage their perspiration (Ezek. 44:18–19)

Aaron's sons Nadab and Abihu were senior men who should have understood the high standards and important symbolism of the role of priest. Yet they carelessly ignored God's holiness and paid a heavy price (Lev. 10:1–3).

The High Priest

The high priest was the chief priest and leader of the Levitical priesthood. All officiating priests played a mediator role, but the high priest in particular provided the highest level of interface between man and God. He would be the only one to enter the Most Holy Place behind the veil, and then only once a year on the Day of Atonement. Because of his closer proximity to God, there were additional qualifications for the high priest. He also had to be even more careful to maintain his ritual cleanliness (Lev. 21:10–15).

The high priest's dress was particularly striking and deeply meaningful. First an undergarment of fine linen over which a blue robe with a hem of gold bells and pomegranate was fixed. Over the robe was a magnificent colored and decorated ephod (long vest). Over the ephod was a "breastplate of judgment" held by a gold chain and decorated with rows of precious stones and the names of the sons of Israel. The breastplate had a place to hold the Urim and Thummim, of which we don't know a great deal. Scholars have suggested that the Urim and Thummim were possibly used as casting stones to determine God's will in the form of a yes or no (Exod. 28:30; Num. 27:21; Ezra 2:63). A turban and a crown topped off the high priest's special dress. The crown (tiara or diadem) included a front facing plate of solid gold on the forehead inscribed with the words "HOLINESS TO THE LORD" and was tied to the turban with a blue cord (Exod. 39:30).

The entire Levitical priesthood and the role of the high priest in particular were a type and a shadow of the incredible future to come.

When we look at the dress of the high priest and aspects of his consecration, it's hard not to see a link with royalty—the distinctly regal vestments, which were far superior to the general priesthood, and the holy crown or diadem. The high priest was not a king and had no executive power in the nation, yet he was dressed and anointed as a king might be. He alone would enter the Most Holy Place as "Holiness to the Lord" and make atonement for the sins of the nation. A deep-thinking Israelite may not have understood the true significance of the ceremony but must have realized that there was something other-worldly being pictured here.[3]

The entire Levitical priesthood and the role of the high priest in particular were a type and a shadow of the incredible future to come. It was a teaching mechanism for ancient Israel and remains so today.

The Civic Roles of a Priest

As previously noted, the role of a priest and a Levite in Israel was not confined to ceremonial duties and tabernacle service only. The job description for priests and Levites was very broad. Some of the civic roles they fulfilled included:

Teachers:

Moses had given the Levites the custody of the law from the outset (Deut. 31:9). They were to be the teachers of Israel. (2 Chron. 17:8–9; 35:3). They taught God's commandments, statutes, and judgments. They taught the history of the nation. They taught people the concept of sin, forgiveness and worship (Mal. 2:7). Levites were an indispensable source of religious knowledge for the people, and the channel through which spiritual life and understanding of God was communicated (Ezek. 44:23).

Judges:

When a matter was too hard for local elders to resolve, the priests and Levites were called on to make final rulings in an official judicial capacity (Deut. 17:8–13). Priests were required to determine the punishments for murder and serious civil matters (Deut. 21:5; 2 Chron. 19:8;1 Chron. 23:2–5).

Civil Leadership:

God wanted his people to look up to the Levites as positive examples and leaders in the nation. At times it was a calling to a frontline executive role, quite unlike the idea of a priest that comes to mind today. The Levites were men of action who inspired others. A striking example is God's direction for the priests to rally and motivate the troops in times of national crisis and war (Deut. 20:1–4). Priests were also the trumpet-bearers, right in the thick of battle (Num. 10:8–9; 31:6). When Moses found the people with the golden

---

[3] Interestingly, Moses, as the nation's leader, was not given a special dress code. This is not what we would expect if this was a manmade construct.

calf, he called on the Levites to deal with the offenders (Exod. 32:26–28). We see the leadership shown by Phineas in dealing with a crisis (Num. 25:6–13).

The Levites were men to be reckoned with. It was they who defended the new king in the time of Joash (2 Chron. 23:7). They were the armed gatekeepers of the temple (1 Chron. 9:17–27), described as valiant men (2 Chron. 26:17).

Management and Accounting

Another role the priests played was to supervise the management and accounting of finances for various projects. The priests oversaw the treasury used to build the temple and during later refurbishments (1 Chron. 26:20, 24, 26; 29:7–8; 2 Kings 12; Ezra 8:24–30). Whenever someone trustworthy and responsible was needed, the priests and Levites were called upon (1 Chron. 9:26).

Health inspectors:

Priests played the role of physicians and health inspectors for their communities (Lev. 13–15). If a person had an infection or disease, they came to the priests for inspection. If buildings or other items were contaminated, the priest would determine the best course of action. In these roles, priests were a vital part of the community.

Musicians

David later reorganized the Levites and particularly chose talented Levites as musicians to glorify God (1 Chron. 16:4–9; 23:5; 2 Chron. 5:11–13). Some were relieved of all other duties so they could concentrate on their music (1 Chron. 9:33).

Other Responsibilities

The priests and Levites fulfilled other responsibilities. Priests were involved in blessing the people on various occasions (Num. 6:23; 2 Chron. 30:27). Levites would have been responsible for organizing the service and celebrations during the festival seasons. These were major events centered on the tabernacle that had to be carefully managed.

Understanding the importance of the role of the priests and Levites in ancient Israel helps us appreciate why God harshly reprimanded them for failing to do their duty. Their influence was enormous.

> Her priests have violated My law and profaned My holy things; they have not distinguished between the holy and unholy, nor have they made known the difference between the unclean and the clean; and they have hidden their eyes from My Sabbaths, so that I am profaned among them. ... Therefore I have poured out My indignation on them; I have consumed them with the fire of My wrath; and I have recompensed their deeds on their own heads," says the LORD GOD. (Ezek. 22:26, 31)

The book of Malachi is also an indictment on the priests for failing to fulfill their leadership role. They failed to lead and teach the people, and God's judgment on them was hard (Mal. 1:6; 2:1–9).

The Spiritual Symbolism

Although the general opinion today depicts the old Levitical priesthood and tabernacle system as archaic and irrelevant, God's detail in establishing its structure is a clear sign there is far more than meets the eye at first reading. It is another example of God's glory in concealing a matter—and the reward in its uncovering (Prov. 25:2).

The tabernacle and priesthood represented a window into God's realm, which is timeless.

The tabernacle and priesthood represented a window into God's realm, which is timeless. Each and every detail had meaning and purpose. And only by looking at these Old Testament systems can a person fully understand what the New Testament writers were expounding. The book of Hebrews explains the deeper significance of the priestly system. It identifies Jesus as the true High Priest and a minister of the true sanctuary of God in heaven:

> Now this is the main point of the things we are saying: We have such a High Priest, who is seated at the right hand of the throne of the Majesty in the heavens, a Minister of the sanctuary and of the true tabernacle which the Lord erected, and not man. (Heb. 8:1–2)

Ancient Israel understood that the high priest, after purifying himself, would go before the God of Israel and pray for the nation's sins to be forgiven (Lev. 16:12–16). The future offering of Jesus and his presentation to the Father were being symbolized in type (John 20:17). But the ancients had no idea that one day, direct access to God would be available to individuals:

> But into the second part the high priest went alone once a year, not without blood, which he offered for himself and for the people's sins committed in ignorance; the Holy Spirit indicating this, *that the way into the Holiest of All was not yet made manifest while the first tabernacle was still standing.* (Heb. 9:7–8)

At the time of Jesus' death, the temple veil was torn from top to bottom (Matt. 27:51). The writer of Hebrews again explains the significance of the veil as a depiction of the flesh of Jesus by which the gulf between God and man is spanned:

> Therefore, brethren, having boldness to enter the Holiest by the blood of Jesus, by a new and living way which He consecrated for us, through the veil, that is, His flesh, and having a High Priest over the house of God, let us draw near with a true heart in full assurance of faith. (Heb. 10:19–22)

Christians can now come boldly to the throne of grace because of the efficacy of Jesus, our righteous High Priest:

> Seeing then that we have a great High Priest who has passed through the heavens, Jesus the Son of God, let us hold fast our confession. For we do not have a High Priest who cannot sympathize with our weaknesses, but was in all points tempted as we are, yet without sin. Let us therefore come boldly to the throne of grace, that we may obtain mercy and find grace to help in time of need. (Heb. 4:14–16)

The writer of Hebrews also explains how Jesus, who was a Jew and not a Levite, could become our spiritual High Priest in the order of Melchizedek, and how this was foreshadowed long ago in the writings of Moses and David (Gen. 14:18; Ps. 110:4, Heb. 6:20; 7:1–17).

It is valuable exercise to read the entire book of Hebrews. It shows how perfectly these old systems shadowed God's plan of redemption.

New Testament Priesthood

The significance of the Old Testament firstborn system and the selection of Levi as the firstborn priestly tribe also becomes clear in the New Testament and further opens our eyes to God's plan for the church.

God's original intent was for the collective nation of Israel to be a firstborn among nations. At the foot of Mount Sinai, God identified the entire nation of Israel as a nation of priests (Exod. 19:5–6). His desire was for Israel to collectively model the role of priests (mediators, teachers, judges, guides, etc.) to the world, leading other nations to the true God.

But Israel rejected God's invitation and was found not worthy (Matt. 22:1–8). And God used their stumbling as an opportunity to open the doors to the gentiles (Rom. 11:1–11). Gentiles (other nations) were now invited to be a part of the church of the firstborn and can be grafted into spiritual Israel (Rom. 11:13–24).

Jesus is described as the firstborn of many into the family of God (Rom. 8:29), and the church is described as the church of the firstborn, made up of the elect or chosen ones:

> But you have come to Mount Zion and to the city of the living God, the heavenly Jerusalem, to an innumerable company of angels, to the general assembly and church of the firstborn who are registered in heaven. (Heb. 12:22–23)

The "church of the firstborn" is a significant statement. Just as the "firstborn" Levites were specially selected to serve the nation, Peter describes the church in the same priestly terms:

> But you are a *chosen generation, a royal priesthood, a holy nation, His own special people,* that you may proclaim the praises of Him who called you out of darkness into His marvelous light. (1 Pet. 2:9)

The firstborn received a greater blessing and a privileged role of leadership in the family. This is the promised reward of the faithful elect (Rev. 3:12; 7:15).

> Grace to you ... and from Jesus Christ, the faithful witness, the firstborn from the dead, and the ruler over the kings of the earth. To Him who loved us and washed us from our sins in His own blood, and has made us (a kingdom of) priests to His God and Father, to Him be glory and dominion forever and ever. (Rev. 1:4–6)

The ancient structure of the priesthood that God outlined to Moses thousands of years ago is not irrelevant to modern Christians.

Logically, if the church is described as "firstborn" or "firstfruits," there must be future siblings, else the term has no meaning. The concept of the firstfruits and the greater harvest of the latter fruits is further expanded on in the meaning of the holy days.

This subject is a complete study in itself and can only be touched on here. But even at a high level, it confirms the deep meaning God built into ancient Israel's ceremonial and societal structures.

The ancient structure of the priesthood that God outlined to Moses thousands of years ago is not irrelevant to modern Christians. The ultimate fulfilment of the priesthood and tabernacle systems will be in the future kingdom of God, and the role of priest is set to continue long into the future:

> Blessed and holy is he who has part in the first resurrection. Over such the second death has no power, *but they shall be priests of God and of Christ*, and shall reign with Him a thousand years. (Rev. 20:6)

The Sacrificial System

You shall offer peace offerings, and shall eat there, and rejoice before the LORD your God. —Deuteronomy 27:7

The concept of sacrificing an animal is an ancient idea God endorsed before the nations even existed. Shortly after God expelled Adam and Eve from Eden, we see Abel making an offering to God of a firstborn of his flock and it being accepted (Gen. 4:4). From those earliest times and continuing after Noah, sacrificing remained a central practice of all ancient Near East religions.

While we may understand the intent of a sacrificial system in a theoretical sense, it is not easy to imagine living in a culture where sacrifices were a part of life. Ritualistic blood sacrifices are off-putting and foreign to our modern way of thinking, coming across as some sort of archaic fear-based system for the uneducated masses. But we must put aside our own perspective and first seek to understand the historical and cultural context.

> *The sacrificial system God gave Israel was perfectly aligned to the culture of the day.*

We live at a time in history when most people eat meat, but few are involved in meat production. Seeing the actual slaughter of an animal would be distressing to a modern city dweller. Yet for most of history, it has been a blessing and a joy to be able to kill the "fatted calf" with no associated negativity. And in the ancient Near East, offering a valuable animal to a deity was a natural and meaningful thing to do, accepted at all social levels and across cultural and national boundaries.

The sacrificial system God gave Israel was perfectly aligned to the culture of the day—so much so that the Israelites often made additional sacrifices at the old pagan high places in Canaan, even when God told them *not* to do so (Deut. 12:2–4; 2 Kings 16:4; 17:10, etc.).

Intent of the Heart Paramount

The sacrificial system appears so different from our New Testament theology that it presents as a different religion to many Christians. It's as if the God of Israel was more interested in outward legalistic ritual than what went on in a person's heart.

But that's not how Jesus saw it. Jesus knew that God had never changed. The intent of the heart has always been paramount to God (Deut. 5:29; 6:5–6). Jesus castigated the religious leaders of his day for not comprehending this important point—something they *should* have understood. Quoting from the Old Testament prophet Hosea, Jesus said:

> But go and learn what this means: "I desire mercy and not sacrifice." (Matt. 9:13)

Scripture shows the righteous people of old understood this point from the law:

> Samuel said: "Has the LORD as great delight in burnt offerings and sacrifices, as in obeying the voice of the LORD? Behold, to obey is better than sacrifice, and to heed than the fat of rams." (1 Sam. 15:22)

> For You do not desire sacrifice, or else I would give it; You do not delight in burnt offering. The sacrifices of God are a broken spirit, a broken and a contrite heart—these, O God, You will not despise. (Ps. 51:16–17)

It was not as if God didn't want the people to sacrifice to him—he did. He knew sacrifices were a powerful teaching device for the people, but he wanted them done with the right attitude. God was never impressed with the size of a sacrifice, only with the attitude of the heart. It was upsetting to God to see hypocrites coming to him with sacrifices:

> "To what purpose is the multitude of your sacrifices to Me?" says the LORD. "I have had enough of burnt offerings of rams and the fat of fed cattle. I do not delight in the blood of bulls, or of lambs or goats. ... Bring no more futile sacrifices; incense is an abomination to Me. The New Moons, the Sabbaths, and the calling of assemblies—*I cannot endure iniquity and the sacred meeting.*" (Isa. 1:11, 13)

God expresses the same thoughts through the prophet Amos:

> I hate, I despise your feast days, and I do not savor your sacred assemblies. Though you offer Me burnt offerings and your grain offerings, I will not accept them, nor will I regard your fattened peace offerings. Take away from Me the noise of your songs, for I will not hear the melody of your stringed instruments. (Amos 5:21–23)

These sentiments God expressed through the prophets reflect the original intent of the law, which was for Israel to learn to love God with all their heart, not simply act out external rituals as one might to a pagan god.

Purpose of the Sacrificial System

God gave the sacrificial system to teach Israel several key concepts underlying the worship of God. It was built on practices that God had given early in the history of man.

Firstly, sacrifices and offerings were first and foremost an expression of faith in God, as the example of Abel shows (Heb. 11:4). Offering a sacrifice to the God of Israel was an outward acknowledgment of God's sovereignty in a person's life and his willingness to put his trust in him.

Secondly, sacrifices were a powerful way of teaching the serious nature of sin and how to achieve atonement and reconciliation with God.

> For the life of the flesh *is* in the blood, and I have given it to you upon the altar to make atonement for your souls; for it *is* the blood *that* makes atonement for the soul. (Lev. 17:11)

The first recorded animal sacrifice was made by God when He clothed Adam and Eve with garments of skins (Gen. 3:21). The symbolism of the animals that had now died because of Adam and Eve's sin was clear. Noah was later taught the significance of God making man in his image and that the shedding of man's blood must also be accounted for with blood (Gen. 9:5–6). For these reasons, blood carried a special significance and was not to be consumed (Lev. 17:12–14). The Levitical sacrificial system was built on these principles and taught the need for redemption and God's willingness to forgive in a practical way.

God gave the sacrificial system to teach Israel several key concepts underlying the worship of God.

Thirdly, sacrifices were an expression of gratitude. After the flood, Noah's natural reaction was to offer burnt offerings in thankfulness that humankind had been spared (Gen. 8:20). God gave Israel specific sacrifices to perform as an expression of thanksgiving for what he had provided and his desire to fellowship with his people (Lev. 22:29).

Finally, the sacrificial system was to help Israel understand God's holiness and specialness. Because God was holy, all things had to be done with reverence and in the way God decreed. Formal sacrifices could only occur in specific places by authorized people and with designated types of animals. God put in place the categories of acceptable sacrificial animals long before Moses (Gen. 4:4; 7:2; 8:20).

Types of Sacrifices

There were five specific types of sacrifices and offerings, each with a different emphasis and meaning (Lev. 7:37–38).

Burnt offering (Lev. 6:8–13)

This type of offering represented building and maintaining a relationship with God. A male animal without blemish was offered and completely burned up. Given with a right repentant attitude it was a pleasing aroma to God (Lev. 1:17). Burnt offerings were done morning and evening at the tabernacle.

Grain or cereal offering (Lev. 6:14–23)

These offerings were given by an individual to God as an act of thankfulness. A voluntary portion of a crop was offered and the rest to be eaten by the priests.

Fellowship or peace offering (Lev. 7:11–36)

This was an offering symbolizing fellowship and peace with God. The participant kept most of the animal for their own consumption. The offering symbolically represented the individual's covenant with God by the blessing of enjoying a meal in the presence of God. These sacrifices were done in a spirit of rejoicing (Deut. 27:7).

Two other types of offering were given as an expiation for sins:

Sin or purification offering (Lev. 6:24–30)

These offerings were presented to make atonement for sin of an individual or the nation. This type of offering was generally done for the congregation as a whole. A sin offering of this type was offered for the nation on the Day of Atonement.

Guilt or trespass or reparation offering (Lev. 7:1–10)

This offering was given to provide compensation or restitution for sin. A portion was burned with rest given to the priests.

Personal Sacrifices Were a Special Event

When reading through the various types of offerings in Leviticus, a person might mistakenly assume that individual sacrificial offerings were required regularly, as if every time a person sinned, they would need to make an offering and atone for the sin (like going to regular confession with a priest as in some religions.) But this was neither the intent nor the reality. Presenting an animal to God as a sacrifice was reserved for special occasions and not something that most individuals did very often. We know that for a number of reasons.

Firstly, statutory sacrifices were to be performed only at the tabernacle (Lev. 17:8–9; Deut. 12:1–14). Therefore to make an offering, the individual needed to travel to where the tabernacle was located at that time. Canaan is not geographically large, but it would still have taken many days of travel for most people in the nation to reach the tabernacle. Regular sacrificing was therefore prohibitive for most people for reason of distance.

Secondly, God did not intend sacrifices to financially burden the people. The sacrifice of a premium animal was an expensive exercise that an average person could only afford on special occasions. The associated travel time and potential loss of income would also be an added cost. God was fully aware of the costs involved, and to ensure the system was available for all, he allowed the poor of the community to offer a lower-cost animal and for their offering to be fully accepted (Lev. 5:7, 11; 12:8; 14:21). He also allowed each person to *give as he was able* to prevent economic hardship (Deut. 16:17).

Sacrifices at the tabernacle were special occasions for families.

Thirdly, the tabernacle had limitations. It didn't have the capacity to handle a massive number of offerings each day. The size of the tabernacle, the size of the altar, and the requirement to only have the sons of Aaron presiding, restricted the number of daily sacrifices possible. The tabernacle operated for hundreds of years before the larger temple was constructed in Jerusalem, and even with the enlarged temple, there were still capacity limits for sacrifices.

Sacrifices at the tabernacle were therefore special occasions for families. Far from being an impost, they were memorable times for all the family to look forward to. The ideal was to travel to the tabernacle three times per year to celebrate the festival seasons, but not all could afford the time or cost of travel. Attendance was dependent on the blessings God had given the family:

> But if the journey is too long for you, so that you are not able to carry the tithe, or if the place where the LORD your God chooses to put His name is too far from you, *when the LORD your God has blessed you*, then you shall exchange it for money, take the money in your hand, and go to the place which the LORD your God chooses. (Deut. 14:24–25).

Traveling to the tabernacle and temple is reflected in the lives of certain individuals. For example, Elkanah, the husband of Hannah and father of Samuel, traveled only once per year to the tabernacle to perform his annual sacrifice (1 Sam. 1:3, 21).

Joseph and Mary traveled to Jerusalem once per year at the Feast of the Passover (Luke 2:41). This may have been all they could afford. Joseph and Mary were not of the wealthier class and lived a long way from Jerusalem.

Certainly, if someone felt burdened by a weighty issue or sin, they could come to the tabernacle at any time and present themselves to God. Or if someone wished to voluntarily make a special vow to God, they would come to the tabernacle with appropriate offerings (Num. 6; Acts 21:23–24). But for most Israelites, a trip to the tabernacle was a special event.

What Israel Understood

It's clear from the many scriptural examples of offerings being presented that the godly people of old understood the fundamental intent of these sacrifices—namely:

- That sin has consequences, separates people from God, and must be atoned for. Even unintentional sins could not be ignored (Lev. 4:2–3).
- That God provided a substitutionary way of paying the penalty for sin. When a person sinned, a lamb would be sacrificed in their stead.
- That the sacrifices were to be accompanied by a humble and repentant heart (Ps. 51:16–17). When they hypocritically went through the motions, simply trying to win God's favor, he didn't listen (Isa. 1:11–16).
- That the intent of the sacrifice was reconciliation and restoration (Lev. 4:20, 26). The ceremonies of Passover and the Day of Atonement focused on this.

Even with a limited view of God's plan, his desire for forgiveness, atonement, and reconciliation was clear. These are key principles Christians today understand. The symbols have changed, but the intent has not.

The entire Mosaic system looked forward to the Messiah (Heb. 10:1–4, 11–14). At the outset of his ministry, John the Baptist saw Jesus walking toward him and spoke words that must have puzzled his listeners: "Behold! The Lamb of God who takes away the sin of the world!" (John 1:29). How much John understood at that time is not clear, but he obviously grasped the significance and typology of Jesus as a sacrificial lamb.

The New Testament makes it clear that full understanding was not given to the people of old. Even though prophets like David and Isaiah wrote about a future Messiah as an atoning sacrifice, they didn't understand the depth and scope of what they were writing about (1 Pet. 1:10–12; Eph. 3:8–10; 1 Cor. 2:7). These things were specifically hidden by God from both the people of old and the principalities of heaven. Even Satan later was confused as to the purpose behind Jesus' sojourn on this earth (Matt. 4:1–7).

Not a Punishment

A comment by God in Jeremiah is sometimes interpreted as proof that God gave the Israelites the sacrificial system as some sort of punishment or burden:

> For I did not speak to your fathers, or command them in the day that I brought them out of the land of Egypt, concerning burnt offerings or sacrifices. But this is what I commanded them, saying, "Obey My voice, and I will be your God, and you shall be My people. And walk in all the ways that I have commanded you, that it may be well with you." (Jer. 7:22–23).

But it is a mistake to read a negativity into these verses that is not implied. As noted earlier, sacrifices were extant throughout all civilizations of the ancient world and were seen as a natural expression of worship. These verses are simply highlighting priorities. God was confirming that he gave the sacrificial system after the main body of law and emphasizing that trusting and obeying him was of far more value than ritualistic sacrifices—a sentiment expressed elsewhere in the Old Testament (1 Sam. 15:22; Ps. 51:16; Hosea 6:6).[1]

From the perspective of the priests who were doing the butchering work, it is also hard to see how their work would be any more of a problem than it might be for a modern butcher doing similar work for a living. The butchering work in the tabernacle was for the younger men only and was rostered. The on-duty priests also received special portions of the offering for themselves (Num. 8:23–25; 18:8–19).

New Testament Theology Based on the Sacrificial System

A Christian can more fully grasp the depth of God's redemptive plan for humanity by looking at the rituals and symbols of the Mosaic sacrificial system. It was a plan ordained from the foundation of the world (1 Pet. 1:20; Rev. 13:8).

---

[1] This concept is further discussed in the chapter *New Testament Terminology*.

We are indebted to the writer of Hebrews, who ties together the symbolic meaning of the sacrificial system with the reality of Christ. The blood of bulls and goats could never take away sin—they were symbolic (Heb. 10:4). But God did promise to forgive their sins (e.g., Lev. 4:20; 5:10; 16:30; Ps. 86:5). He did this knowing it looked forward to the future sacrifice of his son (Heb. 9–10).

The symbolism of the sacrifice and the blood continued to carry enormous significance in the New Testament era. On the evening of his death, Jesus introduced the new symbols of the new covenant clarifying what the old system had shadowed:

> *The symbolism of the sacrifice and the blood continued to carry enormous significance in the New Testament era.*

> And when He had given thanks, He broke it and said, "Take, eat; this is My body which is broken for you; do this in remembrance of Me." In the same manner He also took the cup after supper, saying, "This cup is the new covenant in My blood. This do, as often as you drink it, in remembrance of Me." For as often as you eat this bread and drink this cup, you proclaim the Lord's death till He comes. (1 Cor. 11:24–26)

After Jesus' death, the teaching purpose of the sacrificial system ended. But even then, Jewish Christians still used the temple system up until its destruction (Acts 21:26). They would have done so with a deeper appreciation of the ceremonial system, recognizing the true significance of the rituals. But the system and the earthly priesthood were only ever meant to be temporary until their ultimate fulfillment in the atoning sacrifice of Jesus (Heb. 10:11–12).

The Holy Days

The feasts of the LORD, which you shall proclaim to be holy convocations, these are My feasts. —Leviticus 23:2

All cultures, ancient and modern, have their national days of remembrance and ritual. People cherish such days. They are designed to evoke patriotic emotion and remind a nation of its heritage, culture, and spiritual roots.

Ancient Israel was no exception. God gave Israel a schedule of annual statutory holy days rich with meaning and purpose. These days had great significance for the people of the time, reminding them of God's providence in the great events of their history and of the need for him to remain central in their nation's affairs. As we saw earlier, internal biblical evidence shows these days were times of great joy when the people were faithful and kept them.

In addition, unlike the commemorative days of most cultures, these days were uniquely forward-looking. While ancient Israel could not have understood it at the time, the holy days were a shadow of future events for Israel and the world. These deeper meanings can now be understood in the light of New Testament theology. Two significant events of the New Testament era are connected to these holy days: the death and resurrection of Jesus the Messiah, and the "official" launch of the New Testament church. Far from being irrelevant and outdated, these days continue to have great meaning for modern Christians.

> *The holy days were a shadow of future events for Israel and the world.*

The Festival Seasons

The holy days are listed in several sections of the books of Moses, the primary points of reference being Leviticus 23, Numbers 28–29, and Deuteronomy 16. There was nothing pagan in the origin of these days (Lev. 18:1–3). God outlined the holy days directly to Moses at Mount Sinai (Exod. 23:14–16) and specifically claimed them as his own:

> And the LORD spoke to Moses, saying, "Speak to the children of Israel, and say to them: 'The feasts of the LORD, which you shall proclaim to be holy convocations, *these are My feasts.*'" (Lev. 23:1–2)

The entire nation would look forward to these times, both young and old (Deut. 16:14). They were called *feasts,* because other than the solemn Day of

Atonement, they were to be occasions of joy and celebration (Deut. 12:5–7). They were attractive to the people and, at the same time, spiritually uplifting and a reminder to stay faithful to the God who had given them so much.

The holy days centered on an annual calendar designed to align with the seasons and harvest cycles of the land of Canaan.[1] Canaan had two major harvests: the early to middle spring harvest of grains and the latter autumn harvest of grapes and fruit. The holy days were grouped into three festival periods spanning these seasons:

> Three times you shall keep a feast to Me in the year: You shall keep the Feast of Unleavened Bread (you shall eat unleavened bread seven days, as I commanded you, at the time appointed in the month of Abib, for in it you came out of Egypt; none shall appear before Me empty); and the Feast of Harvest, the firstfruits of your labors which you have sown in the field; and the Feast of Ingathering at the end of the year, when you have gathered in the fruit of your labors from the field. (Exod. 23:14–16)

These three festival seasons became known by various names: the feasts of Unleavened Bread, Firstfruits, and Ingathering.

Feast of Unleavened Bread

This weeklong feast started with the celebration of the Passover meal and marked the start of the early spring harvest. Unleavened Bread was held at the beginning of the year in the early spring (month of Abib[2]) when the first grain crops planted before winter were starting to ripen.

Feast of Firstfruits

Variously called Feast of Weeks, Feast of Harvest, or Pentecost (Greek), this late spring festival was held at the end of seven weeks of harvesting the grains. The festival was a harvest celebration.

Feast of Ingathering

The third season of holy days includes the Feast of Trumpets, Day of Atonement, and the weeklong Feast of Tabernacles, all held in the seventh

---

[1] For a brief summary of the Hebrew calendar, refer to Appendix "The Hebrew Calendar."
[2] Abib means "tender green ears."

month of Tishri. This autumn festival period coincided with the latter fruit harvest of the land.

The first of the holy days, Passover, was introduced while Israel was still in Egypt. The other days were given in the wilderness where there was clearly no harvest cycle and no access to grains and fruit trees. Scripture implies that Israel did keep the days in some fashion before arriving in Canaan (Num. 9:4–5; Lev. 16), but the festivals were specifically given to align with the land where they were headed. After crossing the Jordan, the manna ceased, and they then relied on the produce of the land. From that time on the days were kept in alignment with the harvest seasons.

> Now the children of Israel camped in Gilgal, and kept the Passover on the fourteenth day of the month at twilight on the plains of Jericho. *And they ate of the produce of the land on the day after the Passover, unleavened bread and parched grain, on the very same day.* Then the manna ceased on the day after they had eaten the produce of the land; and the children of Israel no longer had manna, but they ate the food of the land of Canaan that year. (Josh. 5:10–12)

A brief overview of the individual holy days and their significance follows.

Passover

The first holy day period of the year started with the Passover ceremony, which fell on the evening of the first day of the Feast of Unleavened Bread.

The children of Israel ate the first Passover meal in Egypt under stressful circumstances. Nine terrible plagues had decimated the Egyptians, and God promised the Israelites that the tenth and final plague would be the one Pharaoh would respond to and set them free (Exod. 11).

God instructed each Israelite family to prepare for the evening by selecting a male lamb without blemish, and then, on the fourteenth of Abib, slaughtering the lamb, ensuring no bones were broken (Exod. 12:1–12, 46). The blood of the lamb was to be used to mark the lintels and doorposts of their homes to protect them from the destroying angel:

> Now the blood shall be a sign for you on the houses where you are. *And when I see the blood, I will pass over you;* and the plague shall not be on you to destroy you when I strike the land of Egypt. (Exod. 12:13)

God told the people to roast the lamb inside their homes and eat it with unleavened bread and bitter herbs and be dressed and ready to leave in the early hours of the morning. The ceremony was an annual reminder of this incredibly significant event.

> For the LORD will pass through to strike the Egyptians; and when He sees the blood on the lintel and on the two doorposts, the LORD will pass over the door and not allow the destroyer to come into your houses to strike you. And you shall observe this thing as an ordinance for you and your sons forever. It will come to pass when you come to the land which the LORD will give you, just as He promised, that you shall keep this service. And it shall be, when your children say to you, "What do you mean by this service?" that you shall say, "It is the Passover sacrifice of the LORD, who passed over the houses of the children of Israel in Egypt when He struck the Egyptians and delivered our households." (Exod. 12:23–27)

The Passover was a time to remember the great salvation God had performed for the nation. The Israelites understood that the lamb was substitutionary, sacrificed to protect the people with its blood.

Passover was the only ceremony where males were required to be circumcised. Foreigners and strangers were welcome to participate in eating the Passover but first had to commit to the God of Israel by being circumcised (Exod. 12:43, 48).[3]

New Testament Significance

The true significance of the Passover becomes clear in the life and death of Jesus. Jesus was the perfect fulfilment of the symbolism of the Passover. Jesus our Passover was sacrificed for us (1 Cor. 5:7).

Jesus was the perfect fulfilment of the symbolism of the Passover

At the outset of his ministry, John the Baptist described Jesus in terms of a sacrificial lamb (John 1:29). He was the male lamb without blemish, whose bones were not broken, by whose blood we are saved (1 Pet. 1:19). To remove any doubt about the prophetic typology, Jesus was crucified at the time of the Passover sacrifice (John 18:39; 19:14). The puzzling prophecies of Isaiah, particularly around Chapter 53 (called the *Forbidden Chapter* in some Jewish circles), become perfectly clear:

---

[3] Even before Moses, circumcision was understood to be a sign of a commitment to God (Gen. 17:10–11). Moses also taught Israel the spiritual parallels to a circumcised heart (Deut. 10:16; 30:6).

> Surely He has borne our griefs and carried our sorrows; yet we esteemed Him stricken, smitten by God, and afflicted. But He was wounded for our transgressions, He was bruised for our iniquities; the chastisement for our peace was upon Him, and by His stripes we are healed. All we like sheep have gone astray; we have turned, every one, to his own way; and the LORD has laid on Him the iniquity of us all. He was oppressed and He was afflicted, yet He opened not His mouth; He was led as a lamb to the slaughter, and as a sheep before its shearers is silent, so He opened not His mouth. (Isa. 53:4–7)

Understanding that the door would be open to gentiles, and knowing the temple would be destroyed, Jesus instituted new symbols for the Passover on the evening before his death. Instead of the need for a physical lamb, he replaced the blood and flesh of the lamb with a bread and wine service symbolizing his own flesh and blood (Matt. 26:26–28). And for Christians since, the service has enhanced significance as we put our trust in Jesus Christ for our salvation (1 Cor. 10:16–17).

Feast of Unleavened Bread

The Feast of Unleavened Bread follows from the Passover ceremony.

> You shall keep the Feast of Unleavened Bread (you shall eat unleavened bread seven days, as I commanded you, at the time appointed in the month of Abib, for in it you came out of Egypt. (Exod. 23:15)

This weeklong festival builds on the events of the original Passover evening and commemorates the leaving of Egypt (Exod. 12:17). After hundreds of years of bondage, the Israelites would be freed from oppression and on their way to the land of promise.

> And you shall tell your son in that day, saying, "This is done because of what the LORD did for me when I came up from Egypt." It shall be as a sign to you on your hand and as a memorial between your eyes, that the LORD'S law may be in your mouth; for with a strong hand the LORD has brought you out of Egypt. (Exod. 13:8–9)

Celebrating these days of unleavened bread were a reminder of the affliction that the nation bore for so many years and of the role God played in their salvation:

> You shall eat no leavened bread with it; seven days you shall eat unleavened bread with it, that is, the bread of affliction (for you came out of the land of Egypt in haste), that you may remember the day in which you came out of the land of Egypt all the days of your life. (Deut. 16:3)

The people of old understood how leaven worked—that even a little bit of leaven would change the nature of bread entirely. Leaven was generally not used in sacrificial offerings (Lev. 2:11; 6:17).

New Testament Significance

A Christian will not miss the significance of the unleavened bread. Jesus broke bread at the last Passover meal and identified it symbolically as his own body (Matt. 26:26). Earlier in his ministry, Jesus described himself as the bread of life:

> *Jesus described himself as the bread of life.*

> I am the bread of life. Your fathers ate the manna in the wilderness, and are dead. This is the bread which comes down from heaven, that one may eat of it and not die. I am the living bread which came down from heaven. If anyone eats of this bread, he will live forever; and the bread that I shall give is My flesh, which I shall give for the life of the world. (John 6:48–51)

The New Testament also reinforces the association of leaven with sin (Matt. 16:6; Luke 12:1). Paul warns how a little leaven can spread through a believer's life:

> Your glorying is not good. Do you not know that a little leaven leavens the whole lump? (1 Cor. 5:6)

Paul then goes on to instruct the gentile Corinthian church to keep the Feast of Unleavened Bread with the right attitude:

> Therefore purge out the old leaven, that you may be a new lump, since you truly are unleavened. For indeed Christ, our Passover, was sacrificed for us. Therefore let us keep the feast, not with old leaven, nor with the leaven of malice and wickedness, but with the unleavened bread of sincerity and truth. (1 Cor. 5:7–8)

The Feast of Unleavened Bread has a focus on the transforming power of Jesus as the bread of life in the life of a Christian.

Wave Sheaf Ceremony

Included within the weeklong days of Unleavened Bread is a minor ceremony that has great significance in later New Testament theology. When the first crops were ripening in the month of Abib, God directed that a *first sheaf* of the early crop be symbolically cut, brought into the tabernacle, and dedicated to God before the harvest began. It was the first portion of the firstfruits harvest.

The offering, known as the wave sheaf, was offered with a young male lamb without blemish.

> Speak to the children of Israel, and say to them: "When you come into the land which I give to you, and reap its harvest, then you shall bring a sheaf of the firstfruits of your harvest to the priest. He shall wave the sheaf before the LORD, to be accepted on your behalf; on the day after the Sabbath the priest shall wave it. And you shall offer on that day, when you wave the sheaf, a male lamb of the first year, without blemish, as a burnt offering to the LORD. (Lev. 23:10–12)

The wave sheaf ceremony once again points to Jesus. After his resurrection, Jesus was accepted by the Father and became the first of the firstfruits of God's family (1 Cor. 15:20). Jesus is called the firstborn of creation and the firstborn of those who have fallen asleep (Col. 1:15–18). Just as the first harvest of the year could not begin until the first sheaf of the firstfruit harvest was offered, Jesus told His followers that he had to leave and go to his Father before the Holy Spirit could come to them and the spiritual harvest work of the church could commence (John 16:5–14).

> *The wave sheaf ceremony once again points to Jesus.*

Feast of Firstfruits/Pentecost

The Feast of Firstfruits (Pentecost) was held fifty days after the wave sheaf offering (Lev. 23:15–21).[4] It came at the end of seven weeks of harvesting the first crops of the year:

> You shall count seven weeks for yourself; begin to count the seven weeks from the time you begin to put the sickle to the grain. Then you shall keep the Feast of Weeks to the LORD your God with the tribute

---
[4] Pentecost means "fiftieth" in Greek.

of a freewill offering from your hand, which you shall give as the
LORD your God blesses you. (Deut. 16:9–10)

The ancient Israelites understood this was a harvest festival, a time to give thanks to God for the firstfruits of the year:

You shall keep ... the Feast of Harvest, the firstfruits of your labors which you have sown in the field. (Exod. 23:15–16)

Israel also understood that firstfruits generally were special to God and highly significant in the ceremonial system. Firstfruits applied not just to produce but also to the firstborn of families and animals—all of which were dedicated to God (Exod. 13:2; Num. 18:12, 15; Deut. 18:4). This Feast of Firstfruits reminded the Israelites just how special the firstfruits were in God's eyes.

New Testament Significance

Jesus and the New Testament writers used the symbolism of the harvest extensively to explain God's plan for humanity. Jesus looked at the spiritual work to be done and likens himself to the master of a great harvest:

The harvest truly is great, but the laborers are few; therefore pray the Lord of the harvest to send out laborers into His harvest. (Luke 10:2)

It was highly significant that the Holy Spirit arrived on the day of Pentecost. On that first day alone, as the spiritual harvest started, 3,000 were added to the church (Acts 2:41). The Feast of Pentecost is a day that reminds Christians of the incredible opportunity it is to be one of the firstfruits in God's great plan of redemption.

It was highly significant that the Holy Spirit arrived on the day of Pentecost.

Of His own will He brought us forth by the word of truth, that we might be a kind of firstfruits of His creatures. (James 1:18)

The great calling of the church of the firstborn is spoken about in Hebrews (Heb. 12:22–24). By definition, if there is a first great harvest of firstfruits, there must also be a latter harvest and latter fruits to follow.

Feast of Trumpets

The autumn festivals start with the Day of Trumpets on the first day of the seventh month. This day is noted as a memorial of the blowing of trumpets:

> Speak to the children of Israel, saying: "In the seventh month, on the first day of the month, you shall have a sabbath-rest, a memorial of blowing of trumpets, a holy convocation." (Lev. 23:24)

Trumpets were used to announce important events. To an ancient Israelite, especially one at the time of Moses, a memorial of blowing of trumpets would have been associated with the events of Mount Sinai when the arrival of God on the mountain was announced with a heavenly trumpet blast that shook the people (Exod. 19:18–20). It was a time when God himself came down to his people.

New Testament Significance

The Feast of Trumpets has great significance to Christians. Jesus made it clear that trumpets would signal his return to rule the nations of this earth. It will not be an event this world will welcome:

> Then the sign of the Son of Man will appear in heaven, and then all the tribes of the earth will mourn, and they will see the Son of Man coming on the clouds of heaven with power and great glory. *And He will send His angels with a great sound of a trumpet,* and they will gather together His elect from the four winds, from one end of heaven to the other. (Matt. 24:30–31)

The followers of Jesus, on the other hand, will rejoice. It will be a time when both the dead and living in Christ will be changed into spirit and rise to meet him.

> Behold, I tell you a mystery: We shall not all sleep, but we shall all be changed—in a moment, in the twinkling of an eye, at the last trumpet. *For the trumpet will sound,* and the dead will be raised incorruptible, and we shall be changed. (1 Cor. 15:51–52)

> For the Lord Himself will descend from heaven with a shout, with the voice of an archangel, and *with the trumpet of God.* And the dead in Christ will rise first. Then we who are alive and remain shall be caught up together with them in the clouds to meet the Lord in the air. And thus we shall always be with the Lord. Therefore comfort one another with these words. (1 Thess. 4:16–18)

This will be the start of the millennial reign of Christ over this earth supported by the faithful (Rev. 2:26; 20:4; 2 Tim. 2:12).

Day of Atonement

The Day of Atonement was not a feast day like the other holy days but a day of solemnity. It was a day of "affliction" where people restrained from all work and humbled themselves by fasting (Lev. 16:31). At the tabernacle an elaborate ceremony took place that involved the high priest mediating on behalf of the nation and asking God to forgive the sins of the people.

Unlike the Passover ceremony, which involved personal participation, the Day of Atonement was collective, with the high priest representing all the people. The details of the ceremony are outlined in Leviticus 16. It was the only day the high priest could ceremonially enter the Holy of Holies in the tabernacle.

On that day, the high priest, dressed in full ceremonial garments, selected two goats as a sin offering and presented them to God in the Holy Place of the tabernacle. Lots were cast over the two goats. One goat was selected to be sacrificed later as an offering for the people. The other goat would live. It was called the Azazel goat, sometimes incorrectly called the "scapegoat."

Before dealing with the two goats, God instructed the high priest to make atonement for himself. He went behind the veil into the Holy of Holies and sprinkled the blood of a bull on the lid of the ark of the covenant to atone for his own sins. After the first ceremony, he sacrificed the first goat and entered the Holy of Holies a second time. This time he was a mediator, sprinkling the blood of the goat to atone for the sins of all the people.

After completing the second ceremony, the high priest was to lay his hands over the live goat and confess out loud all the transgressions and sins of the people. The Azazel goat was then to be led away by a strong man into the wilderness and set free.

What would the Israelites have understood from this day? The fasting and ceremony would have driven home the serious nature of sin and the need to be forgiven and reconciled to God. They would have seen the high priest's role as a mediator on their behalf as he went in directly to that Most Holy Place where they knew God's presence resided. The live Azazel goat was associated with evil that was banished, carrying all the sins of the nation.

We can thank the writer of the book of Hebrews for expounding our understanding of the Day of Atonement.

New Testament Significance

We can thank the writer of the book of Hebrews for expounding our understanding of the Day of Atonement (Heb. 9). People today need to be reconciled to God just as the people of ancient Israel did. But now we have a perfect spiritual high priest, Jesus Christ, our mediator and intercessor who opened the veil to heaven so we can have direct access to God our Father.

The Azazel goat aligns with the character of the great accuser Satan, who has deceived the whole world (Rev. 12:9). At a future time, he will be bound and put into a place of darkness where he can no longer deceive the nations (Rev. 20:1–2, 10).

Feast of Tabernacles

The annual holy days concluded with the weeklong Feast of Tabernacles (or Feast of Booths), the last and greatest harvest festival of the year, primarily a fruit harvest:

> You shall observe the Feast of Tabernacles seven days, when you have gathered from your threshing floor and from your winepress. (Deut. 16:13)

Tabernacles was a time to rejoice but also for the people to reflect on their original sojourn in the wilderness on their way to the promised land. The word for "tabernacle" in Hebrew, *sukkah*, means "a tent" or "temporary dwelling." During their forty years of wandering, the Israelites dwelt in temporary dwellings and relied totally on the God's providence. To remind the people of those days, God instructed them to create temporary brush arbors and celebrate under them for seven days during this festival:

> *Tabernacles was a time for the people to reflect on their original sojourn in the wilderness on their way to the promised land.*

> And you shall take for yourselves on the first day the fruit of beautiful trees, branches of palm trees, the boughs of leafy trees, and willows of the brook; and you shall rejoice before the LORD your God for seven days. You shall keep it as a feast to the LORD for seven days in the year. It shall be a statute forever in your generations. You shall celebrate it in the seventh month. You shall dwell in booths (tabernacles) for seven days. All who are native Israelites shall dwell in booths, that your generations may know that I made the children of Israel dwell in

booths when I brought them out of the land of Egypt: I am the LORD your God. (Lev. 23:40–43)

It was also a time to celebrate and to be thankful to God for their great blessings:

> And you shall spend that money for whatever your heart desires: for oxen or sheep, for wine or similar drink, for whatever your heart desires; you shall eat there before the LORD your God, and you shall rejoice, you and your household. (Deut. 14:26)

After the seven-day festival was complete, an additional holy day was kept making a total of eight days:

> You shall keep the feast of the LORD for seven days; on the first day there shall be a sabbath-rest, and on the eighth day a sabbath-rest. (Lev. 23:39)

This eighth day was the crowning end to the joyous feast of tabernacles.

An Israelite who meditated on this feast would have been reminded of their temporal nature and the need for God's ongoing guidance and protection in their lives. God's choice to dwell among his people in his own tabernacle was significant within the context of that time (Exod. 29:45–46). The prophets later spoke of a future time when God would once again dwell with his people—this time permanently (Ezek. 37:26–27).

God's requirement to have his law read publicly at the Feast of Tabernacles every seventh year (in the sabbatical year) also served to remind the people of their gracious God who had provided their system of law and their permanent home in the promised land (Deut. 31:10–11).

New Testament Significance

Christians today can understand several different aspects of this festival. The feast is a strong reminder of the temporary nature of this life. Paul likens our mortal bodies to living in a tent, waiting for our permanent habitation:

> For we know that if our earthly house, this tent, is destroyed, we have a building from God, a house not made with hands, eternal in the heavens. For in this we groan, earnestly desiring to be clothed with our habitation which is from heaven. (2 Cor. 5:1–2)

Peter also refers to his physical life as living in a tabernacle:

> Yes, I think it is right, as long as I am in this tent, to stir you up by reminding you, knowing that shortly I must put off my tent, just as our Lord Jesus Christ showed me. (2 Pet. 1:13–14)

At the same time, we express our gratitude to God for his blessings, kindness, and providence as we sojourn this life in our mortal bodies while looking forward to the permanent kingdom of God when God will tabernacle among his people (Rev. 21:3).

Tabernacles is a strong reminder of the temporary nature of this life.

The eighth day has special significance. It was the day when Jesus stood up and invited everyone to come to him to receive the living waters of eternal life:

> On the last day, that great *day* of the feast, Jesus stood and cried out, saying, "If anyone thirsts, let him come to Me and drink. He who believes in Me, as the Scripture has said, out of his heart will flow rivers of living water." (John 7:37–38).

Holy Day Order

There is much more for a Christian to explore in the understanding of these days. For example, it has been observed that the order of the holy days throughout the year has an inherent meaning in its own right. This becomes clearer in the light of New Testament theology. Consider the following:

God's plan for the salvation of humanity starts with the first holy day Passover. Because of Jesus' death and resurrection, we have the hope of a future life. Christians are then required to live a different way of life, partaking of Jesus as the bread of life, represented by the Days of Unleavened Bread.

What follows is the work of the church during this age, represented by the seven weeks of harvesting and the firstfruits harvest being finalized at the Day of Pentecost (Matt. 9:38).

Later in the year is the Feast of Trumpets, depicting the return of Christ when the firstfruits of this age will rise to meet him and will rule with him in a millennial reign. Satan will be restrained at this time and the people reconciled to God, represented by the Day of Atonement. The Feast of Tabernacles and the eighth day follows, aligning with the thousand-year reign of Christ and a final great harvest of humanity.

A Shadow of Things to Come

Just like the original design of the tabernacle and the priesthood, the holy days were a shadow of future events:

> For the law, having *a shadow of the good things to come*, and not the very image of the things, can never with these same sacrifices, which they offer continually year by year, make those who approach perfect. (Heb. 10:1)

> So let no one judge you in food or in drink, or regarding a festival or a new moon or sabbaths, *which are a shadow of things to come*, but the substance is of Christ. (Col. 2:16–17)

The story of Israel's journey to the promised land was also a shadow (a parallel) of a believer's life in Christ. In biblical terms, Egypt is a type of this world and the hold of sin. Just like Israel in Egypt, we need God's saving power to free us from bondage. And also like ancient Israel, we are warned against a lack of belief:

Just like the original design of the tabernacle and the priesthood, the holy days were a shadow of future things.

> For who, having heard, rebelled? Indeed, was it not all who came out of Egypt, led by Moses? Now with whom was He angry forty years? Was it not with those who sinned, whose corpses fell in the wilderness? And to whom did He swear that they would not enter His rest, but to those who did not obey? So we see that they could not enter in because of unbelief. Therefore, since a promise remains of entering His rest, let us fear lest any of you seem to have come short of it. (Heb. 3:16–4:1)

Israel's flight from Egypt provides many more "shadows" of the reality fulfilled in Christ. Paul uses the typology of the crossing of the Red Sea as a symbol of a person's baptism and their faith in Jesus:

> Moreover, brethren, I do not want you to be unaware that all our fathers were under the cloud, all passed through the sea, all were baptized into Moses in the cloud and in the sea, all ate the same spiritual food, and all drank the same spiritual drink. For they drank of that spiritual Rock that followed them, and that Rock was Christ. (1 Cor. 10:1–4)

Israel's sojourn in the wilderness also parallels our life in Christ and shows that life will not be easy, even with God on our side. The *manna* God provided the children of Israel during their wandering is particularly significant. Manna symbolizes the "spiritual food," a "type" of the bread of life, Jesus, and our need for him to sustain us (John 6:58). Israel's crossing the Jordan River points to the believer's physical death, leading to eternal life in the spiritual promised land.

How incredible it is that these events that occurred so long ago, can still have such relevance and teaching power in the life of a Christian in the twenty-first century. They clearly confirm God's master plan and his guiding hand in history.

The holy days God gave Israel were days rich with meaning and are worthy of further study. They were a reminder for ancient Israel of their heritage and God's providence in their history. They continue to have significance for Christians today and are a reminder of the central role Jesus has played in God's plan for salvation. [5]

---

[5] Two other celebratory times are mentioned in Scripture: Purim and Hanukkah. These are not God-initiated holy days but specifically Jewish festivals. Both festivals celebrate Jewish survival against extreme odds. Purim is a celebration of the victory of the Jews over their enemies in the time of the Persian Empire (Esther 9:18–32). Hanukkah—also called the Feast of Dedication or the Festival of Lights—celebrates the rededication of the temple after the Maccabees regained control over Jerusalem from the Seleucids in the second century BCE. (The books of Maccabees, which outline the story, is not included in the Tanakh or in the canon of most Bible translations.) God does not criticize the establishment of these days—Jesus is specifically noted going into the temple on the Feast of Dedication (John 10:22).

Ceremonial Uncleanness

Speak to all the congregation of the children of Israel, and say to them: "You shall be holy, for I the Lord your God am holy." —Leviticus 19:2

As demonstrated in a previous chapter, the Mosaic purity laws offered substantial public health benefits in the form of cleanliness, hygiene, quarantine, and sanitation practices.

But some of the purity regulations have attracted criticism—in particular those that went beyond any obvious health benefit and declared a person unclean based on certain activities. For example, people were declared ceremonially unclean when they had sexual relations, men were unclean if they had a nocturnal emission, women were unclean during their monthly period and after having a baby (Lev. 12:2, 5, 16–18). Such ideas seem oppressive, intrusive, and plain bizarre, more along the lines of something we would expect from the Pharisees of Jesus' day.

These regulations also seem at odds with the enlightened and progressive laws we see in other parts of the law of Moses. On the surface they seem impractical and even impossible to keep. How do we reconcile these ritualistic purity laws with the pragmatic and rational mind of God?

Why Such a System?

Unlike the Pharisees, God has always been a big-picture person—gracious and sensible. He had no desire to burden people or trip them up with an impossible and arbitrary list of daily dos and don'ts.

God had no desire to burden people or trip them up with an impossible and arbitrary list of daily dos and don'ts.

The criticism of the purity system comes from not understanding both the intent of the system and the application. Recall that God's intent for the purity laws were twofold:

1. to teach Israel the importance of being *holy* as God's special people
2. to teach the importance of *physical* cleanliness and hygiene.

There is an overlap of these two purposes and the concept of being "clean" or "unclean" had both a physical and a ceremonial application. It is the ceremonial application that is most often misunderstood.

Ceremonial Cleanness Connected to the Sanctuary

The primary purpose of being ceremonially clean had to do with preparing to *come before the Lord* at the tabernacle (sanctuary).

> *The primary purpose of being ceremonially clean had to do with coming before the Lord at the tabernacle.*

Because God is holy, he wanted Israel to be both physically and ceremonially clean when they *came before him* to worship. This was to reinforce the reality of God's holiness and their own calling as his special people. As God had said, "by those who come near me I must be regarded as holy" (Lev. 10:3).

To reinforce his holiness in the eyes of the people, God set certain standards for those who would come before him. People not only had to be physically clean and free from ailments, they also had to restrain from sex, not be recovering from childbirth, not have any recent contact with the dead or unclean people or unclean items, etc. Anyone who was "unclean" in this way (either physically or ceremonially) could not participate in worship at the temple until they were "clean".[1] Visiting the tabernacle in a knowingly unclean state was a serious matter. It showed disrespect to God and defiled the sanctuary.

This direct link between ceremonial cleanliness and being at the sanctuary is noted in the law:

> Thus you shall separate the children of Israel from their uncleanness, lest they die in their uncleanness *when they defile My tabernacle* that is among them. (Lev. 15:31)

> But the person who eats the flesh of the sacrifice of the peace offering that belongs to the LORD, *while he is unclean*, that person shall be cut off from his people. Moreover the person who touches any unclean thing, such as human uncleanness, an unclean animal, or any abominable unclean thing, and *who eats the flesh of the sacrifice of the peace offering that belongs to the LORD*, that person shall be cut off from his people. (Lev. 7:20–21)

---

[1] Note the previously mentioned example of the men who could not present an offering at Passover because they had contact with a dead body (Num. 9:6–7).

> Whoever touches the body of anyone who has died, and does not purify himself, *defiles the tabernacle* of the LORD. (Num. 19:13)
>
> But the man who is unclean and does not purify himself, that person shall be cut off from among the assembly, *because he has defiled the sanctuary of the Lord.* (Num. 19:20)

Bible commentaries reinforce the association of ceremonial cleanness with worship at the tabernacle:

> God required that his people observe purification rites *when they came into his presence for worship*. Ritual purity was intended to teach God's holiness and moral purity; thus purification rituals functioned to *prepare individuals to approach God*.[2] (Bakers. Emphasis mine).
>
> To be ritually pure means to be free from some flaw or uncleanness that would bar one from contact with holy objects or places, *especially from contact with the holy presence of God in worship*. God is the ideal of purity, and those who are to come in contact with God's presence are also to be pure. ... *Purity qualified one to participate in worship*, an activity central to the life of ancient Israel.[3] (Holman. Emphasis mine)

This connection of ceremonial uncleanness to the sanctuary explains why the purity laws were not a burden to the people. Visiting the sanctuary was an irregular event for most people and therefore being ceremonially clean was generally not necessary for daily life.

Being ceremonially clean was generally not necessary for daily life.

Reminder of God's Holiness

Even the earlier fathers of Israel understood the importance of being ceremonially clean when coming into God's presence. When planning to come before the Lord at Bethel, Jacob directed his family to "purify themselves" and "change their garments," showing respect for God (Gen. 35:2–3).

Moses gave this same directive at Mount Sinai as Israel prepared to come before God:

---

[2] Bibliog: (Bakers 2013, Purity. The Law of Moses. p 1383)
[3] Bibliog: (Holman 2015, Purity. p 1321)

> Moses went down from the mountain to the people and sanctified the people, and *they washed their clothes.* And he said to the people, "Be ready for the third day; *do not come near your wives.*" (Exod. 19:14–15)

On that occasion, just as we would wash and smarten up in readiness to meet an important person, Israel was told to be properly prepared to come into God's presence.

Note the instruction to *not come near your wives*. This again, was not putting a negative connotation on marital relations; it was simply a sign of respect to God that they would abstain from sexual relations before coming before him.

> *Even the earlier fathers of Israel understood the importance of being ceremonially clean when coming into God's presence.*

History tells us that, for most of the pagan gentile nations at that time, sex played a major part in religious worship. God, on the other hand, made it clear to Israel that sex should play no part in worship to him. God wanted them to be physically and mentally prepared and have their minds focused on the upcoming important occasion of visiting the tabernacle.

The Levitical priests in particular, had to understand the importance of God's holiness. They were held to higher standards because they served in the inner court of the tabernacle, interfacing between the people and God.

> Speak to Aaron and his sons, that they separate themselves from the holy things of the children of Israel, and that they do not profane My holy name by what they dedicate to Me: I am the LORD. Say to them: "Whoever of all your descendants throughout your generations, *who goes near the holy things* which the children of Israel dedicate to the LORD, while he has uncleanness upon him, that person shall be cut off from My presence: I am the LORD. (Lev. 22:2–3)

Even then, God was always willing to overlook a technical breach of the purity laws when the attitude of the person was right as the case of Aaron's breach showed (Lev. 10:16–20). Consider also God's grace in the days of Hezekiah when many came to keep the Passover in an unclean state:

> For there were many in the assembly who had not sanctified themselves ... For a multitude of the people ... had not cleansed themselves, yet they ate the Passover contrary to what was written. But Hezekiah prayed for them, saying, "May the good Lord provide

atonement for everyone who prepares his heart to seek God, the Lord God of his fathers, though he is not cleansed according to the purification of the sanctuary." *And the Lord listened to Hezekiah and healed the people.* (2 Chron. 30:17–20)

No Association with Sin

It is important to emphasize that being ceremonially unclean had nothing to do with being in a state of sin. This point is obvious, considering what being "unclean" entailed. Aside from illness and diseases, many activities relating to ceremonial uncleanness were a part of everyday life. Often, the one declared unclean was not responsible for their condition. A woman could hardly be guilty for having her regular monthly period. Neither could a person with a skin ailment be guilty because of his condition, or a husband and wife be guilty for having sexual relations.

Being ceremonially unclean had nothing to do with being in a state of sin.

Clearly, no negativity is associated with any of these things elsewhere in the law. Some activities that created a state of uncleanness were in fact blessings from God—like a woman giving birth to a baby.

Unfortunately, the English word "unclean" creates a negative connotation which is not in the original concept of holiness. Being unclean was not a moral judgment on the individual, it was simply denoting a level of purity and preparedness God was looking for in those that came before his presence.

Private, Self-Managed System

Another area of misunderstanding is that the purity laws were designed to be mostly *private* and *self-managed*. While there were times when priests needed to be advised for public health reasons, most of the time no one would need to know what went on in the private life of another individual and whether they were ceremonially unclean or not. It was generally between the individual and God.

Many of the purity laws that operated in the Second Temple period were Pharisaical extensions that had no basis in the law of Moses— a case in point being Jesus' disagreement with the Pharisees over handwashing (Mark 7:1–8). Edersheim describes the complex process of Pharisaical handwashing, which required them to hold their hands and fingers

The purity laws were designed to be private and self-managed.

at a certain angle and let the water run down and drip off the wrist in a certain way.[4] This sort of tedious ritual did not come from the law of Moses.[5] The Pharisees had turned a personal purity system into a publicly managed regime where they would police others for not complying with their man-made rules.

God's system, on the other hand, was not about outward show—it was personal. Consider the following practicalities in the system God gave Israel:

- He did not command separation or isolation for most ritual uncleanness. In most cases, the simple solution to ritual uncleanness was to wash and wait until evening.
- An unclean person could go about their regular, everyday life; people could look after them when sick, and husband and wife didn't have to sleep in separate beds. A woman going through her normal monthly cycle would refrain from going to the tabernacle and having marital relations, but it was a private matter[6]—no one outside the marriage needed to know.

Purity laws did not in any way diminish the great joy of a woman having a baby, and people could still visit and hold the infant. Furthermore, the mother would have a well-deserved rest from doing other things. She simply could not go to the tabernacle until the prescribed period had passed:

> If a woman has conceived, and borne a male child, then she shall be unclean seven days; as in the days of her customary impurity she shall be unclean. And on the eighth day the flesh of his foreskin shall be circumcised. She shall then continue in the blood of her purification thirty-three days. *She shall not touch any hallowed thing, nor come into the sanctuary until the days of her purification are fulfilled.* (Lev. 12:2–4)

Consider the positive example of Hannah, who was thrilled to welcome baby Samuel. She chose not to come to the tabernacle for several years until Samuel was weaned (1 Sam. 1:21–23). But her husband, Elkanah, when he entered the tabernacle once a year to offer a sacrifice, needed to be ceremonially clean.

---

[4] Bibliog: (Edersheim 1993, 482)
[5] The story is told of the famous Rabbi Achabah, who was put into prison. His water ration was reduced, and he took what little water he was given to wash his hands before eating rather than drink it, saying that he would rather die than commit a sin. Another rabbi said, "It is better to go four miles to get water than to incur guilt by neglecting hand-rinsing before you eat" Bibliog: (Chabad 2022).
[6] Note that Leviticus 15:19 is incorrectly translated in the King James Version, incorrectly implying that a woman must be separated from others during her menstrual cycle.

Not a Burden on Daily Life

It was never God's intention for the ceremonial purity laws related to the tabernacle to be a burden in normal daily life. For most Israelites, visiting the tabernacle was *not a regular occurrence*. For many it was simply too far away.

When they could visit, it was an exciting occasion to look forward to. At such times, an individual was required to be ceremonially clean and properly prepared in mind and body.

The Pharisees *added* to the law of Moses and extended the scope of the purity laws. They promoted the idea that the Jews should adopt the temple purity laws in their everyday lives, making them a burden. As noted by the Center for Online Judaic Studies:

> The Sadducees believed that the purity laws were primarily laws pertaining to the temple, while the Pharisees extended them to all aspects of daily life.[7]

This was not God's original intention. He knew that many Israelites would be in a state of ceremonial uncleanness nearly all their working life because of their type of work or where they lived—butchers, leatherworkers, physicians, or soldiers fighting for months at a time. Being ceremonially unclean didn't stop them from going about their normal lives.[8]

Neither was there any guilt to be associated with being in an unclean state. Only when planning to visit the sanctuary on holy days like Passover and for personal sacrifices would a person examine and prepare themselves to ensure that God was foremost in their mind.

Neither was there any guilt associated with being unclean.

High-handed disregard for God's laws meant being put out of Israel, but if someone made a mistake in these ceremonial matters and went to the tabernacle unclean, they could be forgiven once they became aware of it (Lev. 5). For a person who was unavoidably ceremonially unclean at Passover time, they were able to hold a second service a month later (Num. 9:6–13).

---

[7] Bibliog: (Center for Online Judaic Studies 2023, Sadducees)
[8] Deut. 23:10–14 presents the scenario of uncleanness in a military camp situation. The context is one of camp toileting hygiene and not related to presentation at the tabernacle. Bibliog: (Craigie 1976, 299)

Practical and Meaningful

God designed the ceremonial purity laws to train the heart of the individual to properly appreciate his holiness. There are some aspects of the ceremonial law that we don't understand for reasons that are probably cultural, but mostly it is not hard to see how the system would work in a practical sense. Our confidence that the purity laws were not burdensome comes from the positive nature of God and the practical reflection of that nature in the life of Jesus Christ. There is also no evidence of Pharisaical-type rules intruding into people's daily lives in the narrative of the Old Testament Scriptures.

The ceremonial cleanliness system was a meaningful part of the worship system for God's chosen people. But by the time of Jesus, *man-made* purity laws of segregation and burdensome rituals became a great issue dividing Jews and gentiles—an issue that had to be met head-on and solved before the church could become truly unified.

PART 7: More Difficult to Understand

When a person takes the time to properly consider the historical setting and cultural context, the vast majority of the laws in the Mosaic system are understandable and consistent with God's values and character.

But parts of the historical narrative and some individual laws can be confusing and hard to understand. This section will review some of these areas in light of God's character and the foundational principles he outlined for his law.

Why the Attraction of Paganism?

For My people have committed two evils: they have forsaken Me, the fountain of living waters, and hewn themselves cisterns—broken cisterns that can hold no water. —Jeremiah 2:13

Israel's attraction to the pagan religions of the surrounding nations was the single most negative issue that plagued the nation. From their earliest days in the promised land right down to the final captivity of the nation of Judah by the Babylonians, the pagan gods were like a magnet to them. The Israelites would worship the God of Israel for a time until the allure of the pagan religions would once again entice them away. What was it about these pagan practices that Israel found so attractive?

God Predicted the Problem

God knew from the outset that attraction to the cultic practices of the nearby nations would be a major problem for Israel. Even before they entered the land, God reminded the Israelites multiple times of the dangers of the worship of other gods:

> You shall not go after other gods, the *gods of the peoples who are all around you*. (Deut. 6:14)

> Take heed to yourselves, lest *your heart be deceived*, and you turn aside and serve other gods and worship them, lest the LORD'S anger be roused against you. (Deut. 11:16–17)

Yet despite multiple warnings, the people started drifting from God early in their history:

> They would not listen to their judges, but they played the harlot with other gods, and bowed down to them. *They turned quickly from the way in which their fathers walked*, in obeying the commandments of the LORD; they did not do so. (Judg. 2:17)

What was it about God that Israel wanted to reject? Why wasn't Israel proud of their God who had done such wondrous things for them? Even the pagan nations, whose gods repeatedly let them down, held fast to their deities through thick and thin—they did not change their gods as Israel did. Gods like Baal, Asherah, Molech, and Chemesh remained in the gentile nations for centuries. God later expressed his bewilderment at what Israel was doing:

> "For pass beyond the coasts of Cyprus and see, send to Kedar *and consider diligently, and see if there has been such a thing. Has a nation changed its gods, which are not gods?* But My people have changed their Glory for what does not profit. Be astonished, O heavens, at this, and be horribly afraid; be very desolate," says the LORD. "For My people have committed two evils: They have forsaken Me, the fountain of living waters, and hewn themselves cisterns—broken cisterns that can hold no water." (Jer. 2:10–13)

Through Isaiah, God noted the utter absurdity of it all:

> Who but a fool would make his own god? ... He uses part of the wood to make a fire. With it he warms himself and bakes his bread. Then—yes, it's true—he takes the rest of it and makes himself a god to worship! He makes an idol and bows down in front of it! ... The poor, deluded fool feeds on ashes. He trusts something that can't help him at all. Yet he cannot bring himself to ask, "Is this idol that I'm holding in my hand a lie?" (Isa. 44:10, 15, 20 NLT)

We can feel the exasperation in God's words. He had given Israel intelligent laws that could make people wise—laws that would build a strong nation with the potential to be a light to the world—and here they were doing nonsensical things like making gods of wood.

It's easy from our twenty-first-century position to be critical of the Israelites and assume that we would behave differently in the same position. But while the Israelites were a hard-hearted people, the environment of the day was dramatically different from our world. Examining the historical context reveals that multiple factors contributed to Israel's attraction to the gods of other nations. Each confirms just how different the God of Israel was compared to the gods of the day.

God Was Invisible

Firstly, unlike the gods of the nations around them, represented by idols and images, the God of Israel had no visible representation. He had instructed that no images were to be involved in his worship (Exod. 20:3–5). While this might seem a minor issue to us, it would have been difficult for the people of the time to accept.

Moses knew it was natural for people to want to make images of their gods and to assign supernatural attributes to natural objects:

> Take careful heed to yourselves, *for you saw no form* when the LORD spoke to you at Horeb out of the midst of the fire, lest you act corruptly and make for yourselves a carved image in the form of any figure: the likeness of male or female, the likeness of any animal that is on the earth or the likeness of any winged bird that flies in the air. (Deut. 4:15–17)

Incredibly, idolatry had resurfaced right at Mount Sinai. Despite all the wondrous works they had seen since leaving Egypt and with the thundering and lightning still present on the mountain and the frightening power of God's voice still ringing in their ears, they built themselves a golden calf and pronounced it the God of Israel (Exod. 32:4). They wanted a god they could see with their eyes like what they had seen in Egypt. All the nations around them created impressive images of their gods that they could point to and focus their attention on—and Israel naturally wanted to do the same.

> *Trusting in a God with no visible form was difficult.*

Trusting in a God with no visible form was difficult. Neither did Israel like their king being "invisible." Years later, the elders came to Samuel and asked for a king to "be like all the nations." They wanted one they could see, who would "go out before us" (1 Sam. 8:20). It was not easy to worship and trust in a god with no visible expression.[1]

God Was Mostly Silent

In addition to being invisible, God was mostly silent. On the one occasion at Mount Sinai when he spoke out loud to the people, they were terrified and told Moses, "Don't let God speak directly to us, or we will die!" (Exod. 20:19 NLT; see also Deut. 5:23–28). And so, starting with Moses, God spoke to Israel through his prophets (Heb. 1:1). Even then it was a somewhat distant and irregular form of communication,[2] and the prophets God chose as his spokesmen were often not impressive in appearance or manner.

In contrast, the prophets and priests of the pagan religions claimed to speak on behalf of their gods on a regular basis. It was not uncommon for believers

---

[1] When Roman General Pompey conquered Jerusalem around 63 BC, he was curious to see for himself the God who had inspired such fanaticism, so he entered the Holy of Holies in the temple. When he came out, he exclaimed in surprise that it was only an empty room!

[2] God did at times respond to priestly enquiries through the Urim and the Thummim, but this was a limited and irregular form of communication.

to pay mediums and sorcerers so they could be advised of the will of the gods (2 Kings 23:24; Isa. 8:19). It was something God had warned Israel against (Lev. 19:31; Deut. 18:10–14).

The true God did not operate through mediums. He had given his law, and his instructions were clear: obey me and seek me with all your heart, and things will go well for you. He was subtle and wanted to be sought out. In many ways, the God of Israel was easy to forget:

> And of whom have you been afraid, or feared, that you have lied and not remembered Me, nor taken it to your heart? *Is it not because I have held My peace from of old that you do not fear Me?* (Isa. 57:11)
>
> These things you have done, and I kept silent; you thought that I was altogether like you. (Ps. 50:21)

The God of Israel wanted a relationship based on trust and an internal change of the heart. The pagan way was built around the human senses—statues that impressed the eyes, imposing and impressive buildings, physical experiences and rituals that excited the senses and induced fear and awe in their recipients.

In many ways, the God of Israel was easy to forget.

Demanded Exclusivity

The God of Israel also made another statement which was radically out of sync with the polytheistic cultic beliefs of the time. He demanded first to be above all other gods (Exod. 20:3). Even more outrageous, God demanded exclusivity of worship and boldly stated that other gods were nonexistent:

> For you shall worship no other god, for the LORD, whose name is Jealous, is a jealous God. (Exod. 34:14)
>
> To you it was shown, that you might know that the LORD Himself is God; there is none other besides Him. (Deut. 4:35)
>
> Now see that I, even I, am He, and there is no God besides Me. (Deut. 32:39)

The idea that there was only one god would not have seemed logical to people of the time. After all, there were different nations spread far and wide and different forces in the world. *How could one god be doing all this? Multiple gods must be involved.* Yahweh had developed a reputation as a powerful god, but he was only the god of Israel, not the god of other nations. He was one of many gods in the Levant.[3] The concept of localized or territorial gods were held in all these cultures. There were gods of the land, gods of the hills, gods of the valley, and gods with specialty focus. Most people strongly believed it was unwise to ignore these gods, offend them, and bring down their curses. Note the perspective of the Syrians:

> Then the servants of the king of Syria said to him, "Their gods *are gods of the hills*. Therefore they were stronger than we; but if we fight against them in the plain, surely we will be stronger than they." (1 Kings 20:23)

After he was healed during the time of Elisha, Naaman the Syrian asked for bags of Israelite soil so he could worship Yahweh when he was at home. In Naaman's mind, a person could not worship the God of Israel without a link to the land of Israel (2 Kings 5:17). Later, after the northern kingdom's captivity, the people who repopulated the land asked the king of Assyria for help understanding the local gods:

Even more outrageous, God demanded exclusivity of worship and boldly stated that other gods were nonexistent.

> Then the king of Assyria commanded, saying, "Send there one of the priests whom you brought from there; let him go and dwell there, and let him teach them the rituals of the God of the land." (2 Kings 17:27)

Consider how different the worship of the One True God was to the religious mindset of these cultures. The founding fathers of Israel (Abraham, Isaac, Jacob) had worshipped the same God irrespective of where they were—in Mesopotamia, Canaan, or Egypt.

God told Israel many times not to fear the traditional gods of the land, but they continued to do so. It's why we often see many kings of Israel worshipping both Yahweh and the Baals, trying to cover all bases (e.g., 2 Chron. 15:17). Only a few kings, like Hezekiah and Josiah, attempted to remove these pagan high places. It would have been difficult for the people to ignore all the legends surrounding these regional and national gods and put their trust only in the God of Israel.

---

[3] Bibliog: (Albright 1994, 115-144)

Interestingly, when Israel entered the promised land, God changed the system of worship. Instead of each family sacrificing locally, they were now directed to a central system of worship (Lev. 17:3–4; Deut. 12:8–14). God's new instruction was directly related to opposing the concept of localized gods:

> *They shall no more offer their sacrifices to demons, after whom they have played the harlot.* This shall be a statute forever for them throughout their generations. Also you shall say to them: "Whatever man of the house of Israel, or of the strangers who dwell among you, who offers a burnt offering or sacrifice, *and does not bring it to the door of the tabernacle of meeting,* to offer it to the LORD, that man shall be cut off from among his people." (Lev. 17:7–9)

The Lure of Sex

The immorality of the pagan cultic practices was another trap, particularly for the males of Israel. The Canaanite gods were often worshipped by rituals involving sex. Temple prostitution was a way of gaining the favor of the gods. Furthermore, there was no judgment by those gods against sexual immorality as there was with the God of Israel. God had specifically warned Israel not to be involved with such practices, but the lure of sexual promiscuity would have been difficult to ignore (Deut. 23:17; Hosea 4:10–19). During the reign of King Josiah, there is even mention of cultic male prostitutes operating in the nation (2 Kings 23:7).

> *The Canaanite gods were often worshipped by rituals involving sex.*

In comparison the God of Israel didn't want sex to be involved in any part of his worship. He even told Israel to abstain from sex with their wives before coming before him to make their offerings. The contrast could not have been greater.

The sexual lure of the pagan religions was still affecting the church in New Testament times. Paul had to write and tell believers to reject the sexual immorality in the religions around them (1 Cor. 6:13–20).

Formulas and Magic

Another powerful pull from the pagan religions was the idea that the gods could be induced to fulfill a person's will by following prescribed rituals. Obedience to a standard of moral behavior was not necessary—just follow a formula, and the gods would respond. And doing certain extreme actions could manipulate the gods for specific purposes.

This is sometimes called *sympathetic magic*—the idea that a person could act out a ritual on the earthly plane that would force the gods to act on the cosmic plane. Ritual prostitution, for example, was more than just an appeal to the sexual appetite. It was a powerful enactment of fertility to turn the will of the gods. Female priestesses represented Ashtarte, and the males represented Baal. The cultic sexual union was a magic that would bind Baal to cause Ashtarte to be fertile, thereby giving fertility to the soil and the promise of a good season.[4]

Child sacrifice in particular was powerful magic. It was a way of compelling the gods to do your will by giving up that which is most precious to you. We see this in action with the pagan king of Moab:

> And when the king of Moab saw that the battle was too fierce for him, he took with him seven hundred men who drew swords, to break through to the king of Edom, but they could not. *Then he took his eldest son who would have reigned in his place, and offered him as a burnt offering upon the wall*; and there was great indignation against Israel. So they departed from him and returned to their own land. (2 Kings 3:26–27).

In the eyes of the King of Moab the powerful magic achieved its goals; Israel departed.[5] Some suggest that Jehoram, the evil king of Israel, also believed in the power of this magic, which may explain his hasty exit.

Worship of the true God was in stark contrast to these pagan transactional rituals.

Worship of the true God was in stark contrast to these pagan transactional rituals. God is never indebted to man and cannot be controlled or bribed. No incantation can force him to do anything. Even the proper temple rituals meant nothing to him if not done with a pure heart (Isa. 1:11–17). The pagan gods, on the other hand, provided an appealing, formula-driven, sensual approach that didn't require a change of heart. They were works-based religions like most religions of history.

Easy Yet Difficult

Israel didn't grasp the nature of the relationship God was asking of them. He

---
[4] Bibliog: (Holman 2015, Canaan. p 259)
[5] The story of the Moabite victory was found written on the famous Mesha or Moabite Steele, now located in the Louvre.

was a God who was kind, merciful, and gracious and who wanted to be loved and trusted. He could not have been more different from the frightening and hedonistic pagan gods who had to be appeased. In essence God simply said: "If you want to be blessed, keep my commandments and my laws—put your trust in me."

The way of life God prescribed to Israel was, therefore, both easy and hard at the same time. It was easy in one sense because it was a system of light governance. But it was hard to put their total trust in one God. It was so much easier to trust in the gods their eyes could see, and in their human leaders, armies, alliances, wealth, temple, feelings, and prescribed formulas. The challenge is understandable. Even today, truly trusting in God remains the most difficult thing anyone can do.

What about the Canaanites?

It is not because of your righteousness ... that you go in to possess their land, but because of the wickedness of these nations that the LORD your God drives them out from before you. —Deuteronomy 9:5

"You talk about this kind and loving God of yours, but what about the Canaanites?" That is a question many agnostics and atheists ask believers. *How could a loving God order the extermination of the Canaanites in favor of his own chosen people?*

Many Bible believers have asked the same troubling question when they read God's directive concerning the people of Canaan:

> But of the cities of these peoples which the LORD your God gives you as an inheritance, you shall let nothing that breathes remain alive, *but you shall utterly destroy them:* the Hittite and the Amorite and the Canaanite and the Perizzite and the Hivite and the Jebusite, just as the LORD your God has commanded you. (Deut. 20:16–17)

Yet this same God describes himself as "merciful and gracious, longsuffering, and abounding in goodness and truth" (Exod. 34:6). How can these commands be reconciled with such high ideals? This question has been a stumbling block to many people and is one of the main arguments atheists use to demonstrate that the God of the Bible has serious credibility and character problem.

A Bible believer might state at the outset of such a discussion that God is our Creator, and so he can do what he wants. "The LORD gives, and the LORD takes away" as Job says (Job 1:21). And that is certainly true, but that's not helpful to the question at hand. The question is not whether God has the right or authority to do what he does, the question we seek to understand is *why*.

God Is Consistent

We must first be reminded that the God of the Bible is not capricious, nor is he random, vindictive, or unreasonably angry. His standards are defined, and his actions are *predictable*. God's character was evident in the early years of human history. He had such high hopes for humankind and was discouraged to see their deterioration into depravity:

> Then the LORD saw that the wickedness of man was great in the earth, and that every intent of the *thoughts of his heart was only evil continually.*

> And the LORD was sorry that He had made man on the earth, and He was grieved in His heart. *So the LORD said, "I will destroy man whom I have created* from the face of the earth, both man and beast, creeping thing and birds of the air, for I am sorry that I have made them." (Gen. 6:5–7)
>
> The earth also was corrupt before God, and the earth was filled with violence. (Gen. 6:11)

The Creator God looked down on his magnificent creation with a mixture of grief, unbelief, and anger when he saw what people were capable of. He had patiently watched humans descend into depravity and violence for over 1,500 years and was so upset that he decided to destroy all flesh except for Noah and his family. So after a final 120 years of witness and warning by Noah, the world at that time was washed away—men, women, children, and most of the animal world (Gen. 6–7).

The God of the Bible is not capricious, nor is he random, vindictive, or unreasonably angry.

What happened in the time of Noah was a *judgment* decreed by the Creator God because of extremely evil behavior. In God's eyes the destruction was warranted because he expected certain minimum human standards. He had taught humanity right from wrong, but they ignored their creator and descended into violence and depravity.

After the event, God said he wouldn't bring a flood like that again, even though he would have known that somewhere in the future, humanity would once again go down the same negative path.

Sodom and Gomorrah

Some 600 years later, the people living near the Dead Sea also descended into depravity. An outcry had come up to God, and the people of Sodom and Gomorrah and three other cities were destroyed. Again, this was a judgment because their behavior was abominable in God's sight (Gen. 18:21).

Once again God didn't act rashly in a fit of anger. To be sure his judgment was correct, he came down to personally verify the situation (Gen. 18:21). Abraham knew God's nature was just, and he would not punish people unfairly. "Shall not the Judge of all the earth do right?" Abraham queried (Gen. 18:25). Abraham's questioning shows that he knew the people were corrupt, and he spent some time "bartering" with God to bring down the threshold number. God finally agreed not to destroy the cities if only ten righteous people could be found. But even this low cut-off was not met, and God once again executed judgment upon an evil culture. There was no capriciousness or randomness here—God was again consistent. His standards had not changed since the days of Noah.

Unchanging Standards

Further down the track of history, hundreds of years after Sodom, the major city of Nineveh in Assyria came under a similar judgment for the same behavior, and had they not repented, the same fate would have befallen them (Jon. 1–4).

> *God's judgments are consistent and predictable and based on his righteous character.*

Even God's own special nation, Israel—a nation he had invested so much love and time into—when they eventually descended into depravity, terrible things happened to men, women, and children alike at the hands of foreign armies (Ezek. 22). If it wasn't for God's love for the founding fathers and a remnant of righteous people, God would have destroyed Israel because of their consistent debased behavior (Mal. 3:6; Hosea 11:9).

Other nations have received the same fate. Sometimes God used natural events, as he did at Sodom, but mostly he used the sword of other nations as his executive punishment. Israel was punished by the Assyrians for their behavior (Isa. 10:5). When Assyria then descended into violence and depravity, God used Babylon to punish them (Isa. 10). Later God used the Babylonians to punish Judah (Ezek. 21).

These examples demonstrate God's judgments are consistent and predictable and based on his righteous character.

> *His judgment fell on evil people because of what they did, not because of who they were.*

Atheists have compared the God of Israel with despots like Hitler, Pol Pot, or Stalin, but there is no comparison. These tyrants killed innocent people for their own evil purposes with ideologically driven biases and prejudices. The God of the Bible, on the other hand, has never been a respecter of persons (Deut. 10:17; Rom. 2:11). His judgment fell on evil people *because of what they did*, not because of who they were. God judged all people by the same standard, both gentiles and Israelites.

The Sins of the Canaanites

Circling back to the question of the Canaanites, we see the same debased behavior triggering the same predictable response from God. Some have said that God unjustly picked on the Canaanites so that he could clear out the promised land for the Israelites. This is incorrect. The pronouncement against the Canaanites was a specific judgment because of vile behavior that had been going on for a very long time.

God had been patient with these people for hundreds of years. He specifically held Israel in slavery in Egypt until these people reached a time when judgment against them was overdue. Speaking to Abram hundreds of years prior, God said:

> Know certainly that your descendants will be strangers in a land *that is* not theirs, and will serve them, and they will afflict them four hundred years. And also the nation whom they serve I will judge; afterward they shall come out with great possessions. Now as for you, you shall go to your fathers in peace; you shall be buried at a good old age. But in the fourth generation they shall return here, *for the iniquity of the Amorites is not yet complete.* (Gen. 15:13–16)[1]

God gave the people of Canaan time to either change, or become deserving of their fate. Their destruction was not related to any sense of superiority of the Israelites. As Moses said:

> It is not because of your righteousness or the uprightness of your heart *that* you go in to possess their land, *but because of the wickedness of these nations that* the LORD your God drives them out from before you. (Deut. 9:5)

Moses was under no illusions that Israel was deserving of the promised land. It was given to them because of God's promise to their forefathers.

Canaanite Judgment Was Unique

God's judgment against the Canaanites was specifically because of their base behavior. Other surrounding nations did not fall under the same judgment. God specifically told Israel to not harm or interfere with the nations of Moab, Ammon, and Edom as they came through (Deut. 2:4–6, 9, 19). Israel was also allowed to make treaties with other nations outside Canaan (Deut. 20:10–16).

---

[1] "Amorites" was a general name for the seven nations of the land of Canaan (Josh. 24:15; Acts 13:19).

But the Canaanites were to be totally destroyed.

The Canaanites had over 40 years of advanced warning. God ensured they heard about the great events in Egypt and during the exodus:

> This day I will begin to put the dread and fear of you upon the nations under the whole heaven, who shall hear the report of you, and shall tremble and be in anguish because of you. (Deut. 2:25)

The people of Canaan knew that God's judgment was targeted specifically at them and not other nations. This was confirmed by the actions of the people of Gibeon. The Gibeonites pretended to be from a far country to avoid destruction. They knew they would be spared if Israel believed they lived outside Canaan (Josh. 9). Rahab had earlier confirmed that the Canaanites knew exactly where Israel was headed:

The people of Canaan knew that God's judgment was targeted specifically at them and not other nations.

> "*I know that the Lord has given you the land*, that the terror of you has fallen on us, and that all the inhabitants of the land are fainthearted because of you. For we have heard how the Lord dried up the water of the Red Sea for you when you came out of Egypt. (Josh. 2:9–10)

The Bible does not disclose if any other Canaanites turned to God, but the story of Rahab demonstrates that they could have been spared if they had repented and turned to God. Alternatively, they could have left the land.

What Had the Canaanites Done?

When the practices of the Canaanites are examined, God's strong response becomes understandable. The Canaanites had incorporated vile practices in their cultic practices, including sacrificing their own children:

> You shall not worship the LORD your God in that way; *for every abomination to the LORD which He hates they have done to their gods;* for they burn even their sons and daughters in the fire to their gods. (Deut. 12:31)

The Canaanites were also involved in every form of debased sexual behavior. This was supposedly to emulate the appalling behavior of the gods themselves. Chapter 18 of the book of Leviticus warned Israel against such an extreme list of immorality that it makes a person wonder why God even had to spell it out:

incest with a mother, a sister, a daughter-in-law, a sister-in-law, aunts, uncles, and cousins; rampant pedophilia, homosexual practices, bestiality, child sacrifice—the list is extreme. God confirmed that *all* these appalling things were being practiced by these people:

> Do not defile yourselves with any of these things; *for by all these the nations are defiled*, which I am casting out before you. For the land is *defiled*; therefore I visit the punishment of its iniquity upon it, *and the land vomits out its inhabitants*. You shall therefore keep My statutes and My judgments, and shall not commit any of these abominations, either any of your own nation or any stranger who dwells among you (*for all these abominations the men of the land have done, who were before you, and thus the land is defiled*), lest the land vomit you out also when you defile it, as it vomited out the nations that were before you. (Lev. 18:24–28)

There can be no doubt that these people had a severe judgment coming. When a people burn their children in honor of their gods, when every form of sexual perversion is practiced and accepted publicly at every level of society, when violence and cruelty are widespread, God graphically describes the land "vomiting" out such a people, just as a body heaves under a load of internal poisons. God's judgment against such a people is a warning for all societies that follow suit (v. 29).

> *There can be no doubt that these people had a severe judgment coming.*

A Modern Perspective

We can also put this into a modern perspective. If such acts as those practiced by the Canaanites were broadcast on today's news, and it was seen to be endemic in a foreign country somewhere, there would be a universal outcry for swift and tough military action to intervene in that country.

Witness the international outcry we saw over ISIS when the world saw their beheadings, murders, debasement of women and other vile behavior. Western world leaders convened and agreed to do what was necessary to destroy the ISIS menace. They made a collective judgment that a society based on such standards should be destroyed and agreed to "wield the sword" against them. Yet in many ways, the terrible actions of ISIS were mild compared to the depth of depravity in Canaan.

What was decreed by God on the Canaanites was not genocide. Genocide is the unwarranted, indiscriminate killing of a people. This was a judgment of capital punishment that well and truly fit the crime. Just as the execution by the state of an evil person is not murder, it is a right and proper judgment to remove such evil from the earth.

No Delight in Deaths

Richard Dawkins, the well-known English atheist, massively distorted the reality of what occurred in Canaan with his emotional comments, saying that ancient Israel engaged in "ethnic cleansing" and "bloodthirsty massacres" that were carried out with "xenophobic relish."[2] His outrageous comment does not reflect God's attitude or what actually happened. Neither God nor the Israelites took any delight in the destruction of these people.

We are told multiple times in Scripture that God takes no pleasure in the death of wicked people (Ezek. 18:32). This attitude is proven by his long-suffering attitude toward evil people and his willingness to quickly change his mind when such people repent. Despite being on par with Sodom and Gomorrah, God's willingness to change his mind about Nineveh amply demonstrates this attitude in practice.

> *Neither God nor the Israelites took any delight in the destruction of these people.*

It is also abundantly clear that Israel did *not* want to do the job God told them to do. There was no thought of eagerly wanting to wipe out these people. Israel had to be pushed to do the job. Despite Israel's half-hearted attitude, God still wanted them to remove these evil people from the land. In the end they didn't do as God commanded.

Clear and Present Danger

There is another aspect of God's decree to consider. Not only were the Canaanites well deserving of their punishment, but they were also a clear and present danger to Israel, a direct threat to Israel's existence:

> When the LORD your God cuts off from before you the nations which you go to dispossess, and you displace them and dwell in their land, take heed to yourself that you are *not ensnared to follow them*. (Deut. 12:29–30)
>
> But of the cities of these peoples which the LORD your God gives you *as* an inheritance, you shall let nothing that breathes remain alive, but

---

[2] Bibliog: (Dawkins, The God Delusion 2006, 248)

> you shall utterly destroy them: the Hittite and the Amorite and the Canaanite and the Perizzite and the Hivite and the Jebusite, just as the LORD your God has commanded you, *lest they teach you to do according to all their abominations which they have done for their gods, and you sin against the LORD your God.* (Deut. 20:16–18)

By removing these people from the land, God was keeping his people safe from a very real threat. Their enemies' destruction was necessary to give Israel the best possible chance of survival. As often stated today, the first priority for a nation's leaders is to protect their citizens from harm. The apostle Paul confirms the God-given authority of the state for that purpose, even to go to war if necessary (Rom. 13:4).

Great leaders like Winston Churchill knew that it was necessary to bomb European cities during the war to stop the spread of evil Nazism. This resulted in the destruction of much of Europe and many civilian casualties. The alternative (as Churchill stated) was "for the whole world, including the United States, including all that we have known and cared for, will sink into the abyss of a new Dark Age."[3]

Once they had cleansed the land, God did not want Israel to be a conquering, empire-building nation. They were to be a light to the world. God's ideal for Israel was for other nations to be attracted by their morally sound, free, and prosperous society and voluntarily want to be like them (Deut. 4:5–8).

The Israelites' *failure* to execute God's command fully was one of their greatest blunders, and it resulted in long-term injury to the nation (Judg. 1:28; 2:1–3).

Why the Use of Soldiers?

Why did God choose to use Israel to execute judgment on these people? Why not some supernatural event like the fire and brimstone he used on Sodom and Gomorrah instead of having Israel's soldiers do the job? This is probably the most difficult question to answer, and the Bible does not provide one—but we can make some factual observations:

Comments from God imply he did not originally intend for Israel to do all the fighting. At the outset God said:

> For My Angel will go before you and bring you in to the Amorites and the Hittites and the Perizzites and the Canaanites and the Hivites and the Jebusites; and I will cut them off. ... I will send My fear before

---
[3] Bibliog: (S. W. Churchill 1940)

> you, I will cause confusion among all the people to whom you come, and will make all your enemies turn *their* backs to you. And I will send hornets before you, which shall drive out the Hivite, the Canaanite, and the Hittite from before you. I will not drive them out from before you in one year, lest the land become desolate and the beasts of the field become too numerous for you. Little by little I will drive them out from before you, until you have increased, and you inherit the land. (Exod. 23:23, 27–30)

Had Israel trusted God, they would have had it a whole lot easier:

> Then I said to you, "Do not be terrified, or afraid of them. The LORD your God, who goes before you, *He will fight for you*, according to all He did for you in Egypt before your eyes." (Deut. 1:29–30).

The fact that the Israelites had to do much of the hard fighting work themselves would have certainly served as a warning and reminder of the terrible consequences of sin. Maybe God wanted this lesson driven home to these hard-hearted people.

Moses, Joshua, and others who recorded the narrative of the conquest apparently thought it was acceptable for the Israelite soldiers to do what God commanded of them. No one was wringing his hands over the soldiers having to kill the Canaanites. Those who fought (like Caleb) were national heroes. They knew that this was a sentence on a debased people. It was nothing like the rape and pillage of much of history. There was no personal hatred or vengeance involved. Nor was it done with any delight. It was a judgment decreed by God to be executed swiftly.

The Women and Children

There is one final difficult question: Why did God command Israel to destroy the women and the children?

Consider that if the woman and children had been spared, how long before a new crop of adults just like their predecessors would have appeared? Without a doubt, if the Canaanite women were left alive, they would have remained a major threat to Israel. Women were no less guilty than men, and in many cases, they were the principal instigators. Earlier, when Midian tried to entrap Israel, it was mainly the women who caused the men to go astray (Num. 31:16).

What would have been the result of leaving the children of these debased people alive? Only God knows the answer, but it clearly seems negative. At the end of the day, we must trust his judgment. God has a different perspective on life and death to us and holds the keys to a future resurrection.

Whatever the perspective, remember that just like today, when a community becomes corrupt, there are consequences for every member of the population, even children. When God brought famine and drought on Israel because of their sins, adults and children suffered alike.

> *God has a different perspective on life and death to us and holds the keys to a future resurrection.*

Today we both reap the benefits of godly people around us, and we also suffer as a community when our society deteriorates into sin. Witness the terrible suffering of children in countries like Germany and Japan when their leaders went off the rails. We saw the same in countries like Afghanistan, Iraq, and Syria. The fate of children throughout history has always rested with their parents.

The Goodness and Severity of God

For those who take the time to read the entire narrative of the Old Testament, God's goodness and righteousness comes through loud and clear. From the start, God's intent has always been for humanity's good. He demanded just laws and just rulers. He demonstrated kindness for the poor, the oppressed, the downtrodden, the orphans and widows. He desired a positive, free society for all. He pleaded with people to repent of their evil ways that he might not judge them. He quickly relented from doing harm when people repented.

> *There are times when all people must consider both the goodness and severity of God.*

But in God's eyes there does come a point in a society's downward spiral when a total reset is required. God's judgment against the Canaanites was just and warranted. These are the times when all people must consider both the goodness *and* severity of God (Rom. 11:22).

Sins of the Fathers

Fathers shall not be put to death for their children. —Deuteronomy 24:16

One of the key principles of justice reviewed earlier is the concept of personal accountability. The law of Moses forbade children being punished because of the sins of their fathers (Deut. 24:16).

Despite this clear instruction, there has been criticism that the law was inconsistent. Earlier in the same book of Deuteronomy, right in the heart of the Ten Commandments, is a statement from God that seems contradictory to the law that disallowed kin punishment. It reads as if God was vowing to harshly punish children and grandchildren for the sins of their fathers:

> For I, the LORD your God, am a jealous God, *visiting the iniquity of the fathers upon the children to the third and fourth generations of those who hate Me*, but showing mercy to thousands, to those who love Me and keep My commandments. (Deut. 5:9–10)

Later in Deuteronomy, other statements also appear out of line with the original law. Children will suffer because of their parents' sins:

> If you do not obey the voice of the LORD your God, to observe carefully all His commandments and His statutes which I command you today, that all these curses will come upon you and overtake you ... Cursed shall be the *fruit of your body* ... You shall beget sons and daughters, but they shall not be yours; for *they shall go into captivity*. (Deut. 28:15, 18, 41)

But God is not double-minded, and Moses would not have contradicted himself within a few chapters of the same book, so we must assume that these Scriptures are addressing different scenarios.

The answer to the seeming contradiction is noted in a parallel verse:

> The LORD is longsuffering and abundant in mercy, forgiving iniquity and transgression; *but He by no means clears the guilty*, visiting the iniquity of the fathers on the children to the third and fourth generation. (Num. 14:18)

Here Moses confirmed that God is merciful and forgiving to those who *change* their negative behavior. But for those *guilty* of continuing the evil practices of their fathers, there would be negative outcomes.[1]

Law of Consequences

God has created a universe modeled on his own standards of right and wrong. And in this universe are natural laws. One of those laws is what we might call the *law of consequences*. There are natural consequences to certain ways of life. Paul describes the principle this way: "God is not mocked; for whatever a man sows, that he will also reap" (Gal. 6:7). And what a person sows and reaps will often affect others around them.

The sin of adultery demonstrates this well. The matter of a man or woman caught having an affair with another person doesn't end with them. The mental and emotional injury on innocent partners and children can affect them for a lifetime. Similarly, the decisions of a drunk driver who kills an innocent person can have devasting effects on other people. The natural consequences of sin are evident all around us. Envy leads to hate, and hate leads to violence and wars. Lust leads to immorality, and immorality leads to distrust and broken families. Innocent people regularly suffer as collateral damage from the sins of others.

> *It is the simple reality of life that the consequences of parents' sins will automatically flow to those under their care.*

When God stated that he will visit the sins or iniquity of a family member on another, he was *not* talking about punishing a person for something they haven't done. It is the simple reality of life that the consequences of parents' sins will automatically flow to those under their care—just as millions in this world today suffer from the law of consequences from the decisions of previous generations.

Israel's rejection of God's laws over a long period of time led to a total breakdown in society and eventual captivity. Their leaders lost sight of God and the whole nation went astray and became cursed. There were terrible consequences for everyone—guilty and innocent alike.

Learned Patterns of Behavior

But there is a deeper understanding of the effects of the "sins of the fathers"

---

[1] The phrase "to the third and fourth generation" appears to be a Hebrew expression rather than a precise period of time. It may have originated from three or four generations living in one household, which was common in ancient times.

and how they flow on through following generations and societies.

The *example* of parents has an enormous influence on their children. It's an influence that can either be positive or negative. Parents with patterns of bad behavior, like immorality, anger, alcoholism, gluttony, or even laziness, so often pass these behaviors to their children. Many times Scripture relays how kings of Israel walked in the *sins of their father* (1 Kings 15:3, 26; 22:52–53; 2 Kings 3:2–3; 14:3–4; 21:20–22; 23:37; 24:9). A child who grows up in an environment of ongoing sin and breaking of God's laws has the propensity to take on their parent's destructive pattern of behavior. They then become *guilty in their own right*.

> *Children can also learn to "hate God" like their parents. It's hard to break such a negative cycle.*

This is visiting the iniquity of the fathers onto the next generation. It can be in both the *consequences* and the *learned behavior* from the parents. Children can also learn to "hate God" like their parents (Deut. 5:9). It's hard to break such a negative cycle. In the same way, those who have suffered abuse as a child will sometimes themselves become perpetrators of abuse.

But even if the parent's example was poor, in the spirit of the law of Deuteronomy 24:16, the person must be accountable for their own actions. Being a victim is not an excuse for ongoing bad behavior.

Breaking the Cycle

Even if the negative behavior of the parents is passed on to their children and grandchildren, the cycle can be broken. Ahaz was a king of Judah who did *not* do what was right in the sight of God, yet his son Hezekiah *did*. Conversely, righteous King Hezekiah had a son, Manasseh, who was the evilest of all the kings of Judah.

People are free moral agencies, and God holds each one accountable for their own sins. God will not force someone to sin because of their parents, nor will he tempt someone to sin (James 1:13). Quite the opposite. God greatly desires for people to break the cycle of bad behavior. Far from wanting to punish people for the sins of their fathers, consider God's impassioned plea later to Israel:

> Say to them: "As I live," says the LORD God, "I have no pleasure in the death of the wicked, but that the wicked turn from his way and live.

> *Turn, turn from your evil ways! For why should you die, O house of Israel?"*
> (Ezek. 33:11)

He goes on to state that people do not have to be trapped in their past bad behavior. Each has freewill and will be judged for their own doings:

> When I say to the wicked, "You shall surely die," *if he turns from his sin and does what is lawful and right,* if the wicked restores the pledge, gives back what he has stolen, and walks in the statutes of life without committing iniquity, *he shall surely live; he shall not die.* None of his sins which he has committed shall be remembered against him; he has done what is lawful and right; he shall surely live. Yet the children of your people say, "The way of the LORD is not fair." But it is their way which is not fair! When the righteous turns from his righteousness and commits iniquity, he shall die because of it. But when the wicked turns from his wickedness and does what is lawful and right, he shall live because of it. Yet you say, "The way of the LORD is not fair." *O house of Israel, I will judge every one of you according to his own ways.* (Ezek. 33:14–20).

Some of the greatest achievers in Old Testament history broke out of their negative environments to be a blessing to others. Consider Ruth, Rahab, Noah, Abraham, and Moses. They came out of environments that were idolatrous and immoral. They turned to God despite their background.

The law of Moses affirms that each person will ultimately be held accountable for their own sin. Bearing the guilt of sin is altogether different than suffering the physical consequences of the sins of others.

The Trial by Ordeal for Jealousy

This is the law of jealousy ... when the spirit of jealousy comes upon a man, and he becomes jealous of his wife. —Numbers 5:29–30

The book of Numbers includes a strange ritual concerning jealousy that seems out of character with other aspects of the Mosaic law (Num. 5:11–31). A ritual of this style is generally called a *trial of ordeal*, where a person's innocence or guilt is determined by a series of tests. Trials of ordeal have been used throughout history as far back as the Code of Hammurabi. Most such ordeals have included painful or life-threatening rites where the person would supposedly be divinely protected if they were innocent. Often, the participant would be harmed whatever the outcome.

While the Mosaic jealousy ritual does not harm the participants, it is still a procedure that people find either disturbing or perplexing. A summary of the ritual is as follows:

- If a man develops jealousy toward his wife because of real or imagined unfaithfulness, he may bring her to the priest at the sanctuary.
- The priest makes some "bitter water" by mixing water with some dust from the floor of the tabernacle.
- The priest explains the oath the woman will take. The oath states that if the woman is innocent, then the bitter water will have no effect. If she is guilty, she will become infertile.
- The woman agrees to the oath.
- The priest writes the curses on a scroll and then blots off the words into the bitter water.
- The woman drinks the water.
- If the woman is guilty, the curse will take effect; otherwise she will continue to bear children.

As seen earlier, the Mosaic law took a strong stance against adultery because of its highly destructive effects on the family and society (Exod. 20:14). Why God included this additional procedure for jealousy is unclear, but it certainly would have reinforced the importance of marriage faithfulness.

Protection for the Woman

In the context of the ancient world, the rage of a jealous husband would be frightening for a vulnerable woman. Solomon described a jealous husband's fury as unappeasable (Prov. 6:34–35). He later posed the question, "Who is able to stand before jealousy?" (Prov. 27:4). Jealousy needed to be dealt with.

But what could be done to defuse a husband suspicious of his wife without proof? While someone today might reject the trial of jealousy ordeal as misogynist, unfair, or just plain weird—for the culture of the time, it may have solved a difficult problem for the woman in the best way possible. It provided a way to depower a jealous husband for the protection of the woman.

This procedure confirmed that a jealous husband could not act unilaterally on a suspicion. If he had concerns, he and his wife had to approach the priests and follow the prescribed process. Even though such a process would not be accepted in our world, there were several benefits to the procedure God outlined.

> *The ordeal may have solved a difficult problem for the woman in the best way possible.*

Firstly, the process stopped a negative situation from deteriorating further. In that sense it acted as a circuit-breaker and provided the opportunity for the woman to prove her innocence.

Secondly, the process protected the woman rather than threatened her. The authority to act was taken *out of the hands* of the jealous husband. When they arrived at the sanctuary, the matter was put into the hands of the priest, who would be the mediator between them and God. Having to deal with a priest was not unusual. Priests were the interface between the people and the God of Israel and were trusted authorities in many civil and religious matters.

Thirdly, regardless of whether the woman was innocent or guilty, no harm was done to her by any man. The stress of the situation would be difficult, but the process itself was not threatening. The drink did her no harm.

Lastly, the process put the outcome entirely in God's hands. There was nothing for the husband or priest to do—the process relied solely on a miracle from God to bring judgment. Only if God deemed her guilty of adultery did the curse of sterility theoretically take effect.

Once the process was complete, a man could not continue to bring the matter up. He had brought his concerns to the highest authority, and it was now in God's hands.

Because of the reference to the sanctuary and dust from the tabernacle floor, some commentators suggest that this ordeal may have only been relevant in the wilderness. There is also no evidence of it being in use later when attending the tabernacle would have been difficult for people living at a distance.

Certainly, the forty years in the wilderness was a time when people were living within close proximity of one another, and tensions did arise. Regardless, the unique and harmless way such an emotive matter was defused set a wise precedent from which many judgments could be applied.

> *The authority to act was taken out of the hands of the jealous husband.*

We should also consider this law in light of the question the Pharisees posed to Jesus about divorce. As Jesus so insightfully confirmed, it was because of the hardness of their hearts that such laws needed to be given (Matt. 19:8). The same could be said for this law of jealousy.

Love Your Enemies. Really?

You shall not hate your brother in your heart. You shall surely rebuke your neighbor, and not bear sin because of him. —Leviticus 19:17

We saw earlier that the teaching to *love your enemies* was not a new command from Jesus, but a restatement of a principle given in the heart of the law of Moses (Exod. 23:4–5). It is also expressed elsewhere in the Hebrew Scriptures (Prov. 24:17–18, 29; Prov. 25:21–22). A vengeful and unforgiving heart toward others, even enemies, has never been acceptable in the sight of God (Lev. 19:17–18).

But critics of the Old Testament point out that there are many incidents where godly people of old didn't seem to live up to this high ideal. David in particular, is singled out for criticism for what appears to be a vengeful attitude toward his enemies in the so-called "imprecatory" psalms. These psalms invoke curses for the punishment of the psalmist's enemies. And there are several psalms in that style (e.g., Psalms 7, 35, 55, 58, 59, 69, 109, 137, 139).

In many ways David's attitude was outstanding and commendable. When Saul became David's enemy, David didn't retaliate as one would expect. When he had the opportunity to kill Saul, he refrained (1 Sam. 24). When Saul died, David wept (2 Sam. 1). Later, when David's son Absalom rose against him, David's attitude was one of sorrow, not of anger and revenge (2 Sam. 18:33).

Yet at other times, David seems to operate by a different standard. For example, his final advice from his deathbed to his son Solomon was to bring the troublesome Shimei down to the grave with blood (1 Kings 2:8–9). He said something similar about Joab (1 Kings 2:5–6). How do we reconcile these different mindsets of David, called a man after God's own heart (1 Sam. 13:14)?

There are also other examples in the Old Testament where enemies were not treated with kindness or blessings. The righteous prophet Samuel certainly didn't show love to Agag, Israel's enemy, when Agag was brought before him—Samuel had him hacked to pieces (1 Sam. 15:33). Jeremiah the righteous prophet also called on God to curse his enemies (Jer. 18:19–23).

The Problem Broadens

But criticism of individuals not loving their enemies is not limited to Old Testament times. Some even disparage Jesus for not living up to his own teaching. The same Jesus who taught people to "love your enemies, bless those who curse you, do good to those who hate you," at times seemed to do the opposite. On one occasion, Jesus castigated the Pharisees, pronounced curses (woes) on them, and called them "whitewashed tombs, snakes, a brood of vipers" (Matt. 23:13–17, 23–24, 27, 31–33). He certainly did not bless them.

> *Some even disparage Jesus for not living up to his own teaching.*

On one occasion his disciples saw how Jesus had offended them and questioned him on the matter (Matt. 15:12).

Paul is also criticized like David for some of his imprecations. In his letter to Timothy, Paul asks God to bring misfortune onto Alexander, the coppersmith, for the harm he had done to him (2 Tim. 4:14–15). Yet Paul taught the church to bless their enemies on other occasions (Rom. 12:19–20).

Either all these people (including Jesus) are hypocrites, or there is more to the understanding of what it means to *love your enemies*.

No Delight in the Death of the Wicked

Scripture teaches that the value of loving one's enemies originates from God himself. As Jesus said, God sends the rain on both the just and the unjust and is kind to the unthankful and evil (Matt. 5:45; Luke 6:35). God's desire is always for change, not destruction. He has never taken any delight in punishing those who turn against him (Ezek. 33:11). Righteous Job understood that it was not in God's nature to rejoice in the destruction of evil people:

> If I have rejoiced at the destruction of him who hated me, or lifted myself up when evil found him (indeed I have not allowed my mouth to sin by asking for a curse on his soul) … Oh, that I had one to hear me! (Job 31:29–30, 35)

Years later Jesus expressed a similar attitude. He cried over Jerusalem that had killed the prophets and rebelled so much against God. He did not rejoice at the thought of the city's demise (Matt. 23:37). Such an attitude is not intuitive to human nature. It is natural for a person to be delighted when their enemies come to grief. But God does not think this way. His patience, longsuffering, and willingness to forgive the worst of sins is incredible. He rejoices when evil people turn from their wicked ways. Consider how readily he accepted Abraham's request to forgo the destruction of the cities of the plain, even if only ten righteous people could be found (Gen. 18:22–32), and how quickly he changed his mind about destroying Nineveh when the people repented (Jon. 3:10).

God's attitude of looking and hoping for the best in people is *who he is*. He is the Father in the parable of the prodigal son who greatly rejoices at seeing positive change in the lives of his sons and daughters (Luke 15:20).

But such an attitude should not be confused with being soft on sin or being endlessly accepting of evil ways. God is a God of justice and will only tolerate evil for so long. There will come a time to execute judgment. Before that time, he will send messengers to warn those who are heading for destruction. Such warnings will often be strong and harsh, but they are done in love, in the hope that there will be change.

Rebuking Your Neighbor

In this same spirit of desiring change, God included a well-known directive in the law of Moses for his people: to *love their neighbors*—not to hate them in their hearts, not to hold a grudge, or take vengeance.

At the same time, he included an often-overlooked directive that goes a long way to explain the conundrum of David's, Paul's, and Jesus' actions:

God instructed Israel that it was perfectly acceptable to rebuke or correct a neighbor.

> You shall not hate your brother in your heart. *You shall surely rebuke your neighbor,* and not bear sin because of him. You shall not take vengeance, nor bear any grudge against the children of your people, but you shall love your neighbor as yourself: I am the LORD. (Lev. 19:17–18)

Notice that God here instructs Israel that it was perfectly acceptable to *rebuke or correct* a neighbor as long as they didn't hate that neighbor in their hearts. In other words, if the rebuke was done in a genuine spirit of outgoing concern, without malice or a spirit of vengeance, it was acceptable to do so and even encouraged. Paul instructed Timothy to do likewise:

> Those who are sinning *rebuke in the presence of all*, that the rest also may fear. I charge you before God and the Lord Jesus Christ and the elect angels that you *observe these things without prejudice, doing nothing with partiality.* (1 Tim. 5:20–21)

Rebuking a person is not retaliation. Done in the proper spirit, it reflects a sincere desire to see a person change. Jesus followed this directive, as did Paul. There was no contradiction in their actions. Jesus did not rebuke out of spite or revenge and did not delight in putting others down. He rebuked the Pharisees to wake them up from their blatant hypocrisy.

Stephen also called out the Pharisees for what they were—stiff-necked murderers—and he died for his harsh words (Acts 7:51–60). Yet Stephen was a man filled with the spirit of love and compassion. His final words asked God to forgive his attackers for what they had done. God has always chastened those he loves, including ancient Israel (Prov. 3:11–12). As all parents know, to correct a wayward child is to show true love.

Paul applied this principle when dealing with an immoral situation in Corinth. He told the Corinthian Christians to remove a sinning man from the congregation so that he would wake up and change (1 Cor. 5:5). In the same vein, Paul wanted Alexander, the coppersmith, to be punished so that he would learn and repent of his ways (1 Tim. 1:20). His statement had nothing to do with personal hatred or a desire for revenge.

These examples affirm what love means in a biblical sense. Godly love is not being "nice" to everyone. True love is honest and without pretense, just as Jesus was. Godly love does what is best for the other person, even if they don't see it that way at the time. It has been said that *agape* love is sometimes tough love—but it is true love.

Understanding the Term "Enemy"

When we talk about loving one's enemies, we also must consider what is meant by the term "enemy." Enemy is an emotive word that tends to imply an evil person. But the word "enemy" does not insinuate judgment on another person's character. An enemy may or may not be an evil person. It simply refers to someone who is an adversary or shows hostility toward another. God is called an enemy to those opposed to him (Lam. 2:4–5).

Most people who are personal adversaries in life are not evil. They may be angry, upset, misguided, and have all sorts of reasons for their stance. They may not know what they are doing, as Jesus said of the soldiers executing him. The law teaches us to respond to such people in love, not in a spirit of retaliation. (A person should also keep in mind that an adversary may be in the right, and they may be the ones in the wrong—something that must be carefully considered before rebuking another.)

> *Loving enemies does not mean supporting evil people in their plans or making a common cause with them.*

But some enemies are most definitely evil, and in ancient times, many of those enemies hated the God of Israel. Some of these were serious threats to the nation. The command to love one's enemies was not a directive to bless such evil people who hate God. Look how the prophet Jehu criticized righteous King Jehoshaphat of Judah for his joint operations with evil King Ahab of Israel:

> Should you help the wicked and love those who hate the LORD? Therefore the wrath of the LORD is upon you. (2 Chron. 19:2)

Doing good to persecutors and loving enemies does not mean supporting evil people in their plans or making a common cause with them. If we see such people in personal trouble, we must help them. We are to pray for them. But otherwise, throughout Scripture, we are told to have nothing to do with people practicing evil and to keep away from them. Paul even gave the same exhortation to the church (1 Cor. 5:11; 2 Thess. 3:6).

Justice and Evildoers

One final point to consider in this matter of loving enemies has to do with the role of the state. As discussed earlier, individuals are to not seek personal vengeance, but they can seek justice. And the state does have a God-given responsibility to deal with evildoers (Rom. 13:1–4). It is an essential part of a just society. Multiple times throughout the Prophets God expressed his displeasure when leadership did not carry out their responsibility to defend the weak (Jer. 7:5–7; 21:12; 22:3; Isa. 10:1–2; Zech. 7:10–13).

The state has a God-given responsibility to deal with evildoers.

An impartial state dealing with a matter for the public good is not the same as an individual taking emotive vengeance. God expects the justice system and the state to execute judgment impartially and dispassionately on evildoers, including military responses in times of war if necessary.

When considering the behavior of Samuel, David, Solomon, and other leaders of Israel, we must keep in mind they were the appointed judges and executors of the nation, and God expected them to bring judgment on evildoers—and they rightly did so. Several imprecatory psalms are written from David's position as the executor of his nation. While David may not have been perfect in everything he said, there was no personal hatred or revenge involved. David had to deal with evil leaders in the surrounding nations, and it was right and proper for him to ask God to bring these people to swift and hard judgment (Ps. 139:19–22). David was also clear in his psalms that God was the ultimate judge—David was confident God would do what was right.

Some criticize David for his tough final words on Joab and Shimei, but it was David's softheartedness that created the original problem, not his harshness. Joab had been a loyal commander to him for decades, and David could not bring himself to address Joab's murder of Abner. David had known all along that it was not right that these men had not been brought to justice. David's failure to execute justice for Absalom's act of murder also got him into enormous strife (2 Sam. 19:5–6). Personally loving one's enemies should not be confused with the necessity to bring evildoers to justice. It was something that David as king and judge should have done for the good of the nation.

Despite his personal failings, David was fiercely loyal to God. Unlike many other kings, he never swayed from acknowledging the true God of Israel. His imprecatory psalms in particular reflect his aversion to evil people who were seeking to harm him and others in the nation. In David's mind if someone was an enemy to the God of Israel, then he was an enemy to David (Ps. 139:21). David prayed for God to defend his own name and deal with these evildoers.

One psalm that ties together this seeming conflict of attitudes is Psalm 139. This is one of the criticized imprecatory psalms where David expresses his hatred of evildoers. But in context, it is a beautiful psalm of a man who has surrendered himself to God and fully trusts in God's righteous judgment. Jesus himself quotes from some of these "imprecatory" psalms, as did Paul (John 15:25; Rom. 11:9–10; 15:3).

Today as we see heinous crimes committed in our own countries and elsewhere, it is also right and proper for all righteous people to pray that God uses the executive leaders of the world to bring evil people to swift judgment.

God Hardens Hearts?

Therefore He has mercy on whom He wills, and whom He wills He hardens.
—Romans 9:18

The book of Deuteronomy includes a story of God's actions against certain pagan kings, which some find troubling. As the children of Israel traveled toward Canaan, Moses sent a proposal to King Sihon of Heshbon for the Israelites to pass peacefully through his land. But Moses then relates that God hardened the king's heart so that he would engage Israel and be beaten in battle:

> And I sent messengers ... to Sihon king of Heshbon, with words of peace ... But Sihon king of Heshbon would not let us pass through, for the LORD your God *hardened his spirit and made his heart obstinate*, that He might deliver him into your hand, as it is this day. (Deut. 2:26, 30)

The same thing happened to Og, the king of Bashan (Deut. 3:1–3). God somehow made Sihon and Og pick a fight with Israel, which they had no hope of winning. In the book of Joshua, God hardened the kings in the land of Canaan similarly, which also led to their destruction (Josh. 11:18–20).

The most well-known instance of God hardening a person's heart is with Pharaoh at the time of the exodus from Egypt. God told Moses in advance that he would harden the heart of Pharaoh so that he would not free the Israelites, and it took ten plagues before Pharaoh finally allowed them to leave (Exod. 4:21). People have been troubled with the idea that God might manipulate a person against their will to achieve his goals—as if people are pawns in a game.

> *Free will is an integral part of God's plan for humans.*

The hardening of a person's heart also seems contradictory to the scriptural evidence presented elsewhere that God is not a controlling or manipulative being. As covered earlier, free will is an integral part of God's plan for humans, and we see his consistent respect for the free will of both righteous and evil people throughout Scripture.

God Does Not Override Freewill

To answer the dilemma, we must understand what it means for God to harden someone's heart. It is not what many think. There is no evidence in Scripture, nor in God's character, that he ever takes control of a person against their will. In every case of hardening, pride, ego, or sin is involved, and God simply works with the character weaknesses of the person involved.

Humans filled with pride or arrogance are easily manipulated by external influence. An egotistical leader puffed up with their own importance is easily hardened by those who oppose and stand up to them. Nebuchadnezzar was such a pride-filled leader (Dan. 4:30). He reacted furiously when Shadrach, Meshach, and Abednego refused to obey him. He was not used to being defied. His rage was so out of control that his own men died in executing his orders (Dan. 3:19–22).

Even human beings can manipulate pride-filled people relatively easily. Many an egotistical leader has been brought down by the flattery of sycophants who encourage them to do things that are not sound. In contrast, a humble and contrite heart is not affected by flattery and cannot be hardened by others.

God holds people accountable for their own actions, even those he hardens.

Satan and his demons possess and manipulate people against their will (Mark 5:2–5; Luke 8:28–29). God does not use such techniques. God and Satan have nothing in common. God holds people accountable for their own actions, even those he hardens (Rom. 2:5). He is just and would not hold someone accountable if their actions were out of their control.

Examples of Hardened Hearts

At various times in history, God has used the major character failings of an individual to achieve his own greater purpose.

King Rehoboam was someone God hardened for his purpose. We know that because of what occurred. God had previously prophesied that Israel would divide into two nations after Solomon (1 Kings 11:31). God knew that the people were already suffering under the burdens imposed by Solomon, and it wouldn't take much for the northern tribes to once again break off from the house of David.

God achieved his prophetic aims by having Rehoboam's young crony advisors stroke the new king's pride and ego. They appealed to the king's vanity and encouraged him to exert his new power (1 Kings 12:8–11). When he did so, the people rebelled. God saw Rehoboam's arrogance and used it for his purpose. Rehoboam's free will was not overridden.

Another instance occurred at the time of King Ahab of Israel. In this case, Scripture gives a heavenly insight into how God worked to achieve his goals. Ahab was an evil ruler, and God finally decreed that enough was enough. He wanted Ahab to go up to battle and lose his life so that his prophecy of calamity against him could be fulfilled.

How would God get Ahab to go into battle? God called on his heavenly council and asked for input (1 Kings 22:19–20). An idea was presented to use Ahab's lying priests to persuade Ahab to go up to battle by telling him he would be successful (vv. 21–22). God accepted the plan, and it worked. God knew that this hard-hearted king so hated God's prophet Micaiah that even when he heard Micaiah say that the council of the other prophets was a deception, he would still go up to battle. Once again God used the character weaknesses of a person for his greater purposes.

The Case of Pharaoh

God prophesied to Abraham hundreds of years previously that his people would be enslaved and come out of slavery with many possessions. For that great purpose, God raised up a hard-hearted and stubborn leader who would be there at the time.

By the time of Moses, Egypt's wealth and power had grown, and the status of the pharaoh was that of a god. A supreme god-ruler like Pharaoh, accustomed to absolute unchallenged power, would not take kindly to anyone making demands of him. To harden Pharaoh's heart, it would only need Moses to appear before Pharaoh with a demand to "let my people go" (Exod. 5:1–2). A proud and obstinate self-willed king like Pharaoh would immediately be infuriated. God could confidently predict the man's reaction because he knew the

God softened and hardened Pharaoh's heart by applying and removing external pressure upon a proud and hard-hearted ruler.

man well (Exod. 3:19). (We might imagine a similar result if such demands were made on the modern North Korean dictator.) Pharaoh reluctantly softened when the plagues were upon him, but every time the pressure was lifted, Pharaoh went back to his natural hard-hearted self.

God softened and hardened Pharaoh's heart, not by some mind control nor by overriding Pharaoh's free will, but by applying and removing external pressure upon a proud and hard-hearted ruler whom he knew extremely well. This is why Scripture tells us that Pharaoh was responsible for hardening his own heart in response to God's actions (Exod. 7:13; 8:15, 19, 32; 9:7, 34). Even later pagan Philistine priests understood that Pharaoh was accountable for his actions at the time of the exodus:

> Why then do you harden your hearts as the Egyptians and Pharaoh hardened their hearts? When He did mighty things among them, did they not let the people go, that they might depart? (1 Sam. 6:6)

God raised up Pharaoh for a great purpose related to a promise he gave to Abraham. But Pharaoh had no reason to complain. He had not been treated unfairly, and all his decisions were made by his own free will.[1] He was an evil man who had killed the children of Israel and harshly oppressed the Israelites. He fell under the righteous judgment of God because of his actions (Exod. 6:6; 7:4; 12:12). King Sihon and King Og would have been the same.

Hardening and Softening

The apostle Paul referenced what happened to Pharaoh and notes that it is God's prerogative as Creator to work as he wills with his creation:

> What shall we say then? Is there unrighteousness with God? Certainly not! For He says to Moses, "I will have mercy on whomever I will have mercy, and I will have compassion on whomever I will have compassion." So then it is not of him who wills, nor of him who runs, but of God who shows mercy. For the Scripture says to the Pharaoh, "For this very purpose I have raised you up, that I may show My power in you, and that My name may be declared in all the earth." Therefore He has mercy on whom He wills, and whom He wills He hardens. (Rom. 9:14–18)

Some read a concept of randomness into Paul's statement as if God is a despotic leader who rewards or kills according to his mood of the moment. But God does not operate randomly according to a whimsical fancy, as some might interpret these verses. God acts according to his *will*, and his will operates in line with his predictable and understandable character and righteousness. God does not harden righteous people. Hardening occurs

---

[1] Note that Pharaoh himself knew that he had personally sinned by his actions (Exod. 9:27, 34).

through the "deceitfulness of sin" (Heb. 3:13).

God's own people of Israel hardened their hearts against God's will, and God was angry with them (Ps. 81:10–13; Zech. 7:11–13; Heb. 3:8–11). It was not what he wanted.

God could have softened Israel's hardened hearts, and he did many times. But softening a person's heart is usually a painful process. The harder a person's heart, the more external pressure is needed to soften that heart. Multiple times, God brought calamity on the nation of Israel to soften them and wake them up. And each time it worked. But they would soon forget God, and their hard hearts would return. In the end God left them in their stupor, and they were taken into captivity (Jer. 11:14; Rom. 11:7–10). This same hard-heartedness was still evident in the Jews at the time of Jesus centuries later (Matt. 13:13–15). God in his great wisdom then decided to use Israel's hardened hearts to bring salvation to the gentiles (Acts 28:24–28).

God will always respond to a soft heart.

It is God's prerogative to harden or soften according to his will. But it is a will that is always righteous and just. No one can ever accuse God of hardening them against their will. It is comforting to know that God will always respond to a soft heart:

> But on this one will I look: on him who is poor and of a contrite spirit, and who trembles at My word. (Isa. 66:2)

All this reinforces why a soft and humble heart is a prerequisite of the kingdom of God (Matt. 18:3–4).

Hard-to-Understand Mosaic Laws

Incline your ear to wisdom, and apply your heart to understanding.
—Proverbs 2:2

The majority of the laws of Moses make perfect sense once we seek to understand the cultural context and apply the consistent values of God.

However, a small number of statutes and judgments remain difficult to understand. These are laws that seem at odds with other laws, overly punitive, or inconsistent with the underlying moral principles expressed elsewhere. The difficulty in understanding them most likely relates to having incomplete historical data on the cultural and religious practices of the ancient world. The problem cannot relate to any inconsistency in God's standards. The premise Jesus held to—that the entirety of the law was based on truth, love, justice, mercy, and faith—must be our starting point.

While we can attempt to explain these passages today, they may remain obscure until more historical information comes to light.

Woman's Hand "Cut Off"

The book of Deuteronomy presents a strange scenario accompanied by a harsh penalty that seems out of line with the standards of justice reflected elsewhere in the law:

> If two men fight together, and the wife of one draws near to rescue her husband from the hand of the one attacking him, and puts out her hand and seizes him by the genitals, then you shall cut off her hand; your eye shall not pity her. (Deut. 25:11–12)

To consider that such an unlikely incident might actually occur is one matter, but to have the need for such a written judgment is even harder to understand. For this reason, it is more likely that this judgment (like so many others) represents a teaching principle of law.[1] To be consistent, this judgment must be compared with the other *lex talionus* provisions in the law.

Recall the earlier *eye for an eye* chapter, where it was shown that the saying was not to be interpreted literally but existed to ensure that compensation was to be proportional to the harm inflicted. The emphasis on *not pitying* was also previously explained. It was a directive to the judge to be objective and not allow their decision to be swayed by emotions.

---

[1] Jesus also spoke about cutting off hands in a symbolic sense (Matt. 18:8).

In this case, there would be the need to determine the cost to the woman of the damage she did to a man's genitals. The law gives the judge direction by putting the value of the genitals as comparable to the loss of a hand. This value could be used to determine the level of monetary or otherwise compensation. While not entirely satisfactory, the explanation is consistent with other sections of the law.

Some commentaries have suggested that the word translated "hand" may instead be referring to a woman's hair and a punishment of being shaved. That interpretation is left for scholars to debate. (Refer footnote.[2])

Barred for Generations

Throughout the law there is a strong emphasis on impartiality and equality. There is also the principle of a child not being held accountable for the sins of their fathers. Yet one section of law seems to contradict these principles. It stipulates that certain people are to be barred from entering "the assembly of the Lord" for multiple generations because of their ethnicity or family problems:

> He who is emasculated by crushing or mutilation shall not enter the assembly of the LORD. One of illegitimate birth (of a forbidden union)[3] shall not enter the assembly of the LORD; even to the tenth generation none of his descendants shall enter the assembly of the LORD. An Ammonite or Moabite shall not enter the assembly of the LORD; even to the tenth generation none of his descendants shall enter the assembly of the LORD forever. (Deut. 23:1–3)

At the outset, note that this law is only related to the male lineage and not female. The masculine references used within the law confirm that. Neither is it directed at someone who may have a wife of another heritage. Consider the example of King David. David's great grandmother was Ruth the Moabitess, which was less than the ten generations removed from a Moabite ancestor, confirming the law being directed at males only (Ruth 4:21–22).

The question that must be answered is what the term "assembly of the Lord" refers to in this context. The law elsewhere states that a stranger who turns to God can become like a native-born (Exod. 12:48). Isaiah also confirms that foreigners and eunuchs who turned to the Lord were most welcome (Isa. 56:3–

---

[2] Bibliog: (Grisanti 2012, p702), Bibliog: (Benner 2022, Deut. 25:11-12)
[3] The Hebrew word *mamzer*, translated as "illegitimate or of forbidden union" in some Bible versions, is only used twice in the Old Testament and is of doubtful meaning.

7). And we have the example of Zelek, an Ammonite, who became one of David's mighty men (1 Chron. 11:39). There were also numerous foreigners in Israel whom God esteemed. All this seems to work *against* the idea that the meaning of the term "assembly of the Lord" in this chapter is a general reference to the entirety of Israel.[4]

There are several scholarly opinions on how this law is to be interpreted. One explanation is to interpret the term "assembly of the Lord" in the context of Deuteronomy 23 as a reference to holding office in Israel, not to general participation. This interpretation would be consistent with other aspects of the law where specific attributes were necessary to be eligible for certain leadership roles—for example, only Levites could fulfill priestly roles, only a native-born Israelite could be king, and those with certain defects could not be priests.[5]

Centuries later, Nehemiah interpreted this law to mean those of mixed heritage must be separated from the Israelites (Neh. 13:1–3). But the specific example he noted was Tobiah the Ammonite (an unbeliever), who was wrongly given residence in the temple precinct (vv. 4–8). Tobiah opposed the reconstruction of Jerusalem and had fought Nehemiah all along (Neh. 4:7). The general separation of the mixed multitude may have been overzealous on Nehemiah's part because God had always welcomed believing foreigners to be part of Israel. But the situation in Nehemiah's day may have involved *unbelieving* foreigners who would have caused serious problems for the fledgling reconstituted nation.

Rebellious Son

One particular Mosaic law prescribes a harsh punishment for a son who blatantly rebelled against his parents:

> If a man has a stubborn and rebellious son who will not obey the voice of his father or the voice of his mother, and who, when they have chastened him, will not heed them, then his father and his mother shall take hold of him and bring him out to the elders of his city, to the gate of his city. And they shall say to the elders of his city, "This son of ours is stubborn and rebellious; he will not obey our voice; he is a glutton and a drunkard." Then all the men of his city shall stone him to death with stones; so you shall put away the evil from among you, and all Israel shall hear and fear. (Deut. 21:18–21)

---

[4] Bibliog: (Grisanti 2012, p680)
[5] Discussed in the earlier chapter *The Priesthood*.

While this judgment reinforces just how seriously the family hierarchy was to be taken, it seems excessive in its response. But there are some important points to be noted:

Firstly, it is written with the most extreme case in mind. For parents to even consider such a drastic action would be extraordinary. Secondly, *both* the father and mother had to agree to bring such a charge. Thirdly, we note that parents were not allowed to act alone. They had no right to take the life of their children as was the case in other ancient cultures.[6] They had to come before the elders of the city for a judgment. When they did, they would need to prove the case that their son was indeed worthy of death. It was not a foregone conclusion.

While this law strongly reinforced the command to honor parents, not one instance of such a drastic punishment ever being applied is recorded in Israelite or Jewish history.[7]

Altars and Sacrificial Locations

In the book of Deuteronomy, we find a clear instruction that sacrifices were to be only offered at the central sanctuary once Israel dwelt in the promised land:

> Take heed to yourself that you do not offer your burnt offerings in every place that you see; but in the place which the Lord chooses, in one of your tribes, there you shall offer your burnt offerings, and there you shall do all that I command you. (Deut. 12:13–14)

In what appears to be a violation of this instruction, we see a number of God's servants in the post-conquest years offering individual sacrifices at places other than the central sanctuary. Notable examples include Gideon, Manoah, Samuel, David and Elijah. At various times these men offered sacrifices away from the tabernacle. God was clearly supportive, and in some cases specifically instructed them to do so (Judg. 6:25–26; 13:16–19; 1 Sam. 16:2–3; 2 Sam. 24:18).

An explanation for the seeming contradictory behavior may be found in a command God gave earlier to all the Israelites at Mount Sinai. Here God made allowance for a simple style of stone and earthen altar on which an individual could offer special sacrifices to God:

---

[6] Infanticide was a right of parents in many ancient cultures Bibliog: (Obladen 2016).
[7] Bibliog: (Prager 2022, Deuteronomy 329-331)

> Then the Lord said to Moses, "Thus you shall say to the children of Israel: ...An altar of earth you shall make for Me, and you shall sacrifice on it your burnt offerings and your peace offerings, your sheep and your oxen. In every place where I record My name I will come to you, and I will bless you. And if you make Me an altar of stone, you shall not build it of hewn stone; for if you use your tool on it, you have profaned it. Nor shall you go up by steps to My altar, that your nakedness may not be exposed on it." (Exod. 20:22–26).

The tabernacle with its major bronze altar was constructed only a few months after this regulation was given at Mount Sinai. It is very clear in the Mosaic law that once the tabernacle was constructed, all formal and official sacrifices and celebrations were to be centered around the sanctuary just as Deuteronomy 12 confirms. Was this Exodus 20 command only given for the short interim period until the tabernacle was operational? Or was it a standing provision that allowed an individual, at special times, to offer thanks to God via sacrifice? [8]

It would seem reasonable to assume, based on the scope and importance given to this Exodus 20 law of sacrifice, that it was a permanent provision that could be invoked when needed. The very design of these humble altars did not present any competition to the formal sacrificial system and statutory holy day events held at the sanctuary. Individuals were clearly commanded to go to the central location and present to the priests for all such occasions.

It is also apparent that God's design for these temporary simple stone and earthen altars, with no steps, was in direct opposition to the pagan "high" places. (Refer footnote.[9])

Jubilee Release of Servants

Scripture presents a quandary in the year of Jubilee. The Jubilee (fiftieth) year is noted as a joyous time when those in servitude are released (Lev. 25:10, 39–40). On first consideration, the release of servants in the fiftieth year would seem redundant since Hebrew servants could only be held six years and would have been released the previous (forty-ninth) year as part of the annual sabbatical provisions (Deut. 15:12). It is doubtful, as some have suggested, that the Jubilee release related to those servants engaged in the intervening twelve

---

[8] Critical scholars have generally interpreted the tension between these verses in Exodus 20 and Deuteronomy 12 as support for the Documentary Hypothesis theory, denying the authorship of Moses.
[9] Benjamin Foreman supports the ongoing coexistence of Exodus 20 and Deuteronomy 12 sacrifices in a 2019 *Tyndale House Bulletin* journal article. Bibliog: (Foreman 2019)

months. The wording of the Jubilee also denotes a far more dramatic concept of liberty and freedom.

The dilemma is resolved when we understand the intent of the Jubilee Year. The Jubilee was focused on land servitude and release, whereas the focus of the annual sabbaths were on general debt servitude release.

Over the course of fifty years, landowners may have lost control of their property. Some may have sold the long-term lease of their land by choice. Others may have been forced to sell due to financial difficulty, ill health, mismanagement, drought, misfortune, or family reasons, etc. Instead of being masters, they would become a hired hand, possibly on their own property, without the right to the profits of the land.

The Jubilee Year was, in a very real sense, a year of freedom and release for these former landowners:

> And if one of your brethren who dwells by you becomes poor, and sells himself to you, you shall not compel him to serve as a slave. As a hired servant and a sojourner he shall be with you, and shall serve you until the Year of Jubilee. And then he shall depart from you—he and his children with him—and shall return to his own family. He shall return to the possession of his fathers. (Lev. 25:39–41)

The Jubilee would have been a dramatic once-in-a-lifetime event for all family landowners—to no longer to be hired servants but once again masters of their own family lands. This is the freedom from servitude the Jubilee is referring to. (Refer footnote.[10])

---

[10] Michael Harbin presents a case in support of this interpretation in a 2012 *Tyndale House Bulletin* journal article. Bibliog: (Harbin 2012).

New Testament Terminology

Paul ... speaking in them of these things, in which are some things hard to understand. —2 Peter 3:15–16

There are a number of New Testament phrases and terms that, on first reading, might give the false impression that the writer was disparaging the Mosaic law. Most of these questionable areas are attributed to Paul, who Peter confirmed was a complex writer and, at times, hard to understand (2 Pet. 3:15–16).

To ensure a correct understanding of historical terminology, we must consider the context, the audience, and whether the explanation is consistent with the broader perspective of Scripture.

A review of some of those commonly noted expressions follows.

"Curse of the Law"

In his passionate explanation to the Galatians on how no one is justified by works, Paul used a phrase that has been misunderstood. Paul quoted from Deuteronomy, where it states that a person who does *not* do the things written in the law will be cursed:

> For as many as are of the works of the law are under the curse; for it is written, "Cursed is everyone who does *not* continue in all things which are written in the book of the law, to do them." (Gal. 3:10; see also Deut. 27:26)

The curse is the penalty or sentence that comes on a person for breaking the law. Paul continues, stating that faith, *not* law-keeping, justifies a person, and he referenced the Old Testament prophet Habakkuk and the book of Leviticus to support his case:

> *But that no one is justified by the law in the sight of God is evident*, for "the just shall live by faith." Yet the law is not of faith, but "the man who does them shall live by them." (Gal. 3:11–12; see also Hab. 2:4; Lev. 18:5)

Paul then explained that the curse (or penalty) is removed—not by works but by Jesus' sacrifice on the cross:

> Christ has redeemed us from the curse of the law, having become a curse for us (for it is written, "Cursed is everyone who hangs on a

tree"), that the blessing of Abraham might come upon the gentiles in Christ Jesus, that we might receive the promise of the Spirit through faith. (Gal. 3:13–14)

The curse Paul was referring to cannot be the law itself because the curse came on those who did *not* do what the law prescribed (v. 10). As Paul noted, a man who followed them will *live* by them (v. 12; Lev. 18:5). To otherwise think that God gave a law that cursed those who kept it is not theologically sound.

"Weak and Beggarly Elements"

In his epistle to the Galatians, Paul used a term sometimes equated with the law of Moses:

> But then, indeed, when you did not know God, you served those which by nature are not gods. But now after you have known God, or rather are known by God, how is it that you turn again to the *weak and beggarly elements*, to which you desire again to be in bondage? You observe days and months and seasons and years. I am afraid for you, lest I have labored for you in vain. (Gal. 4:8–11)

The English Standard Version (ESV) translates "weak and beggarly elements" as "weak and worthless elementary principles of the world." The New International Version (NIV) uses the phrase "weak and miserable forces."

It is hard to imagine any scenario where Paul would describe the holy days and festivals that God gave Israel—the ones David rejoiced in and Jesus himself observed—in such disrespectful terms. Paul elsewhere spoke positively about the law (Rom. 7:12).

It is far more reasonable and contextually sound to deduce that Paul was referring to certain gentiles in Galatia who were returning to their old pagan ways that had formerly enslaved them. As Paul said at the outset, "Indeed, when you did not know God, you served those which by nature are not gods" (Gal. 4:8).

"Yoke of Bondage"

Paul uses a phrase in Galatians that is sometimes cited to support the idea that Paul thought of the law of Moses as burdensome and oppressive. The term is "yoke of bondage", and it's often taken out of context:

> Stand fast therefore in the liberty by which Christ has made us free, and do not be entangled again with a *yoke of bondage*. (Gal. 5:1)

The context here is not the broader law but specifically the wrong Pharisaical idea that a person needed to be circumcised to be *justified* in the sight of God (vv. 2–6). This was a part of the ongoing struggle Paul had with "those of the circumcision"—who believed that physical works could somehow make a person right in the sight of God.[1] Paul stated that attempting to use the law in this way would *alienate* one from Christ and his grace (v. 4).

This yoke was again the subject when the apostles came together in Jerusalem to discuss the matter of circumcision as related to salvation:

> And certain *men* came down from Judea and taught the brethren, "Unless you are circumcised according to the custom of Moses, you cannot be saved."
>
> Now therefore, why do you test God by putting a yoke on the neck of the disciples which neither our fathers nor we were able to bear? (Acts 15:1, 10)

Circumcision of itself cannot be the yoke of bondage being referred to here. Circumcision has been practiced for millennia, right up to modern times. It was of itself easy to bear. And neither were other ceremonial aspects of the written law "unbearable," as we previously reviewed.

In the broader context of the New Testament, it is evident that the unbearable yoke was the false idea that a person could justify themselves in the sight of God by their works. This was a key tenet of the Pharisees' teaching, one that Jesus had previously criticized (Matt. 23:4). Their tedious interpretations of the law were an attempt to show God just how "righteous" they were (Luke 18:11). The very idea of a person having to continually "prove" to God how "good" they are would definitely be an unbearable burden.

"Handwriting of Requirements That was Against Us"

Depending on the translation being used, a verse from the book of Colossians has an expression that can be confusing:

> And you, being dead in your trespasses and the uncircumcision of your flesh, He has made alive together with Him, having forgiven you all trespasses, having wiped out the *handwriting of requirements that was*

---

[1] Justification by works is an inherently illogical idea. In no legal context can future law-keeping cover past offenses.

against us, which was contrary to us. And He has taken it out of the way, having nailed it to the cross. (Col. 2:13–14 NKJV)

Some have interpreted the "handwriting of requirements" that were "against us" and "contrary to us" as the law of Moses. But as we have amply seen, God did not give the law of Moses for negative reasons. He was not "against" the people of Israel. He gave them his teachings "for their good" (Deut. 6:24; 10:13).

The confusion arises from the expression "handwriting of requirements." It comes from a technical Greek term not used elsewhere in the New Testament. It refers to a legal "certificate of indebtedness." Other modern English translations make the meaning of the verse clear:

> Having forgiven us all our trespasses, by canceling the record of debt that stood against us with its legal demands (vv. 13–14 ESV)

The New International Version (NIV) phrases it as "canceling the charge of our legal indebtedness."

It was not the law of Moses that was contrary to us, but our sins. Paul likens our sins to a record of legal debt against God that we cannot on our own hope to clear. Peter made a similar comment (Acts 3:19). We would be dead in our trespasses except for Jesus clearing that debt by his sacrifice on the cross. The record of our sins was symbolically nailed to the cross with Jesus as he took upon himself the sins of the world. Jesus' death and resurrection gives us hope of a new life which we otherwise could never deserve.

"Enmity Contained in Ordinances"

In chapter 2 of his letter to the Ephesians, Paul specifically addresses the gentile Christians. He writes of the former "enmity" between Jew and gentile that was created by a *"wall of separation"* and *"commandments contained in ordinances"*:

> For He Himself is our peace, who has made both one, and has broken down the middle wall of separation, having abolished in His flesh the enmity, *that is,* the law of commandments *contained* in ordinances, so as to create in Himself one new man *from* the two, *thus* making peace, and that He might reconcile them both to God in one body through the cross, thereby putting to death the enmity. (Eph. 2: 14–16)

Some have confused this "wall" and these "ordinances" with the written law of Moses. But as we have highlighted multiple times[2], the written law of Moses did not create any enmity between Jew and gentile. It decreed one standard of law for all people in the land (Lev. 24:22), and included clear directives that gentiles were to be loved as one of their own (Lev. 19:34). The Mosaic law also welcomed gentiles to worship and sacrifice to the God of Israel (Num. 15:14–16).

The set of rules that treated gentiles as second-class citizens was an entirely man-made construct that developed after the Babylonian captivity. In their misguided zeal for "purity", the Jewish religious leaders created segregation ordinances that resulted in a great divide between Jew and gentile. This gulf was further reinforced by a physical wall of separation created within the Second Temple precinct—a wall which the First Temple did not have.

Through his death and sacrifice, Jesus removed these man-made barriers between Jew and gentile and brought the entire church together as one unified body (Gal. 3:28). In this way, Jesus restored the original intent of the law—which was designed to be a unifying force to bring all people to the true God.

Peter came to understand that this was the way God has always been:

> In truth I perceive that God shows no partiality. But in every nation whoever fears Him and works righteousness is accepted by Him. (Acts 10:34–35)

---

[2] Refer subject index: wall of separation; gentiles, segregation

PART 8: Final Perspectives

This final section presents some summary thoughts on why God gave the law in the format that he did, and why his covenant with Israel failed to achieve God's objectives the first time around.

It concludes with a brief look at the role of the law in the future kingdom of God and its relevance for a modern Christian. Knowing the consistent character of God, it will not be surprising to learn that the foundational principles and teachings God espoused thousands of years ago still have application for all people and for all times.

Why Was It Written This way?

The spirits of the prophets are subject to the prophets. —1 Corinthians 14:32

As noted in an earlier chapter, how the Mosaic law code is presented in the books of Moses appears disorganized to our modern minds. It does not conform to the standard we would expect today for such an important work.

We would at least expect related sections of law to be grouped logically, but often, they are not. Narrative is often intertwined with law code, format varies, and topics are sometimes hard to follow. It has been said that in some ways, reading the law of Moses is like reading the Congressional Record of the United States Congress or the transcript of Parliament,[1] where formal dialogue on law is intermixed with comments and side discussions.

Because of the irregular structure, some scholars have concluded that this points to the law being delivered over a long period of time by different writers and suggests the work of men rather than that of a sovereign deity. But is it valid to critique an ancient work against modern standards? Are there other explanations as to why the law of Moses might be presented to us the way it is?

Some observations and speculation might be helpful.

God's Ways Are Not Our Ways

An often-ignored foundational point on this topic is the understanding that the true God is *totally unlike* the God of most people's imagination. He doesn't do things how we might naturally expect: "My thoughts are not your thoughts, nor are your ways my ways" the Lord says (Isa. 55:8). The whole idea that God's primary method of communication throughout the ages would be via flawed human beings is nothing like we would naturally expect from so great a being. Why didn't he deliver his message directly himself?

> *The true God is totally unlike the God of most people's imagination.*

Consider the prophets of old: Despite having untold numbers of angelic messengers at his command, God primarily chose men who were often far from perfect to deliver his witness and warning to the nations. Angels rarely

---

[1] Called "Hansard" in some Commonwealth countries.

spoke. And some of his prophets—like Elijah, Jeremiah, and Ezekiel—were unusual, to say the least. They were not the greats of the world, yet God chose them to be his representatives. We see the same pattern with the Hebrew Scriptures. God chose to deliver his written revelation to man by using multiple human writers across a period of hundreds of years.

It is the same in the New Testament era. We would not naturally expect a wild-looking wilderness character like John the Baptist to be the envoy of the long-awaited Messiah. Later, when Jesus declared he would build his church, he again chose a motley group to do the job. These men, including fishermen, a zealot, and a tax collector of all people, were not the greats of their day. They often struggled to understand what Jesus wanted of them. Yet the church was built, and we can thank these men and others for the written testimony of the New Testament Scriptures. Jesus himself never wrote a word.

It's not at all intuitive that God would do things this way.

When considering the law of Moses, the same recurring pattern is evident. Despite its importance, the law is not presented in a way we might naturally expect. Neither was it supernaturally given to Israel already written. God instead chose Moses—a reluctant messenger who initially pushed back at God's calling—to be the intercessor between God and the nation. God spoke the words to Moses, and Moses transcribed them for posterity. Other than the Ten Commandments, which God wrote himself on stone, we can thank Moses for writing the first books of the Bible. And the result reflects both God and the style of his human messenger.

Inspiration, not Control

How did God ensure that these human writers would pass on the correct message? While all Scripture is "God-breathed" (2 Tim. 3:16 ESV), inspiration did not involve God taking control of the minds and hands of his prophets and forcing them to structure and format words precisely to his bidding. God has never operated in that way. As Paul insightfully wrote, "The spirits of the prophets are subject to the prophets" (1 Cor. 14:32), meaning each human agent has a sovereign mind and spirit that God respects and doesn't override. While he grants his Holy Spirit to *enhance* a person's abilities, the Holy Spirit is a *helper*, not a controller (John 14:26). The Holy Spirit does not "possess" a person or force them against their will. God inspired his prophets, but then left them to present the testimony in their own words.

The influence of the individual sovereign mind of the writer is clearly evident throughout all the books of the Bible. We see the different personalities of the authors coming through. Their backgrounds, education levels, language proficiencies, locations, professions, etc., all influenced the style and format of their writing. Highly educated Isaiah is called the Shakespeare of the prophets in contrast to the simpler style of Amos the farmer. Paul's writing is complex and academic, different from James and others. Luke's testimony is the personal testimony of a physician. David's words arose from his unique personality and perspective of God. God inspired their written words, but they were the author's own.

> *God inspired his prophets, but then left them to present the testimony in their own words.*

The books of Moses are the same. While the content reflects the hand of God, the format and style reflect the personal involvement of Moses and others. Bible scholar Michael Heiser summarizes the process of inspiration well:

> We need to embrace a Providential view of inspiration. Inspiration is not an event. It's a process guided by Providence knowing that God made his own choices in terms of the hands that would touch the text and produce it in its final form for us. And it has its own goals. All of this occurred under God's watchful eye and produced something he was satisfied with, because it accomplished his goals. God doesn't care if Scripture as it was inscripturated (as it was written down) specifically addresses all our questions. He cares only that it accomplishes his ends.[2]

How God inspires goes a long way toward explaining why we have what we have. If we have any criticism of the format or style of the Mosaic law, we should realize that Moses was not perfect—but he did accomplish what God desired of him, and we have proof of that in our hands today: words that have changed the world.

Recording of the Ancient Text

Another point that may explain some of the seemingly "disordered" sections of the early books of Moses is the circumstances surrounding their origin and how the writings have been handled and passed down since the original autographs.

---

[2] Bibliog: (Heiser 2019, Exodus 21-23 Part 1)

The record tells us that Moses wrote over *multiple decades*. God gave the original law code at Mount Sinai, and Moses wrote down what he received at that time (Exod. 24:4). Forty years later, as he neared death, he was still adding to the record (Deut. 31:9, 22). Sometime in the interim period, God also asked Moses to record the narrative of Israel's journey from Egypt to the promised land (Num. 33:2).

Moses also may have drawn on relevant written testimony when it was available, just as any author would do today. Genesis, for example, seems to reference earlier genealogical records. Scholars have observed notations (Heb. *toledoths*) in the book, which point to some original records Moses may have drawn on to write or assemble the book of Genesis.[3] A *Book of the Wars of the Lord* is also mentioned in Numbers (Num. 21:14–15). It would have been Moses' responsibility to bring together these earlier records (including oral records) while maintaining the integrity of the earlier authors.

Considering the leadership role Moses had during this time and the many other matters he had to deal with, Moses may have only written as he was able. The point here is to acknowledge that Moses' writing would not have been a logical uninterrupted progression from start to finish. And the text we have confirms that. It appears to have been written piecemeal, and multiple drafts may have been done. Editorial comments were also added after Moses, including the story of his death in Deuteronomy 34.

> *Moses' writing would not have been a logical uninterrupted progression from start to finish.*

Transmission of the Text

It's also relevant to consider how the text was transmitted and its order. The original medium Moses used (either papyrus or parchment) had limitations on scroll size.[4] Scrolls could potentially be ordered differently as they were rearranged, and future copies and translation work done.

Before his death, Moses handed his writings to Joshua, who made copies of them. Joshua was probably the one who added the record of Moses' death and

---

[3] There are 11 such structural notations in Genesis: 2:4 (heavens and earth); 5:1(Adam); 6:9(Noah); 10:1(sons of Noah); 11:10(Shem); 11:27(Terah); 25:12(Ishmael); 25:19(Isaac); 36:1,9(Esau); 37:2(Jacob).

[4] The original medium Moses wrote on is unknown. Both papyrus and parchment were known in ancient Egypt. Moses most likely carried writing instruments and materials from Egypt along with the many other tools the tabernacle artisans had available in the wilderness.

other edits (Josh. 8:32; 24:26).[5] Then later unknown editors, possibly Ezra, would have overseen the conversion from the ancient Paleo-Hebrew script into the Hebrew mostly seen in the Dead Sea Scrolls. Again, this may have further impacted the text's style, format, and order before the final Old Testament canon.

It is easy to criticize the format and style of the books of Moses. But when considering its origins in ancient times and what was involved, we will do well to appreciate the enormous effort that went into preserving the ancient text we have today.

God Wants to Be Sought Out

One final thought. Considering the law code's broad scope across moral, civil, and ceremonial matters, it is extremely concise. God could have easily outlined far more detail to Moses and created a far more extensive law code—more in line with the style of the Jewish Talmud or like our own detailed national law codes. Instead, God chose to present his principles and laws *concisely*, which at times has the tendency to make aspects of the law seem trivial to the casual observer.

While there are benefits in this conciseness for preservation and transmission through the ages, it more importantly speaks volumes about God's perspective of man and the nature of the relationship he desires. He knew that understanding such an important document presented in this way would require thought, meditation, and cultural and situational interpretation. Simply reading the letter of the law would never impart deep understanding. God made humans in his own image and had full confidence that a person with the right heart and attitude would be able to discern his intent. It confirms God's fundamental respect for the intelligence of man.

As stated many times, God has never been interested in a shallow, ritualistic connection with people. He has always desired a deep relationship of the heart and mind. Such a relationship requires passion, effort, and an eagerness to seek God. He has always wanted his people to seek him with diligence, and he rewards those who do so with understanding:

> Seek the LORD your God, and you will find Him if you seek Him with

---

[5] Acknowledging Moses as the author of the books of the Pentateuch should not be understood too narrowly. Moses was the person who received the words of the law from God and wrote them down, but that did not preclude scribal help or later editing of the accompanying narrative. Anachronisms in the early books confirm that later scribes updated the text. God was more than capable of ensuring that the text continued to meet his purpose.

> all your heart and with all your soul. (Deut. 4:29)
>
> And you will seek Me and find Me, when you search for Me with all your heart. (Jer. 29:13)

The words Moses wrote down for us admirably achieve the purposes God set for them, and we can be grateful to Moses and all the faithful men and women who followed and helped preserve the text we have with us today.

> Moses indeed was faithful in all His house as a servant, for a testimony of those things which would be spoken afterward. (Heb. 3:5)

Why the Old Covenant Failed

Because [I found] fault with them ... because they did not continue in My covenant, and I disregarded them, says the Lord. —Hebrews 8:7–9

Much has been written on the "impossibility" for an individual to keep the law of Moses, implying the law was doomed to fail from the outset. Most comments along these lines are based on the false premise that the complicated and contradictory laws of Judaism were, in fact, the laws of Moses, which they most certainly were not. As we have amply seen, the actual written law of Moses was *not* impossible to keep. It was a positive and empowering system of personal responsibility and light governance.

But that aside, there is an even bigger underlying false premise: one that implies that an individual must be able to keep a law perfectly for that law code to be of value. This is a patently silly idea. *Of course* it was impossible for a human to keep the law of Moses perfectly. It is also impossible for a human to keep Jesus' Sermon on the Mount teachings perfectly. Neither is it possible for an individual to keep the law of their own nation perfectly. Humans will always make mistakes, no matter the system of law. But knowing that all people will slip and fail at times is no excuse to reject a sound structure of law.

> *Of course it was impossible for a human being to keep the law of Moses perfectly. It is also impossible to keep Jesus' Sermon on the Mount teachings perfectly.*

God was under no illusions that Israel would be perfect. He has always been rational and pragmatic. He knew every individual human would sin at some stage. Many of the "heroes" of faith had spectacular moral failures. *For this reason* the merciful God of Israel built a system of forgiveness into the law. The tabernacle and the mercy seat were central to the worship system. Atoning sacrifices were available to all, and God promised to forgive (e.g., Lev. 4:20).

The Fault Lay with the People

God himself tells us exactly why the old covenant failed. It was not due to his neglect, and neither was it the fault of the enlightened law system he had graciously given them. The fault lay with the people:

> For if that first covenant had been faultless, then no place would have been sought for a second. Because *[I found] fault with them ... because*

they did not continue in My covenant, and I disregarded them, says the Lord. (Heb. 8:7–9)

What God seemed surprised at was not that Israel would sin, but the level at which they rejected him. He demonstrated that he was more than willing to forgive or overlook their mistakes and did so many times. But their ongoing lack of belief and stubborn rejection of him for centuries, pushed the long-suffering God to a breaking point. They were indeed a "stiff-necked people," as he called them (Exod. 32:9).

> *God himself tells us exactly why the old covenant failed. The fault lay with the people.*

The people's hard-heartedness and lack of trust in God led to their downfall, *despite* God's mercy and special care:

> Then the LORD said to Moses: "How long will these people reject Me? And how long will they *not believe Me*, with all the signs which I have performed among them? (Num. 14:11)

> I will make a new covenant ... not according to the covenant that I made with their fathers ... My covenant which they broke, *though I was a husband to them,* says the LORD (Jer. 31:31–32)

> Therefore the LORD said: "Inasmuch as these people draw near with their mouths and honor Me with their lips, but have *removed their hearts far from Me.* (Isa. 29:13)

Jesus spoke on this topic on multiple occasions, likening Israel to those invited to a great wedding but who despised the incredible opportunity they were being offered (Matt. 21:33–41; 22:1–14). His cry over Jerusalem sums up God's yearning for his people to only turn back to him:

> O Jerusalem, Jerusalem, the one who kills the prophets and stones those who are sent to her! How often I wanted to gather your children together, as a hen gathers her chicks under her wings, but *you were not willing*! (Matt. 23:37)

Was Israel Doomed to Fail?

Some suggest that there was no real hope for Israel to remain faithful to God and that the people were doomed to fail from the start. One of Moses' comments is used to support this idea:

> Yet the LORD has not given you a heart to perceive and eyes to see and ears to hear, to this very day. (Deut. 29:4)

At face value, this verse seems to imply that God somehow held Israel in a double bind: On one hand, being angry with them for their disloyalty, but at the same time, blocking them from succeeding. But a God of truth, love, mercy, and grace does not operate this way. As we've seen throughout the narrative, God did not withhold anything from these people. His overwhelming love had been evident since Egypt and he expressed his longing for his people to put their trust in him (Deut. 5:29; 32:29; Ps. 81:13). Moses was simply referring to the negative inclination of the people's hearts that were still evident after forty years of wandering (Deut. 31:21).

> *God did not withhold anything from these people. His overwhelming love had been evident since Egypt.*

The Bible consistently teaches the *individual* to oversee and manage their own heart. Israel *blocked* or *hardened* their hearts against God and prevented the words of God from penetrating deep inside, and the people remained that way for centuries (Jer. 5:21; Ezek. 12:2). The entire context of Moses' summary comments in Deuteronomy chapters 29 and 30 was a warning against having such a heart. As David later wrote:

> Do not harden your hearts, as in the rebellion, as in the day of trial in the wilderness, when your fathers tested Me; they tried Me, though they saw My work. (Ps. 95:8–9)

It was their own decision to reject God, and his wrath came down upon them accordingly:

> But *they* refused to heed, shrugged their shoulders, and stopped their ears so that they could not hear. Yes, *they* made their hearts like flint, refusing to hear the law and the words which the LORD of hosts had sent by His Spirit through the former prophets. Thus great wrath came from the LORD of hosts. (Zech. 7:11–12)

Parallels with Our Society

It doesn't take a lot of imagination to see the parallels between the decline of ancient Israel and our own Christian heritage societies today. Just as Israel lost sight of their Creator and turned to worthless idols, we are also now rejecting—even despising—the knowledge of God and are working to erase him from our culture. We are replacing the true God with the gods of materialism and narcissistic ideologies.

Other nations are finding this rejection of our Christian values puzzling. So many countries have admired and been attracted to our system of law, freedoms, and values, yet we are now trampling on what has made us strong. Instead of acknowledging that our nations' fundamental strength and vitality originated from our Judeo-Christian heritage and the rule of law outlined in the Bible, our society is increasingly looking for answers to our problems elsewhere. But we won't find them because absolute truth comes only from our Creator.

The same happened to ancient Israel. For centuries other nations stood in awe of the God of Israel and the name of Yahweh struck fear into the pagan cultures (Josh. 2:9; 2 Chron. 14:14; 17:10; 20:29, etc.). Yet in the end, Israel became a morally bankrupt people despised by their enemies. Just as it did not work out well for Israel, neither will it work out well for our Western nations today.

The Law and the Kingdom of God

Now it shall come to pass in the latter days that the mountain of the LORD's *house shall be established on the top of the mountains ... and peoples shall flow to it. ... For out of Zion the law shall go forth, and the word of the* LORD *from Jerusalem.*
—Micah 4:1–2

The most common perspective of the law of Moses is that of a system belonging to a bygone era with no relevance beyond the time of Jesus. But Moses and the prophets taught otherwise. They prophesied of a future time when God's kingdom would be established on this earth and the same teachings and values Moses taught would be spread beyond Israel to all nations. It is a clear demonstration of the timeless nature of the enlightened law of God when its true perspective is understood.

Foretold Long Ago

Even before they entered the promised land, Moses could see the people's propensity to go astray, and he prophesied what would happen in the latter days of the nation. He foretold the curses for disobedience that would come upon Israel and how they would be taken from the land and become a byword among the nations (Deut. 4:27–30; 29:24–28).

But Moses ended his final sermon on an encouraging note. Even though the people would forget the true God, he would not forget them. Their scattering would not be the end of their story. God, in his sovereignty, had determined from the outset that even if Israel deserted him, he would one day achieve his plan for the descendants of Abraham. He promised to rescue them from the furthest parts of the earth where they would be dispersed and bring them back into their land (Deut. 30:1–4). He also prophesied that one day Israel would turn back to God and keep the laws he had given them and be the enlightened nation he always wanted them to be (Deut. 30:5–10).

Some equate this prophecy with the return from exile of the Jews in the time of Cyrus. But the scale of this prophecy is far greater, referencing *all* the tribes of Israel, not just Judah. Also, what occurred at the time of Ezra and Nehemiah was not a permanent revival of the hearts and minds of the people. It was temporary, and in the years that followed, developed into a misguided religion that lost sight of God's values and standards. It was nothing like the permanent change of heart and mind that Moses and multiple later prophets prophesied would one day occur. This prophecy has never been fulfilled in history and will only be realized with the establishment of God's kingdom on this earth.

The Law to Spread to All Nations

Jeremiah prophesied of this future time when the combined nations of Israel and Judah (all the tribes) would come together under a new covenant with the law of God (the Torah) now written in their hearts and minds:

> Behold, the days are coming, says the LORD, when I will make a new covenant with the house of Israel and with the house of Judah ... this is the covenant that I will make with the house of Israel after those days, says the LORD: *I will put My law in their minds, and write it on their hearts; and I will be their God,* and they shall be My people. No more shall every man teach his neighbor, and every man his brother, saying, "Know the LORD," for they all shall know Me, from the least of them to the greatest of them, says the LORD. For I will forgive their iniquity, and their sin I will remember no more. (Jer. 31:31–34)

This promise of a new covenant started its fulfilment with Jesus and the spiritual church of the firstborn. Jesus described his kingdom as a mustard seed that starts small and will one day spread to the whole earth (Matt. 13:31–32). God will once again work with the physical nations of Israel and Judah. Ezekiel also prophesied of this future time and emphasized the role the teachings of God would play:

> Therefore say, "Thus says the LORD God: 'I will gather you from the peoples, assemble you from the countries where you have been scattered, and I will give you the land of Israel.'" ... *Then I will give them one heart, and I will put a new spirit within them, and take the stony heart out of their flesh, and give them a heart of flesh, that they may walk in My statutes and keep My judgments and do them;* and they shall be My people, and I will be their God. (Ezek. 11:17, 19–20)

It is clear from the context that the law to be written in their minds and hearts is the same law Moses received and delivered. The idea of the law residing in the inner person is not new—God always desired his teachings to reside in people's hearts (Deut. 6:6; 11:18; 32:46).

The New Testament provides more detail about these future events, describing how Jesus will return to this earth as Lord of lords and King of kings (Luke 1:32–33; Rev. 11:15). He will make Jerusalem the center of his earthly kingdom. This time is often referred to as the Millennium, a peaceful period of a thousand years where Christ will rule the nations (Rev. 20:6). The prophet Isaiah describes this as a time when not just Israel, but *all nations* will seek to know the great God and learn his ways. It is a time when the law of God (the Torah) will guide all people to God:

> Now it shall come to pass in the latter days that the mountain of the LORD's house shall be established on the top of the mountains, and shall be exalted above the hills; and *all nations* shall flow to it. Many people shall come and say, "Come, and let us go up to the mountain of the LORD, to the house of the God of Jacob; *He will teach us His ways, and we shall walk in His paths." For out of Zion shall go forth the law, and the word of the LORD from Jerusalem.* (Isa. 2:2–3; see also Mic. 4:1–2)

It is clear from the context that the law to be written in their minds and hearts is the same law Moses received and delivered.

It will be a time of world peace:

> They shall beat their swords into plowshares, And their spears into pruning hooks; Nation shall not lift up sword against nation, Neither shall they learn war anymore. (Isa. 2:4).

This law, which will spread out from Jerusalem, will not be focused on power or control but on educating and empowering people with the knowledge on how to have a truly successful life:

> For the earth shall be full of the knowledge of the LORD as the waters cover the sea. (Isa. 11:9)

Even holy days, which help educate people of God's great purpose, will be kept by all nations:

> And it shall come to pass that everyone who is left of all the nations which came against Jerusalem shall go up from year to year to worship the King, the LORD of hosts, and to *keep the Feast of Tabernacles.* And it shall be that whichever of the families of the earth do not come up to Jerusalem to worship the King, the LORD of hosts, on them there will be no rain. If the family of Egypt will not come up and enter in, they shall have no rain; they shall receive the plague with which the LORD strikes the nations who do not come up to keep the Feast of Tabernacles. (Zech. 14:16–18)

The detailed nature of the many prophecies across so many of the prophets, and the fact that there has not been any extensive fulfillment of them in history, confirms that they belong to a time yet in the future when Jesus Christ returns to rule the nations.

A New Heart and Mind

An obvious question comes to mind: If God can put new, receptive hearts and minds into people, why didn't he do so with ancient Israel? Why did he put up with the hard-heartedness for centuries and not just "install" a new heart at that time?

The answer to this question comes from properly understanding what it means to "put the law in their minds and write it on their hearts." This is not something God is going to do by force or coercion. Nor is it some sort of "magic" where a person of poor character with no interest in God suddenly transforms into a person of character. A truly changed heart must always be voluntary without compulsion. God will open minds and provide the Holy Spirit as a *helper*, but the initiative to accept Jesus must start with a receptive and softhearted individual.

A truly changed heart must always be voluntary without compulsion.

Even with Jesus as King of kings, the ways of God will not be natural to man. People will need to be taught God's values, which are embodied in the law. The law will be put into people's minds by godly teachers:

> And I will give you shepherds according to My heart, who will feed you with knowledge and understanding. (Jer. 3:15)

To teach people to love the Lord with all their heart will take patience. God's kingdom will be founded on love, not fear. There will still be hard-hearted people who may be slow to respond (as the previous example of Zechariah 14 shows). But at the end of the day, God will achieve his goals, and his kingdom will succeed.

What will prevent society from failing again? In one word: *leadership*. The perfect, unchanging godly leadership of Jesus Christ supported by his loved and trusted family (the saints) who have the same internal values as he does (Dan. 7:27; Rev. 20:4). The recurring pattern of ancient Israel forgetting God after their godly leaders died will never happen again.

The Law of Moses Today

You have known the Holy Scriptures, which are able to make you wise for salvation through faith which is in Christ Jesus. —2 Timothy 3:15

One of the great setbacks to the Christian movement has been the loss of respect for the Old Testament, and specifically the system of law God gave to Israel.

It's a decline that accelerated in the second half of the twentieth century and, in many ways, is epitomized by the 1980 United States Supreme Court ruling against the display of the Ten Commandments in public schools. While largely symbolic, the ruling demonstrated the changing public opinion in a nation that formerly revered these "ten words", and had them proudly displayed in many of the highest courts of the land. What we are now seeing in our Western world is a civilization that has lost its cultural confidence and is deteriorating into moral confusion. Christianity, so long admired as the source of strength and vitality of our nations, is now seen as a roadblock to social progressivism.

Unfortunately, many Christians also see the Old Testament as mostly irrelevant and don't grasp how the loss of respect for the Hebrew Scriptures has weakened the foundation of Christianity and empowered skeptics to mock the God of the Old Testament.

> *The loss of respect for the Hebrew Scriptures has weakened the foundation of Christianity.*

They have failed to appreciate that the New Testament faith is based on the Hebrew Scriptures, and without the Old Testament, the New Testament loses its foundation. Not only does the New Testament include nearly 300 direct references to the Old (and by some measures 1,000 or more indirect references), but the core Christian concepts of God, faith, justification, salvation, the Messiah, etc., are all grounded in God's Old Testament revelation. Without understanding the origins of core doctrines, the New Testament message can be confused and even contradictory. Far from being irrelevant, the Hebrew Scriptures are God's revelation to man and contain wisdom and truths that have application for all cultures and all times.

Historical Confusion

One major misunderstanding that developed in the centuries before Christ is the false idea that the law of Moses was a system of justification by works. It never was, as Paul was at pains to explain. Abraham was declared righteous by his faith not by works, and Israel was saved by God's grace before they had even received the law. This misguided idea on the role of the law infiltrated the church via Pharisaical Judaism and was a heresy Paul addressed in several letters (Rom. 4:1–5; Gal. 2:16). The integrity of the law of Moses was further undermined by the myriad of contradictory rules that Judaism had added to the original laws of God but were often presented as being from God.

This negative baggage surrounding the law of Moses has resulted in the great principles and teachings contained in the law being lost in technical theological arguments. Instead of approaching the books of Moses as a source of wisdom and guidance to life, too often the study of the law deteriorates into arguments over which parts of the law are to be "kept" and which are to be "done away." This way of thinking is a by-product of the justification by works argument—where individuals are trying to determine which laws are efficacious for salvation and which are not. But this is not how God has ever wanted his law and teachings to be viewed. Law-keeping of itself could never, and will never, save anyone. That's never been its purpose.

> *All the negative baggage surrounding the law of Moses has resulted in the great principles and teachings contained in the law being lost in technical theological arguments.*

All this has led to confusion over Paul's writings, with some accusing him of being contradictory—sometimes seeming to uphold the law, and other times seeming to discard it. But when we understand the context of the New Testament heresies, the matter becomes clear: Paul was a strong supporter of the written law as God intended it to be understood, but he had no time for those seeking to twist and distort the original intent of God's teachings. "The law is good if one uses it lawfully," Paul noted to Timothy (1 Tim. 1:8).

Why God Gave His Law

Putting aside the complex and often confusing theological arguments and looking at the simple statements of Scripture reveals the reason God gave his law to Israel. It is not hard to understand—the law was an expression of his grace. He loved these people, and so he revealed to them a way of life based on truth that would lead to true success.

> And *because He loved your fathers*, therefore He chose their descendants after them; and He brought you out of Egypt with His Presence, with

> His mighty power. ...Therefore know this day, and consider it in your heart, that the LORD Himself is God in heaven above and on the earth beneath; there is no other. You shall therefore keep His statutes and His commandments which I command you today, *that it may go well with you and with your children after you,* and that you may prolong your days in the land which the LORD your God is giving you for all time. (Deut. 4:37, 39–40)

God wanted undeserving Israel to be his special people—to represent his standards and be a leading light among the nations. As the ultimate source of truth, God knows what works and what doesn't. Man does not naturally know this:

> There is a way that seems right to a man but its end is the way of death. (Prov. 14:12)

As God said to Joshua:

> This Book of the Law shall not depart from your mouth, but you shall meditate in it day and night, that you may observe to do according to all that is written in it. *For then you will make your way prosperous, and then you will have good success.* (Josh. 1:8)

The moral directives, principles, and teachings God gave Israel were designed to lead to positive outcomes because they align with the reality of his character and his design for humankind.

An Expression of Faith

Directly connected to the wrong understanding of the role of the law is the confusion surrounding the concept of "obedience." Attempting to "obey" laws is commonly put in the same category as a person trying to earn salvation. But again, the simple concepts expressed in Scripture are being lost in theological confusion. Scripture (both Old and New Testaments) never presents obedience to God in that way.

Abraham's obedience was not his attempt to show God how "righteous" he was. Abraham obeyed because he *believed* God and *trusted* that what God told him to do was for his good. His obedience was an outward demonstration of the fruits of his faith (Heb. 11:8–10).

And this makes perfect sense. Knowing that God is sovereign and has an individual's best interests at heart, a person should carefully listen to and act on *every* word that proceeds out of the mouth of God (Deut. 8:3; Matt. 4:4).

Belief that God knows best has always been a positive motivation for obeying God—not a motivation of terror or trying to prove how good we are, or point-scoring to impress God—but obedience that demonstrates we really do put our trust in him and tremble at his every word (Isa. 66:2).

This is an easy-to-understand concept. If a person today, for example, engages a financial advisor, doing what their advisor counsels demonstrates they do indeed trust them. And vice-versa, if a person proceeds to ignore their advisor's recommendations, it is evidence that they do *not* trust their advisor, and the relationship will soon fail. In the same way, Abraham obeyed because he *believed* in the promises God had given him. James spoke to this exact issue for Christians:

Abraham obeyed because he believed God and trusted that what God told him to do was for his good.

> What does it profit, my brethren, if someone says he has faith but does not have works? Can faith save him? If a brother or sister is naked and destitute of daily food, and one of you says to them, "Depart in peace, be warmed and filled," but you do not give them the things which are needed for the body, what does it profit? Thus also faith by itself, if it does not have works, is dead. (James 2:14–17)

James then specifically uses the example of Abraham to show how his trust in God was confirmed by his actions:

> Was not Abraham our father justified by works when he offered Isaac his son on the altar? *Do you see that faith was working together with his works, and by works faith was made perfect?* And the Scripture was fulfilled which says, "Abraham believed God, and it was accounted to him for righteousness." And he was called the friend of God. You see then that a man is justified by works, and not by faith only. (James 2:21–24)

In other words, faith is *action-oriented*. It is easy to say, "I believe you, Lord," but that is just the start of the journey. The proof is in the deeds. When properly understood, there is no conflict between faith and works—works are simply the demonstration of a person's living faith.

When an individual is called by God and comes to know Jesus Christ, it is natural to ask, "What do you want me to do, Lord?" and "How do I live my life in a way that honors and pleases you?" Such a person will carefully listen to the master's instructions and do everything he asks of them because they believe in and trust him implicitly. Their motivation for obedience is the love, trust, and gratitude for what God has done for someone so unworthy. But their confidence in their eternal future will always depend on God's grace.

Applicability of the Law Today

What relevance does the law of Moses have for today's Christian? Well, if we approach the law as a revelation from God and a guide to life, it has enormous relevance. The core of Christian ethics is to be like God—and the law contains godly instruction, teaching, wisdom, and revelation that has value for people of all ages.

The core of Christian ethics is to be like God.

What people have generally not appreciated is the timeless nature of God's teachings. While the law he gave to Israel was written to the culture of the day, God has never been trapped in the time warp of ancient times. From the outset, he encouraged people to seek him, meditate on, and treasure the wisdom and truth in the underlying principles of the law and adapt them to the times in which they lived.

In that sense, God's commandments are *exceedingly broad* (Ps. 119:96). How can anyone, for example, deny that the Ten Commandments are a recipe for a morally sound people and a stable, free, and happy society? And the principles behind the judgments remain a source of wisdom because they reflect the

The law contains instruction, teaching, wisdom, and revelation that has value for people of all ages.

mind of God. The statutes are part of God's revelation to man. Consider what was covered earlier about the ongoing relevance of the holy days in teaching God's great master plan for humanity. Even studying the temporary sacrificial system and Levitical priesthood can open our eyes to God's great plan of salvation and the role of Jesus the Messiah. Jesus was the ultimate end goal, the purpose[1], of the law (Rom. 10:4).

And if there are civil or ceremonial laws that we don't see any relevance for today, rather than asking, "Do I have to keep this law?" a far more valuable

---
[1] Greek *telos*

approach is to ask, "What was the intent behind this particular law? What does it teach me about the heart and mind of God? How can this guide me to live a godly life? How does this apply to me?" This is how James saw the law:

> But he who looks into the *perfect law of liberty* and continues *in it*, and is not a forgetful hearer but a doer of the work, this one will be blessed in what he does. (James 1:25).

Those who approach the law this way will find depth, understanding, and guidance for life in every part of it—even in those seemingly trivial jots and tittles that otherwise have no connection to our culture.

The people of Israel never grasped this depth of the teachings they were given. They were hard-hearted and treated God as one would treat a pagan deity, trying to appease him with legalistic rituals and formulas instead of a loyal heart. Yet all along, God desired for Israel to take his instruction into their hearts and use it as a guide and inspiration for life. He desires the same for spirit-filled Christians today.

Speaking of those *same* laws, the writer of Hebrews connects the words of Jeremiah directly to us:

> But the Holy Spirit also *witnesses to us*; for after He had said before, "This is the covenant that I will make with them after those days, says the LORD: *I will put My laws into their hearts, and in their minds I will write them*," then He adds, "Their sins and their lawless deeds I will remember no more." (Heb. 10:15–17)

Paul understood this perfectly, teaching that the *entire Old Testament system* is profitable for instructing a Christian in the path to a godly way of life:

> You have known the Holy Scriptures, which are able to make you wise for salvation through faith which is in Christ Jesus. *All Scripture* is given by inspiration of God, and is profitable for doctrine, for reproof, for correction, for instruction in righteousness, that the man of God may be complete, thoroughly equipped for every good work. (2 Tim. 3:15–17)

All of it has great value. This is exactly what we would expect from a great God who can see the end from the beginning. For this reason, Paul wrote that he *delighted in the law of God* in his heart (Rom. 7:22).

David, too, approached the law this way. He saw it as *a lamp to his feet and a light to his path* (Ps. 119:105). He wanted to know God deeply and took notice of every word. He longed to understand how he could develop a heart and mind just like the God he loved. A person who has the same approach today will be blessed.

Conclusion

Hopefully, this book has given you, the reader, an added appreciation for the enlightened system of law that God graciously gave the nation of Israel thousands of years ago. While much more could be added, I hope what has been presented serves to strengthen your faith in the greatness of God and confirm the consistency and immutability of his character. As has been rightfully observed: there is only one God—and the God of the Old Testament is the God of the New. The Christian faith is the worship of the God of Genesis—a God that Jesus perfectly reflected in his life and words.

The law of Moses originated from a God of love and had love as its central value. God wanted Israel to learn to love him with all their heart, soul, and strength and to love one another as they loved themselves (Deut. 6:5; Lev. 19:18). God has never changed. This ancient law had the same command to love that Jesus gives his followers today (Matt. 22:37–40; 1 John 4:11).

> *God has never changed. This ancient law had the same command to love that Jesus gives his followers today.*

The words of Moses also reinforce other great character attributes of God: that he is a God of truth and wisdom who can be trusted. A God full of grace, mercy, and forgiveness. A God who loves justice. A God who is rational and practical. A God who loves freedom. A big-picture God with a purpose and great plan in mind for those who carry his image. And most endearingly, a God who is personal who will listen and respond to the smallest of his children. This is why the greats of old put their faith in God and why we can have the same confidence in him today.

May God continue to bless your ongoing study of his Word and further open your mind to his enlightened way of life.

Appendices

Appendix: Law of Moses or Law of God?

At face value, the term "law of Moses" implies that Moses, not God, was the author. Joshua was the first to use the phrase (Josh. 8:31–32). The term is later used by such Bible greats as David, Ezra, Nehemiah, Daniel, and Malachi (1 Kings 2:3; Ezra 3:2; Neh. 8:1; Dan. 9:11; Mal. 4:4). Paul and Luke continue the same terminology in the New Testament (Luke 2:22; 1 Cor. 9:9). Even Jesus described the law as the *law of Moses* (John 7:23).

The Ten Commandments were given by God, but what about the rest of the law? If it was fully or even partially the work of men, it's inherent value can be rightly questioned. Did Moses play a part in the law's development as some suggest?

Moses Never Claimed Authorship

Despite the law often being referred to as the *law of Moses*, Moses never claimed that he was the source of any part of the law. Moses consistently said he took *all* his instructions from God and presented himself as the intermediary:

> Beware that you do not forget the LORD your God by not keeping *His commandments, His judgments, and His statutes* which I command you today. (Deut. 8:11)

> And the LORD *commanded us to observe all these statutes*, to fear the LORD our God, for our good always, that He might preserve us alive, as it is this day. Then it will be righteousness for us, if we are careful to observe all these commandments before the LORD our God, *as He has commanded us.* (Deut. 6:24–25)

The books of Leviticus and Numbers use the phrase "the Lord spoke to Moses" dozens of times as God gave the extensive details of the law. Moses then passed on what he was given:

> So Moses told the children of Israel everything, *just as the LORD commanded Moses.* (Num. 29:40)

On his visits to the mountain, Moses said he received more than just the Ten Commandments:

> Then the LORD said to Moses, "Come up to Me on the mountain and be there; and I will give you tablets of stone, *and the law and*

commandments which I have written, that you may teach them." (Exod. 24:12)

So He declared to you His covenant which He commanded you to perform, the Ten Commandments; and He wrote them on two tablets of stone. *And the LORD commanded me at that time to teach you statutes and judgments,* that you might observe them in the land which you cross over to possess. (Deut. 4:13–14)

God's ownership of all aspects of the law is reinforced by his own words:

Therefore you shall observe all *My* statutes and all *My* judgments, and perform them: I am the LORD. (Lev. 19:37)

Surprisingly, even God himself calls his own law the *law of Moses*, while simultaneously confirming that he was the author. Speaking through the prophet Malachi, he states:

Remember the law of Moses, My servant, which I commanded him in Horeb for all Israel, with the statutes and judgments. (Mal. 4:4)

In summary, Scripture is clear that these laws were not the invention of Moses or any other man but originated from God himself. The *law of Moses* is the *law of God*. There is no difference. The term *law of Moses* is used simply to identify the role that Moses played as God's messenger.[1]

People Asked for a Mediator

One reason Moses is so closely associated with the law originates from a request from the Israelites. God may have originally intended to deliver the entire law directly to the people. But when he spoke the Ten Commandments out loud, the people were so terrified they asked that God not speak directly to them anymore. Instead, they requested that Moses be the interface between them and God (Deut. 5:25–27). God agreed to this arrangement (Deut. 5:28–30). He told the people to stay home and that he would give Moses the commandments and the rest of the law:

Go and say to them, "Return to your tents." But as for you (Moses), stand here by Me, and *I will speak to you all the commandments, the statutes, and the judgments which you shall teach them*, that they may

---

[1] There are other terms used throughout the Bible to refer to the Old Testament law, including "the law of God," "the law of the Lord," "the book of the law," and "the Book of the Covenant." Refer to Appendix "Biblical Terms for the Law" for more detail.

> observe them in the land which I am giving them to possess. (Deut. 5:30–31)

As the one who received and delivered God's law to Israel, Moses' name became intrinsically associated with the law. The term *law of Moses*, therefore, is not a statement of authorship but of responsibility. It was Moses' role to receive the words of God, teach them to the people, and oversee their transcription for posterity.

Appendix: Laws Before Moses

Not all the laws Moses delivered to the Israelites were new. There is evidence of a system of worship and a system of law being in place long before Israel arrived at Mount Sinai. We are not told how this system was structured, but we do see ceremonial aspects in play early. For example:

- Abel, the son of Adam and Eve, sacrificed animals (Gen. 4:4).
- Firstlings and firstborn had importance (Gen. 4:4; 27:19–32).
- Noah sorted animals into clean and unclean (Gen. 7:2).
- Noah built an altar and offered sacrifices of clean animals (Gen. 8:20).

Abraham paid a tenth of his spoil to Melchizedek, the priest of Salem, hinting at an understanding of tithing and the role of a priesthood (Gen. 14:18–20).

Right and wrong and sin were also understood from the beginning:

- Cain was punished for the sin of murder (Gen. 4:10).
- God despaired of the "wickedness" of man long before Moses, implying man knew better (Gen. 6:5–7).
- Sodom and Gomorrah were judged because of their sins (Gen. 13:13).
- Joseph understood that adultery was a sin (Gen. 39:7–9).
- While Israel was still in Egypt, the midwives knew right from wrong and "feared God" even more than the Egyptian Pharaoh (Exod. 1:17).

Abraham lived according to a defined structure of law, although we don't know the extent of that system. This is evident in a comment God made to Isaac:

> And in your seed all the nations of the earth shall be blessed; because Abraham *obeyed My voice and kept My charge, My commandments, My statutes, and My laws."* (Gen. 26:4–5)

Whatever Abraham's pre-Sinaitic law system included, it must have been entirely compatible with the laws given to Moses centuries later. We can confidently make that assertion because Moses (who wrote this comment in Genesis) would have otherwise had to distinguish what he meant by Abraham's statutes, commandments, and laws and differentiate them from those he delivered to Israel. Moses also acknowledged the existence of a structured system of law *before* the law was given at Mount Sinai:

> If you diligently heed the voice of the LORD your God and do what is right in His sight, give ear to His *commandments and keep all His*

> *statutes*, I will put none of the diseases on you which I have brought on the Egyptians. (Exod. 15:26)
>
> And the LORD said to Moses, "How long do you refuse to keep *My commandments and My laws?*" (Exod. 16:28)

This includes the Sabbath, with the people instructed to refrain from collecting manna on that day:

> Moses said, "Eat that today, for *today is a Sabbath to the LORD*; today you will not find it in the field. Six days you shall gather it, but on the seventh day, the Sabbath, there will be none." (Exod. 16:25–26)

Moses was also judging the people according to a standard of law before Mount Sinai. When his father-in-law, Jethro, asked Moses why he alone judged the people, Moses answered:

> Because the people come to me to inquire of God. When they have a difficulty, they come to me, and I judge between one and another; and I make known the *statutes of God and His laws*. (Exod. 18:15–16)

Despite their slide into captivity in Egypt and their subjection to Egyptian rules and laws, the Israelites were an intelligent people who had retained their genealogies and history. They knew the details of the story of their father, Abraham, and the promises to his descendants. They knew of the God of Abraham, Isaac, and Jacob, and cried out to him for relief (Exod. 2:23–25). Centuries later, Luke documented the lineage of Jesus back to Adam (Luke 3:23–38), confirming that records were retained even through the captivity years. Israel also maintained a record of the early stories of Genesis during their captivity, either orally or in some early textual form. Moses drew on this when he compiled the book of Genesis.

It therefore makes sense on the evidence, that the giving of the Ten Commandments and statutes at Sinai were at least in part a restatement of laws given from creation and known by the ancients. Most of the Ten Commandments can be described as natural laws built into the reality of the universe God has created for man. They represent truth from a God of truth.

Appendix: Biblical Terms for the Law

There are several terms used throughout Scripture to identify the Old Testament law. They include:

- the law of Moses
- the law of God
- the law of the Lord (Yahweh)
- the book of the law
- the Book of the Covenant
- the Book of the Law of the Lord (Yahweh)

Our modern Western world naturally interprets terms like these in a precise manner, assuming strict definitions when it comes to matters of law. For that reason, some have used these different terms to categorize the law of the Old Testament into various sections.

But it is highly problematic to read into the ancient text a technical preciseness of language and terminology that simply didn't exist at that time. The Bible was written over an enormous period of time, by multiple authors, across different cultures and languages, and for different audiences. The authors wrote in the context of their time. It is not surprising, therefore, to find that the same law is called by many different terms.

The books of Ezra and Nehemiah demonstrate this well. Ezra interchanges the terms *law of Moses* and *law of the Lord (Yahweh)*:

> This Ezra came up from Babylon; and he was a skilled scribe in the *Law of Moses, which the* LORD *God of Israel had given*. ... For Ezra had prepared his heart to seek the *Law of the* LORD, and to do it, and to teach statutes and ordinances in Israel. (Ezra 7:6, 10)

Nehemiah similarly interchanges the terms *law of God* and the *law of the Lord (Yahweh)*:

> Also day by day, from the first day until the last day, he read from the *Book of the Law of God*. (Neh. 8:18)

> And they stood up in their place and read from the *Book of the Law of the* LORD *(Yahweh)* their God for one-fourth of the day; and for another fourth they confessed and worshiped the LORD their God. (Neh. 9:3)

Nehemiah then confirmed that the book of the law he was referring to was indeed the law given by Moses:

> These joined with their brethren, their nobles, and entered into a curse and an oath to walk in *God's Law, which was given by Moses* the servant of God, and to observe and do all the commandments of the LORD our Lord, and His ordinances and His statutes. (Neh. 10:29)

David links the terms *law of God* with Moses' law:

> Only may the LORD give you wisdom and understanding, and give you charge concerning Israel, that you may keep the *law of the LORD your God.* ¹³ Then you will prosper, if you take care to fulfill the statutes and judgments with *which the LORD charged Moses concerning Israel.* Be strong and of good courage; do not fear nor be dismayed. (1 Chron. 22:12–13)

Joshua, who first used the term *law of Moses*, later used the term *law of God* (Josh. 24:26).

The New Testament has the same substitution of terms. Luke wrote that Mary and Joseph observed the rituals of the *law of Moses*, which he later refers to as the *law of the Lord*:

> Now when the days of her purification according to the *law of Moses* were completed, they brought Him to Jerusalem to present Him to the Lord. ... So when they had performed all things according to the *law of the Lord*, they returned to Galilee, to their own city, Nazareth. (Luke 2:22, 39).

The law of Moses was also referred to as a "book." Moses described it both as the *Book of the Covenant* and the *Book of the Law*:

> Then he took the *Book of the Covenant* and read in the hearing of the people. And they said, "All that the Lord has said we will do, and be obedient." (Exod. 24:7)

> If you obey the voice of the LORD your God, to keep His commandments and His statutes which are written in this *Book of the Law*, and if you turn to the LORD your God with all your heart and with all your soul. (Deut. 30:10)

The book was to be carried beside the ark of the covenant:

> So it was, when *Moses had completed writing the words of this law in a book*, when they were finished, that Moses commanded the Levites, who bore the ark of the covenant of the LORD, saying: "Take this *Book of the Law*, and put it beside the ark of the covenant of the LORD your God, that it may be there as a witness against you. (Deut. 31:24–26)

In the time of Hezekiah, the book is called the *law of the Lord* and its contents noted, confirming it was the same book Moses wrote:

> The king also appointed a portion of his possessions for the burnt offerings: for the morning and evening burnt offerings, the burnt offerings for the Sabbaths and the New Moons and the set feasts, as it is written in the *Law of the Lord*. (2 Chron. 31:3)

During the reign of King Josiah, Hilkiah found this Book of the Law which had been lost and handed it to the king. The record again confirms that this was the same book written by Moses. Here it also called the Book of the Covenant:

> Now when they brought out the money that was brought into the house of the LORD, Hilkiah the priest found the *Book of the Law of the LORD given by Moses*. ... The king went up to the house of the LORD, with all the men of Judah and the inhabitants of Jerusalem—the priests and the Levites, and all the people, great and small. And he read in their hearing all the words of the *Book of the Covenant* which had been found in the house of the LORD. (2 Chron. 34:14, 30)

The contents of this book are referred to as the *words of the covenant* and are again identified as the same law given by Moses:

> Then the king stood in his place and made a covenant before the LORD, to follow the LORD, and to *keep His commandments and His testimonies and His statutes* with all his heart and all his soul, to perform the *words of the covenant that were written in this book*. (2 Chron. 34:31)

All these examples confirm that the *law of Moses* was indeed one and the same as the *law of God* and the *law of the Lord*. These are the same words Moses wrote down in "book" form and delivered to the children of Israel not long before his death.

Appendix: The Hebrew Calendar

The statutory holy days outlined in the law of Moses are noted as falling on specific dates of a calendar. Today this biblical calendar is generally referred as the Hebrew (or Jewish) calendar. It is a lunar-solar (lunisolar) calendar aligned to the seasons and harvest cycles of the land of Canaan.

But the law of Moses does not include instructions on how to implement the calendar. A calendar was obviously in use, with reference to months and days, but the necessary calendrical rules are not outlined. While Israel was still in Egypt, God simply announced that the first month (Abib) of the year would be in the spring when Passover was kept (Exod. 12:2).

There was a calendar of some sort already known to the Israelites prior to Mount Sinai. The creation account notes that God gave the heavenly bodies for calendrical purposes, implying ancient origins (Gen. 1:14). Noah is noted as using a calendar (Gen. 7:11; 8:4, 5, 13), and there are hints in Scripture that the Israelites had been accurately tracking time prior to the exodus (Exod. 12:41). The Hebrew calendar, therefore, seems to have been in operation long before Moses.

The Hebrew calendar has the start of each month occurring on the New Moon (Num. 28:11; 29:6; 10:10). A lunisolar calendar is quite different from a solar calendar like the one we use today. Our Gregorian calendar has twelve fixed months per year. To keep it in sync with the orbit of the earth around the sun, a leap year with an extra day is added every fourth year along with occasional time clock adjustments. In the Hebrew calendar, the 30-day (approximately) lunar cycle doesn't divide well into a 365 day (approx.) solar year, so keeping the calendar in sync with the seasons requires more dramatic adjustments. To do this, an additional thirteenth (intercalary) month must be inserted approximately every 3 years.

There are many other rules and decisions needed to maintain a calendar. Calendars must be calculated in advance so that people can plan ahead for festivals etc. For example, people living in more northern parts of ancient Israel needed to have a substantial advance notice of the new year so that they could attend Passover in Jerusalem. A future calendar became especially relevant in the Second Temple period when Jews scattered in far-off lands had to plan their journey months in advance to be in Jerusalem for the celebrations.

Because God provides no way to astronomically identify the first month of Abib or precisely when to add the additional month, such decisions must by necessity be by decree. To keep everyone united on the same calendar, such decisions require a central authority. To give calendrical authority to individuals would otherwise be a source of confusion.

From the time of Moses, the calendrical authority would logically have been given to the high priest supported by the Levites. (The feasts were to be "proclaimed at their appointed times" Lev. 23:4). While there are no hints of calendar disputes in ancient Israel, contentions arose after the return from Babylon between various sects of Judaism, on who had the calendrical authority.

The primary purpose of a calendar is sometimes lost in technical arguments. A calendar exists to *bring people together*, and to achieve that goal a central authority is needed. Paul notes that it was the Jews who were entrusted with the *oracles of God* (Rom. 3:2). We have them to thank for the preservation of the Old Testament Scriptures. Jesus also implicitly accepted their role in the administration of the calendar by his attendance at various holy days at the temple.

While calendrical disputes remain, the most widely used modern Hebrew calendar accepted in the world today is the one initially established by Rabbi Hillel II in the fourth century CE. He is credited with establishing a fixed calendar that allowed dispersed Jews to know in advance the dates of upcoming years and holy days.

Appendix: Further Insights from the Psalmist

The longest chapter in the Bible is the beautiful Psalm 119. The author of the psalm is not specifically noted but has been traditionally identified as David. Regardless of the authorship, the inspired heart of the psalmist, and his deep love of God's word as expressed in the law of Moses, comes strongly through.

> I have rejoiced in the way of Your testimonies, as *much as* in all riches. I will meditate on Your precepts, and contemplate Your ways. I will delight myself in Your statutes; I will not forget Your word. (Ps. 119:14–16)

> Open my eyes, that I may see wondrous things from Your law. (Ps. 119:18)

> My soul breaks with longing for Your judgments at all times. (Ps. 119:20)

> Your testimonies also *are* my delight *and* my counselors. (Ps. 119:24)

> I will run the course of Your commandments, for You shall enlarge my heart. (Ps. 119:32)

> Give me understanding, and I shall keep Your law; indeed, I shall observe it with *my* whole heart. Make me walk in the path of Your commandments, for I delight in it. (Ps. 119:34–35)

> Behold, I long for Your precepts; revive me in Your righteousness. (Ps. 119:40)

> And I will walk at liberty, for I seek Your precepts. (Ps. 119:45)

> I will speak of Your Testimonies before kings and will not be ashamed. (Ps. 119:46)

> And I will delight myself in Your commandments, which I love. My hands also I will lift up to Your commandments, which I love, and I will meditate on Your statutes. (Ps. 119:47–48)

> I remembered Your judgments of old, O LORD, and have comforted myself. (Ps. 119:52)

Your statutes have been my songs in the house of my pilgrimage. (Ps. 119:54)

Teach me good judgment and knowledge, for I believe Your commandments. (Ps. 119:66)

The law of Your mouth *is* better to me than thousands of *coins of* gold and silver. (Ps. 119:72)

Give me understanding, that I may learn Your commandments. (Ps. 119:73)

Let Your tender mercies come to me, that I may live; for Your law *is* my delight. (Ps. 119:77)

Unless Your law *had been* my delight, I would then have perished in my affliction. I will never forget Your precepts, for by them You have given me life. (Ps. 119:92–93)

I have seen the consummation of all perfection, *but* Your commandment *is* exceedingly broad. (Ps. 119:96)

Oh, how I love Your law! It *is* my meditation all the day. You, through Your commandments, make me wiser than my enemies; for they *are* ever with me. I have more understanding than all my teachers, for Your testimonies *are* my meditation. I understand more than the ancients, because I keep Your precepts. (Ps. 119:97–100)

How sweet are Your words to my taste, *sweeter* than honey to my mouth! Through Your precepts I get understanding; therefore I hate every false way. (Ps. 119:103–104)

Your word *is* a lamp to my feet and a light to my path. (Ps. 119:105)

Your testimonies I have taken as a heritage forever, for they *are* the rejoicing of my heart. I have inclined my heart to perform Your statutes forever, to the very end. (Ps. 119:111–112)

I hate the double-minded, but I love Your law. (Ps. 119:113)

Therefore I love Your commandments more than gold, yes, than fine gold! Therefore all *Your* precepts *concerning* all *things* I consider *to be* right; I hate every false way. (Ps. 119:127–128)

Your testimonies are wonderful; therefore my soul keeps them. The entrance of Your words gives light; it gives understanding to the simple. I opened my mouth and panted, for I longed for Your commandments. (Ps. 119:129–131)

Trouble and anguish have overtaken me, *yet* Your commandments *are* my delights. The righteousness of Your testimonies *is* everlasting; give me understanding, and I shall live. (Ps. 119:143–144)

Consider how I love Your precepts; revive me, O LORD, according to Your lovingkindness. The entirety of Your word *is* truth, and every one of Your righteous judgments *endures* forever. (Ps. 119:159–160)

Great peace have those who love Your law, and nothing causes them to stumble. (Ps. 119:165)

My soul keeps Your testimonies, and I love them exceedingly. I keep Your precepts and Your testimonies, for all my ways *are* before You. (Ps. 119:167–168)

I long for Your salvation, O LORD, and Your law *is* my delight. (Ps. 119:174)

Bibliography

Adams, John. 1775. *III. To the Inhabitants of the Colony of Massachusetts-Bay, 6 February 1775.* Founders Online. 6 Feb. Accessed 2023. https://founders.archives.gov/documents/Adams/06-02-02-0072-0004.

—. 1780. "John Adams and the Massachusetts Constitution." *Government of Massachusetts.* https://www.mass.gov/guides/john-adams-the-massachusetts-constitution#-john-adams-and-the-rule-of-law-.

—. 1798. *John Adams to Massachusetts Militia.* Founders Online. 11 Oct. Accessed 2023. https://founders.archives.gov/documents/Adams/99-02-02-3102.

Adams, Samuel. 1778. *Samuel Adams, Letter to John Scollay 1776. The Life and Public Services of Samuel Adams Vol III. P115.* Boston: William Wells. Massachusetts Spy 1778,.

Albright, W. F. 1994. *Yahweh and the Gods of Canaan: A Historical Analysis of Two Contrasting Faiths.* Indiana: Eisenbrauns.

Allsop, Justice James. 2016. "Values in Law: how they influence and shape rules and the application of law." *Hochelago Lecture, Faculty of Law.* Hong Kong: University of Hong Kong. http://classic.austlii.edu.au/au/journals/FedJSchol/2016/15.html.

Bakers. 2013. *Bakers Illustrated Bible Dictionary.* Grand Rapids. MI: Baker Publishing Group.

—. 2012. *The Baker Illustrated Bible Commentary.* Grand Rapids. MI: Bakers Publishing Group.

Barnes, Albert. 1983. *Barnes Notes on the Old and New Testaments.* Baker Books.

Beale, G.K. 2008. *We Become What We Worship.* IVP Academic.

Benner, Jeff A. 2022. *Ancient Hebrew Research Center. Hebrew Word Studies.* Jun. Accessed 2023. https://www.ancient-hebrew.org/studies-words/what-is-torah.htm.

—. 2022. *Ancient Hebrew Research Centre. Deut 25:11-12 Cut off Hand.* https://www.ancient-hebrew.org/studies-verses/deuteronomy-25-11-12-cut-off-the-hand.htm.

Biblical Archaeology. 2023. *The Tel Dan Inscription: The First Historical Evidence of King David from the Bible.* https://www.biblicalarchaeology.org/daily/biblical-artifacts/the-tel-dan-inscription-the-first-historical-evidence-of-the-king-david-bible-story/.

Block, Daniel I. 2011. *How I love YourTorah, O Lord!* Eugene, OR: Cascade Books, A Division of Wipf & Stock Publishers.

Block, Daniel. I. 2012. *The Gospel According to Moses.* Eugene. OR: Cascade Books. An Imprint of Wipf & Stock Publishers.

Butt, Kyle. 2015. "Deuteronomy 22:28-29 and Rape." *Reason and Revelation* 9 Vol 35. No. 8.

Center for Online Judaic Studies. 2023. *Overview Background.* Accessed Aug 2023. https://cojs.org/overview-_background/.

Chabad. 2022. *Rabbi Akiba in Prison.* Accessed June 2023. https://www.chabad.org/library/article_cdo/aid/111935/jewish/Rabbi-Akiba-in-Prison.htm.

—. 2022. *The 39 Melachot.* Accessed June 2023. https://www.chabad.org/library/article_cdo/aid/102032/jewish/The-39-Melachot.htm.

Chabad. Menachem Posner. 2022. *15 Wise Sayings of Hillel the Elder.* Accessed May 2023. https://www.chabad.org/library/article_cdo/aid/5906623/jewish/15-Wise-Quotes-of-Hillel-the-Elder.htm.

Chabad. Yehuda Shurpin. . 2022. *What Does 'Eye for an Eye' Really Mean?* Accessed Oct 2023. https://www.chabad.org/library/article_cdo/aid/479511/jewish/What-Does-Eye-for-an-Eye-Really-Mean.htm.

Chesnutt, Charles. 2009. *Origins of Bankruptcy.* https://chapter7-11.com/origin%20of%20bankruptcy.html.

Churchill, Sir Winston. 1940. *Their Finest Hour.* 18 Jun. https://winstonchurchill.org/resources/speeches/1940-the-finest-hour/their-finest-hour/.

Churchill, Winston S. 1956. *A History of the English Speaking Peoples. Vol 1. The Birth of Britain.* London: Cassell & Company Ltd.

Clarke, Adam. 1810. *Acts 15:10 Commentary.* https://www.studylight.org/commentaries/eng/acc/acts-15.html.

Columbia Heart Surgery. 2016. *Heart Disease was Common in Ancient Egypt Too.* 18 Feb. https://columbiasurgery.org/news/2016/02/18/heart-disease-was-common-ancient-egypt-too-0.

Convict Records. 2023. *Convict Records of Australia.* https://convictrecords.com.au.

Cornell. 2023. *LII Legal Information Institute.* https://www.law.cornell.edu/wex/rational_basis_test.

Craigie, P. C. 1976. *The Book of Deuteronomy.* MI: Wm. B. Eerdmans Publishing Co.

Dammery, Richard John Edward. 1991. *Law Code of King Alfred.* https://www.repository.cam.ac.uk/items/a5b9f0e5-3b11-4785-a4e4-7435dbacf49a.

D'Aubigne, J.H.Merle. 2012. *History of the Reformation of the 16th Century Vol III. Translated H.White.* Project Gutenberg (https://www.gutenberg.org/files/41253/41253-h/41253-h.htm).

Davis, John J. 1971. *Moses and the Gods of Egypt.* Indiana: BMH Books.

Dawkins, Richard, interview by Tony Jones. 2012. *Q&A ABC https://www.youtube.com/watch?v=kwPeyssjIPY* (10 April).

—. 2006. *The God Delusion.* New York: Houghton Mifflin.

Edersheim, Alfred. 1993. *The Life and Times of Jesus the Messiah.* Hendrickson Publishers.

Feiler, Bruce. 2009. *America's Prophet.* New York: HarperCollins.

Foreman, Benjamin. 2019. "Sacrifice and Centralisation in the Pentateuch." *Tyndale House Tyndale Bulletin.*

Franjo Gruber, Jasna Lipozenčić, Tatjana Kehler. 2015. *History of venereal diseases from antiquity to the renaissance.* https://pubmed.ncbi.nlm.nih.gov/25969906/#:~:text=Clay%20tablets%20from%20Mesopotamia%2C%20Egyptian,that%20these%20diseases%20were%20considered.

Frankl, Viktor E. 2008. *Man's Search for Meaning.* Great Britain: Rider, a Random House Group Company.

Franklin, Benjamin. 1840. *The Writings of Benjamin Franklin. 10:297.* Botson: Tappan, Whittemore and Mason.

Freeman, James M. 1875. *Handbook of Bible Manners and Customs.* New York: Nelson & Phillips.

Froese, Paul. 2004. "Forced Secularization in Soviet Russia: Why an Atheistic Monopoly Failed." *Journal for the Scientific Study of Religion.* Wiley.

Gane, Roy E. 2017. *Old Testament Law for Christians.* Michigan: Baker Academic.

Gojko Barjamovic, Thomas Chaney, Kerem Coşar, Ali Hortaçsu. 2019. *Trade, Merchants, and the Lost Cities of the Bronze Age.* 27 Mar. Accessed Jun 2023. https://academic.oup.com/qje/article/134/3/1455/5420484.

Graham, Billy. 2013. *Answers.* Billy Graham Evangelistic Assoc. Accessed 2023. https://billygraham.org/answer/is-it-true-that-the-god-of-the-old-testament-is-different-from-the-god-of-the-new-testament/.

Grisanti, M. A. 2012. *Expositor's Bible Commentary: Numbers-Ruth (Revised Edition) Vol 2.* Zondervan.

H, Merrill. Eugene. 2008. *Kingdom of Priests.* Michigan: Baker Academic.

Harbin, Michael A. 2012. "The Manumission of Slaves in Jubilee and Sabbath Years." *Tyndale House Tyndale Bulletin* 63 (1).
Harrison, R. K. 1980. *Leviticus: an introduction and commentary.* Illinois: InterVarsity Press.
Hays, Jeff. 2018. *Disease and Health Problems in Ancient Egypt.* Sep. https://factsanddetails.com/world/cat56/sub404/entry-6405.html.
Heiser, Dr Michael. 2019. *Naked Bible 290: Exodus 21-23 Part 1.* 19 Sep. https://nakedbiblepodcast.com/podcast/naked-bible-290-exodus-21-23-part-1/.
Hendrickson, Mark. 2013. "The Pandora's Box of Pregressivisn: Positive Law." *Forbes*, 30 May.
Henry, Matthew. 1994. *Matthew Henry's Commentary on the whole Bible: complete and unabridged.* Hendrickson Publishers.
Henry, Patrick. 1776. *Virginia Declaration of Rights. 1776. Item 15.* Red Hill Patrick Henry National Memorial. 12 June. Accessed 2023. https://www.redhill.org/primary-sources/virginia-declaration-of-rights/.
Herman, Dr. M. 2017. *TheTorah. The Origins and Use of the 613 Mitzvot.* Project TABS. Accessed Apr 10, 2023. https://www.thetorah.com/article/the-origins-and-use-of-the-613-mitzvot.
Herrman, Virginia. Smith, Adam. 2023. "The Alphabet". *Expedition Magazine. V64.3. PennMuseum.* . 2 Aug. Accessed Aug 2023. https://www.penn.museum/sites/expedition/the-alphabet/.
Hess, R. S. 2008. *The Expositor's Bible Commentary. Genesis-Leviticus (Revised Edition) Vol 1.* Michigan. USA: Zondervan.
Holman. 2015. *Holman Illustrated Bible Dictionary.* Nashville. TN: B&H Publishing Group.
Hughes, Graham. 1996. *Common Law Systems.* Oxford: Oxford University Press.
Hughes, J. Donald. 2014. *Environmental Problems of the Greeks and Romans: Ecology in the Ancient Mediterranean (Ancient Society and History).* Maryland: John Hopkins University Press; 2nd edition.
Issler, Klaus. 2017. *Biola University. Talbot School of Theology. Faculty Blog.* What Does the Old Testament Say About Loans and Interest Parts 1-5. 22 Nov. Accessed 2023. https://www.biola.edu/blogs/good-book-blog/2017/what-does-the-old-testament-say-about-loans-and-interest-part-1.
Jacobs, Joseph, and Ludwig Blav. 1906 (orig). *Jewish Encyclopedia.* Accessed July 2023. https://www.jewishencyclopedia.com.

James-Clark, Kelly. 1993. *Philosophers Who Believe: The Spiritual Journeys of Eleven Leading Thinkers.* Inter-Varsity Press.

Jefferson, Thomas. 1786. *Thomas Jefferson Memorial. Northeast Portico.* Accessed 2023.
https://www.nps.gov/thje/learn/photosmultimedia/quotations.htm.

—. 1819. *Thomas Jefferson to John Adams, 10 December 1819.* Founders Online. 10 Dec. Accessed 2023.
https://founders.archives.gov/documents/Jefferson/03-15-02-0240.

—. 1820. *Thomas Jefferson to William Charles Jarvis, 28 September 1820.* 28 Sep. https://founders.archives.gov/documents/Jefferson/03-16-02-0234.

Jennings, Timothy R. 2017. *The God-Shaped Heart.* Michigan: Baker Books.

Keren, Rachel. 2022. *The Shalvi/Hyman Encyclopedia of Jewish Women. Torah Study.* https://jwa.org/encyclopedia/article/torah-study.

King, L. W. 2012. *Code of Hammurabi.* CreateSpace Independent Publishing Platform.

Kitchen, K. A. 2006. *On the Reliability of the Old Testament.* Michigan: Wm. B. Eerdmans Publishing Co.

Knight, Douglas A. 2011. *Law, Power, and Justice in Ancient Israel.* Kentucky: Westminster John Knox Press.

Kuntz, Kenneth J. 1974. *The People of Ancient Israel.* New York: Harper & Row Publishers.

Lawler, Andrew. 2016. *City of Biblical Abraham Brimmed With Trade and Riches.* 11 Mar.
https://www.nationalgeographic.com/adventure/article/160311-ur-iraq-trade-royal-cemetery-woolley-archaeology.

Lebbert, Rev Jean E. 2015. *A Positive Approach: Freeing the Ten Commandments from Negative Language.* CreateSpace Independent Publishers.

Lee, Prof. Dr. F. N. 2006. *King Alfred the Great and our Common Law.* Kent. U.K.: Bexley Christian Publications.

Lewis, C.S. 2002. *Mere Christianity.* London: Harper Collins .

Lewis., C. S. 1996. *The Collected Works of C.S.Lewis. God in the Dock.* MI: Eerdmans Publishing.

Lincoln, Abraham. 1863. *Gettysburg address delivered at Gettysburg Pa. 1863.* 19 Nov. https://www.loc.gov/resource/rbpe.24404500/?st=text.

Locke, John. 1690. *Second Treatise of Government.* Project Gutenberg Ebook 2003 https://www.gutenberg.org/files/7370/7370-h/7370-h.htm.

Loizides, Antonius. 2015. "Draco's Law Code." *World History Encyclopedia.* 12 Jun. https://www.worldhistory.org/Dracos_Law_Code/.

Madison, James. 1788. *Federalist No 62.* https://guides.loc.gov/federalist-papers/text-61-70.

—. 1788. *Judicial Powers of the National Government.* Founders Online. 20 June. Accessed 2023. https://founders.archives.gov/documents/Madison/01-11-02-0101.

Mahoney, Timothy. 2020. *Literacy in Ancient Israel - New Findings Show More Educated than Previously Thought.* . 23 Oct. https://www.patternsofevidence.com/2020/10/23/literacy-in-ancient-israel/.

Marx, Karl. 1848. *Communist Manifesto. Chapter 2. Proletarians and Communists.* https://www.marxists.org/archive/marx/works/1848/communist-manifesto/ch02.htm.

McMillen, S. MD, Stern, David MD. 2000. *None of These Diseases.* Michigan: Revel 3rd Edition.

Metaxas, Eric. 2017. *If You Can Keep It.* New York: Penguin Books.

National Archives. 1776. *Declaration of Independence: A Transcription.* 4 July. Accessed Jun 2023. https://www.archives.gov/founding-docs/declaration-transcript.

National Constitution Center. 2023. *The United States Constitution - Full Text.* Accessed Jun 2023. https://constitutioncenter.org/the-constitution/full-text.

National Geographic. 2022. *Democracy Ancient Greece.* 20 May. Accessed Apr 2023. https://education.nationalgeographic.org/resource/democracy-ancient-greece/.

National Justice Museum. 2023. *The Bloody Code.* https://www.nationaljusticemuseum.org.uk/museum/news/what-was-the-bloody-code.

National Library of Medicine. 2016. *Estimation of country-specific and global prevalence of male circumcision.* 1 Mar. Accessed Apr 2023. https://www.ncbi.nlm.nih.gov/pmc/articles/PMC4772313/.

—. 2022. *Hyssopus Essential Oil: An Update of Its Phytochemistry, Biological Activities, and Safety Profile.* 13 Jan . Accessed Jun 2023. https://www.ncbi.nlm.nih.gov/pmc/articles/PMC8776447/.

—. 1993. *Infectious diseases during the Civil War.* 16 Apr. Accessed Aug 2023. https://pubmed.ncbi.nlm.nih.gov/8513069/.

—. 2017. *The mythos of laudable pus.* 13 Jul. Accessed Jun 2023. https://www.ncbi.nlm.nih.gov/pmc/articles/PMC5538214.

New World Encyclopedia. 2022. *New World Encyclopedia.* Accessed 2023. https://www.newworldencyclopedia.org.

Obladen, M. 2016. *From Right to Sin: Laws on Infantcide in Antiquity.* https://doi.org/10.1159/000440875.

Peterson, Jordan, interview by James Altucher. 2018. *12 Rules to Life, A Solution to Suffering Podcast* (1 Feb).

Petrovich, Douglas. 2017. *The World's Oldest Alphabet: Hebrew As the Language of the Proto-consonantal Script.* Jerusalem: Carta Jerusalem.

Poythress, Vern S. 1991. *The Shadow of Christ in the Law of Moses.* New Jersey: Presbyterian and Reformed Publishing Company.

Prager, Dennis. 2022. *The Rational Bible, Deuteronomy.* Washington DC: Regnery Faith.

—. 2018. *The Rational Bible, Exodus.* Washington. DC: Regnery Faith.

—. 2019. *The Rational Bible, Genesis.* Washington. DC: Regnery Faith.

Queensland Government. 2023. *Criminal Code Act 1899.* https://www.legislation.qld.gov.au/view/html/inforce/current/act-1899-009.

Queensland Supreme Court. 2022. *Direction 23 General Summing up Directions.* 9 Sep . https://www.courts.qld.gov.au/__data/assets/pdf_file/0010/85465/sd-bb-23-general-summing-up-directions.pdf.

Rabinowitz, Louis. 2007. *Encyclopedia Judaica 2nd Ed.* Detroit: Macmillan Reference USA in conjunction with Keter Publishing House. Jerusalem.

Radmacher, E.D, R.B. Allen, and H.W House. 1999. *Nelson's New Illustrated Bible Commentary.* Nashville. TN.: Thomas Nelson.

Reagan, Ronald. 1981. *Reagan Quotes Speeches. Inaugural Address.* 20 Jan. https://www.reaganfoundation.org/ronald-reagan/reagan-quotes-speeches/inaugural-address-2/.

Renn, Stephen. D. 2005. *Expository Dictionary of Bible Words.* Massachusetts: Hendrinkson Publishers.

Roberts, Robert. 1899. *The Law of Moses. As a Rule of National and Individual Life and the Enigmatical Enunciation of Divine Principles and Purposes.* Birmingham: Frank Juckes.

Rushdooney, Rousas John. 1973. *The Institutes of Biblical Law.* Presbyterian and Reformed Publishing Company.

Schlessinger, Laura. 1998. *The Ten Commandments.* New York: HarperCollins Publisher.

Sefaria. 2023. *The Contemporary Torah 2006. Commentary.* https://www.sefaria.org.

Shakespeare, William. 2015. *The Complete Works of William Shakespeare.* New York: Barnes & Noble Inc.

Smith, Adam. 1859. *The Theory of Moral Sentiments*. Scotland: printed for Andrew Millar, in the Strand; and Alexander Kincaid and J. Bell, in Edinburgh.

Steinsaltz, Adin. 1976. *The Essential Talmud*. New York: Basic Books Inc.

Strobel, Lee. 2000. *A Case for Faith*. Michigan: Zondervan.

Templeton, Charles. 1996. *Farewell to God. My Reasons for Rejecting the Christian Faith*. Toronto: McClelland & Stewart.

The Guardian. 2015. *Angela Merkel pledges to cut German immigration figures but rejects limit.* 14 Dec. https://www.theguardian.com/world/2015/dec/14/angela-merkel-pledge-cut-german-immigration-figures.

The Rule of Law Education Centre. 2022. "What is the Rule of Law." *The Rule of Law Education Centre.* https://www.ruleoflaw.org.au/what-is-the-rule-of-law/.

United Nations. 2018. "The costs of corruption: values, economic development under assault, trillions lost." *United Nations News.* 9 Dec. https://news.un.org/en/story/2018/12/1027971.

United States Govt. 2023. *Title 18. Crimes and Criminal Procedure. Ch. 51 Homicide. Section 1111.* https://www.law.cornell.edu/uscode/text/18/1111.

Univ. of Maryland. Francis King Carey School of Law. 2016. *Charging the Poor: Criminal Justice Debt & Modern Day Debtors Prisons. Neil Sobol.* . Accessed Jun 2023. https://digitalcommons.law.umaryland.edu/cgi/viewcontent.cgi?article=3701&context=mlr.

University of Leipzig. 2023. *Ebers Papyrus.* https://www.ub.uni-leipzig.de/en/about-us/exhibitions/permanent-exhibition/ebers-papyrus/.

Vine, W. E., Unger, M. F., & White, W., Jr. 1996. *Vines Complete Expository Dictionary of Biblical Words. Vol 1.* Nashville: Thomas Nelson.

Washington, George. 1789. *George Washington to Edmund Randolph 1789.* 28 Sep. https://www.loc.gov/resource/mgw2.022/?sp=177&st=text.

Washington, George. 1939. *The Writings of George Washington. Washington to Marquis De Lafayette 1788 29:410.* Washington D.C.: U. S. Government Printing Office, 410.

Whiston, William. 1989. *The Works of Josephus.* MA: Hendrickson Publishers, Inc.

Wilbur, David. 2016-2022. *Does the Torah Prohibit Polygamy?* Accessed Dec 2023. https://davidwilber.com/articles/does-the-torah-prohibit-polygamy.

Williams, Peter J. 2015. *Does the Bible Support Slavery?* 30 Oct. https://www.bethinking.org/bible/does-the-bible-support-slavery.
Witherspoon, John. 1906. *John Witherspoon. Thanksgiving Day Proclamation 1782.* New York: David Walker Woods. Pub: Fleming H. Revell Co. .
Wright, Christopher. J. H. 2004. *Old Testament Ethics for the People of God.* Illinois: inter Varsity Press.
Yancey, Philip. 1988. *Disappointment with God.* Grand Rapids. MI: Zondervan.
—. 1999. *The Bible that Jesus Read.* Michigan: Zondervan.
Zeigler, Sarah L. 2017. *The First Amendment Encyclopedia. Sunday Blue Laws.* Sep. Accessed Jun 2023. https://www.mtsu.edu/first-amendment/article/1243.

Index of Subjects

613 Commandments, 17
Abraham, 39, 100, 104, 116, 118, 128, 137, 190, 193, 202, 208, 290, 295, 321, 342, 362, 408, 413, 430, 437, 477
  justified, 67, 467, 468
Achan, 250
Adam and Eve, 205, 208, 341, 372, 374, 477
adultery
  commandment, 151
  consequences, 423
  Jesus' mercy, 183
  Jesus' teaching, 42
  penalty, 184, 203
agape. *See* love
Amorites. *See* Canaanites
animal welfare, 344
ark of the covenant, 142, 146, 235, 350, 355, 357, 358, 359, 360, 389, 480
Assyria, 250, 287, 290, 291, 408, 414
Atonement, Day of, 59, 282, 365, 375, 381, 389
avenger of blood, 245, 249, 255, 257
Baal, 215, 362, 404, 408, 410
Babylon, 14, 53, 238, 296, 306, 314, 404, 414, 483
Beatitudes, 40
birthright. *See* firstborn
Boaz, 257
bribery, 168, 241
Caleb, 121
  the Kenizzite, 235
calendar, 56, 381, 482

Canaan, 108, 189, 220, 251, 269, 282, 289, 342, 376, 381, 435, 482
Canaanites, 86, 215, 328, 329, 412, 415, 419
capital punishment, 151, 173, 184, 245, 248, 249, 250, 258, 272, 319, 418
ceremonial system. *See* worship system
ceremonial uncleanness, 395
circumcision, 68, 139, 235, 339, 383, 400, 448
cities of refuge. *See* sanctuary cities
citizenship, 234
clean and unclean animals, 338, 477
concubines, 112, 194
David
  as king, 60, 99, 221, 235, 244, 289, 350, 367
  confirms Moses, 19
  desire to build temple, 128
  forgiven, 185
  imprecatory psalms, 429, 433
  multiple wives, 112
  perspective of the law, 60, 67
  shewbread incident, 38
Deborah, 202, 219, 244
Decalogue. *See* Ten Commandments
dietary laws, 338
divorce, 43, 110, 185, 272, 274, 316
economic
  effect, 278, 281, 283, 285, 293

framework, 291
system, 287
education, 308
Egypt, 10, 13, 25, 149, 167, 188, 279, 287, 300, 309, 362, 415, 437, 477, 478
  diseases of, 332, 340
  exodus from, 8, 25, 27, 52, 83, 111, 137, 210, 235, 260, 288, 298, 311, 382, 393, 435
elders, 215, 216, 218, 220, 245, 259, 274, 359, 366, 443
  role of, 193, 241
environment
  caring for, 341
equality
  modern confusion, 170
  under law, 165, 169, 246
exodus. *See* Egypt exodus from
eye for eye. *See* justice
Ezra, 456, 462, 479
faith
  example of Abraham, 67, 467
  importance of, 187
  justification, 67, 191, 446
  related to law, 33, 66, 189, 281, 374, 440, 468
family
  God's plan, 192, 195, 197
  heirarchy, 206
  importance of, 192, 199
  in Israel, 193
fear of God, 196, 349
Feast of Booths. *See* Tabernacles
Feast of Firstfruits. *See* Pentecost
Feast of Harvest. *See* Pentecost
Feast of Weeks. *See* Pentecost
firstborn, 208, 372
  birthright, 208
  ceremony, 209

  church of, 369, 387
  Jesus, 386
  nation, 195, 209
  priesthood, 210, 361
firstfruits, 208, 370, 387, 392
foreigners
  categories of, 236
  citizenship, 234, 237
  equality under law, 36, 165
  love towards, 167, 319
  servitude, 327
  social welfare, 300
  welcome, 227, 232, 296, 306, 357, 441
forgiveness, 63, 105, 116, 131, 132, 139, 178, 179, 182, 183, 190, 252, 259, 277, 354, 360, 366, 368, 377, 379, 401, 430, 432, 458, 472
freedom, 1, 135, 291, 296, 297
  civil rights, 223
  defined, 96, 227
  God's perspective, 94, 111, 231, 472
  Jubilee, 282, 445
  moral virtue, 96
  of religion, 226
  of speech and assembly, 230
  requires law, 95, 153
  Sabbath, 278, 279
gentiles, 124, 294
  included, 71, 126, 238, 370, 384, 414, 439
  segregation, 2, 36, 357, 358, 402, 448
Gibeonites, 329, 416
gleaning, 143, 303
God
  aligned to reality, 91
  character is knowable, 74

desires to be understood, 75
gracious, 112
just and righteous, 106
lover of freedom, 94
master plan, 115, 199, 347, 394, 470
of love, 82
of vengeance, 104
personal, 118
pragmatic, 107
rational and coherent, 88
unlike our expectations, 126
zealous and motivated, 114
God's values
law an extension of, 75
unchanging, 80
wanted Israel to emulate, 75
golden calf incident, 51, 127, 367, 406
government
God's plan, 214, 287, 306
modern style, 224, 293
grace, 248, 271, 448, 470
God's, 66, 79, 82, 113, 128, 137, 278, 230, 298, 349, 354, 369, 460, 467
old covenant, 83
prior to Jesus, 28
relationship to law, 25, 137, 138, 467
hardened hearts, 435
health and hygeine, 333
Hebrew calendar. See calendar
Herod, 355, 357
Hezekiah, 55, 190, 290, 360, 398, 408, 424
high priest, 217, 242, 355, 360, 362, 365, 368, 389, 483
death of, 259
dress, 365
Jesus, 116, 259, 358, 368
standards, 364
holiness of God, 348
holy days, 142, 216, 312, 380, 447, 464, 470, 482, See specific days
Jesus kept, 355
purpose, 116
typology, 380, 393
humility, 25, 124, 125, 130
idolatry, 253, 404, 406
impartiality, 36, 164, 165, 175, 235, 240, 433
inheritance laws, 54, 108, 202, 204, 208, 236, 256, 282, 284, 321
interest
commercial loans, 294
foreigners, 237, 294
poor not charged, 301
Isaac, 118, 190, 193, 208, 408, 469, 477
Jacob, 118, 190, 193, 208, 209, 397, 408
jealous, description of God, 115, 407, 422
jealousy trial by ordeal, 426
Jeroboam, 57
Jerusalem, 55, 57, 209, 235, 290, 329, 354, 357, 370, 376, 377, 430, 442, 448, 459, 463, 464, 480, 482
Jesus
confirms Moses, 20
critical of Pharisees, 32, 35, 103, 110, 163, 399, 429
firstborn of many, 211, 370
glorified, 349
grace and truth, 28
harmony with the Father, 79
High Priest, 368

humility, 124, 126
King of kings, 463
life and legacy, 2, 4, 123
like Moses, 24, 26
merciful, 179, 183
mission, 115
our Passover, 383
parables, 155
personal, 118
perspective of the law, 32, 88, 144
pragmatic, 107
redeemer, 260
respectful of temple, 355
Sabbath, 37, 278, 279
Sermon on the Mount, 40
supporter of women, 200
the bread of life, 385
unchanging values, 74, 78, 80
Jethro, 19, 362, 478
Jewish calendar. *See* calendar
John the Baptist, 377, 383, 453
Joseph, 209, 309, 477
Joseph and Mary, 186, 209, 377, 480
Josiah, 16, 190, 408, 481
Jubilee
year of, 278, 282, 283, 284, 293, 306, 342, 444
Judah
kingdom of, 16, 22, 53, 57, 190, 284, 314, 404, 414
tribe of, 25, 235
Judaism, 14, 70, 155, 161, 167, 296, 338, 458, 467
judgments, 142, 173, 262
application of, 155
defined, 155
difficult, 440
Paul's use of, 156

judicial system, 240
justice
defined, 99, 185
eye for eye, 44, 171
God of, 99, 104, 105, 177, 251
harsh examples, 252
principles of, 164
relationship to mercy, 101
role of redeemer, 256
role of the state, 433
weightier matter of law, 34, 66
kidnapping, 151, 319, 328
kinsman redeemer. *See* redeeming kinsman
Kosher, 338
land
ownership, 282, 292, 342
redeeming, 283
law of Moses
term defined, 8, 14
lending laws, 294, 301, 302, 305
levirate marriage, 195, 256, 257
Levites, 170, 205, 210, 235, 243, 282, 361
income, 296
roles, 218, 242, 366
Levitical cities. *See* sanctuary cities
liability. *See* tort laws
liberty. *See* freedom
literacy, 312
love
a decision, 87
agape, 82, 85, 432
commanded, 84, 270
God of, 2, 82, 134, 138, 198, 472
law of Moses, 46, 69, 84, 87, 93, 120, 144, 145, 373, 467
marital, 198, 201
neighbor, 154, 167, 262
of enemies, 429

of family, 192, 198
of foreigners, 36, 319
recipricol, 84, 196
marriage, 194, 198, 199, 201, 269, 272
  ceremony, 193
  faithfulness, 426
  forced, 273
  God with Israel, 196
  levirate. *See* levirate marriage
  male role, 204, 206
  proof virginity, 274
  rights, 326
  spiritual parallels, 199
  time of war, 276
Melchizedek, 362, 364, 369, 477
mercy, 39, 145, 248, 271, 277, 354, 360, 459
  application, 101, 102, 131, 175
  God's, 63, 82, 182, 460
  Jesus, 183
  Joseph example, 186
  relationship to justice, 101
  weightier matter of law, 34, 66, 179
mercy seat. *See* ark of the covenant
Messiah, 4, 36, 39, 116, 119, 121, 123, 260, 353, 354, 360, 377, 380, 453, 470
monarchy
  Israelite, 107, 214, 215, 219, 220, 245
Moses
  author, 312, 420, 453, 455, 456
  compared to Jesus, 24
  educated, 332
  historicity, 19, 25
  interacting with God, 109, 119, 127, 348, 350, 354, 357, 359, 363, 397, 406, 435

  Jesus support of, 20
  perspective of the law, 47, 91
  reputation, 1
  seat of, 32, 33
  veil, 71
Mount Sinai, 8, 48, 107, 127, 141, 279, 348, 354, 357, 359, 369, 388, 397, 406, 455, 477, 482
natural law, 92, 147, 423, 478
near kinsman. *See* redeeming kinsman
negative law, 152, 154, 228
Nehemiah, 56, 295, 442, 462, 479
new covenant, 69, 71, 102, 238, 379, 463
Noah, 28, 374, 413, 425, 477, 482
old covenant, 8, 40, 49, 54, 61, 69, 102, 135, 179, 190, 203, 238
  basis, 83
  personal, 118
  unique, 139
  why it failed, 458
oral law, 14, 15
paganism. *See* idolatry
Passover, 116, 170, 235, 312, 377, 381, 382, 392, 398, 482
  circumcision required, 234
  complaints, 54, 108
Paul
  background, 65, 234
  hard to understand, 446, 467
  imprecations, 430
  perspective of the law, 65
penalties. *See* sentencing and penalties
Pentateuch, 8
Pentecost, 116, 303, 381, 386, 387
polygamy, 110, 112
poor

caring for, 11, 23, 131, 166, 278, 295, 300, 376, 421
priesthood, Levitical, 27, 205, 242, 361, 362
  typology, 363, 371, 470
priesthood, Melchizedek. *See* Melchizedek
public health, 331
purity laws. *See* ceremonial uncleanness
Rahab, 121, 126, 190, 202, 206, 236, 277, 416
redeeming kinsman, 245, 255
  Jesus as redeemer, 260
Rehoboam, 57, 436
Ruth, 121, 256, 257, 284, 425, 441
Sabbath
  breaking, 252, 253, 284
  freedom, 279
  God's intent, 37, 143, 151, 189, 227, 280, 293, 303
  Jesus, 2, 37, 107, 278, 279
  origin, 147, 278, 279, 312, 478
  rest, 322, 344
  Talmud, 280
sabbatical year, 278, 280, 282, 284, 293, 344, 445
sacrificial system, 372, *See* worship system
  purpose, 374
  types of sacrifices, 375
  typology, 378
Samuel, 54, 111, 216, 219, 220, 224, 243, 377, 400, 406, 429, 433
sanctuary. *See* tabernacle
sanctuary cities, 243, 258
sentencing and penalties, 248
Sermon on the Mount, 12, 40, 177, 458

servitude, 250, 315
  daughter, 326
  debt, 285, 320
  foreigners, 327
  involuntary, 317, 320
  Jubilee release, 444
  legal protection, 323
  reasons for, 320
  redeeming from, 256
  time of war, 329
  vocation, 321
  voluntary, 317, 320
  wife, 327
  working conditions, 322
  year of release, 281, 305
sex
  God's purpose, 204, 270, 277
  male and female, 201, 205, 270, 271, 277
sexual morality, 147, 194, 204, 269
  desire, 270
  false accusation, 274
  Jesus, 43
  pagan cultic practices, 362, 398, 409, 416
  penalties for misconduct, 271
  STDs, 333, 340
sexual violence, 272
slavery. *See* servitude
  definition, 315, 316, 319
  historical, 319, 323, 329, 330
  translation from Hebrew, 317
social welfare, 300
Sodom, 104, 128, 413, 414, 418, 477
Solomon, 55, 57, 112, 221, 237, 244, 289, 308, 328, 356, 359, 436
statutes
  defined, 142

tabernacle, 183, 203, 214, 334, 354, 360
   design, 355
   God's dwelling place, 119, 351, 356
   importance, 354
   typology, 116, 358, 368
Tabernacles, Feast of, 56, 303, 390, 464
Talmud, 15, 18, 156, 456
temple
   first, 16, 55, 119, 128, 354, 356, 359, 367, 376
   second, 15, 203, 238, 355, 357, 358, 369, 379, 394, 399, 483
Ten Commandments, 8, 12, 86, 120, 137, 141, 146, 192, 227, 271, 312, 466, 470, 475, 478
theocracy, 216
tithe, 33, 296, 304, 376
torah
   meaning, 135, 308
Torah, 8, 14, 17, 65, 135, 314, 463
tort laws, 262
Trumpets, Feast of, 381, 387
Ugarit, 88, 162
unclean. *See* ceremonial uncleanness
Unleavened Bread
   Feast of, 55, 312, 381, 384
usury. *See* interest

vengeance, 175, 176, 433
   definition, 104
   God of, 104
   personal, 44, 172, 177, 257, 420, 431
wages, 158, 292, 302, 323
wall of separation, 357, 449
wave sheaf ceremony, 386
wealth
   creation, 9, 279, 288, 289, 291, 293, 296, 298, 342
widows. *See* poor
   protection for, 255, 284
women
   and the law of Moses, 200, 203
   bold towards Moses, 109
   curse of Eve, 205
   distinctive role, 204
   family, 192
   God's respect for, 201
   inheritance laws, 284
   times of war, 276
   violence against, 272
worship system, 347
   not burdensome, 3, 33, 37, 48, 55, 57, 280, 351, 376, 378, 395, 401, 447
year of release. *See* sabbatical year
Zelophehad, daughters of, 108, 202, 284

Index of Scriptures

Genesis
1:14 *482*
1:26 *94, 114*
1:27 *201*
1:27–28 *201*
1:28 *341*
1:31 *114, 345*
2:15 *341*
2:18–24 *192*
2:18 *201*
2:24 *110, 201*
3:16 *205*
3:17–19 *205*
3:21 *374*
3:24 *359*
4:4 *208, 372, 374, 477*
4:10 *249, 477*
6–7 *413*
6:5–7 *413, 477*
6:6 *250*
6:11 *413*
7:2 *374, 477*
7:11 *482*
8:4 *482*
8:5 *482*
8:13 *482*
8:20 *374, 477*
9:5–6 *249, 259, 374*
9:6 *257*
12:3 *9, 116*
13:2 *288, 295*
13:13 *477*
14:18–20 *362, 477*
14:18 *369*
15:2–3 *321*
15:6 *67, 137*
15:13–16 *415*
15:16 *269*
17:8 *342*
17:15–17 *118*
17:17 *128*
17:19 *202*
18:1–15 *118*
18:11–15 *128*
18:12 *118*
18:18 *239*
18:19 *100*
18:21 *413*
18:22–32 *104, 430*
18:25 *128, 413*
21:6 *118*
24:35 *288*
26:4–5 *477*
26:13–14 *288, 295*
27:19–32 *477*
27:33 *209*
27:34 *209*
29:18 *193*
29:20 *193*
29:22 *193*
35:2–3 *397*
39:7–9 *477*
48:18 *209*
49:3–4 *209*

Exodus
1:15–21 *202*
1:17 *477*
2:1–10 *19*
2:11–15 *22*
2:21 *19*
2:22 *19*
3:1 *362*
3:8 *49*
3:11 *25*
3:13–14 *80*
3:15–17 *27*
3:16 *193, 241*
3:19 *437*
3:21–22 *288, 322*
4:10–14 *22*
4:21 *435*
4:22 *195, 210*
4:22–23 *209*
4:25–26 *22*
5:1–2 *437*
6:6 *260*
6:16–20 *19*
7:13 *438*
8:15 *438*
8:19 *438*
8:32 *438*
9:7 *438*
9:27 *438*
9:34 *438, 438*
11 *382*
12 *108*
12:1–12 *382*
12:2 *482*
12:13 *382*
12:17 *384*

12:19 *238*	**20:1** *146*	**21:36** *264*
12:23–27 *383*	**20:2** *150*	**22:1–3** *252, 320*
12:38 *235*	**20:2–3** *189*	**22:2–3** *265*
12:43 *383*	**20:3–5** *405*	**22:3** *323*
12:46 *382*	**20:3** *407*	**22:5** *263*
12:48 *170, 235, 236, 238, 328, 383, 441*	**20:6** *183*	**22:6** *263*
	20:8 *279*	**22:10–13** *263*
	20:8–11 *312*	**22:14** *263*
12:49 *165*	**20:8–10** *322*	**22:16–17** *272, 273*
13:1–2 *209*	**20:11** *147, 279*	**22:20** *253*
13:2 *387*	**20:12** *193, 203*	**22:21–23** *300*
13:8–9 *334*	**20:14** *426*	**22:25** *294, 301*
13:21 *356*	**20:15** *292*	**22:26–27** *302*
15:20 *202*	**20:16** *292*	**23:1** *266*
15:26 *473*	**20:17** *43, 204, 292*	**23:3** *167*
16:25–26 *478*	**20:18–20** *8*	**23:4–5** *45, 268, 429*
16:28–29 *147*	**20:20** *197*	**23:4** *85*
16:28 *473*	**20:22–26** *444*	**23:7** *266*
18:4 *19*	**21:2** *322*	**23:8** *168*
18:5 *19*	**21:2–4** *327*	**23:10–12** *280*
18:13 *26*	**21:5–6** *321*	**23:10–11** *281, 342*
18:13–14 *27*	**21:7** *326*	**23:11** *304*
18:15–16 *478*	**21:8–11** *326*	**23:12** *303, 344*
18:16 *311*	**21:16** *319, 328*	**23:14–16** *380, 381*
18:21–22 *241*	**21:18–19** *264, 325*	**23:15** *384*
19 *8*	**21:20** *324*	**23:15–16** *387*
19:5 *137, 189, 341*	**21:20–21** *325, 325*	**23:19** *161*
19:5–6 *210, 369*	**21:22–25** *151, 265*	**23:23** *420*
19:13 *250*	**21:22–23** *172*	**23:27–30** *420*
19:14–15 *398*	**21:22–27** *174*	**24:3–4** *15*
19:15 *269, 362*	**21:26–27** *324*	**24:3–8** *120*
19:16 *348*	**21:28–30** *264*	**24:4** *455*
19:18–20 *388*	**21:29** *174*	**24:7** *480*
19:21–23 *348*	**21:29–30** *259*	**24:9–10** *350*
20 *8, 141*	**21:33–34** *262*	**24:9–11** *359*
20:1–2 *137*	**21:35** *264*	**24:12** *475*

Scripture Index 505

25–27 *354*
25:8 *119, 354, 356*
25:19–20 *355*
25:21–22 *357, 359*
26 *355*
26:1–14 *354*
27:1–8 *356*
27:9–18 *355*
28 *363*
28:2 *363*
28:4–6 *309*
28:40 *363*
28:42–43 *364*
29:9 *170, 362*
29:30 *362*
29:35 *362*
29:37 *362*
29:44 *362*
29:45 *119*
29:45–46 *391*
30:22–38 *354*
30:30 *27*
31 *354*
31:13 *278*
31:15 *253*
31:18 *146*
32:1–6 *127*
32:4 *22, 406*
32:9–11 *26*
32:9–10 *127*
32:9 *459*
32:11–13 *25*
32:11–12 *127*
32:15 *146*
32:15–16 *146*
32:26–28 *367*

32:27 *250*
32:32 *26*
33:3–7 *119*
33:7–11 *357*
33:11 *119*
33:19 *102*
33:20 *348*
34:6 *28, 82, 91, 412*
34:8 *348*
34:12 *215*
34:14 *407*
34:21 *292*
34:28 *146*
34:29 *349*
35–36 *355*
35:25–26 *309*
35:30–35 *309*
38:9–20 *355*
38:21 *354*
39 *363*
39:4–5 *159*
39:30 *365*
40:2 *354*
40:20–21 *146*
40:30 *334*
40:34–38 *356*

Leviticus
1:17 *375*
2:11 *385*
4:2–3 *377*
4:20 *377*
4:26 *377*
5 *203, 401*
5:1 *247*
5:7 *376*

5:11 *376*
6:1–5 *252*
6:8–13 *375*
6:14–23 *375*
6:17 *385*
6:24–30 *375*
7:1–10 *375*
7:11–36 *375*
7:20–21 *396*
7:37–38 *375*
8:6 *364*
8:30 *350*
10:1–2 *350*
10:1–3 *365*
10:3 *350, 396*
10:9 *365*
10:11 *167*
10:16–20 *398*
11:27–28 *334*
11:29–32 *334*
11:32–34 *334*
11:35 *334*
11:40 *334*
11:44–46 *339*
12:2 *395*
12:2–4 *400*
12:3 *339*
12:5 *395*
12:8 *209, 376*
12:16–18 *395*
13 *335*
13–14 *335*
13–15 *367*
13:45 *335*
13:46 *335*
13:47–59 *335*

14:1–6 338
14:2–3 335
14:8–9 335
14:11 335
14:21 376
14:34–52 336
14:40–48 336
14:47 336
14:48–53 338
15 334, 362
15:16 269
15:31 269, 396
16 355
16:12–16 368
16:31 389
17:7–9 409
17:8 238, 357
17:8–9 376
17:11 374
17:12–14 374
18:1–3 352, 380
18:3 13
18:5 138
18:18 195
18:19 334
18:24–25 269
18:24–28 417
19:2 77, 348, 353
19:13 292
19:14 159
19:15 100, 166, 240
19:16 265
19:17–18 42, 429, 431

19:18 44, 143, 144, 172, 177, 267, 319, 472
19:27 162, 362
19:28 162, 362
19:31 407
19:32 193
19:33–34 167, 234, 319
19:34 36, 450
19:35–36 266, 292
19:37 475
20:1–3 254
20:7 351
20:10 185
20:14 250
20:26 351
21:1–4 364
21:5 162
21:7 364, 364
21:9 250
21:10–15 365
21:16–23 364
21:20 364
22:2–3 398
22:3 254
22:18 238, 357
22:27 345
22:28 345
22:29 374
23:1–2 380
23:3 279
23:10–12 386
23:15–21 386
23:24 388
23:39 391

23:40 50
23:40–43 391
24:11–12 253
24:12–20 172
24:17–22 171
24:18 172, 174
24:21 172
24:22 165, 324
25 342
25:1–7 280
25:5 344
25:7 344
25:8–9 282
25:10 278, 282
25:11 342
25:14–17 294
25:20–22 281
25:23 237, 342
25:23–24 282
25:23–28 292
25:25 193, 256
25:25–28 284
25:29–30 237, 292
25:29–31 282
25:29 292
25:32–34 282
25:32–35 283
25:35–36 294
25:35–37 301
25:39 320
25:39–41 445
25:44 236
25:44–46 327
25:45–47 237
25:47 237, 296, 328
25:47–55 237

Scripture Index 507

25:47–48 *256*
25:48–49 *255*
25:50–52 *284*
25:55 *318*
26:1–13 *190*
26:7–8 *220*
26:11–12 *356*
26:13 *52, 315*

Numbers
1 *193*
1:50–53 *362*
1:52–53 *356*
2 *119*
2:2 *193, 356*
3:1–4 *362*
3:5–10 *363*
3:12–13 *210, 361*
4 *363*
4:4–6 *355*
4:17–20 *356*
4:18 *254*
4:46 *193*
5:5–8 *256*
5:11–31 *426*
6 *377*
6:2 *203*
6:23 *367*
8:23–25 *363, 378*
9:2–4 *108*
9:6–7 *396*
9:6–13 *401*
9:7 *54, 108*
9:9–11 *108*
9:14 *238*
9:15–17 *356*

10:8–9 *366*
10:10 *482*
11:11–15 *47*
11:16 *193, 241*
12:3 *25, 125*
12:10 *22*
12:11–14 *26*
13:3–6 *235*
14:11 *119, 459*
14:18 *83, 422*
14:27 *53*
15:14–16 *238, 450*
15:14–15 *357*
15:16 *36, 234*
15:27–29 *252*
15:30 *238*
15:30–31 *253*
15:32–34 *252*
15:37–38 *160*
15:39–40 *161*
16:3 *350*
16:44–49 *127*
17:10 *355*
18:8 *170*
18:8–19 *378*
18:12 *387*
18:15–18 *210*
18:15 *387*
18:23–24 *211*
19:11–12 *334*
19:13 *397*
19:15 *334*
19:20 *254, 397*
20:10–12 *22*
25 *121*
25:1–5 *271*

25:6–8 *271*
25:6–13 *367*
26:55 *108*
27:1–6 *202*
27:1–2 *203, 246*
27:2–4 *54*
27:4 *109*
27:6–7 *109*
27:18–21 *27*
28:11 *482*
29:6 *482*
29:40 *474*
31:6 *366*
31:16 *420*
31:20–23 *336*
31:24 *336*
31:25–54 *288*
32:12 *235*
33:2 *311, 455*
33:55 *236, 237*
35:2–5 *283*
35:9–15 *258*
35:12–27 *255*
35:16–21 *259*
35:25–28 *259*
35:29–30 *258*
35:30 *180, 259*
35:31 *174*
35:33–34 *250, 258*
36 *109*
36:2–9 *256*
36:6–9 *236*
36:7 *282*

Deuteronomy
1:13 *218, 241, 308*

1:16 *100, 193*
1:17 *240, 241*
1:29–30 *420*
1:31 *193*
2:4–6 *415*
2:9 *415*
2:19 *415*
2:25 *416*
3:1–3 *435*
3:23–26 *22*
4:1 *164*
4:2 *218*
4:5–6 *9*
4:5–8 *48, 216, 232, 419*
4:6 *91, 308, 314*
4:7 *119*
4:9–10 *311*
4:13–14 *475*
4:14 *155*
4:15–17 *406*
4:24 *115*
4:25–29 *105*
4:27–30 *462*
4:29 *457*
4:31 *182*
4:35 *407*
4:37 *468*
4:39–40 *468*
4:40 *86*
5:1 *164, 167*
5:9–10 *422*
5:9 *424*
5:15 *37, 279, 280, 312, 322*
5:25–27 *475*
5:29 *372*
5:30–31 *476*
6:1–2 *155*
6:5 *9, 60, 144, 206, 472*
6:5–6 *84, 182, 372*
6:5–7 *120*
6:6 *76, 134, 167, 463*
6:6–20 *167*
6:6–7 *344*
6:7 *308*
6:8–9 *310*
6:9 *313*
6:10–11 *295*
6:14 *404*
6:20–23 *137, 311*
6:24 *86*
6:24–25 *474*
6:25 *139*
7:3–4 *236*
7:6 *9, 348*
7:7–8 *83*
7:9 *102*
7:10 *104*
7:12–14 *49*
7:14 *281*
7:15 *333, 337*
7:16 *237*
8:1 *164*
8:2 *135*
8:3 *188, 298, 299*
8:5 *197*
8:7–9 *288*
8:11 *474*
8:18 *289*
9:5 *415*
9:6 *83*
9:20 *26*
10:2 *355*
10: 12–13 *86*
10:12–13 *138, 196*
10:12 *144, 183*
10:15 *193*
10:16 *139, 383*
10:17 *36, 166, 168, 414*
10:18 *167*
10:19 *167*
10:21–22 *138*
11:1 *138*
11:10–11 *188*
11:11–12 *342*
11:13 *144*
11:13–14 *188*
11:16–17 *404*
11:18 *121, 463*
11:18–20 *138*
11:18–21 *310*
11:20–21 *313*
12:1–14 *376*
12:2–4 *362, 372*
12:5–7 *381*
12:13–14 *362, 443*
12:29–30 *418*
12:31 *416*
12:32 *18*
13:1–5 *253*
13:3 *144*
13:11 *245, 251*
14:1 *162, 195*
14:21 *237*

Scripture Index 509

14:22 *292, 296*
14:22–25 *296*
14:24–25 *376*
14:26 *391*
15:1–3 *237*
15:1–4 *281, 305*
15:6 *288, 294*
15:7–8 *301*
15:7–10 *305*
15:11 *268, 296*
15:12–15 *281*
15:12–18 *305*
15:12 *322, 444*
15:13–14 *322*
15:16 *323*
15:18 *323*
16:3 *312, 385*
16:9–10 *387*
16:11 *303*
16:11–12 *322*
16:13 *390*
16:14–15 *303*
16:14 *380*
16:17 *303, 376*
16:18 *240, 242*
16:19–20 *166*
16:19 *241*
17:2–5 *253*
17:6–7 *246*
17:7 *252*
17:8–12 *218*
17:8–9 *218, 242*
17:8–13 *366*
17:10 *243*
17:11 *167, 243, 310*
17:12–13 *243*

17:13 *251*
17:14–20 *112*
17:14 *189*
17:14–15 *237*
17:14–17 *289*
17:15 *169*
17:16–20 *221*
17:17 *112*
17:18–20 *60, 165*
17:18–19 *219, 311*
17:19–20 *23*
18:1 *363*
18:4 *210, 387*
18:10–14 *407*
18:18–19 *24*
19:6 *259*
19:11–12 *259*
19:14 *267, 292*
19:15 *168, 246, 320*
19:16–21 *172*
19:16–19 *246*
19:18–21 *252*
19:18–19 *266*
19:19 *252*
19:20 *251*
19:21 *175, 250*
20:1–4 *219, 366*
20:4 *189*
20:5–9 *220*
20:8 *220*
20:10–11 *329*
20:10–16 *415*
20:12–15 *329*
20:16–17 *412*
20:16–18 *419*
20:19–20 *344*

21:1–9 *258*
21:5 *243, 366*
21:10–13 *277*
21:14 *277*
21:15–16 *208*
21:17 *209*
21:18 *204*
21:18–21 *442*
21:22 *250*
21:22–23 *251, 336*
22:1–3 *268*
22:1 *344*
22:4 *268, 344*
22:5 *271*
22:6–7 *343*
22:8 *265*
22:9–11 *158*
22:10 *159*
22:13–17 *275*
22:18–21 *275*
22:21 *252*
22:22 *203*
22:23–24 *272*
22:25–27 *273*
22:25 *274*
23:1–3 *441*
23:2 *364*
23:3–8 *237*
23:12–14 *335*
23:15–16 *324*
23:19–20 *294*
23:20 *237, 294*
23:24–25 *304*
24:1 *185, 272, 276*
24:1–4 *194*
24:1–3 *313*

24:6 302
24:10–11 302
24:12–13 302
24:14–15 302
24:15 292
24:16 169, 422
24:19–22 304
25:2–3 251
25:4 156, 292, 323
25:5–10 195
25:9–10 255
25:11–12 440
25:13–16 267, 292
26:11 50
26:11–12 304
27:1–3 313
27:7 375
27:8 313
27:15 254
27:17 267
28:1–14 9, 49, 190
28:1–2 189
28:1 288, 289
28:3–6 287
28:7 220
28:8 287
28:11 287
28:15 50, 422
28:18 422
28:27 333
28:41 422
28:60 333
29:4 460
29:9 49, 289
29:10–15 120
29:24–28 462

30:5–10 462
30:6 144, 383
30:9–10 51
30:10 480
30:11–14 49
30:14 134
30:19–20 232
31:9 15, 366, 455
31:10–11 391
31:11 310
31:12 203
31:16 231
31:19 312
31:21 460
31:22 312, 455
31:24–26 313, 481
31:29 232
32:4 99, 251
32:6 87, 195
32:35 104
32:39 250, 407
32:46–47 91
32:46 134, 463
33:29 50
34:10 27

Joshua
1:7–8 51
1:8 91, 289, 468
2:9–10 416
2:9 461
2:11 188
5:10–12 382
5:14–15 119
6 121
7:15 250

7:25 250
8:29 251
8:31–32 474
8:32 456
8:34–35 16
9 416
9:27 329
10:27 251
11:18–20 435
14 121
14:2 282
17:13 328
18 282
18:8–9 313
19 282
20:1–9 258
20:4 259
22:8 288
23:1–2 215
23:13 237
23:14 54
24:1 215
24:14 13
24:15 415
24:25–26 313
24:26 456, 480

Judges
1:28 419
2:1–3 419
2:7 215
2:10–11 215
2:16–17 218
2:17 313, 404
3:7 313
3:11 215, 289

Scripture Index 511

3:30 *215, 289*
4:4–5 *202*
4:4 *219*
4:4–6 *244*
4:21 *206*
5 *202*
5:24–27 *206*
5:31 *215, 289*
6–8 *220*
7 *220*
8:13–14 *313*
8:22–23 *219*
8:28 *215*
21:25 *215*

Ruth
1–4 *121*
2 *303*
3:10 *256, 257*
4:1–6 *284*
4:1–9 *292*
4:3 *203*
4:10 *254*
4:21–22 *441*

1 Samuel
1 *121*
1:3 *377*
1:11 *202*
1:21 *377*
1:21–23 *400*
2:18 *243*
3:19 *219*
3:20 *243*
6:6 *438*
7:15–17 *243*

8:1–3 *244*
8:3 *241*
8:4–5 *54*
8:4–8 *215*
8:5 *220*
8:5–8 *226*
8:7–9 *112*
8:7 *119, 216*
8:10–18 *289*
8:11–18 *225*
8:19 *220*
8:19–20 *244*
8:20 *220, 406*
8:21–22 *289*
12:12 *216*
13:7–13 *219*
13:14 *60, 429*
15:22 *373, 378*
15:33 *429*
16:7 *134*
21:1–6 *38*
24 *429*
25:2–18 *206*

2 Samuel
1 *429*
5:11 *290*
6:1–2 *360*
6:10–11 *235*
6:18 *219*
7:5–7 *128, 356*
8:11–12 *289*
8:15 *99*
12:1–6 *345*
12:13 *185*
14:4 *203, 246*

15:2–4 *244*
18:33 *429*
19:5–6 *434*
20:14–22 *206*

1 Kings
2:3 *474*
2:5–6 *258*
2:8–9 *429*
3:9–14 *308*
3:16–28 *244*
3:16 *246*
4:34 *308*
5:1 *290*
5:11 *290*
8:9 *355*
8:62 *56*
8:66 *56*
9:11–14 *290*
9:26–27 *290*
10:8 *290*
10:14–29 *290*
11:3 *112*
11:8 *237*
11:31 *436*
12:4 *225, 290*
12:8–11 *436*
12:27 *58*
12:32–33 *58*
19:18 *121, 191*
21:1–3 *284*
21:17–19 *284*
21:27–28 *129*
22:19–20 *437*

2 Kings
3:26–27 *410*
16:4 *372*
17:10 *372*
17:27 *408*
18:14 *291*
22:14 *202*
23:7 *405*
23:24 *407*

1 Chronicles
2:34–35 *236, 321*
4:10 *121*
4:15 *235*
5:1 *209*
9:17–27 *367*
9:26 *367*
9:33 *367*
11:39 *442*
12:4 *329*
13 *350*
13:12 *350*
15 *350*
21:26 *219*
22:12–13 *480*
23:14–17 *19*
23:2–5 *365*
23:4 *244*
23:6 *219*
28:12 *355*
28:19 *355*
29:10 *195*
30:21–22 *55*

2 Chronicles
1:12 *289*
5:7–8 *359*
5:10 *355*
6:18–21 *356*
6:32–33 *358*
7:1 *356*
8:7–9 *329*
8:14 *219*
9:20–22 *290*
14:14 *461*
15:9 *58*
15:15 *58*
16:9 *118*
17:8–9 *366*
17:10 *461*
19:2 *433*
19:6 *240*
19:8 *366*
20:29 *461*
23:7 *367*
26:16–21 *350*
26:17 *367*
26:18 *219*
30:1 *55*
30:17–20 *399*
30:27 *367*
31:2 *219*
31:3 *481*
31:20 *55*
32:27 *290*
34:14–18 *16*
34:14 *481*
34:30 *481*
34:31 *481*
35:3 *357, 366*
36:20–21 *285*

Ezra
3:2 *474*
6:16–17 *56*
6:22 *56*
7:6 *479*
7:10 *479*

Nehemiah
1:7 *20*
3:7 *329*
4:7 *442*
5:1–12 *295*
8:1 *474*
8:8 *167, 310*
8:18 *479*
9:3 *479*
10:29 *480*
12:43 *56*
13:1–3 *442*

Esther
4:16 *202*
9:18–32 *394*

Job
1:21 *412*
31:29–30 *430*
31:35 *430*
42 *349*

Psalms
1:1–2 *64*
7:1–17 *369*
8:3–4 *115*
19:7–11 *61*
19:14 *64*

25:4–5 *61*
25:9–10 *61*
32:1–2 *63*
33:5 *100*
37:30–31 *61*
40:8 *61*
50:21 *407*
51:1 *63, 83*
51:6 *134*
51:16–17 *63, 373, 377*
51:16 *378*
57:10 *182*
63:6 *64*
78:38–39 *182*
81:10–13 *439*
89:14 *101, 248*
95:8–10 *191*
95:8–9 *460*
99:1 *360*
99:6 *27*
103:8 *182*
103:8-10 *186*
103:11 *182*
103:17 *182*
105:26 *20*
110:4 *369*
111:10 *90, 197, 351*
112:1–3 *296*
119:14–16 *62, 484*
119:18 *484*
119:20 *484*
119:24 *484*
119:32 *484*
119:33–36 *62*
119:34–35 *484*
119:40 *484*
119:45 *484*
119:46–48 *62*
119:46 *484*
119:47–48 *484*
119:52 *484*
119:54 *485*
119:66 *485*
119:72 *485*
119:73 *485*
119:77 *485*
119:92–93 *485*
119:96 *163, 470, 485*
119:97–100 *485*
119:98–100 *62*
119:103 *62*
119:103–104 *485*
119:104 *62*
119:105 *62, 137, 471, 485*
119:111–112 *485*
119:113 *485*
119:125 *62*
119:127 *62*
119:127–128 *485*
119:129–131 *486*
119:143–144 *486*
119:159–160 *486*
119:165 *486*
119:167–168 *486*
119:174 *486*
139:19–22 *434*
139:21 *434*
143:5 *64*
145:18 *121*
148 *345*

Proverbs
1:7 *89*
1:8 *204*
3:11–12 *432*
3:12 *197*
6:6–11 *292*
6:20 *204*
6:34–35 *426*
12:10 *345*
14:12 *85, 468*
24:17–18 *429*
24:29 *429*
25:2 *368*
25:21–22 *45, 178, 429*
27:4 *427*
28:1 *98*
28:26 *86*
31:10–31 *203*
31:16 *203*

Ecclesiastes
3:11 *114*

Isaiah
1:11 *69, 373*
1:11–16 *377*
1:11–17 *410*
1:13 *373*
1:17 *248*
1:18 *89, 182*
1:23 *241*
2:4 *464*
6:1–5 *349*

6:3 *348*
8:19 *407*
9:7 *28, 100*
10 *414*
10:5 *414*
11:1–3 *351*
11:9 *464*
29:13 *459*
30:18 *101*
37:15–16 *360*
41:8 *119, 128*
41:21 *89*
42:21 *4, 39*
43:25 *183, 266*
44:10 *405*
44:15 *405*
44:20 *405*
45:6 *150*
45:19 *92*
46:9–11 *117*
46:10 *91*
53:4–7 *384*
55:8–9 *124, 149*
55:8 *452*
56:3 *235*
56:6–7 *235*
57:11 *407*
57:15 *125, 348*
61:1–2 *278*
61:8 *99*
63:12 *20*
63:16 *195, 260*
64:8 *195*
66:2 *125, 439, 469*

Jeremiah
2:5 *54*
2:8 *76*
2:10–13 *405*
3:6–7 *129*
3:12 *183*
3:14 *196*
3:15 *465*
3:16 *357*
4:22 *76, 87*
7:22–23 *378*
9:23–24 *76*
9:24 *101*
11:14 *439*
15:1 *20*
17:9 *86*
17:10 *134*
18:19–23 *429*
22:3 *248*
29:13 *457*
31:9 *195*
31:31–32 *459*
31:31–34 *463*
31:32 *196, 207*
33:6–9 *105*
34:8–10 *285*
34:8–11 *285*
34:13–15 *284*

Lamentations
2:4–5 *432*
3:22 *183*

Ezekiel
1:28 *349*
10:1–2 *359, 360*

11:17 *463*
11:19–20 *463*
18:32 *250, 418*
20:13 *284*
20:21 *284*
21 *414*
22 *414*
22:26 *368*
22:31 *368*
33:11 *105, 250, 425, 430*
33:14–20 *425*
37:26–27 *391*
44:18–19 *365*
44:20 *162*
44:22 *364*
44:23 *366*
44:25 *364*
47:21–23 *239*

Daniel
3:19–22 *436*
4:30 *436*
7:13–14 *28*
7:27 *465*
9:11 *474*
10:7–10 *349*

Hosea
1:2 *276*
6:6 *69, 103, 378*
10:12 *248*
11:1 *52*
11:4 *52*
11:9 *414*

Amos
5:12 *241*
5:21–24 *103*
5:21–23 *373*

Jonah
1–4 *414*
3–4 *104*
3:10 *430*

Micah
6:3 *54*
6:6–8 *103*
6:8 *34, 101, 248*
7:18 *182*

Nahum
1:2 *104*

Zechariah
7:9–11 *248*
7:11–13 *439*
7:11–12 *460*
14:16–18 *464*

Malachi
1:6 *368*
2:1–9 *368*
2:7 *242, 366*
2:15 *194*
2:16 *43, 110*
3:6 *80, 414*
4:4 *20, 474, 475*

Matthew
1:5 *202*
1:18–19 *186*
4:1–7 *378*
4:4 *299*
5:1–11 *40*
5:4 4 *85*
5:9 *198*
5:17–18 *41*
5:17 *46*
5:20 *41*
5:21 *41*
5:21–22 *42*
5:27 *41*
5:29–30 *173*
5:31 *41*
5:31–32 *43*
5:33 *41*
5:33–37 *44*
5:38 *41*
5:38–42 *44, 177*
5:43 *41*
5:43–45 *45*
5:45 *430*
6:9 *198*
6:26 *343*
7:12 *45, 145*
9:12–13 *37*
9:13 *179, 373*
9:38 *392*
11:28–29 *126*
11:29 *131*
12:1–2 *38*
12:1–13 *107*
12:3–4 *38*
12:5–7 *38*
12:7 *179*
12:11–12 *38*
12:12 *280*
12:14 *42*
13:13–15 *439*
13:14–15 *54, 160*
13:31–32 *463*
13:35 *116*
15:3–9 *103*
15:6–9 *16*
15:7–8 *103*
15:12 *16, 430*
16:6 *385*
17:1–3 *26*
17:3 *21*
17:24–25 *355*
17:27 *355*
18:3–4 *125, 439*
18:8 *440*
18:21–22 *182*
19:3 *110*
19:3–7 *316*
19:4–6 *110, 192, 194*
19:7–8 *110*
19:8 *43, 428*
19:10–12 *270*
20:28 *260*
21:15–16 *26*
21:28–46 *71*
21:33–41 *459*
22:1–14 *71, 459*
22:1–8 *370*
22:36–40 *84, 144*
22:37–39 *84*
22:37 *88*
22:39–40 *45*
22:40 *86*

23 *106*
23:1–3 *33*
23:2 *32*
23:4–5 *33*
23:4 *448*
23:5 *161*
23:13 *33*
23:13–17 *430*
23:16–22 *44*
23:16–19 *90*
23:23 *33, 66, 164, 178, 179, 187*
23:23–24 *430*
23:25–33 *34*
23:27 *430*
23:31–33 *430*
23:37 *430, 459*
24:30–31 *28, 388*
25:27 *295*
26:26–28 *384*
26:26 *385*
26:64 *28*
27:51 *369*
28:10 *198*

Mark
1:44 *335*
2:27 *37*
3:4–5 *280*
3:24 *79*
5:2–5 *436*
7:1–6 *352*
7:1–8 *399*
7:3–5 *35*
7:6–8 *35*
7:6 *36*

7:9 *16*
7:9–13 *42*
10:14 *26*
12:32–33 *144*
12:34 *144*
12:38–40 *36*
12:40 *303*

Luke
1:32–33 *463*
2:22–24 *210*
2:22 *474, 480*
2:25–38 *121*
2:39 *480*
2:41 *377*
2:49 *115*
3:23–38 *478*
4:18–19 *278*
5:14 *335*
6:11 *42*
6:34–35 *301*
6:35 *430*
8:10 *155*
8:28–29 *436*
9:54 *28*
10:2 *387*
10:26 *16*
10:29–36 *268*
11:42 *34, 66, 164*
12:1 *385*
12:6 *343*
12:14 *27, 184*
13:15 *38*
13:16 *280*
15:20 *129, 431*
16:29–31 *39*

17:14 *335*
18:11 *448*
19:23 *295*
20:37 *20*
21:1–4 *130*
24:27 *24*

John
1:1–2 *81*
1:12 *198*
1:17 *28*
1:29 *377, 383*
1:45 *24*
2:16 *355*
3:14 *20*
3:16 *82*
3:17 *105*
4:9 *36*
4:34 *79*
5:18 *42*
5:45–47 *34*
5:46 *20*
6:15 *27*
6:38 *79*
6:48–51 *385*
6:58 *394*
7:16 *79*
7:19 *4, 20, 37*
7:23 *474*
7:24 *100*
7:37–38 *392*
8:4–6 *184*
8:19 *76, 184*
8:32 *96*
8:34–36 *260*
8:58 *80*

9:16 *37*
10:10 *115*
10:22 *394*
10:30 *2, 79*
14 *198*
14:6 *29*
14:7 *2, 79, 126*
14:23 *118*
14:26 *453*
15:25 *434*
16:5–14 *386*
17:21 *2*
18:31 *32, 184*
18:36 *27*
18:39 *383*
19:14 *383*
20:17 *368*

Acts
1:6–7 *28*
2:41 *387*
3:19 *449*
3:22–26 *24*
5:33 *42*
7:21–22 *21*
7:22 *25, 309, 332*
7:32 *348*
7:51–60 *432*
7:54 *42*
9:4–5 *66*
10:28 *36*
10:34–35 *450*
13:19 *415*
13:20 *215*
13:38–39 *68*
15:1 *448*

15:10 *448*
18:15 *32*
18:18 *44*
21:23 *44*
21:23–24 *377*
21:26 *379*
22:2–3 *65*
22:25–29 *234*
24:26 *168*
26:4–5 *65*
28:24–28 *439*
28:25–28 *54*

Romans
2:5 *436*
2:11 *414*
2:14–15 *92*
2:29 *139*
3:1–2 *314*
3:2 *483*
3:19–20 *181*
3:27–28 *68*
4:1–5 *467*
4:2–3 *67*
4:3 *137*
4:6–8 *67*
4:9–10 *68*
7:7 *69*
7:7–12 *181*
7:12 *70, 447*
7:22 *471*
8:19 *197*
8:21 *197*
8:29 *370*
9:1–5 *70*
9:14–18 *438*

9:15 *102*
9:31–32 *68*
10:4 *470*
11:1–11 *370*
11:7–10 *439*
11:9–10 *434*
11:11 *71*
11:13–19 *238*
11:13–24 *370*
11:22 *104, 421*
12:17–21 *176*
12:19–20 *430*
13:1–4 *176, 433*
13:4 *419*
13:9–10 *69*
14:13 *160*
15:3 *434*

1 Corinthians
1:10 *194*
1:22–23 *124*
1:27–28 *130*
2:7 *378*
5:5 *432*
5:6 *385*
5:7 *383*
5:7–8 *385*
5:11 *433*
6:9–11 *277*
6:13–20 *409*
8:9–13 *160*
9:1–2 *157*
9:3–7 *157*
9:8–10 *157*
9:9 *474*
9:10 *158*

9:14 *158*
10:1–4 *393*
10:16–17 *235, 384*
11:7–12 *204*
11:24–26 *379*
14:32 *453*
15:9–10 *71*
15:20 *386*
15:51–52 *388*

2 Corinthians
3:7–11 *71*
3:14–17 *71*
5:1–2 *351*
6:14–15 *159*

Galatians
1:13–14 *17, 70*
2:16 *467*
3:13–14 *260, 447*
3:28 *238, 450*
4:6–7 *198*
4:8 *447*
4:8–11 *447*
5:1 *447*
5:14 *69*
6:7 *423*

Ephesians
2:14–16 *449*
2:19 *238*
3:8–10 *378*
5:22–33 *198*
5:25 *207*
5:28 *201*
5:30–33 *199*

5:31–33 *201*
6:1–3 *194*

Philippians
2:7–8 *124*
3:4–6 *66*
3:7–9 *66*

Colossians
1:15–18 *386*
2:13–14 *449*
2:16–17 *393*
3:11 *238*

1 Thessalonians
4:16–18 *388*

2 Thessalonians
3:6 *433*

1 Timothy
1:8 *70, 467*
1:20 *432*
2:5–6 *260*
5:8 *261, 292*
5:17–18 *158*
5:18 *323*
5:20–21 *431*

2 Timothy
2:12 *388*
3:15–17 *471*
3:16–17 *144*
3:16 *453*
4:14–15 *430*

Titus
1:5 *194*
1:10–11 *70*
1:13–14 *17*
2:13–14 *260, 353*

Hebrews
1:1–3 *81*
1:1 *406*
2:11 *198*
2:17 *260*
3:5 *457*
3:8–11 *439*
3:13 *439*
3:16–4:1 *393*
3:19 *69*
4:14–16 *369*
6:20 *116, 369*
7:22 *71*
7:26–27 *259*
8:1 *116*
8:1–2 *358, 368*
8:4–5 *358*
8:6 *71*
8:7–9 *459*
9 *116, 390*
9–10 *379*
9:4 *355*
9:7–8 *369*
9:24 *358*
10:1 *359, 393*
10:1–4 *377*
10:4 *379*
10:11–14 *377*
10:11–12 *379*
10:15–17 *471*

10:19–22 *369*
10:30–31 *104*
10:31 *349*
10:38 *191*
11 *190*
11–12:1 *122*
11:1 *191*
11:4 *374*
11:6 *187*
11:8–10 *468*
11:23–24 *20*
12:1 *190*
12:16 *209*
12:22–24 *28, 387*
12:22–23 *370*
13:8 *80*

James
1:13 *424*
1:17 *80*
1:18 *387*
1:25 *471*
2:8–12 *232*
2:13 *102*
2:14–17 *469*
2:21–24 *469*

1 Peter
1:10–12 *378*
1:13–16 *353*
1:15–16 *77*
1:18–19 *260*
1:19 *383*
2:9 *370*

2 Peter
1:13–14 *392*
3:9 *105*
3:15–16 *446*

1 John
1:5 *81*
3:1 *198*
4:8 *82*
4:18 *196*

3 John
2 *288*

Jude
9 *20*

Revelation
1:4–6 *370*
1:7 *28*
1:16 *349*
2:26 *388*
3:12 *370*
4:8 *348*
5:6–14 *359*
7:15 *370*
11:15 *463*
12:9 *390*
13:8 *124*
15:3 *312*
15:4 *348*
19:9–10 *199*
19:11–16 *80*
20:1–2 *390*
20:4 *388, 465*
20:6 *371, 463*

20:10 *390*
21:3 *359, 392*
22 *116*

www.ingramcontent.com/pod-product-compliance
Lightning Source LLC
Chambersburg PA
CBHW071947070526
44583CB00015B/1098